# Night Fires

Kathy Priddis

Raider Publishing International

New York        London        Johannesburg

Cover painting by Kathy Priddis, oil on wood panel, inspired by the artist's visit the village of Kateri.

ISBN: 1-93538396-5
Published By Raider Publishing International
www.RaiderPublishing.com
New York London Johannesburg

Printed in the United States of America and the United Kingdom

Uwa da uba ga gargadi,
Kun ga auren tilas babu kyau
Shi yakan saka yara gantali
*Boom-de-boom-boom! [kalangu drum]*

*Mothers and fathers, here's a warning*
*If you force a marriage*
*Young people will roam*

— Hausa song played on the kalangu drum

# Night Fires

Kathy Priddis

# PART 1
*Kaduna*

# CHAPTER 1

He had authority, this big Igbo. When he said, "Hadissa, you know how it must be," it was quite clear what he meant. She had always known it was futile, transitory, but starved of love and denying her own code of conduct, had resisted the truth of it. Even at their first meeting, crouched together over the torn body in the feverish intensity of the operating theatre, she had yearned towards him. His intent gaze above the mask, his moist, slightly pendulous lower lip trembling with effort. A woman's life fast ebbing away beneath their hands. His inadvertent touch, together on the wounded flesh; hers, on his forehead, wiping the beads of sweat. A necessary, shadowed intimacy, a crux point of life and death in a hot, windowless room.

Watching the muscles on his bare, glistening arms and conscious of his warm, vibrant energy, she felt insignificant, out of count.

Finally, his hands stilled, his voice muffled beneath the mask. He made an ambiguous comment about how this woman on the table might have children waiting at home, unaware. Was this an oblique reference to his wife? She knew he was married.

Sluicing the blood afterwards, masks discarded, she asked, "Is she in danger, then, your wife? Is that what you meant?" There had been riots, nation-wide.

The sun streamed through the dusty windows making the dirty white plaster of the walls glow like new décor. Sweat circles under their arms and across their chests. Hubbub outside, but not their business. Their shift was over.

"No, Hadissa, I was talking about that woman. My wife's safe enough. She's well away," his eyes flirtatious, "on my farm in Lagos. I go back whenever I have leave. Check the stock. See my children."

She hadn't asked, how many children, or how old. Nebulous, anonymous beings. Yet she was curious about his marriage and still moved by his touch. *Yes*, she thought, *but do*

3

*you love her?* It seemed important to know, and some days later, in bed with him in the Nurses Home, she asked him. Her hand playing over his wet, hairless chest, passionately needing to hear from his own mouth how he might justify his infidelity. Craving a denial.

"Do you love her, then, this wife of yours?"

Outside the street erupted. A shot, a scream. A bin crashed to the ground, glass exploded – a window, a flying bottle. The sound of running feet, then silence. Covering his black nakedness with the crumpled, regulation sheet, he had gone to the window and peered out into the pulsating darkness. Turning, his eyes were uneasy, hooded, secretive. His was an arranged marriage, he said, the land given in token. 'Love' was not a word he recognized. She was his *wife*, and pre-empting her, added, he would never take another. As a Christian he had renounced polygamy. It was all she needed to know, he said, except that one day he must go back. In flesh, if not in spirit.

"What, make your life there?"

He shrugged. "I mean a job in Lagos."

That had been months ago. She had stilled her questions, the subject closed between them. Until last night when, with cautious wariness, he had given her his quietus.

"You could have told me before we made love!" Bitterly humiliated, she almost screamed the words. Dragging herself back on the pillow, scrambling with her legs to find purchase on the mattress, feeling she must get up, meet him at his own base level. Shouting at each other in the dark, their faces lit to chiaroscuro by the hurricane lamp. Both conscious that outside people were being maimed and killed. Sirens blared; in the corridor a whisper of feet, muffled exclamations, the front door slamming.

He was sullen, implacable. "You've known all this from the beginning."

Her tears wet on her cheeks, her hair in disarray, she raised her head and looked at him coldly, almost with hate.

"You also have known," she said quietly. "So why now, suddenly?"

She spoke with dignity; and with his head hanging, he answered her. He'd become afraid. Someone in authority had found out, taken him aside, told him he had good prospects if he kept his record clean.

4

Stung, she threw the words at him. "And what of *my* record and its cleanliness?"

Guilt in his eyes, he collected his things and left. Unaware of the careful shutting of the door, she knew by the settling stillness of the room that he was gone. If she went now she would find him at the hospital, but instead she lay down as if to sleep, smelling his smell on the sheets and hugging the pillow to her face. Trying to drown out the sounds outside and in her head. For a while, in the accusing emptiness of the Nurses' Home, she had slept, but woke to misery.

She had felt soiled before, but never like this. Her wantonness, her promiscuity, filled her with shame, but his attraction to her, like the electricity, was spent. She was consumed by anger at his treatment of her. She would wipe his name from her mind as he, with one stroke, had wiped hers from his. She lay with the covers pulled up to her chin, the night sky creating a thin film of light over the pillow, damp with the tears of her dreams. She had woken once, sharply awake, hearing her name: *Hadissa, Hadissa...* Now she loathed this room where she had been so happy.

*God help me, I've got to get away from here!*

She was on the bus. Somehow, she had got up, showered, and put on her uniform as precisely as ever. The streets were teeming, everyone on their way to work, or home from the night shifts. The rising sun was obscured by a red miasma of dust and fumes and smoke from the night fires. An armoured car blocked an entrance to a side road. Litter lined the streets. Outside every shop, scavenging dogs ripped at the black plastic sacks and bulging cartons. Snarling, as *they* had snarled last night, tearing at the mounds of rubbish.

*God help me, I hate Kaduna. But I cannot get away...*

She hurried down the corridor towards casualty. People lay silently hunched against the walls. They might have asked, "Where were you?" but their forgiving, pain-filled eyes slid away, watching the sweating medics. A never-ending stream of patients, the consulting rooms full.

Hadissa loathed the casualty department. She hated the machete wounds, the dangling limbs, the blood, the shock, the desperate, restrained moaning. During a moment's hiatus the relatives crowded around her, bewildered, asking inarticulate questions. "Where is God in all this?" "Is this in his plan?" She

5

had no answer for them. She was asking the same questions. Were it not for the endless conflict, there was so much else that could have been done, small operations to change people's lives.

She worked all day without a break. Again, she heard her name called in the same crooning voice, *Hadissa, Hadissa,* and she turned, but it was nothing. As night fell, a girl-child was carried in and laid on her lap, small, unconscious, innocent, her face and her fragile arms lacerated by shrapnel. Hadissa held her close, peering for signs of life in the tired, shattered face, in the empty, unseeing eyes.

*Shall I ever, now, have a child?* She laid her gently on the trolley, for she was fainting, fainting...

Her head of department stood over her, a patina of red dust on his polished shoes. Unlike the junior medics who covered their feet with green plastic covers and dressed in rough cotton tunics, Mr Boseh always wore western dress. A tall man with a barrel chest, imposing, dignified. She dared not meet his eyes or face his disapproval. His first words seemed to confirm it.

"You must go away, Hadissa," he said gravely. "Here, drink this." His voice was deep; the vowels wide in classic fashion, each syllable accentuated. He squatted down in front of her and handed her a plastic cup of water from the blue fountain. Thankfully, she drank, but this surrender of his dignity filled her with unease.

"You're worn out, Hadissa." He raised his hand as if to touch her knee. But no, of course he wouldn't touch her. "It's obvious to us all. You've not been yourself for days. Now get up – slowly, now; slowly. That's right." He stood up. "Now, Hadissa, you must pack your bags. I want you to go to Kateri. You need a change of scene, so it may as well be you."

Kateri, her own village. She was horrified, and for the first time her eyes met his. His wide pockmarked face, so familiar from months of working next to him in the crisis atmosphere of the operating theatre, or listening to him in tutorials, now seemed the face of a stranger. Was this an oblique way of dismissing her?

"You are sending me home?"

"Ah, of course, you come from Kateri, don't you? I'd forgotten that, if indeed I ever knew it. What a coincidence! Yes, but not in disgrace, Hadissa. Why, do you think you have failed us somehow? No, no," – not waiting for an answer – "It's where the new clinic is sited. Didn't you know? When were you last home?"

"A while ago. I heard nothing about a clinic."

"Well, it's a new venture. And you have family there?"

"My twin brother. And... my mother." Ah, what would her mother think of her? "But I hadn't thought to go back..."

He folded his arms over his stethoscope. "Your training will continue there, Hadissa. Do good work and it will be counted in your favour."

"Work?"

"Of course. What did you expect? A holiday?" He smiled at her encouragingly. "No, someone has to go, so as I say, it may as well be you. You're just right for it. Why, you're a most acceptable part of this team! Everyone knows how dedicated you are. We all think the world of you."

"Go back..." Her tone was mournful, defeated.

He looked at her sternly. "Hadissa, right now you must go where you're told. Who knows, the finger of God may be pointing..."

Hadissa put her head down and began to cry openly, her words muffled by her sobs. "You don't need me. I'm useless. I don't belong anywhere! I'm all used up, for Christ's sake!"

Boseh turned from her as if losing patience and affronted by her tears, muttering almost angrily, "Nurse, what better way is there of being used up, than for Christ's sake?"

\* \* \*

She thought she had left the place for good. Kateri, an anonymous place, featureless, a bush village like any other. A place to stop for vegetables and drinks. Halfway between two cities, a place she would rather forget...

She had no choice. She dared not disobey her consultant, and in a strange way, she was grateful, though her head was throbbing. She would be able to kiss John-Sunday, but seeing her mother would be agonising. She would simply be confirming in her eyes how stupid she had been to leave home. Since the loss of her father, her mother had become prejudiced against the city. Yet, if she returned, not as a prodigal daughter, but as an official hospital delegate, it might just be enough to protect her from the

7

worst of her reproaches. Her uniform, at least, might impress her, lift her spirits. She cared about status. She never looked below the surface of things. She hated it when matters forced themselves under her nose, thwarting her marketplace boasts.

Hadissa swallowed two aspirin from the packet in her bag and crunched the acrid tablets with distaste. *Maybe God's hand is in all this. At least my father isn't there. I won't have to suffer...*

As the bus sped along the dusty, potholed road, she began to recover and to notice the familiar points of reference that punctuated this fifty-mile journey from Kaduna. It was noon, the sun high in the sky, making a mirage of the russet veld and blueing the elephantine back of the plateau of Jos. Through the opaque, dusty windows, on the hard shoulder, fleeting, transient images. Wood-stacks, tomato stalls, women carrying huge burdens of kindling-wood, their bare feet scuffing the dust, impervious to the burning concrete. A solitary tree, where cattle sheltered in dark-pooled shadows, the cattleman motionless, balancing on his staff, one leg crooked over the other knee. A brief glimpse of the coarse yellow sole of his foot. Tableaux caught in time.

The bus jolted and balked at the potholes and the driver gave a high cackling laugh. "Praise be, another one, hold on!" Turning his head to observe his passengers, rolling his eyes in mock fright, testing their endurance. They appraised him silently, slumped in their seats, their arms slack around their bundles and baskets. Sweating, anxious, but glad to be on the day bus instead of the evening one – long since discontinued because of the fighting. Everyone hated the road, and not just because of its pitted surface.

*I am alone in a crowd on this bus.*

After a while she slept, her pashmina over her head, but woke as they slowed for Kateri. The bus bumped and rolled along the dry grass verge, and she was dropped off. She stood irresolute, her head fuzzy with sleep. She debated whether to go straight to her mother's hut or, as the hospital's official representative, keep a certain distance. She was still reluctant to face her mother and be forced to listen to her censure, her loneliness. She wanted desperately to see John-Sunday, but she knew that at this time of day he would be out in the field.

The bus ground its gears and set off. She stood at the

side of the road, watching it disappear into the dusty distance until obscured by other vehicles racing past, horns blaring, making her ears ring. The heat was immense and she longed for a drink of water. In the deep darkness of the shacks, darker faces watched her. The pastor appeared, hurrying to greet her, a film of sweat on his face. A stranger – the old one long since moved on.

"Praise God, you got here safely! Come to my hut. My wife will have refreshment for you." His accent, staccato and unidentifiable, proved he was not a local man. They slithered down the gravel bank towards the concrete houses set back from the road. Where the borehole had been was ringed by shack fencing, but the church remained, a familiar, pale pink concrete hangar. Children gathered round and Hadissa paused, thinking she must surely recognise some of them, but the pastor slapped them away, and they walked on alone.

*Are You helping me? Is this in Your plan?*

The instructions from her consultant had been clear. "You'll have four full days. Take part in whatever is going on. Get them to take you into the bush. See how things are there. Observe and make notes, get statistics. How you spend the rest of your time is your own business, but the work must be done. You must understand, Hadissa, the clinic is a vital project for the poor of our region, and we're dependent on an English diocese for funds. So see how the development is going on. Especially, they'll want to know about the day surgery unit and post-operative facilities. We need this hospital, and we have to prove it!"

"And then? I come back to work?"

"Hadissa... Consider working there. Think about it. Think about making it your home again."

\* \* \*

The pastor's wife was dressed in a traditional, brightly patterned *kanga* and her feet were bare. It made Hadissa glad of her uniform, despite its shabbiness, and that her shoes were polished leather. They marked her as a person of consequence, and set her apart. Later, followed by a gaggle of runny-nosed children, the pastor's wife took her over to the clinic, a large single-storey, concrete villa set inside a high, compound wall. As she unlocked the iron gates, they scraped across the dry ground, raking up the sand.

Hadissa remembered this place as a partially derelict shell where, as children, they had been forbidden to go for fear of the spirits. The walls were cracked and the roof gaped. There was no electricity or running water, but piles of sand and sacks of concrete in the corner of the compound testified to at least a partial refurbishment.

The pastor's wife led her to a room at one side of the compound, unlocked the door and showed her in, and then left. The children clamoured at the netted window, giggling, revealing gapped and broken teeth, flies drinking at their eyes and mouths.

A small, cell-like room. On a low bunk bed, hardly raised from the floor, were a thin mattress and a neatly folded blanket. Beside it, a pitted enamel bowl and two plastic buckets full of greenish water, in which dead flies were floating. Alone at last, she shook out the blanket, draped it clumsily over the window, and began to undress. She scooped out the flies from the bucket, flicking them on to the concrete floor, and washed herself down. When she was dressed, she picked up her camera and left the room, carefully locking the door behind her. The children were still there, strangers to her. She entered the main building and shut the door on them.

Hadissa had always wondered why anyone should choose this spot to build a villa. The rooms, with their high, ornamental ceilings and marble floors, demonstrated how beautiful the house had once been. Now metal pipes and snaking cables hung from the walls, doorframes were missing, and the windows broken. Shards of glass lay on the floor, peppered with red dust, like chilli. Who was he, the man who had lived here? It was surely bizarre to build this once grandiose dwelling so close to the squalor and poverty of the mud-hut village. What was his motive? Readily available servants, no doubt, gardeners for his green plot, a driver for his Cadillac, porters for the wrought-iron gates, house servants for his bodily needs, messengers to fetch and carry. Would that have contented him? How could she judge? No heirs had laid claim to it, which, in itself, spoke of tragedy. An untold story, a mystery, nourished the spirits of this place.

In the evening, the pastor's family invited her to share their food. They were gracious, welcoming, but wary,

10

deferential. She ate in their best room, by the light of a single candle, separate from them. A hot meal of small pieces of chicken in peanut sauce and a bowl of scented rice. Afterwards she went out to join them. A hurricane lamp lit the bare earth in the passage between the concrete houses. One end housed the chicken shacks, the other the family quarters. Bins of maize and plastic bowls lay scattered on the ground among used plates and cooking pots. Numerous small dogs lay prone on the earth or scavenged in garbage cans. The evening was cold, but the fire was already ash, powdered and silvery, for they had only used enough fuel to cook. On a bench against the wall the pastor's wife lay prone, pillowing her elbow, her heavy hips mountainous on a thin sponge mattress, her half-closed eyes glinting watchfully. Hadissa could hear dogs barking up on the hill, the hiss of the flame in its gas, the murmured prayers of the pastor, who sat on a wooden, backless bench, crouched over an open Bible, though it was now far too dark to read.

*   *   *

Hadissa left it as late as possible before going to her mother's hut. Her night vision revealed a starry sky and the sinister, looming shapes of trees and bushes. She did not find the dark oppressive. It matched her mood, as vulnerable as though bathed in spotlight. It was the thought of her mother that oppressed her. Her mother's shame. Yet had they not both been rejected? Both humiliated? She rejected this thought. She did not want to resemble her mother.

The path led up the terracotta hill, away from the road, but the sound of the traffic reverberated even here, ricocheting off the barren rock ahead of her. She held her skirt close to her legs for fear of snakes in the long, yellow grass. Dogs followed at her side, and she kept her hands away from them, for they were unclean. She had almost forgotten what the countryside sky looked like at night, for in Kaduna, unless the power was cut, the stars were obscured by a multitude of lights, streetlights, neon signs, the lamps from high-rise flats and the street fires of rough sleepers. Here the sky was a dark, incandescent blue, the stars like mealy porridge against the heavens.

The path led between circles of mud-huts where shadowy figures of women moved in the light from the dying

11

cooking fires. Behind the palisades of shack-fencing Hadissa could hear the grunting of a foraging sow and the unearthly squeals of her piglets. The dogs barked and yapped in response, nuzzling at the gaps in the planks. Occasionally she heard voices raised in laughter or argument, and a strong smell of petrol from the hurricane lamps overlaid the residual smells of cooking. When the path unexpectedly deviated, she hesitated, thinking she had forgotten the way. Then she realised that, over time, some huts had fallen into disuse, their thatched roofs collapsed within the walls, and new huts had been built and a new path trodden. She passed the village school, the *makaranta*, where she had gone each day with John-Sunday. And Stanley, too, though she could not bear to think of him. She had not lived at home since then.

Eventually she reached her mother's hut. Outside the low door was the figure of her twin, squatting in the dust, reading in the light of a hurricane lamp. He was totally absorbed, the open book between his feet, his hands loose on the ground. Her heart leapt to meet him, and she gazed at him silently, standing quite still under the trees. John-Sunday seemed to sense a presence, for he suddenly looked up. She saw the whites of his eyes and the sudden gleam of his teeth. She moved forward into the circle of light, surrounded by dogs, and greeted him in the singsong Hausa of their tribe.

"John-Sunday, *sannu*!"

He got to his feet, grinning bashfully, wagging his head, then bowed formally. "Hadissa, *sannu kade*! You've come, then!"

"What are you reading, John?"

He closed the book. "Engineering." He shrugged, as self-deprecating as always.

They hugged closely, each inhaling the familiar smell of the other; except for them both there were new smells, too. She smelt of soap and the spices she had eaten, and he, taller than her by a hand's breadth, of the warm, familiar man-smell of his armpits, and the hot dust of the field where he worked.

"You knew I was coming, then," she teased, "before I came?"

There was telepathy between them, yet she was a little strange to him, in her uniform, and he refused to play. "We got word. Momi stayed up, fretting. I told her you might not come

12

tonight, over the path in the dark."

"Snakes…"

His teeth flashed. "I know."

"Tell me, then, how she is."

John-Sunday shrugged and spread his hands. "The same. She lies in the hut…"

"I don't mean this minute, though I should have realised she'd be sleeping. I'm sorry it's so late. I stayed for food with the pastor."

"We thought you might, but it's too late for her now. She sleeps all day, since Dadda left."

Hadissa looked down forlornly, still clutching his hands, the harsh reality of his situation pricking her night vision. She began to examine his fingers, tipping them towards the light to probe his calloused, pink palms.

"Do you know where he is?"

She felt him shrug. "Who knows? Everyone thinks, Abuja."

"Working?"

He pursed his lips and breathed in hard through his nose. "Drinking, more like…"

They were silent.

"And you; how are you, John-Sunday?"

Again he shrugged, the muscles rippling in his neck. "*I* work."

She laughed. "I can see that you do!"

He drew her away from the hut.

"Don't let's wake her," he said. "If she sees you she'll only start crying, then I'll be up all night. You're staying at the pastor's house?"

"No, the old villa."

He frowned. "Are you okay there? The spirits…"

She laughed again. "Ah, John, don't be foolish!"

"Don't mock the spirits," he chided her. "Well, I'll walk you back. But you must come again in the daytime."

They set off, arm in arm. The dogs had disappeared. On the way, Hadissa told him about her new duties. She did not tell him of her broken love affair, for he would be ashamed of her. Yet he must already be ashamed of her because she had neglected her duty to her mother. She was herself, ashamed. She had put off coming, wandering for hours through the empty

13

rooms of the old villa, notebook in her hand, and she had done this, which could have waited a day, instead of going straight to her mother's hut, which should not have waited an hour. Her mother was sick, and she had been brought up to believe that visiting the sick was a strong moral duty, for who knew what would come? Maybe the sickbed would become a deathbed. Yet, although she realised that her mother had turned her face to the wall, she did not think she was actually dying. Even so, the guilt piled up inside her.

Hadissa had always confided in John-Sunday, and now in the anonymous, concealing dark, she told him how she had collapsed in the hospital; nothing serious, she assured him, merely exhaustion. Under his probing, she admitted to a deeper malaise; that she feared she would not be able to finish her training. His questions came thick and fast.

"Why not?"

"Because... because I've come to hate casualty work."

"But *why*, Hadissa?"

"It's pointless, John, futile – people get sent away maimed."

"And so?"

His tone was firm, challenging, almost stern, and Hadissa faltered. Why was he so slow to understand? Then she knew how to say it.

"John-Sunday, the spirit has gone out of me." John-Sunday knew about spirits. "I'm afraid... I'm afraid I'll have to give it up."

"This is bad. Yes, it's bad. And have you prayed?"

Again she hesitated. "I've tried to, John. I don't know... No, I don't know that I've really prayed.

"Well, you should. You should at least pray, Hadissa."

They walked on in silence until they reached the compound. She left him, then, for he would not enter the room where she was sleeping, and after they had parted John-Sunday stood for a long time outside the gates, pondering the things that she had told him. He knew full well how long she had cherished the dream of becoming a nurse, and this gave him an insight as to how she must be feeling. He was full of compassion for her, yet he felt helpless. He longed to help her, but he did not know what to do.

Inside her room, Hadissa lit a stub of candle, took off her

uniform, hung it on the window frame, and put on a cotton shift. Then, exhausted but calm, she knelt on the bare earth. She was thankful to have seen her brother, and she thought she should pray, as he had said, but her heart was like stone. She ought to give thanks for a safe journey, for John-Sunday's love, for his health, for her mother, for her own life. There was much to give thanks for and to praise God for, but she was mute. If she prayed, she thought, her guilt might lift a little. She was apprehensive about what the morning would bring and the weight of her medical duties, but sensed the opportunity within it, too, and she might have prayed that she might be found worthy. She couldn't do it. She knelt for a while on the bare earth, thinking, and wondering why she couldn't pray. She stayed there until her knees cramped, then she climbed into bed, leaving the candle burning on the floor by the mattress. She draped the thin blanket over her arms, shivering slightly, and fell asleep immediately. That night she did not dream.

\* \* \*

*I am writing in my notepad... I rose early and began to explore. Little has changed, except for the new concrete houses on the roadside. The children came again, bickering over who would hold my hands, wanting to touch me. They felt the stuff of my uniform; they pinched and stroked my skin.*

*The man on the mattress under the tree, speaking English to me in a soft voice, gentle, sad. I did not recognise him at first, but when he told me he used to be head teacher in the makaranta, I knew him at once. His illness has aged him. He cannot walk. For three years, he has lain here.*

*– They bring me food, carry me into the hut, empty my slop bucket, they are kind to me but some of the children laugh.*

*Babies and toddlers crowd on to the mattress with us. I bend my head down, respectful.*

*– What is your trouble?*

*He whispers in my ear – I have piles.*

*A simple operation would have cured this. A day in the hospital, a local anaesthetic, and his life could have been returned to him.*

*The old woman in the windowless hut, her face, luminous in the darkness.*

*– I have cataracts, I am fifty-two years of age, I have lain here for nine years, I cannot see. No, I didn't know about the clinic. Praise the Lord; that would be very good, but for others, not for me, my time is past, others have a greater need.*

*And what about my mother?* she thinks *What might she have said, if I'd given her the chance?*

"I am old and ugly, my son is dead, murdered on the road, my husband tormented himself with grief and now he has left, he has abandoned us all, he is drinking his life away in the city, my daughter does not return to me, she who should have been my solace in my old age and done my field-work for me... Perhaps there is no God, perhaps this is a punishment for the sins of my ancestors..."

*The child screaming with the ear infection, the parents shouting – Antibiotics? What are they?*

*I give them the aspirin from my bag, instruct them about dosage, it's not really the best thing for the child, yet it's all I have. I curse my lack of preparation. The abscessed tooth, no more aspirin, the twisted fingers caught in the fan belt, the scars from burning, the spinal injuries, the septic cuts left to rot the limb, the endless stories of miscarriages and still-births, appendicitis peritonitis, typhoid. All things we could treat in the hospital, if it were not for the fighting. But without a vehicle they cannot reach the hospital, they still do not use money except for trade.*

*Why did I not notice all these things when I lived here? I only noticed the road, and the accidents, which happened almost daily.*

*I only noticed what my father did to me.*

This last she writes small, small, and then resolutely crosses it out. Who else might see her words?

*The lack of mains water, the meagre diet of yams, plantain, maize, rice... the lack of greens, scarcely any protein. No breakfast or midday meal, all day in the fields or wherever without food.*

She thinks, *Why do I not know what they do, how they*

*spend their time?* I see I have been blind.

*They come back to start the cooking only when darkness falls. So I fast with them, though my stomach aches. There is no sign of John-Sunday, and I am still afraid to visit my mother.*

Again, remembering, she blacks out the last sentence.

*There is a driver here, Gabriel, and in the afternoon, he drives me into the bush in a truck borrowed from the Deanery, so not always available. It is old, dented, the front bumper missing, and also one door. Up and down over beaten tracks, thirty miles or more of beaten track, dried up riverbed, the vehicle groaning and objecting like an ancient mule. More mud-hut villages spread about in clusters in the flatland of the bush, and the same problems: pot-bellied children, blindness, high infant mortality rate, high incidence of skin diseases, malaria... Yet, far out on the plain, an animist priest looks after orphan children in a disused animal hut, the door the height of the smallest child... Not just AIDS orphans, the fighting.*

Now she finds a clean page, and this, this was for herself.

*I am* awed *by the people here. I want to take them in my arms, this small community, this wonderful, clean, mud-hutted village, which, God forgive me, I hated so much that I could not wait to get away from, where the borehole is broken, the electricity hasn't worked for years, they live by paraffin and wood fires, cook in black cooking pots over heated stones under the night sky, sleep on thin sponge mattresses on the bare earth in unventilated huts, where they need a hospital, they need a hospital.*

*What more can I write? Kaduna, my life there, seems another world. I must come back. And tomorrow, I shall visit my mother. I shall tell her I am coming home. But I will never again live in a hut. And I shall never marry here.*

*I cannot marry. I cannot be found out, not a virgin. So I shall never marry.*

She stares into space...

17

Under the mattress, which she checks for scorpions before she sleeps, something glitters, a small glass pendant on a broken chain. Trapped in the glass is a cross fashioned of tiny shards of silver, so utterly incongruous in this place that she laughs out loud. Who could have been here before her? She takes it and wraps it round her wrist. It will be her talisman.

*Is it I, Lord? Do you need me? Yes, Lord, I will go for you, for I have heard you calling in the night...*

# CHAPTER 2

At this end of the concourse, every face was black. At the desk, someone's papers were causing trouble and the queue had ground to a halt again. The man in front of him half turned to speak, then thought better of it, his eyes widening.

Dan Marsden did not help him out. He had already attracted more than his share of attention. He knew that his height, his pale skin and the red beacon of his hair must seem completely alien to them, and it made him feel in a kind of limbo between what was English, knowable, and therefore safe, and the vast, unknown of Africa. He was already apprehensive about the visit, for due to the conflict in Kaduna, they had been advised not to go to Nigeria. If he hadn't already committed himself he would have turned back, but he knew that if he balked now, Luke would simply go alone. Where *was* Luke, anyway?

He was glad that they were being scrupulous about security, but even so, it was almost comical, this slow rhythm of shuffling men, sliding their bundles and suitcases along the scuffed marble floor. Cheap, black suits, hot-ironed. At the back of the queue thickset women sat quietly on huge pieces of luggage, boxes and old suitcases bound with rope, their eyes vigilant, gauging when they would have to move, waiting for the beckoning male. Some nursed docile children with sleepy, heavy-lidded eyes and rosebud lips, their limp, honey-coloured arms dangling, or clutching for reassurance. The women seemed passive, tranquil, until they caught sight of Dan, when their eyes slid away, not in hostility but hiding their curiosity under a veneer of politeness. Further away people were talking and laughing, but around him an uneasy silence had descended, and he knew it was because of the way he looked, that he was different.

He thought, *Will it be like this in Kaduna?* The fact was, he could not imagine Africa. Or rather Nigeria – his mind refused to be specific – for him it was simply Africa, and he could not imagine it. Wedged in his mind were images dating back to his schooldays, of bare-breasted women boiling indescribable things in black cooking pots, of thatched mud huts, of mysterious masked dances around blazing bonfires, and Christian martyrs – but why that juxtaposition? He had picked up an article by Tutu on white missionaries: how they brought the Bible to the land, then took the land and left the Bible. A half-schooled, half-indoctrinated people, he'd said, with a bleak and uncertain future. But surely things had moved on since then? He suspected exaggeration, and remained sceptical. Yet, dimly, he was conscious that the dignity of a race had been stolen, and that a growing tribalism had taken its place – and religious conflict.

The man in front of him held himself aloof from the rest of the queue, waiting impassively with his hands clasped behind his back, his gleaming almond eyes hooded and seemingly impervious to all that was going on around him. As the queue edged forward, he moved with it, pushing a battered cardboard trunk along the floor with a graceful sliding motion of his whole leg. He was a huge man, built like a rugby player, dressed in a black suit which had seen better days, shiny on the trouser legs and around the elbows. Underneath the fabric of his jacket, his biceps bulged. He waited, Dan thought, as patiently as his slave forebears might have waited, with an immense patience and poise – but then he dismissed the thought as unworthy. He really must stop equating black skins with slavery. He knew it only betrayed his own ignorance. Then the man turned, and Dan saw that he was a priest, wearing a Roman collar.

Outside the sky was grey with rain, like skimmed milk. In his mind's eye, he saw the lush green of English trees transmuted into the burnt scrub of the African plain, and he almost shuddered, but there was no time to dwell on his anxieties, for ahead of him there was a disturbance of some sort, and the sound of a woman wailing. Uniformed officials crowded around her, and the queue halted again as people craned their necks to see what was going on. A man with a sniffer dog arrived, a dusky brown Alsatian, its thick neck encompassed by a wide leather collar. It strained forward on the lead, its tongue lolling, its huge paws slipping on the marble floor, and the woman reared back, her hands to her mouth, her eyes rolling with alarm. She was a large, well-dressed woman, but she looked cowed – slave images again, he thought. Someone took her arm and led her away, her voice now raised in a whine of protest, her thick lips wet and slack, her brown eyes wide with fear, sweat collecting in the folds of skin round her eyes and running down her cheeks like tears. A porter followed, pushing her heavily laden trolley. The man with the dog had disappeared as silently as he had come. Searching the crowd, Dan saw him, both hands holding the dog in check, the animal canting sideways away from him, its nose almost touching the ground, its ears pricked.

Comments rippled down the line, the English vowels slightly distorted, the syllables protracted. Heads wagged in sympathy and concern – and relief, that someone else had been the focus of attention.

"Wrang tick't..."

"How could she have the wrang tick't?"

"Nat the wrang ticket, the wrang desk!"

"She will meez her plane..."

Heads bent as people began to check their paperwork and look up again, reprieved, smiling. The noise level rose. Dan watched as social barriers were broken, backgrounds shared, brief histories, family connections, commonality established. Though not for everyone, he saw, observing the groups merge and change like shifting sand, saw eyes blossom with latent hostility, saw lips tighten into silence. Antagonism even here, then, he thought, and enough to give up a place in the queue. The woman was forgotten, though her wails still echoed down the concourse, where other eyes saw her, and where the faces that turned towards her were white. They won't know she's gone to the wrong desk, thought Dan. They'll just be indifferent – or think the worst. Something illegal, a scam.

At that moment, he caught sight of Luke, standing immobile at the back of the queue, and was immediately irritated. He must have spotted me, thought Dan – how long would he have stood there, and not said hello? Luke nodded, a small, slightly arrogant gesture, economical and spare as always. He was standing with a large flight bag clasped in front of him, his shoulders braced. His jacket was wet, rain-spattered.

\* \* \*

Once above the clouds, Dan relaxed in his seat and allowed his thoughts to merge with the hum of the engine.

Beside him, Luke was reading his newspaper, but Dan didn't want to read. He wanted to try to catch up with himself, to examine the sequence of events that had led him to this moment. There were questions about this trip, for which he would have liked answers, and he knew that he could have asked Luke, but he shrank from that. They had never been intimate and they had lost touch since leaving college. Once they were in Kaduna that would change, for they would be the only whites for miles around.

Nevertheless, he had five hours in which to sort himself out, allowing for interruptions. Beside him, Luke had spread his newspaper across both tables, an intrusion into his minimal space that Dan found galling.

Luke must have sensed something. "You okay?"

"Not much leg room. I think I'll stow this, get some rest." He closed his eyes, as if to sleep.

\* \* \*

As students together at Trinity, Dan and Luke had been under the tutorage of an elderly theologian, Canon Stephen Ashcroft. Stephen had a strong, very certain Christian faith, but in spite of that, and because it was tempered with an utter lack of arrogance or guile, Dan had warmed to him.

Yet Stephen had always expected too much, he thought, plunging back into his memories. At their last session before he'd left college, he'd really gone for him. "Frivolous", "complacent", "intellectually shallow", "more in sorrow than in anger" – the words still rankled. Despite his erudition, Stephen talked in clichés, which Dan found infuriating.

"In the end it's up to you, Daniel. I think you're searching, and if you're sincere and if you persevere, I'm sure you'll find what you are looking for. That's one of the promises of God. He's wrestling with you, as he wrestles with all of us, like stamping on grapes to make good wine, but not so brutal. You've got integrity, so whatever you resolve to do about your life depends on how forgiving you let yourself become about its foundations. Roots, you know, and parentage. And where the shocks have come in the structure, and why. And where the fault lines are in your spiritual landscape."

"Maybe I don't have a spiritual landscape," Dan had

22

muttered rebelliously.

"Then find one."

"Maybe I'm not capable."

"Then you're more exceptional than you think."

In the end, Stephen's overt evangelising had alienated him – unlike Luke, a theology student, who had revelled in it so much he'd gone on to seek ordination – but Dan respected his old tutor and remained fond of him. The more he thought about what Stephen had said, the more aware he became that his views on life lacked substance and solidity. As the only child of elderly parents, he had led somewhat of an isolated existence and had learnt to camouflage his feelings, so he never revealed how hurt he had been by the old man's comments. Not long after he left college, he found a position in a comprehensive school outside Cambridge, teaching mathematics. He was aware that Stephen had retired to Ely, just a few miles up the road, but before meeting up with him again, he wanted to establish himself as a person of greater depth and maturity. For meet him again he would. Occasionally he asked himself, *Why should it matter?* But deep in his heart, he knew it was because Stephen had been the first person in his life who had genuinely cared about him at the deepest level of his being, who reached out to him, for his own sake, where he was.

\* \* \*

His flat was just outside the city centre, opposite the river on Chesterton Lane, and during the day he launched himself into his work with vigour. In the evenings, he ate at a local pub and it was there that he met Ellen, an attractive and vivacious English literature graduate who worked in a solicitor's office in the town. Five weeks later, she moved in with him.

It was a mistake from the first, for he did not have the emotional vocabulary of love. The contrast between their personalities was too great; she was spontaneous and sociable; he was cerebral and introspective. That she was the stronger character made him disinclined to fall in love. As with previous relationships he resented the intrusion into his private space of her feminine presence, her deliberate domestication of his bachelor flat, and they quarrelled over trivia. Both of them were redheads; both had a short fuse. Ellen found him manipulative, selfish, miserly, and sexually over demanding – the list grew daily. She was alarmed by his frequent black moods, which chipped away at any affection she might have had for him, and she told him so coldly.

"You're incapable of making room in your life for anyone else..."

"That's not true! You're not the first, you know! And whose flat is it, anyway?"

"That's just like you!" she retorted, stung by the spite in his voice. "You take every opportunity, don't you, to undermine my self-esteem. I pay my way! I just don't earn as much as you."

And so on and so forth. Blame tumbled about the flat, smudged itself into the wallpaper and made everything tasteless and dull. Eventually, after a particularly vitriolic quarrel, he told her in no uncertain terms that he would be happier alone. He sat on the sofa, his arms crossed mulishly over his chest, his legs twisted into knots, while Ellen, weeping, yet secretly glad things had come to a head, packed her bags and left. They had been together for less than six months, most of which had been stormy.

During the next few days, Dan felt as though a burden had been lifted from his shoulders, and he forgot how objectionable he had been. However, this sense of liberation was not unmixed with a certain panic and the fear that he was emotionally inept, incapable of ever sustaining a relationship. He recalled that previous quarrels with girlfriends had been initiated mostly by him, and that Ellen would not have picked fault with him. Unwelcome, self-revealing thoughts, quickly glossed over.

In the days that followed he began to examine himself furtively, like snatched glances in a mirror, as though fearing what he might discover. He wanted someone to talk it over with, but the only person he could trust was Stephen. He calculated that, to make Stephen partisan, he must bias the story in his own favour, a complication in his character, which he refused to acknowledge. Stephen, on the telephone, was avuncular.

"Oh, you poor chap! How're you feeling?"

"Well, you can imagine, I'm devastated."

"Then you'll have to learn to forgive."

Straight to the heart, that was Stephen, but the word meant nothing to Dan, for he knew he was posing. Yet, what had started as pretence became real – he began to genuinely grieve.

As the weeks of the summer term went by and the first pain subsided, he began to feel guilty about his casuistry with Stephen. Again, he asked himself why it should matter. He recalled Stephen's words during that final session in his rooms, could almost hear his voice, and his mood changed to one of rage against Ellen, the cause of his anguish. As for forgiveness, he could not connect it to his picture of either Ellen or himself. He stopped going to the pub in case he met her there and he didn't follow up his first call to Stephen. Instead, he threw himself single-mindedly into his teaching. His cheeks became gaunt; deep lines developed under his eyes and his pale skin suffered.

By the end of term, he discovered that his rage had all but burnt out. It left behind a residue of anxiety; for once again, he knew that the root of his troubles lay in his own perverse nature. He also suspected that in exaggerating things to Stephen he had blotted his copybook again. Why had he not simply unburdened himself, instead of whining like a child over a stolen treat? As the first days of the holiday passed, he hardly left the flat. His hair became long and greasy and the stubble grew on his chin and down his throat. Late one evening, despairing at his lack of inner resources, he made a second telephone call to Stephen and arranged to go up to Ely.

The risk was that the old man might confront him with unpalatable truths that he was only half inclined to accept, but he refused think about that. At the very least, it would give him a temporary respite from the churning of his mind.

* * *

"Well, Daniel, I'll not beat about the bush. You've just been a bit silly, I think. You've always been a contrary sort of animal, a bit of a misfit, but..." Seeing Dan's dismay, he checked himself, and leant back in his armchair. "Look, you're a good mathematician. Surely, with a bit of logic, you can see your way out of this. These things happen. Put it down to experience, why not?"

"Experience of what, though?" said Dan miserably. "Love? Friendship? What?"

"Life, if you like. Or lust, but you won't enjoy me saying that. On the one hand, I suspect you've been quite brutal to poor

Ellen – you can be very unimaginative, you know, about what other people are feeling. You go around with your heart on your sleeve and your head in the sand." He grinned to take the sting out of his words. "Is that a fair summary, do you think?"

Dan squirmed in his chair. "You don't sound as though like me very much!"

" 'Like' has got nothing to do with it, old son."

"Well, you make me sound very immature!"

"You probably still are, a bit. No crime in that, but what are you now, twenty-four? At your age I was ferrying casualties in the War and already engaged to Verity..."

Dan curbed his irritation. "People don't settle down as early these days. You know that, Stephen."

"You go through the motions, though. You live with each other, which we never did. Well, never mind that." He paused, then said more strongly, "Daniel, you need to do something about this. And I've been bending my mind since you phoned." He smiled. "As a matter of fact I have the germ of an idea, if you'd care to hear?"

"Go on."

"Are you in touch with Luke?" asked Stephen enigmatically. "You know he was priested this year? Seen him, have you?"

Dan shrugged. "Separate ways. You know how it is."

"Yes, you weren't much alike, were you? But I thought you were good friends, nevertheless."

"We lived in the same halls; that's all."

"Well, I'm in fairly close touch. He's serving his title in Warwickshire, and I like to keep an eye..."

*I bet you do*, thought Dan, and groaned inwardly. Was Stephen about to suggest he confide in *Luke*?

"You know he went to Nigeria during his diaconate year? Well, he's kept the link and he's due to go back again shortly. I assume you're a free agent?"

"For the holidays, I suppose so, yes."

"Would you like to go with him?"

Dan was astounded. "What, to Africa?"

"Nigeria, actually, as I said. Kaduna State. Now, Daniel, it's only an idea, but, you know, sometimes it's a good thing to be picked up by the scruff of the neck and put down somewhere quite different. Gives you a new perspective. The place is

26

irrelevant really. You're the kind of person who reacts, rather than responds, to situations, and what matters is that you learn to be a bit more measured, take time to digest things. If you go to Kaduna you'd have to. People live differently there. You'd need to spend time listening, taking things in. It might distract you a bit from what's been going on in your life, perhaps change your outlook. That's the least I'd hope for."

"And what's the most, may I ask, since you're organising my life for me?"

The old man smiled thinly. "Oh no, it's your choice, if you go. But the best that could happen is that you'll learn that you're not always right. Sorry, but I mean what I say. And be a bit more forgiving, both of yourself and others. But I'd also hope that you might realise some specifics, like how other people live out their faith, and find yourself challenged by it. Start to deal with the issues of faith, how they affect your life, instead of continually ignoring them. You know, it sounds to me as though you've never really been tested."

"*Tested*? What on earth are you talking about?"

"Ah well, you need to find that out for yourself."

"But... but what on earth would I *do* there?"

"You might do a bit of work, actually. You're a good teacher, so you tell me, and there's a school in the capital that could use your talents. I'm sure Luke would be only too glad to have you along."

Which was why Dan was now *en route* to Kaduna.

# CHAPTER 3

Always John-Sunday woke to the sound of the dogs. He would brush aside the flimsy curtain, peer through the wire insect net and watch them scampering through the long yellow grass that grew under the wall. Whining and quarrelling, nosing each other's hindquarters, lifting their legs to pee. He would hear the call of the rooster, the sound duplicated by others in the higher reaches of the village but he could tell what time it was by the colour of the night sky and the fading stars and the fact that the road had not yet started.

If he woke during a certain hour of the night, he could listen and not hear the road. There would be, perhaps, an hour or so of complete silence, the lucid, penetrating silence of the bush. The rest of the time the road was a deadening row, a permanent howl, a thunderous rush of sound. He was conscious of it in the fields, and even where his mother lived, more than three miles up the hill into the bush, it was not completely quiet.

If it weren't for the dogs, he could have slept longer, for he was always tired. He would lie under his blanket and watch them through the net, running freely over the hill. He would look for Rufus, who came at the same time each morning, his head muffled in a dirty white *keffiyeh*, riding his bike down the bumpy hillside on his way to the borehole for water for the milk powder. Rufus wanted his numerous children to grow up healthy and have milk regularly, but the borehole was broken, the water stagnant and muddy. Two churns, old paraffin drums, fastened to his handlebars with orange twine, clattered against the bike as he rode past. Day after day, he would ride his bike down to the borehole, but he never serviced the bike and it looked as though it was ready to fall apart. John-Sunday thought he was stupid to let it get into such a condition.

At the corner of the window where the net was broken, John-Sunday could see beetles, crushed against the mud wall, motionless and dry. Every morning he would say to himself, *I must mend the net,* but he never did. He would take care over his mother's nets as a matter of course, for she was terrified of the mosquitoes that came in when the lamp was lit, which carried malaria, but he never got round to mending his own. Perhaps he was more like Rufus than he thought. Perhaps all of them were the same. Too tired and dispirited at the end of a day to do more than just fall into bed.

He knew he should get up. His mother would be in a rage if she woke and found the chickens not fed. He pulled his shirt on over his shorts, and went next door to the latrine, a mud-brick hut over a hole in the ground. The mains had never been connected and the porcelain toilet held candle stubs and boxes of matches. An assortment of buckets stood on the beaten earth, and the place was dark and odorous. Snakes often came in the night, attracted by the smell. He would find them curled under the plank, which was not so good if he had to squat.

Outside, the sun was rising over the hill, pink, like a flower, making the earth glow and the shadows lengthen. John-Sunday picked up the two buckets of water, which he had filled from the river the previous night, and began to climb the track towards his mother's hut. In the past he would often find her already crouched by the stones she used for the fire, trying to light it, her plump hind- quarters touching the earth, her wrap-around skirt soiled from her trip to the river. It would make John-Sunday ashamed to have lain so long, dreaming away the early morning hours in his bed while the heat rose about him. Her flat bare feet, the toes wrinkled and arthritic, grimed with a smattering of mud from the riverbank, would be a reproach to him. It would not be the only reproach. He did not need to imagine what she might say to him. It was always the same over-generous nagging, followed by her equally generous cackling, scornful laugh. Her no-good son, John-Sunday, that's who he was. Lately she had taken to staying in bed. He would take her the water and light the fire himself before going out into the fields.

Sure, she had been just as hard on Hadissa. Given that they were the only ones left, she might have been easier on them. The only time she had expressed herself glad of them was on a Sunday, overseeing them as they smartened themselves for church, shining up their hair with cooking oil. On their way to the service she would give them proud, sideways looks, pleased with them and ready to admit it. But since Hadissa had left for the city and she hardly mentioned Hadissa's name.

On their way to the service, she would give them proud, sideways looks, pleased with them and ready to admit it. But since Hadissa had left for the city, she no longer went to church and she hardly mentioned Hadissa's name.

"She wasn't always like this, it's true, it's true," muttered John-Sunday later that morning. He was hand hoeing a field of yams, and he spoke the words out loud, a symptom of his loneliness. "She was better before Stanley was taken." He didn't reproach her. If he said anything, she'd only start crying again. Crying for her dead son – *He'm gone to the Lord!* But in the end, her faith had not sustained her, for Stanley was her beloved firstborn and her husband had deserted her.

John-Sunday frequently rehearsed the story inside his head, as if by doing so he might understand it better. Unconsciously, instead of the linguistic cadences he had been taught at school he fell into the rough patois of his tribe, a mixture of broken, ungrammatical English that seemed better to serve the events of that time. In his mind, he dropped into it now.

None of it would have happened if their father had not gone Kaduna-way to see about spares for the tractor. There was nothing round Kateri. If something broke, it stayed broke. There were no parts and no mechanics even if they could get parts. Anyway, that's all their Dadda was doing. Then he got caught up in the riots, and was lost for a few days. At Kateri they sat, worried, and scanned the road. They didn't hear if he was safe or not, so eventually Stanley hitched the fifty miles to Kaduna City to look for him. He waited all day beside the road with his thumb up, and a cardboard notice with "KADUNA" writ large. Then he set off walking, but he couldn't walk the whole fifty miles in the heat. Eventually, about mid-afternoon, he got a lift in a truck marked *Praise the Lord Clothing Company*, so that was all right. No harm, either, till they reached the city, by which time it was dark. Then they ran into bandits. Made him get out on the side of the road. Asked the usual question – *are you a Christian?* – and when he had said yes, they shot him.

They were Muslim and he was Christian, so they shot him; that's all it was. That driver, he just turned right around bring him back Kateri. That was a brave act, not just driving on the wrong side of the road in all that traffic, for that was common

30

practice when the traffic was blocked on one side or if there was undue subsidence. Drivers simply crossed the central reservation and proceeded on the other side. Many vehicles showed the results of that chaotic practice. It was nothing new. But turning his back on them, picking up Stanley, and carting him home in an obviously Christian truck in the dark - that was a brave act.

It was all of fifty miles back to Kateri from the place where Stanley got shot, and the driver said that Stanley, he was crying half the way. He stopped, he said, by the roadside, because Stanley was moaning and shedding tears. Then Stanley died, and after that, when the driver was sure that he was dead, and after he'd thanked God for his life, he brought Stanley's bloodstained body home, covered by a brand new second-hand coat from the back of the truck.

They gave Stanley a Christian burial in the plot of land set aside for this, out back of the huts. They wrapped him in a white homespun sheet, dug a deep hole, the pastor said prayers, then they rolled the body into the hole and filled it in. Afterwards, during the praise time, John-Sunday's mother stood up in the Church and wailed. All the other women gathered around her, wailing and ululating, she moaning and tearing her best dress – "He was the apple of my eye; he was the apple of my eye." She said it so many times that John-Sunday became ashamed, both for having to witness her terrible grief, and for his jealousy. He could not bear her saying all the time "he was the apple of my eye," when he was there, also her son. She stopped in the end, choked back her tears, straightened the creases in her dress, smoothed back her hair, which had become dishevelled in her ravings, and said: "The Lord have him now – he's safe," after which she fell silent.

His father was shielded by the Lord all that time, not knowing anything had happened. He holed up in Kaduna for nearly a week, unable to get to a telephone. In any case, there was no telephone at Kateri, though when people saw the telegraph poles by the roadside they assumed the village was well equipped with telephones. Until they realised there were no connecting cables. Kateri villagers called them wish-poles, there twenty years without ever having the connection fixed. Anyway, John-Sunday's father kept off the streets, and then returned to Kateri when he could, arriving in the early hours not knowing Stanley was already in his grave. He stayed all day in the hut and

31

didn't come out until it was nearly dark. He cried his heart out, embraced John-Sunday and said he wished he'd gone to Abuja for the spares. They had heard tell there was a good man there, but not cheap. There was no other mechanic for miles except Muslims, his father said. Since he wouldn't go to a Muslim, he had to go to Kaduna.

That was how John-Sunday recounted the story to himself. That was the reason behind the death. The logic of it and the history. For which there was no answer and no redemption.

John-Sunday didn't dislike Kaduna. He knew which areas were safe and those where it was wiser not to be seen. Everyone could tell at a glance who was Muslim and who not. The Christian Igbo were strong-shouldered, tall as Dinka, round of head with a small wide nose and slightly protruding, full lips. The Muslims, whose ancestors were Fulani from the north, tended to be shorter, more finely built, with narrow faces, aquiline noses and high cheekbones. John-Sunday and his kind always went bareheaded, and they were clean-shaven, but the Muslims were usually bearded and they habitually wore the *keffiyeh* wound around their heads like a turban. John-Sunday feared the Muslims with a huge fear and avoided meeting them whenever possible.

John-Sunday and Hadissa went to school in Kaduna, at St Michael's Anglican Cathedral School. Their first day was terrifying. For two village children who had grown up in the bush, the wide streets and concrete buildings of Kaduna seemed vast, impersonal. The school, itself, terrified them. Everywhere they looked, they saw "SMACK" chalked up, on all the desks, the books, the blackboards, the cupboards, even on the doors, as though the whole regime was punitive. Even afterwards, when he discovered it was only the initials of the school, signifying ownership, in case some wayward pupil was tempted to steal, he found it hard to let go of his initial fear.

He and Hadissa were there five years. They stayed with an aunt in the city and came home to Kateri once a term if there was a lift. It was a good time. He learnt much and made friends. His fees were paid partly by his Dadda, and partly by the church in Kateri, because his father was a close friend of the pastor, and when he was sober had helped him with church projects. The school itself contributed because they were on the lookout for bright students. The few years he spent there were agreeable enough, but he didn't want to dwell on them. He didn't want to remember the studying or the smart uniform or even the football team. All that had gone down the road with Stanley.

Stanley was there before John-Sunday, two years ahead. When he was killed John-Sunday was sent for, and he stayed home afterwards. His mother needed someone to cart for her, do her stint on the market, and work the field. Their father, crazed with grief, left the village, never to return. John-Sunday was sixteen and about to take important exams, but it was more important that the crops survived. Afterwards Hadissa returned to Kaduna to complete her nursing training, but John-Sunday replaced his father in the field, even following in his father's steps as a Sunday school teacher. He enjoyed that. It taught him his Bible in a way that nothing else could have done, and he would tell them the stories of Jesus, and in the Old Testament, the stories of the "chosen people". He would pray with them, earnest, simple prayers, that they would be openhearted to hear God's plan for them.

Yet his new responsibilities were a burden to him until he was allocated the concrete house, which had been given to his father for services rendered, and then he felt they also liberated him. His mother stayed in her old hut, outback of Kateri, but John-Sunday preferred to remain near the hub of village life. The house had two rooms and was cool, winter and summer alike, and the latrine was nearby, but best of all, as a mark of his newly acquired status as head of a family, it had a tin roof. Although it made an appalling noise in the rainy season, it was a great improvement on the usual spider-infested thatch. He was tired of spiders dropping on him when it rained, crawling into the bedclothes. Not that it rained often.

Under his father's strict regime, John-Sunday had few good memories of childhood, and he felt both relieved and guilty when he finally realised he had gone for good. Even as an adolescent he had been aware that his father enjoyed the bottle too much, and when he was drunk his temper was capricious. John-Sunday soon learnt how to make himself scarce or when it was safe to come home, knowing that he would find his father face down on his bed, snoring drunk. John-Sunday quite enjoyed looking at him lying there, for in this somnolent state, he could not be roused, and John-Sunday could study him at his leisure.

He would stand in the doorway of the hut looking down at the prone figure, noting how much paler his father's skin was than the rest of them, and how his hair grew red at the ends when in need of a cut. It disturbed the boy, that his father's skin was not dark and glossy like his own, but paler, more olive, and how the hair grew red at the ends. Some said his father was a throwback to the time of the first white missionaries, but he never remembered who had told him. It was just something that he suddenly understood as fact; that a white missionary had married a black girl, or at least had got her with child, and his father was the result, his colour diluted over several generations. It was not a story John-Sunday much liked, and he did not discuss it with his mother. Instinctively he kept it a secret from Hadissa, for she was having a hard enough time with their father as it was. Something had gone very wrong between the two of them. He had never quite known what had happened and he hadn't wanted to ask, preferring in those days of adolescent reserve to hide his face in the sand. Whatever it was, he didn't think she had ever been beaten as he had been beaten, beyond the point when any punishment should have finished.

Stanley was never beaten. He was his father's son and no mistake, with the same red hair when it was long and his father's volatile temper, his bullying and his penchant for mischief. Yet John-Sunday had loved Stanley and genuinely grieved that he was no longer there. For as long as he could remember, he'd had an older brother, and then, one day, he had none.

He did not pity himself, but gave thanks for what he had, rather than for what was missing. Like most of his tribe, he was stoical, and he knew that God had a plan for him, as he had for all of them. His own plan to become a mechanic had been abandoned, but sometimes, when he could not help himself, he would go up the hill and visit the old tractor, the cause of the trouble. Its tyres were flat and it had sunk into the grass, for it had never been mended. He would stroke the hot corroded paintwork, or sit in the torn, sponge-covered seat, turning the steering wheel, like a child playing at farmers.

He thought that God's plan for Hadissa would most likely turn out all right, even though it was now patently obvious that she didn't like her nursing work. John-Sunday thought it was rather strange, things happening the way they had. For if

Stanley had been dying in Kateri she could have nursed him if she'd been a nurse by then, and if he'd been a mechanic their father wouldn't have gone looking for parts and Stanley would not have died. It seemed to him that God's plan had worked out all wrong, with all the wrong timing, for Stanley, for himself, and for their parents. At times, he even felt guilty to be alive. Some said it was fated, and that was what he had come to believe.

\* \* \*

John-Sunday had reached the end of his day's digging, and he collected up his tools and put them into his homespun sack. From his crop trousers, he untied the lengths of twine, which he used to protect his legs from snakes and insects, and put them in his pocket. The clothes that he habitually wore were basic and utilitarian: tattered, cotton trousers and a white cotton vest, both stained red by the earth.

The sun was setting and a warm yellow glow suffused the sky, darkening the land so that individual valleys and hills merged together in a long, wide sweep of purple. Between John-Sunday and the distant silhouette of the plateau of Jos was a vast, empty land whose immense age, with wonder and awe, he sometimes compared with his own youthfulness. He felt that it would take a great deal of effort on his part to imprint his individuality on the place, and that he was far more likely to sink without trace, as a heavy object is gradually sucked into the viscous water of a borehole.

Some months ago, in preparation for the *fadama* season, John-Sunday had run a line of irrigation pipes from the riverbed to a series of punctured oil cans, which he had sunk into the soil at the edge of the field. The pipes were easily dislodged and he had been forced to repair them several times, sealing the joins with clay from the riverbank, and now he considered walking the few miles to the river to check on them.

As he stood up the sheer massiveness of the land and its vivid, almost pre-natural colours impinged on his consciousness, and he became frightened. Spirits were said to inhabit the fields, the trees, and the dense scrub and though, as a Christian, he had been taught otherwise, he had seen their mysterious fires and could not easily shrug them off. Deciding to wait until daylight before checking his pipeline, he put his head down, shouldered his tools and began to walk quickly across the field back to the village.

* * *

John-Sunday was a child of his time and of his tribe, yet, conditioned by his Christian faith, he hungered for greater things. Since the death of his brother, he had ceased to dream and plan his future, and took each day as it came. Sometimes the hunger was so intolerable he would rage his fist to the sky, and the dream would return, slipping softly into his mind like a snake at a water butt. He would stand motionless, picturing how things might have been, then vent his frustration on the soil. His dream was to have an engineering shop, based at Kateri but supplying all the farmers in the region, providing parts, expertise and training for a new, younger generation of farmers and mechanics. Their diet would improve and there would be less suffering. Making small innovations, such as the irrigation pipe, was a working-out in microcosm of this greater dream, to prove to himself what he could do. It was not his only dream. First, there had to be peace.

John-Sunday was not sophisticated enough to understand the nuances of Christian/Muslim relations or what precisely had caused the unrest of recent years. It was the road, and what took place on it every day, which encapsulated for him the malaise that gripped the whole country. Yet even the road, and the demons that resided there after dark, could not persuade him to be fearful of the area in which he was born. In itself the road was a good thing, the principal route between two major cities, and therefore advantageous to business. In time, even the armed robbers who terrorized it might be subdued by education and work and better health programmes. Given the opportunity, the very impetus towards peace would itself create the climate for change that was so utterly necessary for progress.

If, as a child, John-Sunday had feared the Muslims, he did not fear them now. Peace, for him, meant more than a laying down of arms or some form of complicated coexistence. It meant people of different creeds sharing similar aspirations. It meant respect, a respect born of common suffering and deprivation. Though he could not have articulated it thus, that was his dream.

He was only nineteen.

As for himself, he thought, as he finally reached the safety of his house, meantime and for the meanwhile he would feed the chickens, muck up the soil for the maize plants and the yams, strip maize, strip yams, go hunt bush meat, strip bush meat, do his stint on the market, cut mud-bricks, look after his mother, ride Kaduna-way for bits and pieces, and teach Sunday School. It sounded a varied sort of existence. It also sounded bleak.

One day, he resolved, I will leave here and go study engineering. Then I will be the mechanic for Kateri and everyone will come to me for parts and that will be the beginning of my dream. Then we can have tractors again, and maybe a generator. It's still my plan. But it can't happen yet.

*   *   *

After John-Sunday had eaten, he was more buoyant, and by the time he trudged up the hill to his mother's hut, he had forgotten about malign spirits and was more preoccupied by those that were more benevolent. For months, he had been trying to remember the name of the man with the Christian truck who had brought Stanley home. It had constantly eluded him, though he didn't know why, and he felt that if only he could remember it, the man's spirit might approach and become his friend. He needed friends; he wanted a companion in his work, and he also thought that, if he had someone with whom he could share his dream, it would be more likely to come true.

There was much about that time that he wanted to forget, but there was much to cherish, too. He never wanted to forget his brother's face, but already the sense of it was fading. Except that, sometimes, when he footed a ball with the others, he would see his brother's figure amongst them, lithe and agile, slanted for the kick. It would bring him up short, wondering if he had seen his brother's spirit. Other memories were less whimsical: how his mother's face habitually softened when Stanley, her favourite son, blocked the doorway to the hut at the close of day, but ignored *him* except to scoff. Or how, when he was younger, Stanley and his father had, between them, bullied and teased him till he had cried. The assorted memories, he supposed, of a normal family, and unsavoury though they were, he did not want

37

to completely lose them, and neither did he want to forget the name of the man who had brought Stanley home. Taken together, they were holy things, and he felt ashamed to have forgotten a thing like a name, which was given a man by God and was holy. Then it came to him, the name of the man. How could he have forgotten it, since it was John, like the first part of his name? He remembered then that he had asked him if he had another name, like his own, Sunday, to tack on, and he'd said, yes, it was Holiness. A good name, John-Holiness, he thought.

He was a good man, too. The day he brought Stanley home he had stopped with them and shared food. John-Sunday killed a chicken for all of them that night, and it fed four families. He recalled sobbing uncontrollably as he did it, botching the job, puncturing the flesh so that the goodness dripped away into the fire. They kept silence during the meal to respect the food, but afterwards, when the women had gone and the two of them were sitting by the dying embers, John-Holiness had spoken of a young man he knew who was visiting his church in Nasarawa, a township out-back of Kaduna. A man by the name of Luke, a white man from England.

John-Holiness remembered being irritated by the apparent irrelevance of this piece of information.

"Well, why has he come?" he asked, simply to be courteous, for otherwise he might well have asked, what has that got to do with anything?

John-Holiness said he was mentioning Luke because of the riots that were taking place in Kaduna. The Muslims were on the verge of introducing shariah law, and the Christians were resisting out of fear. Churches and mosques had been burnt and people killed. Luke was trying to persuade the state governor that if he collaborated with the bishop of Kaduna in his projects for peace, it would help both the Muslims understand why the Christians were nervous of shariah, and the Christians to understand why the Muslims thought shariah would be fairer to their people.

"They say shariah is about forgiveness, and Christian law about retribution. Have you heard that?"

John-Sunday, at the time, had been indifferent.

"Of your patience," he'd said politely. "I don't see why you are telling me this. What has it got to do with my brother's death?"

"Well," said John-Holiness, with shy deference, "your brother, God rest him, was killed by the Muslims. Forgive me, I do not want to offend you, but someone needs to help us learn to live together. We have not done very well by ourselves. Maybe someone, and particularly an Englishman, can help us do this thing, for they have worked with us before. And we must do it. It is a thing that must happen some day so we may as well start now."

"Christians will never work alongside Muslims," said John-Sunday mulishly.

"I have thought this, too, but now I am starting to ask, 'why not?' They might, if they could see the point of it."

"It is true someone needs to work to make us understand each other," John-Sunday said, painfully. "But not white men from England. We should find a way, ourselves. You cannot trust the white man. He plunders our country..."

He thought, bitterly, of his own white ancestor with the red hair, but cast the image aside and struggled to find words to express himself.

"Sure, he left behind his own structures of law and order, health, schools and good roads, but he taught us incompletely. Did he share power with us, or give us authority, or make leaders in our communities? No. So when he left we only had systems that we had not properly learnt to use. So now we have to rely on our old, tired systems, and much is corrupt and many people suffer, and you know we are not good at problem solving. You're not a farmer, John-Holiness," he continued, waving his hand towards the darkness of the fields. "But I will give you an example: the land is rich, but we cannot farm it, except by hand hoe. The white man persuaded us to buy tractors instead of using bullocks like the old way, so we in Kateri did this, and then they left without giving us spares or teaching us how to mend them. And the bullocks all gone."

"It was not all their fault," said John-Holiness quietly. "My father was a farmer, and I remember that time. The tractor could do in one afternoon what the bullocks could do in a week. So instead of cultivating more land, the farmers just left off earlier and went home. The Christian farmers, that is. The Muslims just bought more land. My father said no one realised until after the British had gone how much they could have learnt from them if they'd wanted to."

39

"What happened to your farm?"

John-Holiness shrugged, the one-shoulder shrug that was more eloquent than any words. "The Muslims bought us out."

Now John-Sunday remembered something else. He remembered what John-Holiness had said to him as they had prepared to go to the vigil for Stanley.

"Well, I will pray for you tonight and for many nights, and we will pray for you and your family in our church. For I do strongly feel that you must not shut out the thought of meeting this man Luke, because it might be that Luke is in God's plan for you. How, I do not know. But God knows."

\* \* \*

As John-Sunday climbed up the escarpment and took the path to his mother's hut, his thoughts shifted to Hadissa and he felt a mounting disquiet. She was due to graduate the following year, but now that she seemed likely to stay in Kateri, at least for a while, he worried that her graduation might be delayed. He knew she hated the village – not the people, for Hadissa had never hated anyone in her life, but the grinding poverty and, for women especially, the complete lack of any prospects, other than work on the market and walking the slow miles back and forth from the river. The situation with their father should have improved after she had stopped sleeping in the parental hut, but it had become well nigh intolerable and had coloured her perception of village life. Their father had treated her with contempt, and had generally ignored her, even at family times. If she addressed him, he would turn his face away, an expression of malicious glee on his face. She had been right to leave, in spite of their mother's objections and dire warnings. Had she remained she would have been like a bird trapped in a net, totally impeded and unfulfilled. Kaduna should have been a liberation, yet now she was deeply unhappy again. Given what he knew of the daily violence of Kaduna streets he could understand why she now flinched from casualty work, especially losing a brother to the road. She ought to retrain, perhaps become an assistant to a doctor in general practice, or a midwife, or something useful for the clinic, but John-Sunday could not see it happening unless she could train abroad.

He stopped short as if struck, and slapped his thigh. That

was the answer! It would take some organising, and money, too, which they did not have, yet he had heard of some people who had studied abroad, even bush village people, who had become so rich and respected that they no longer liked to admit their village roots, though some were proud to admit it, or too proud not to. After seeing Hadissa that day and sensing her needs, John-Sunday thought that perhaps John-Holiness might have been right, that here was a connecting thread. He would listen out for news of Luke's arrival in Kaduna, and then make an opportunity to meet him, even if it meant contacting the bishop first. He could send a letter with Hadissa when she returned to the city. He did not think that the bishop would refuse him, for had he not wept with them over the news about Stanley? He knew their circumstances, that their father had run away to Abuja. Here, perhaps, was an answer for his sister, and he vowed to try. He would do it for the sake of Stanley and his father, and for Kateri. Most of all he would do it for Hadissa, if it would help. She must come first with him now.

# CHAPTER 4

The 747 banked steeply as it descended to Abuja, and Luke braced himself against the seat in front of him, his eyes intent on the landscape below. It reminded him of his first time in Africa; that thump of excitement in his stomach, a heady mixture of anticipation and fear.

Dan had been quiet throughout the journey, but now Luke was conscious of him craning forward to see, and he leant back to make room. Below were vast swathes of uncultivated land dotted with mud-hut villages. A narrow snake of water twisted its way among the white boulders, vividly orange in the setting sun. Above, a cloud of red dust spiralled into the air before dispersing in the cloud.

"Is that the Saharan wind you were telling me about?"

"No, just a dust storm. It's the wrong time of year for the harmattan. You'd have hated that. It blots out the sun for days."

"It doesn't matter what the weather does," Dan said, surprising himself. "I'm just glad to be here at all." His sallow cheeks were flushed and his eyes glittered with excitement.

The plane took them over the outlying suburbs of the city; grim, sprawling shacks huddled together between sprawling factories, their dirt yards littered with old machinery. These soon gave way to a grid pattern of wide streets, the houses surrounded by extensive green lawns within high compound walls.

"Abuja is rich?"

"Comparatively. A lot of government properties, cultural buildings, things like that. It was meant to be the garden city of Middle Belt Nigeria, but they ran out of cash. Unlike Kaduna, it's mostly Muslim, but a lot of Christians from bush villages come here looking for work. I'm afraid all they find is the bottle. But you'll see for yourself: it's a question of the haves and the have-nots. Those that have, have a lot – 'marble halls' isn't in it! It's very different in the villages, you'll see."

"How different?" Dan braced himself as the plane

42

rocked slightly. It seemed to hang in the air between each downward lurch, as if on invisible steps of cloud.

"Just what you'd expect of any bush village. In spite of the British, there's been surprisingly little change, especially in the countryside. Or if there has, they've reverted now that the Brits have left. The first time I was in Nigeria I spent some weeks in the bush."

"Where did you sleep, in a hut? And what did you eat, bush meat?"

"You joke, but you're not far wrong, and I avoid both when I can. I warn you, it's only one meal a day, but they'll give us the best they have. They'll maybe kill a chicken in our honour. Last time I slept in a room off the new clinic and ate chicken each night for three days. It's quite safe. And in Kaduna we'll sleep in the bishop's compound. It's a fair sized place with guesthouses and shower facilities. Nathan, his manservant, cooks breakfast and supper. You'll be in clover."

"I'm looking forward to it."

For the last time Dan looked around at his fellow passengers. Most were indigenous, dressed either in thin city suits and sparkling white shirts that contrasted starkly with their burnished skins, or else in full-length, richly patterned tunics and voluminous cloaks of animal skin. The men were mostly bareheaded, although some wore turbans or the *fez*, while the women sported patterned headdresses matching their wrap-around skirts, arranged in complicated folds. The only other white person had been sitting directly in front of Luke and Dan, and in the sleepy time after the meal they had struck up a brief conversation with him. They learnt that he was a German Lutheran missionary on his way to Jos. At first he was voluble, but on discovering that Luke was a curate in the Anglican Church, he became more guarded, as if somehow they were in competition.

Dan was irritated. "How on earth can you expect the Muslims to cooperate, if you can't even collaborate as Christians?"

The German became tight-lipped with annoyance and Luke laid a hand on Dan's arm. "Now, come on..." he murmured, "there's a history to all this, you know. Don't let it bother you."

"It doesn't *bother* me, as you put it. It just proves what

I've always thought. More wars are fought over religion…"

"Well, let's not add to it, hey?"

Shame-faced, and recalling Stephen's warning along the same lines, Dan was silenced.

"Go gently," the old priest had said, "both on others and on yourself. Don't be too ready to write off what you don't understand. You need to listen, and let them *know* you're listening, especially if you meet the village leaders. Just sit back and take it all in. They need you to treat them with respect. They'll quickly suss it if you don't, and then all our hopes for working with them will be scuppered."

"I'll be careful." In spite of Stephen's earlier bluntness Dan had been gratified to be asked to accompany Luke on this brief fact-finding trip, and he was anxious to reassure the old man that his confidence had not been misplaced. "You can trust me."

"I know I can."

"By the way," Stephen had said as he left. "You'll not want much in the way of money in Nigeria. You'll be in the hands of your hosts, and, in any case, I doubt if money'll change hands. Take some gifts, useful things like biros or diaries, and toiletries or earrings for the women. You'll be offered gifts in return, but don't be surprised if they seem more expensive than what you've given them. That's the African way. And don't refuse anything you're offered. Except, be a bit careful with the water. In fact, carry bottled water everywhere. And take a bit of extra cash for emergencies – and get some DEET for the mosquitoes. Nigeria is generally hot; there's little variation between winter and summer, but you'll be there at the end of the wet season, not that they see much rain…"

The engine gave a last roar as the plane made its final approach. Almost immediately Dan could see the concrete buildings of Abuja Airport rushing towards them, and, incongruously, a boy with goats on the dry grass at one side of the runway. Then the wheels touched, the plane bouncing on the concrete as if on cushions of air, and the engine surged, its brakes grinding. As they taxied towards the terminal building, the passengers began to open their lockers and take down their bags, ignoring the instructions of the air hostesses to remain in their seats. Dan and Luke stayed where they were, inscrutably law-abiding. The German missionary rose and stretched, picked

44

up his hand luggage, and with a muttered 'wiedersehen', pushed his way up the gangway.

*   *   *

By the time they had retrieved their suitcases, the rosy glow of the setting sun had transformed the large windows of the terminal building to beaten brass. Outside were a stale, residual heat and the odour of gasoline and sewers.

Dan was about to take off his jacket when Luke said, "No, keep it on for the moment. We're being met, and jackets off is too informal here."

"Who's meeting us?"

"Could be Cletus, Area Dean of Kaduna. Or just his driver."

"Well, until he comes..." Dan slipped off his jacket.

They waited on the edge of the deserted pavement for what seemed a very long time, watching the passengers from their flight being collected by assorted vehicles, including a village bus, which drove away lopsidedly, its roof crammed with people and bundles. Eventually a small, battered open-backed truck swung into the precinct with its headlights full on.

"Ah, here they are at last." Luke sounded relieved, and Dan realised he, too, had been anxious.

"We're going in *that*?"

"Looks like it."

"Late, aren't they?" Dan struggled into his jacket, aware of a sour smell from his armpits. "Given that we've got another hundred miles to go."

"African time. Don't worry about it. We're in their hands."

The truck clattered towards them with short jerky movements, then it seemed to gather speed and pulled in so close to them that Dan had to jump back. The tyres skidded against the kerb, scattering the piles of red dust that had accumulated there, and the passenger door swung open to reveal an intensely black, smiling clergyman, dressed in a thick dark suit and a high clerical collar.

"Luke! *Maraba da zuwa!*"

"*Na gode, na gode!*"

They embraced warmly, then Luke turned back to Dan

45

and introduced him.

"Dan, this is Brother Cletus, Area Dean of Kaduna. Cletus, this is Daniel Marsden, all the way from England to see you. You came straight from Kaduna?"

"In *this*?" Cletus gestured contemptuously towards the truck and gave a cackle of laughter. "No, we had a car but we got a flat tyre near Kateri so we left it there. This is the Kateri truck." He spoke in a clipped, singsong voice, the vowels wide, and his words running together like a waterfall. "What else we do?" He shrugged apologetically, spreading his hands. "Now we go straight back to Kaduna, so we oughta get going."

He turned to someone inside the truck.

"Come on down, Amadi, say hello to our guests. This here is Amadi, my driver. Damn-good-driver," he said, slapping him on the back. "His name, it means 'rejoicing', but he don't live up to it. Always frightened, aren't you, Amadi?" Again he cackled with laughter.

Amadi grinned but did not elucidate.

"Come on, folks, let's get going!" Cletus was suddenly abrupt. "Amadi, throw the bags in the back. Gotta long ways to go tonight! Luke, you warned this boy?"

"I'll leave that to you, if you like."

"Warned me about what?" Dan glanced at Luke, who shook his head wryly.

Cletus pulled a lugubrious face, his eyes rolling. "Baandits! On the road. We gotta get back before they spot us!"

"Bandits? You're not serious!"

"Man, fear not, the Lord is with us. Now git on board."

He pulled back the passenger seat to allow Dan to squeeze into the small space behind the front seats, and then climbed in after him.

"You sit in the front, Luke. You're VIP – you c'n take the bullets!"

Amadi was still chuckling under his breath as they turned towards the exit signs and made their way on to the main road, the ancient engine juddering noisily. His knees almost touching his chin, Dan realised that after a few miles he would be completely cramped. Not wanting to fuss, he leant back against the metal sides of the cab and made himself as comfortable as he could. Behind, a raft of blue smoke from the exhaust obscured the view, and he wondered how far they would get before breaking down completely. There was a car at Kateri, halfway to their destination, but with a flat tyre. This, then, was Africa.

After a few miles Cletus leant forward and touched Luke politely on the shoulder.

"You tellin' me you haven't warned him about the road?" He gestured with his thumb towards Dan. His smile was broad and his teeth gleamed in the darkness of the cab, but Dan could see that he was apprehensive.

Luke turned in his seat. "Hey, I didn't want to put him off coming!"

"You not worried, Luke?" Cletus' voice was sober.

Luke regarded him levelly. "You usually pray, Cletus. You prayed today?"

"Of course! But we'll pray again, for the return journey." Cletus lifted his hands. He held them wide apart, as if at the altar, closed his eyes, and in a loud, singsong voice, began to intone.

"Lord, we praise-your-name. Lord, we pray that your blood will cov-ah this vehicle and land-us-safe-Kaduna. We pray that the eyes of the bandits will be closed *shut* against us; that we may pass through like Moses-in-the-Red Sea... Hear us, Lord. A-men."

"A-men, a-men," echoed Joseph softly, his hands taut on the wheel.

Dan was transfixed by the biblical immediacy of the prayer, and alarmed by its implications. "What is it about this road?" He dreaded the answer.

"The road?" Cletus looked at him. "You wan' me to tell you about the road?"

"Well, yes, if..."

"You wan' to know? You wan' me to tell you?"

Dan shrugged. "What's the big deal?"

"Man, I c'n tell you. We just have to hope and pray you don' find out for yourself, but I c'n tell you, then you say youse prayers!" He leant back, folded his arms, and began to speak in the slow voice of the storyteller, emphasizing his words.

"This road, it has two lanes, more'n a hundred miles long, Abuja to Kaduna. British-built, a fine road once, but the rains have long-ago washed it away, and now there's more rock than road. You see, it gets a lotta heavy traffic, so it gets some wear." He gave Dan a sideways glance. "And we as a nation ain't good at problem solving, so the road stays un-mended, like the ve-hicles. They think here that you c'n use a ve-hicle until it dies, and use it anyhow, like I have seen sometimes many people crammed into one ve-hicle, or many oil drums carrying watter in the back of an e-state car. Now it is one thing to load six oil drums empty and quite another to load 'em full of watter!" He laughed and slapped his knee. "So the ve-hicle, it breaks underneath, the axle, or something, and then the car is dead forever. You see them on the roadside, the seats stripped out like bush meat, open to the sky, the paintwork all gone in the heat, burnt out, too, very often. Not just cars, any ve-hicle. Like a dying dawg, they look, splayed out with all its legs gone. And tankers, rolled over, where now people live. They use the feedhole for a window."

"Must be very hot..." murmured Dan, "but if that's all there is to fear..."

"*That's* not what there is to fear!" Cletus interrupted, slapping his knee again. "It's armed robbers you have to fear! If you go at all, you must be back by five o'clock. Night falls, then, and the bandits, that's when they come out."

"It's past six now," said Dan, nervously.

"Man, that is why we are now in some hurry!"

Dan could not resist a feeling of exasperation at this answer.

"We got in at four-fifteen..." he began, then as Luke's hand lifted in protest, he subsided.

"Yes-man, we saw the plane, but Amadi, here, he ain't no good at racin' planes! We knew where you'd be, and hey, we'd prayed."

\* \* \*

By now the sky was sombre with incipient night. In the vast anonymous landscape Dan could see tiny pinpricks of light, and occasionally the paler tinge of smoke rising from night fires and the distinctive, conical silhouettes of nearby mud huts. The traffic hurtled towards them out of the dark, a steady stream of ramshackle cars, transport lorries, trucks and single-decker buses. A van with a tortured engine passed them on the hard shoulder and he saw the rusty underside of it, lit to orange by their own faint headlights – the axle tilting with its uneven load, its wheels skidding on the broken surface, sending stones and gravel onto their bonnet.

Amadi seemed engaged in a personal battle with the road. He held himself rigid, his chin jutting, his elbows wide, wrestling the wheel. He avoided the potholes by swerving abruptly into the path of the nearest vehicle, to the sound of protesting horns and catcalls. Even in the dark Dan could see the glint of their eyes and the flash of white teeth. They were like horses on a racecourse, swerving against each other and away – not quite touching, but close enough for Dan to grit his teeth. He winced and gripped his seat, imagining the sound of scraping metal, his body catapulted through the windscreen into those thundering, mashing wheels. Amadi, too, was not as easy in his mind as Dan had first thought. After each brief encounter he would subside again in his seat, uttering quavering, half-articulated prayers. His strong bare arms were covered with a sheen of sweat. He frequently wiped the wheel with his sleeve and his lips were wet and trembling. He seemed to be on the edge of some private experience, but whether it was extreme glee or extreme terror, Dan could not tell. He watched him nervously until he was weary of watching, then he turned his eyes away, resting them on the backs of the overburdened lorries in front, many of which sported labels such as *Praise God Animal Foods, Amen-Lord Linen Co.*, and *Thank You Jesus Second-hand Peugeot Car Parts.* Even, he saw, *Allah is Great Dry Stores.*

He thought, *I do not begin to understand.*

All this had taken very little time, and after Amadi had settled again, Cletus resumed his story.

"These bandits, then. You're driving along, everything going very fast, then you see them on the skyline, waving their torches – they use flaming bitumen – and you must stop, otherwise they'll shoot at you, and then you end up dead. So you stop, and if you're lucky, they just take what you've got. If you're not, well…" He made a sign across his throat. "Ain't that so, Amadi? Ain't that right? I speak truth, yes?"

"You sho' do!" Amadi nodded. "That's sho' what it's like. That's what it's like or-right!"

"It can't happen often, surely?" Dan quavered.

"Man, ev-ar-y day!"

"But don't the police…?"

Cletus laughed contemptuously. "Hey, they might *be* the police, they're so corrupt! And you cannot tell who is police and who ain't when it's dark and both are armed, and both wear combat gear. You have *got* to pull over and stop. I tell you, man, it's terrifying. Everyone is afraid of the road at night, ain't that so, Amadi? No one cares how fast they drive. They're so frightened; they just want to get off the road."

"I hate to mention it," said Dan quietly. "But *we're* on the road at night."

Cletus touched his arm in the dark, and his voice was kind.

"Daniel," he said, using his name for the first time. "That's why we pray the way we do. You gotta have faith, man. Even some of these bandits, they're Christians."

"Christians?"

"Ab-so-lutely! Don't you have Christians, turned bad? So you gotta pray for them, that they see the Light. They is evil men, but they started off just poor Christians, unable to make a living. Bush village-Christians. Wino-Christians. Ex-prisoners. Daniel, our prisons are *full* of Christians. You don't believe it? Come with me one day and I'll show you."

"What about Muslims? Don't they..."

"Some of them, but they have shariah law. It's very harsh, but it works well for them. And they are not allowed alcohol. That prohibition goes very deep, so they tend not to stray. But, sure, there's trouble on the road from Muslims, but a different sort of trouble. A different sort of bandit. They'll ask if you're a Christian, and if you are, they'll shoot you where you stand. A friend of mine at Kateri, his son, it happened to him."

"Did he die?"

"He died on the road. He was seventeen. It broke the whole family..."

Cletus sat more upright, bracing himself against the shaking of the vehicle as it sped through the night, the twin pools of light from the headlights dancing on the road and up into the darkness as they hit the potholes.

"Look, Daniel, I'm not telling you this to scare you. It's just how it is with us, every day." His voice was normal now, less singsong. "Look, I'll tell you about something that happened last year, give you the picture. These four kids from Kateri were crossing the central reservation, okay? Now Kateri is both sides of the road. It's mostly Muslim on the other side and you can buy things Christian-Kateri don't sell, and there is a soft drinks place with a radio. These kids, well, they should have been quite safe. The central reservation, well, if you've seen it, you'd know it was a safe place to cross. Why, they even grazed their goats there, tied up of course, but it's wide enough. It's a sort of very wide, flat ditch. You know about this, Amadi?"

"I heard tell…"

"Anyway, there they were, standing on the edge of the road, partly in this ditch place, and partly beginning to cross the fast lane. And this driver, this mad Muslim, this evil, evil man, he comes tearing up, and he swerves right over and catches the kids with his car, and down they go. And many people saw how it was done, and that it was done by this Muslim from the other side of Kateri."

He rubbed his hands over his face, his voice was rough with emotion. "You might ask, 'Why did he do that?' I'll tell you. For hate, that's all."

Dan was speechless. He couldn't take his eyes off him.

"See, Kateri church is built on the roadside, and for some reason they built the mosque next to it, don't ask me why. So Muslims cross in front of the church to get to the mosque and Christians cross in front of the mosque to get to market. And the Muslims say it is an offence to them, Christians walking that way. It's become a big issue. It's true they're called to prayer five times a day – though some are not willing – but as Christians *we're* called to pray unceasingly, to live as though Christ is always present even when we don't think he is, I mean when times are bad. And in fact I have discussed this with the imam." He tapped Luke on the shoulder. "Did you know that, Luke? Did you know I talked with the imam? I must tell you, he found the idea ver-ry interesting. He thought Christians prayed only on Sundays. It was news to him, as I think it would be to some Christians, huh? But it is true; it is in the Bible."

He cleared his throat. "Anyway, that night. So a group of men go out to kill that Muslim man and his family. But the pastor gets to hear of it and so out *he* goes that night. He meets them on the road as they are waiting to cross, and he can see who they are, and he names them and says, 'I *know* you' – well, I won't say their names, though I know who they are. And he says to them, 'I *know* you. You, huh – and you, huh – and you, huh.

51

Do you not think there is enough killing already in this village?'
That's what he said. That's what he asked them. 'Do you not
know,' he said, 'that our Lord Jesus Christ tells us to love our
enemies? For yes, I do believe,' he said, 'that this man who
killed these four is mine enemy. But yet I am called by the Lord
to love him and pray for him.' So then they said they would not
listen to him. But he said to them, 'God has a plan for you and
this is not in his plan.' That's what he said to them. Then they
asked him what they should do, for their children lay dead. And
he said to them to go with him in the morning to see the Muslim
leaders, and discuss what must be done. So this was agreed,
though they were weeping. He stayed with them all night and
wept and prayed with them, and read the scriptures, until they
were peaceful again, and crying only in their hearts... Both for
the going of their children and also for the anger that had caused
that criminal act."

Cletus was silent for a moment, and Dan saw the glint of
his tears.

"And in the early morning," he said, almost whispering,
"just as the sun was up but before the five o'clock prayer, he, my
brother in Christ, he talked with the Muslim leaders and said
there must be love and forgiveness between our two peoples and
not revenge."

Dan looked at him.

"You want to know what they said?" asked Cletus. "The
Muslim leaders? I'll tell you. They said this man would be
beheaded for his crime."

"And was he?"

"No, the pastor pleaded with them, until they said he
must at least go away. He must take his family and leave the
village and that what he had done was an insult to Mohammed
and a curse on himself and his family for all their days. And they
would find four young men from their number to be sons to work
for the families who had lost sons for the field. That was an
amazing thing for them to say, for Muslim boys to work
alongside Christians, but they said it. That was not as much
recompense as you might think, for who would now give them
grandchildren? No, their seed would die out. But at least they
had labourers for the field. So it was settled."

"And it was okay?" Dan asked doubtfully.

"Daniel, you are right; it was not okay. It bred

52

resentment, for Muslims and Christians do not like to work together and after the harvest the Muslim boys stopped going. But it was local justice and no one was left ashamed. The whole community saw the justice of it, and marvelled at the Christian power to forgive and start over. There was no need for it to come to court for the spirit of the law was appeased already. And since then so many people started coming to the church – people not just from Kateri but from outback places, that my friend the pastor, he who I am proud to call my brother, said that we must make a church out back of Kateri. And they are building it at Taha, a bush village about thirty miles off the road, across the plain. He is building it and the blood of the four children is sanctifying it."

There was a hush in the cab as he finished, and Luke, who had turned in his seat to listen to the story, reached over and laid his hand over Cletus' clenched fist. Cletus took his hand and held it strongly.

"You know, Luke," he said. "This man who is my brother in Christ, he also works projects for peace but he does not call them projects. It is who he is and how he lives, which is for peace. He does not need a white man to tell him how Jesus says we must live our lives. And he does not need a white man to tell him how to discern God's plan. For he does this himself in his praying, and in the praying he does with all the other pastors when we meet each week with the bishop in Kaduna. Yet I am not saying that your presence is unwelcome. We need your presence. And we need your prayers. And, hey, Luke, we need your mon-eys! But above all we need your solidarity. Yes, man! Talking is not enough. Prayer is much, but not enough. There must be action, and... and problem solving!"

There was quiet in the truck after Cletus finished speaking. Dan fell into a fitful sleep, punctuated by nightmarish images of frantic cries and the metallic crunch of colliding vehicles, of black faces and grinning teeth, but each time he woke it was to continuing darkness and the loud hum of the engine and Amadi's tense figure at the wheel.

\* \* \*

Dan woke as they slowed for Kateri, and Cletus pointed out the church with the mosque next to it. They saw no sign of

53

bandits until they were nearly at Kaduna, though Dan had been dimly conscious of a police presence at the two checkpoints through which they had passed. The ramshackle buildings were lit by enormous single bulbs on heavy cables swung across the road, and scores of lorries were parked haphazardly in the wide, flat ditches that lined the intersection. He was just beginning to think that Cletus' story had been exaggerated when, ahead on the road, he caught sight of flames. He sat up nervously and leant forward.

"There's fire! Fire on the road!"

"We know." Luke's voice was calm. "It's their torches. Take care now. Say nothing."

"*Ya kaddara*! *Ya kaddara*!" groaned Cletus, and Dan was dismayed to see him run his hand quickly over his face. If Cletus was afraid, he who was so used to this road, then what was in store for the rest of them? Suddenly he felt very conscious of his white skin, and very exposed. Luke turned his head.

"Dan, whatever happens," he said quietly, "do exactly as Cletus says. Say nothing. Let him handle it."

"Has this happened to you before?"

"Once. It's best to stay very still and just wait and see. If they make us get out, stay close to me. If it all goes bad on us, we'll run... If we can."

"*Run*? My God, where to!"

Ahead of them several figures blocked the road, using their torches to guide the vehicles into the side. The shrill sound of whistles came to them – like French gendarmes, thought Dan irrelevantly. Many of the drivers were leaning out of their windows and smiling; a pretence at bravado, which he could only admire. Amadi looked haggard, his face almost touching the windscreen, and as the vehicles were hustled on to the hard shoulder, he was muttering prayers under his breath.

"Lord, save us. Lord a-mercy. Lord save us..."

Dan observed that the some of the men wore dark camouflage gear festooned with bullet belts while others were in rough clothes and carried short assegai spears, truncheons or long, rusty, evil-looking machetes. After examining the drivers' papers most were sent on their way, but Dan saw the occupants of one car kneeling beside the road; a family, poorly-dressed with shabby shoes and torn tunics, as thin as paper. They were hugging each other, quivering, their heads down. Then it was their turn. Cletus touched Amadi on the shoulder.

"Stop the truck. Let me out your door, Daniel."

Dan scrambled hastily to one side, screwing himself up into a ball so that Cletus could squeeze past him.

"Turn off the engine, Amadi," he said. "Let them see we mean to stay stopped." He walked slowly forward towards the group of men.

"Surely they'll see he's a priest?" Dan whispered to Luke.

"That's a risk, in itself," murmured Luke.

There was some conversation outside, and then, to his amazement, Dan saw Cletus throw back his head, and they heard his high cackle. He shook hands with the nearest man and then walked with deliberate slowness back to the truck. Amadi wound down the window.

"Luke," Cletus said tensely. "You gotta Bible?"

"What? Yes, I have it right here."

Luke felt in his jacket pocket and brought out a much-thumbed Gideon Bible, and passed it over. "What on earth...?"

"It's okay. They're Christians. They haven't got a Bible, and they'd like one."

Dan exhaled with relief.

"Bibles for bandits. That's a new one! God, what a slogan! You want to write something in it, Luke?" His voice was shrill. "Dedicate it or something?" He felt hysteria mounting.

"Easy, Dan. Try to stay quiet."

Cletus was talking with the man near the ditch and others gathered round, ignoring other vehicles, which sped past without being stopped. Cletus was apparently reading to them.

"They can't read?"

"Probably not."

'Then why do they want a Bible? If they can't even read it...'

'Leave it, Dan.'

Cletus shook the hand of the leader again and then pointed to the people kneeling in the dust. He seemed to be asking, what about them? Suddenly, everyone started shouting angrily and guns were raised. Cletus walked forward and placed himself in front of the small family, spreading his hands protectively. Dan drew in his breath.

"What's he doing, for God's sake? It looked okay.

55

What's he up to?"

Amadi looked at him impassively.

"We might be okay, but they are not. They're Muslims and he's a priest. He must do this."

For a moment, the situation hung in the balance, then the leader of the group beckoned to Cletus, who was gesturing to the family to follow. They scrambled up, hurried to their car and clambered in. They drove slowly away, weaving into the traffic. Still Cletus talked with the men. Dan could no longer speak. He felt completely foreign and far from home. He could not believe what he was seeing.

Finally, Cletus simply turned and walked cautiously back to the truck, his shoulders hunched as if he expected a bullet in his back. He climbed in, making no attempt to get into the rear seat, but squashing Luke against the driver.

"Drive now, Amadi," he said crisply. He sounded exhausted. "Just start the engine and let's go."

"All right?" Amadi asked fearfully.

"Just drive."

The truck started up with a rattle, and they swung gradually away and out into the stream of traffic. Dan felt a cold sweat on the back of his neck as he waited for the smack of bullets. Nothing happened. Amadi drove more tentatively now, as though what he had feared would happen, had happened, and was unlikely to happen again. From his lips there came a stream of praise.

"Thank you, Lord. I just wanna thank you, Lord. Thank-you-thank-you-thank-you, Lord."

They gathered speed and headed on, in the direction of the city.

"What on earth were you reading to them?" asked Luke.

"Oh, part of Psalm 91. You know, 'Thousands shall fall by your side but it will not come nigh you'…"

"Ah, Night Prayer," replied Luke softly. "'You will not fear the terror of the night, nor the pestilence that stalks in darkness…' That was risky!"

"Worth it. Unfortunately, they just saw it as prophecy. Now they think they're safe forever."

Cletus sat with his head bowed, and presently Luke lifted out his arm and put it gently round the other man's shoulders. No one spoke again, and there were no more stories.

City lights were ahead of them. On the hard shoulder people could be seen walking with hurricane lamps and indistinguishable burdens, though Dan saw that some of them carried huge bundles of branches. Then came the first traffic lights, and a huge, half-lit neon sign: "WELCOME TO KADUNA."

# CHAPTER 5

The bishop's compound, a three-acre plot of land within a high wall, was situated on the more prosperous side of the city and well away from any conflict. It consisted of the bishop's single-storey red-tiled house and offices, the guest houses, and a number of other dwellings for household servants. Nathan was both cook and housekeeper and two porters manned the solid iron gates. In front of the house was a large gravelled drive bordered by lawns, and behind it a rectangular enclosed field where Nathan grew vegetables for the kitchen.

Dan's room, which came within a few feet of the perimeter wall, was well appointed, with a separate bathroom comprising a porcelain toilet, a basin and a shower, for which he was grateful, since he was already experiencing a sense of displacement. He reflected that what was considered basic at home, or even poor, would appear as undreamt of luxury here, especially in the countryside, yet during the night there were other, more significant things to disturb him. Tossing on the hard mattress, he heard the rumble of heavy wheels over the uneven road, and in the morning discovered that tanks had been sent out to quell the disturbances. He tried not to imagine what form that quelling might have taken.

Dan threw on a tee shirt, cotton slacks and slip-on sandals and made his way over to the main house, where he was told breakfast would be served. Hibiscus and oleander flowered in the partial shade of small trees, and formal flowerbeds, ringed with low-cut box hedges, spanned the gravel drive. Dan wondered if a member of the British Government had lived there at one time, and scathing of British colonial history that he usually was, he felt unaccountably comforted. His mood quickly changed. Around the corner, between him and the front door, was a pack of small dogs basking in the shade of the building. Seeing him, they leaped up and began to bark furiously, circling around him and snapping at his ankles. The noise was deafening.

Dan wanted to kick them away, but he was afraid they might be prized domestic animals and someone might see. He stood there for some moments, helplessly imprisoned by the circle of snarling dogs. Then he saw Luke, at the open door of the house.

"Just walk through them. They won't hurt you."

"Really."

"They're trained to make a noise, that's all. They're guard dogs."

Luke's sympathetic grin as he ushered him into the house didn't help Dan's mood.

"You might have warned me!" he said mulishly, as they closed the door on the noise.

"I'd forgotten about them." Luke was still amused. "I'm sorry. I'm not laughing at you, really. It happened to me, too, when I first came here. I wanted to tell them to bugger off, give them a kick up the rump, but I was afraid of being seen."

Dan relaxed. "That's precisely what I was thinking."

The small dining room overlooked the field at the back of the house and was laid for breakfast. The walls were covered in photographs, mostly of clergy solemnly grouped together in black clerical suits, dwarfed by a central figure of a tall man dressed like a chief. Abruptly, a door opened behind him, and he turned away. A black man appeared, dressed in blue overalls and a striped apron, carrying plates of food. He greeted Luke effusively, displaying very white and even teeth.

"Welcome, massa! It is very good you come back to us, massa! Yo' m'st welcome!"

"Good morning, Nathan. Dan, this is Nathan. He'll be looking after us while we're here."

They sat down at the table and Dan looked at the food uncertainly. It was unlike anything he had ever seen.

"Have some plantain." Luke passed him the dish. "And this is mashed yam, and there's bread and jam. There are yoghurts and drinks in the fridge, but don't start eating yet. We'll say grace."

Nathan stood by the table and clasped his hands, and Luke closed his eyes to pray.

"Lord, bless this food and those who have prepared it, and help us to be mindful of the needs of others. Amen."

Dan had never said grace in his life, and he reflected with some amusement how apposite it was, and succinct, too, not only to ask for the food to be blessed, which was conventional enough, but, in the same breath, the cook and those who had neither food nor cook. He hoped God was listening. Then he reflected, God had certainly listened on the road, at least to Cletus.

When Nathan had left the room, he remarked, "Nathan called you 'massa'..."

"And?" asked Luke through a mouthful of food.

"Echoes of slavery?"

"Not at all! He'd say it to any guest. He's an employee, not a servant. He certainly would not regard himself as anything else. Added to which, he is a wonderful cook. And you must have noticed the garden? That's his initiative, and quite recent, too. When I first came it was nothing but a dirt yard."

"I thought it dated back to the British."

"Originally, perhaps, though I must confess Nathan does rather try to keep the colonial character. Those box hedges, for instance... but, in the garden, as elsewhere, he wanted to do what was best for the bishop, and he thought that meant aping the British. We may have rather left them to it, but people here still think of us with respect. You can see it in the architecture, too, even in new buildings. And the school here is run like an English grammar school. Anyway, how's the plantain?"

"It's actually quite delicious. Can we get it in England?"

"Certainly, if you know where to look. D'you know Coventry?"

"Never been."

"Well, if you go, try the Foleshill Road."

"How do you know these places, Luke? I thought you were based in Warwickshire."

"So I am, and Coventry's at the heart of it. I was priested in the cathedral."

They ate for some moments in silence. Then the dogs started up again, and Dan could hear Nathan's voice in the kitchen.

"See what I mean?" asked Luke. "The dogs announce everyone. That'll be the secretary arriving. You don't hear the gates from here, but the dogs warn you."

"And where's His Holiness?"

Luke frowned at Dan's levity.

"He's gone to Zaria," he replied. "There's a theological

college there. He left very early this morning, before we were up. And, by the way, you don't call him 'Your Grace' or 'My Lord', or anything…"

"Glad to hear it!"

"And you don't use his given name, either…"

"So what *do* I call him? 'Chief'?"

"*No*, Dan, just call him 'Bishop'. And… wear a jacket, there's a good chap."

\*　\*　\*

After breakfast, Luke came to Dan's room and they sat on the rattan chairs while Luke told him about his itinerary.

"Today I go to the hospital to meet the consultant who's overseeing the medical facilities at Kateri. He's donating his time, but he needs certain items, such as a steriliser, which he can't get here – they're too costly. Coventry NHS Trust will donate  some things second-hand, so I've got to get a shopping list. Want to come? It'll take all day, though."

"If you like. What else have you got to do?"

"Well, tomorrow I'm with the architect to discuss some alterations to the design of the clinic. Ramps, things like that, and a dogleg corridor I don't much like. Then the local newspaper, see how they're reporting the violence. I really wanted to drop in to the Cathedral School this week, but I probably won't have time. I've got to visit Kateri, see how the clinic looks, get some up-to-date photos and see the pastor. Sometime next week I ought to go up to Zaria. As I mentioned, they have a theological college there and one of their students wants to come to England for a year's study. That's OK, but I want to go over his CV. Also, I must see a chap called Gibo in Nasarawa. He's the pastor there and he lost his church buildings in the recent riots. I can't do much for him, but I got to know him quite well the last time I was here, and he's a friend. I'd like to just hear what's been going on and give him a bit of support if I can. I'll probably do that tomorrow and leave Kateri till next week."

"A full programme," Dan commented. "They've given you a lot of responsibility, haven't they, for one so…"

"Young?" Luke smirked slightly. "Yes, well, I suppose they have, but time's short. I can't be running backwards and forwards to Nigeria all the time."

"When you go to Zaria, you'll go on that road?"

"Zaria's north of here, but yes."

Dan grinned. "Back by five?"

"If I can. I may have to stay overnight. Will you be okay?"

"Would it be out of place if I came with you? I'd like to see things."

Luke hesitated. "Well, you can come with me to Nasarawa, if you like. But, Dan, you'll have to take a back seat. Gibo needs to talk, not, forgive me, be argued with. And he doesn't need advice. He'll get by on his own. They'll build up again fairly quickly with whatever they find lying around in the streets. And the bishop will help with funds because it's within the diocese. It'll just be a matter of listening."

"Or I could go to the school. I'd really like that."

Luke leant forward. "Now, there's an idea – I'd forgotten you're a teacher. Okay, try a day, and see how it goes. It'll be very different from what you're used to. There's no real equipment. Do you need much equipment for maths?"

"Just a blackboard, a bit of paper, perhaps."

"You'll get a blackboard, but paper's thin on the ground. I'll fetch you a stack from the newspaper office. Just plain newsprint, but usable. In the meantime, help yourself from the office here, providing you don't take too much. Use it sparingly."

"Both sides."

"You've got it."

# CHAPTER 6

It was dawn on the third day of Hadissa's visit to Kateri, and she was preparing for another incursion into the bush when John-Sunday appeared at the door. She still had not found the courage to face her mother, but John-Sunday insisted that, if she did not go soon, their mother would never forgive her. She promised him that she would be back before sunset, and they would walk up the hill together.

"Good. I'll tell her. It'll get her up if she knows you are coming. She'll want to prepare the food."

Hadissa collected her notebook and her medical bag, and walked with him to the truck where Gabriel and the pastor were deep in conversation. The pastor turned to her as she approached, and greeted her in Hausa.

"Hadissa, *sannu*."

"Pastor, *sannu deh*!"

"*Yaya aiki*?" he asked, referring politely to her mission.

"*Mun gode*! We are just about to leave for Taha."

She waited. He was creasing a paper in his hand, and seemed agitated. She could see beads of sweat beneath his hairline and on his upper lip. Her first thought was that she was not going to be allowed to return to Kaduna, and her heart sank. She put her bag in the truck and smoothed down her uniform, then faced him, trembling slightly.

"*Ina labari*? You have news?"

"*Sai alheri*," he reassured her, meeting her eyes. "Is this the right moment?"

"Tell me."

"Hadissa, the bad news is that the bus to Kaduna has broken down and mending it will take time, *ama*... there's no other competition and so there's no need for them to hurry. I'm afraid you must stay in Kateri a while longer."

Hadissa sighed. "Right, but when do I go back to Kaduna?"

"Well, that's the good news. Some Englishmen were collected from the airport three days ago, and the car that was sent for them is here."

"So why is it here, if...?"

"Because it had a flat tyre, and they took the truck instead. Now a driver is coming from the city to collect the car. He will come with a priest who is going further down the road, and that man will bring a spare tyre, and drop the driver off here. You can go back with him."

"I'd be happy to do that," replied Hadissa, gratefully. "It's most gracious. When does he come?"

He spread his hands. "*Ka yi hakuri.*"

Hadissa looked at him. "Pastor," she said, firmly. "I'm quite happy to be patient. I have work to occupy me. But I do not want to be out in the bush when the car comes from Kaduna."

"There is no need for you to be out in the bush when the car comes from Kaduna, for he will wait for your return before he takes you back."

The pastor smiled as if that could solve all the problems of timing.

John-Sunday stepped forward. "With respect, pastor," he said calmly. "Is the car coming this day or is it coming another day?"

The pastor looked surprised.

"That, my son, is in the hands of God. But I have a letter, left here three days ago, the day the car is having the flat tyre, to say that someone would come in three days. That day is today. But it is as God wills, when the car shall come."

John-Sunday took Hadissa's hands in his.

"Hadissa, most likely the car will come today. But you have this journey into the bush, a round trip of nearly eighty miles, and you've not yet seen our mother. Also, you mustn't be on the road at night."

Hadissa sighed again. Everything was suddenly complicated. Gabriel had been leaning against the bonnet of the jeep while this conversation was taking place, and now he stepped forward.

"Hadissa, I have an answer," he said. "Taha is only thirty miles. With respect, if you speak quickly there, and we come straight back, it will not be too late to see your mother. Then, if the car has arrived, you can set out to Kaduna first light."

"*If* the car has arrived." Hadissa showed her frustration. She had become accustomed to the strict timetable of the hospital shifts, and had completely forgotten how, in the bush, time was so arbitrary.

"And you must bring a gift to our mother," said John-Sunday, encouragingly, "for she will not, now, be able to make a meal for you."

"I can bring something. I have... I have a little cross."

John-Sunday took her arm, and led her out of earshot. She looked at him questioningly. He took her hands in his, stroking the backs of them with his wide thumbs. He bent his forehead to touch hers then gazed intently into her eyes.

"Hadissa," he said, hesitantly, "by the time you return I will have written a letter. Will you take it and deliver it?"

"Certainly. Where to?"

"That's easy. The driver will be from the bishop's compound and the letter is for the bishop. But, Hadissa, I want you persuade your driver to wait for you, so that he can take you to the nursing home afterwards. Will you do that?"

"I can try. Or I could ask him to deliver it."

He looked away. "Hadissa, try to deliver it personally. I want you to deliver it personally. Will you do that?"

"It's important?"

"It's very important."

"Then, of course."

"But he must take you home. Don't try to get home on your own. It's too far, and it's dangerous. Promise me?"

She looked at his anxious face, then lifted his hand and kissed it.

"I promise, brother."

\* \* \*

The car arrived in the late afternoon, an old Peugeot estate pitted with rust stains and weighted low on its back wheels by two petrol drums and the spare tyre. The driver was late rising and it was not until late morning when they left. Hadissa made her farewells quickly and climbed into the passenger seat. Looking back, she saw the pastor rapidly making the sign of the cross.

The driver was morose and uncommunicative. After an

hour of bumping along the road he pulled in to a roadside café, got out and slammed the door behind him. Alone in the car, she watched him order a large glass of beer from the bar and join a group of truckers at one of the plastic tables. There was ribald laughter, and inquisitive glances cast her way. Humiliated, Hadissa felt in her bag for her pashmina and covered her head. In the heat of the car and exhausted by her travels of the previous day, she soon fell asleep.

She slept deeply, and it was not until mid-afternoon, when the driver returned, that she woke. At first she was bewildered, unsure where she was. She could smell the drink on him and was bitterly angry.

"What have you been doing," she cried, "leaving me so long? And it's against the rules for you to drink, you know that!" The driver muttered something inaudible. "I could report you for this!"

"Oh, don't do that, lady, I'll lose my job!" he pleaded. "A man deserves a drink occasionally, doesn't he? Don't worry," he added gruffly, starting the engine, "we're halfway there already. I'll still get you back before dark."

"You wouldn't have *dared* to do it if I'd been a man!" she stated grimly, hating him for frightening her. He made no reply, but he seemed less sure of himself, and she had to be content with that.

By the time they arrived at the city the day was sinking into its brief sullen twilight. Open trucks streamed out of town, crammed with jaded factory workers. It was rush hour, the traffic slowly creeping, bumper to bumper, along the main streets, honking at bicycles and pedestrians, at times completely halted, queuing haphazardly around the traffic islands and on the wider pavements.

Hadissa felt stunned by the pace of life. Kateri had slowed her down, and reluctantly she admitted how refreshed she was by the few days spent in her village. Here people looked strained and edgy. Everyone carried a burden of some sort: rolls of fabric, piles of wood, huge enamel bowls of plantain. A man with two goats, one under each arm. Another with chickens, heads dangling, their eyes opaque. Propped against the high compound walls of private dwellings were the homeless, recumbent in boxes or under makeshift tents. A darkened canopy revealed a pair of gleaming eyes, devoid of expression, then contemptuously averted from her chauffer-driven car. Hadissa felt alienated, adrift in a foreign world, herself homeless. At an intersection vagrants crowded round the car. Ragged runny-nosed children with sweets and comfits peered in with large beseeching eyes, gesticulating with sticks of sugarcane or bread rolls. They banged on the dusty windscreen. Her driver cursed, and looked away.

"Stop a minute," said Hadissa. "I have a little money."

"Why should I?" Sneering at her, hunching his shoulders. "You're going to report me anyway. Anyway, they're just riff-raff."

"I won't report you this time…" she said quietly.

"Good! I didn't think you would, a girl, travelling alone…"

"…And I'm sure they're truly needy."

He ignored her, and she leant back against her seat helplessly, refusing to plead with him.

After a while, trying to be polite, she asked him, "*Ina hanya zuwu* bishop's house?"

However, he scorned the Hausa.

"How *far*? You not been there before, then?"

"No. Can't we take a shortcut?"

He gave a scornful laugh. "Ah, in a hurry again?" She turned from him with dislike. Why was he so objectionable?

"I do have to try to get to the nurses' home before dark."

He spread his hands, implacably fatalistic. "*In sh'allah.*"

Abruptly, they were free of the traffic and on a wide, tree-lined avenue. He speeded up, jolting over the sandy potholed surface of the road, and pulled up at a pair of solid iron gates, sounding his horn. A face appeared at the hatch. The gates slowly opened and they drove in.

Hadissa was overwhelmed by the beauty of the place. It was unlike anything she had seen before. Delicate pink tamarisk trees and oleander lined the spacious lawns and the grass was lush and green with copious watering. In front of her was a low building, roofed with hot red tiles, its doorway and windows shaded by white climbing roses. The immense tranquillity of the place was balm to her troubled spirit. Even the dogs, rising from their supine positions on the gravel to let out a chorus of barks and snarls, underlined by their familiar presence the feeling that here she would be safe and secure. The car ran across the gravel and pulled in at the front of the house.

Hadissa got out. "I won't be long. You'll wait for me?"

"So they told me." He eyed her with disdain. "But I also have a home to go to!"

* * *

Luke answered the door. Standing in front of him was a young woman in uniform, an emerald green cotton shawl falling from her shoulders. Her large eyes were luminous and sombre, but behind her direct gaze he discerned a sense of burden. She held herself stiffly, as if fighting off fatigue.

"Won't you come in?" He held the door wide, but she hesitated, and he noticed that the car still had its engine running.

"I'm only delivering a letter."

Her accent was educated, her voice low. Luke held out his hand. "Shall I take it?" he said. "Who's it for?"

She clasped the envelope closely to her breast. "I was told to deliver it personally. It's for the bishop. Is he there?"

"He's just come in. By the way," he added, "forgive my manners. I'm Luke, and I'm a guest here at the moment."

"I am H-Hadissa, from Kateri," she said, stammering slightly. She had never met a white man before and it embarrassed her to give him her personal name.

"You nurse at Kateri? The bishop will know you?"

"He knew of me once, but we never met. And he may not remember. Is he available, do you think? Because the driver is waiting for me, and he's already cross."

"*Cross*?" Luke repeated indignantly. "He's no right to be cross." He smiled down at her warmly. "Leave him to me. Where's he taking you?"

"Just to the Nurses' Home."

"Of course... Well, come in. Give me the letter and I'll give it to the bishop straight away, then I'll speak to the driver. He'll wait for you, don't worry."

Reluctantly she put the letter in his hand. "You're very kind."

Hadissa waited by the front door. Through the glass porch she saw a table laid for a meal, and in the main reception room a man was seated on the sofa, his face obscured by a partition. A few minutes went by and she began to feel she was

68

intruding. The smells of cooking made her faint with hunger, for she had eaten nothing all day. It was not polite, to arrive at mealtime. Perhaps she should leave. After all, her duty to John-Sunday was done.

At that moment, when she was on the verge of quietly slipping away, her name was called. She turned, her hand on the doorknob. The bishop had come up behind her in his soft slippers. He was an immensely tall man, clad in the white flowing robes of a tribal chief, but with a gold pectoral cross on his breast. He was looking at her with an expression of concern, and he carried her open letter in his hand. Quickly, she went down on both knees to make her respectful obeisance.

"You are from Kateri?"

She nodded, her eyes cast down.

"*Assalama alaikum.*" His voice was grave and deep throated.

"*Alaika salamu,*" she responded formally, her voice faint. She was completely overawed. She felt her hand being taken in his and he helped her up, then led her into the reception room where Luke and the other man were sitting.

Both rose to their feet. Both were white-skinned but it was on Dan that her gaze rested. His hair was an astonishing red, the colour of the earth, the colour of the dust when the harmattan blew, the colour, she thought, incredulously, of her own father's hair when it was long. She gazed at him, transfixed, unaware that she was being impolite, conscious only of her own amazement.

"Hadissa..."

She realised that the bishop was speaking to her, and she dragged her eyes away from Dan, confused.

"...let me introduce our English friends."

Hadissa steadied herself, but she only vaguely heard their names, and when Dan shook her hand she rubbed her skin where his white hand had touched it. Nathan appeared, bearing a tray with tall glasses of fruit juice. He looked at Hadissa suspiciously, but served her civilly enough. Hadissa sat on the very edge of her chair, nursing her glass. Rivulets of condensation ran onto her fingers, and she wiped them on her uniform. Furtively, she examined the two young white men. She could not take her eyes off Dan's red hair and his pale eyebrows. His eyes were green, she noticed, his skin not just white, but creamy, like real milk. He caught her eye and she quickly lowered her gaze. She could almost see her reflection in the tiled floor.

She looked around. The room was well furnished, and could seat a dozen or more. The rattan chairs on which they sat were piled with cushions; the walls plastered, hung with photographs and icons. The glass shutters were open, half-closed vertical blinds shielding them from the heat of the late sun. It was all very different from her mother's mud hut or her bare concrete room in the Nurses' Home.

Listening to the bishop talking to Luke, Dan occasionally glanced over to her. He saw a slim young woman with short, wiry dark hair from which colours flashed like sunlight on a tray of gems. Her skin was a dark chestnut, and her hands were large and efficient-looking, with long, tapering fingers and pale fingernails. She seemed weary, and her body smelled of musk, a heady, not unpleasant smell. She was obviously intimidated by the presence of the bishop and when Nathan appeared at the door to announce the meal, she jumped up, flustered.

"I'm sorry! I must go."

"My dear child!" The bishop stood up and came towards her. "It was unpardonable of us to continue our conversation, but I have to leave again; in fact, straight after the meal, and we had just a little business to conclude. Will you forgive me? See, I have your letter in my hand."

"It's not... it's from my brother."

"Ah, your brother! That wasn't quite clear. He spoke of you with great affection but he did not precisely say he was your brother."

She felt uncomfortable. "He did not mean... He's my twin."

"Oh? Well now, that's unusual. Something to celebrate, hmmm? Come and share our meal, and we'll celebrate John-Sunday's twin sister and Hadissa's twin brother. Come, come..."

He was charming. He gestured towards the dining room and she sensed his hand hovering above the small of her back. She felt she could hardly resist, but by the dining room door she stopped and looked down.

"I may not," she said softly.

She felt they were all looking at her, especially the harmattan man whose name she had forgotten.

70

"But, of course you may! Here, sit here." The bishop pulled out a chair for her.

"But I cannot! I have a driver waiting to take me home."

"Back to Kateri?" he said disapprovingly. "Definitely not! On the road at night? De-fin-itely not!"

She managed to smile. "Not to Kateri, only to the Nurses' Home in the city."

"Ah. But you can't go there, either – there's trouble in the city again. It's what we were speaking of. No, tonight you'll sleep here, then in the morning you can leave as early as you like. Indeed, one of us will take you – not me, I'm afraid. I shall be in Zaria – then you can return, maybe the next day, and we can speak together of this letter."

He turned to Nathan and handed him some coins. "Pay off the driver, Nathan, and get a room ready for our guest. I expect there's one free, across the compound."

*　*　*

Hadissa, marvelling at the quantity of food, took a little of everything. There was chicken in a hot chilli sauce, scented rice, fried plantain with tomatoes and sweet peppers mixed with green olives. She had never seen such variety. The men talked, which surprised her, for it was not usually the custom to talk over food. She herself stayed silent, modestly covering her mouth with her hand at each mouthful, and soon she began to listen to what they were saying. The bishop had been educated in Oxford, but when he became animated his African accent became more pronounced.

"Talk to Nathan," the bishop was saying. "If you really want to understand the impact of the riots. It is un-believah-ble, what that man has suffered! And he's not alone. Hundreds, thousands have been affected. Homes burnt; churches burnt; people have even dis-ah-ppeared. And here am I, running back and forth to Zaria, because they feel threatened by Muslim development in the town. I should be out on the streets with my people!"

"Bishop, are you really setting out tonight?" asked Luke, laying down his fork. He glanced at Hadissa and smiled. "Surely, you also should wait till morning."

"Ah, but if I travel very late tonight the roads will be

71

empty because there's a curfew, and I shall get there unseen, whereas if I travel in the morning it will take me hours, and then, as a Christian bishop, I shall be more noticed." He laughed cheerfully. "And I do not want to be noticed, not even by the police who say they can protect me, because they are known to serve two masters. There will be papers to be examined and I shall be delayed. I may have to go with them to the police station. There will be fines to pay. They'll call it a fee for my protection." He smiled. "And it will be just a little more than I am carrying. So then what do I do? Do I come back here and start over? No, it's better that I go tonight."

He leant forward and took the bowl of rice in his hand, heaping it on to Hadissa's plate.

"My dear, you are eating nothing – have some more of this. Now, I'll tell you a story I heard the other day about a man stopped by the police. They asked him for money to buy wood for their fires. Well, he gave them what he had – he had no option, but of course he didn't have much. So then they looked around to see what they could charge him with. They found nothing wrong with the car – a miracle in itself! – so they charged him for travelling alone at that time of day. 'If you come get an accident,' they said, 'who go tell your people?' So this guy in the car, he said, 'But I am *not* alone! I have Jesus Christ, the Angel Gabriel, the Angel Raphael, and the Archangel Michael.'"

The bishop rocked back in his chair and chuckled. "So they charged him with being over-loaded!"

Luke laughed, wagging his finger at him. "Apocryphal!"

The bishop took Luke's finger and gently bent it back into his hand. "Do not point at me, young man, in case my spirit leaps out to greet you. I need it a little while longer for myself. Yes, it's probably apocryphal, but it makes a good story!"

"Well, what about this curfew, then?" asked Dan. "How will you get by that?"

"I'll take my chance on that, unless I fill my car with angels!"

He laughed at his own joke. "No, but seriously, don't be concerned for me. For am I not under the authority of God, as we all are? I am in his hands. What is there to fe-ah? Death? Why should I fear death? You know," he continued more soberly, "you Europeans have a different idea about death – and sickness,

72

too, for that matter. Sickness, for you, is a temporary aberration, merely an interruption of your busy lives, no more than a nuisance, and you fully expect to get well." He smiled, his eyes gleaming with mischief. "If you don't, your next of kin can always sue!"

Luke protested. "Not usually, Bishop, only if..."

"But I have read it! Always you sue. If you are sick you sue and if you come get an accident you sue – I have read it, Luke. Here we can't sue. We are too close to death all the time, and death is not a matt-ah of money. Even something trivial can lead to death, and very often does. Here, especially in the bush, but also among the urban poor, to reach adulthood is an event. Ask Hadissa."

She looked up, startled at the mention of her name.

"Did you know," he continued, waving his fork at Luke, "that here the average life expectancy is only fifty-three? What is it in your country, seventy-five, eighty? We have seventy deaths per thousand people here. Sickness, here, is much more a reminder of mortality than it is with you. Who knows which fever will prove fatal? Isn't that so, Hadissa?"

"It's... it's not the area of nursing where I work," she replied, conscious of her own voice sounding loud in the room. "It's... it's the area where I should like to work, but I am being trained in A and E. Yet, what you say is true. I have seen it for myself, in Kateri."

"It must be difficult to know how to change things..." remarked Luke. "Your medical facilities are already overstretched just coping with the violence on the streets, and your people hardly have the means to be self-sufficient. Also, forgive me, Bishop, when your infrastructure is, in any case, so..."

He was going to say corrupt, but he stopped, afraid of offending him. It was one thing for the bishop to say it, but quite another for a guest. But he reckoned without the bishop's percipience.

"Corrupt?" The bishop faced him. "Ab-so-lutely! I couldn't agree with you more. But you mention self-sufficiency. There again, we have a different worldview. Here, self-sufficiency is seen as more of a vice than a virtue. In your country you have a free Health Service, yet in the Third World – well, sometimes you refuse help because you want us to help

73

ourselves. But let me tell you something. In Hausa the word for 'refusal' and the word for 'hate' are the same. Remember that builder in Nasarawa?"

Luke laughed and turned to Dan. "The man had done all the work on his own – the foundations, the carpentry, the plastering, all of it. I admired him and said so to my Nigerian guide. Do you know what he said? He said he was the meanest of men. "Does he not know there are people needing jobs, here?" he said. And it's a fact, they all depend on each other, and pay in kind."

"Indeed," said the bishop, "here, the virtue is to be mutually dependent. You think it stifles initiative or makes people overly reliant, but, believe me, it means no one is left unsupported."

"What if the head of the family dies?" asked Dan.

"Well, the community will support them for as long as they can, if not too many die all at once. If that happens, well, you've seen our streets. We have our homeless, as you do. And, yes, they starve there, and yes, they die there. But, you see, Dan, here death is part of life. We don't fear it, as you Westerners do. At least, we may fear the mann-ah of our dying, but not death, itself. Indeed, if a loved one has died, and if we have not faith, what we fear is life itself. Talk to Nathan, he'll tell you. Of course we fe-ah! You think we are fatalistic? Not at all! It's a deep understanding of the frailty of life, and how life can tyrannise us. Both Christians and Muslims regard death as the gateway to Paradise. Christians, especially, look forward to a literal return of Jesus to this earth. They believe – and I am counting myself among them – that our life on earth is provisional, a mere preparation for a more glorious life in heaven." Dan, growing increasingly uneasy by all this talk of faith, looked sceptical. "Daniel, I see you're not with me, but it's true, and therefore we don't insure against it, as you do, or try to turn back the clock. For instance, in our Mothers' Union here in Kaduna…"

He leant forward, a mischievous glint in his eyes.

"You know, Daniel, our clergy cannot manage without the Mothers' Union. These women are formidable! I'd be out of a job," he said, laughing, "if some of these women are ever ordained. They'd take over! They practically run our churches as it is."

He sobered. "But what I was going to say was, that every member, yes, ev-ery member of the Mothers' Union in this city has lost a child, either to sickness or to the violence on the streets. Yet, if there's a death in the community it's these women who move in, right into the house. They prepare the dead for burial; they cook the meals for the visitors; they clean out the house. They sometimes stay for days. I make it my business to know these things. Now, I heard you both were in some danger on the road. Well, our people face it every day! Some go out in the morning never to return! Now, if that happens to one of us, it changes something, but it does not affect our worldview in the way that it would for people in the West. That's what faith does, and I can see you lack this faith. A pity – it's the only real way of living."

"I don't..." started Dan, but the bishop interrupted.

"No, you don't. But with faith, you see, Daniel, there's far less questioning why. We do not ask 'why'! We ask 'how'!" he said, suddenly passionate, fisting his hand on the table. "We believe that God, in his infinite mercy and knowledge, has a plan for each individual, and if something gets in the way of that plan, like sin or violence or lack of basic healthcare, we ask how God can help us change things. Change ourselves, if necessary. Like it or not, it's as true for you as anyone on this earth. That's what we ask, to be changed. And that's what you should ask. Don't you agree, Hadissa?"

During this long speech Hadissa had been trying not to think of her dead brother. Since his death she had not voluntarily evoked his face or his spirit, but listening to the words of the bishop, Stanley's winsome, irrepressible, slightly arrogant face came before her, almost more real than in life. She reflected how his glad energy and enthusiasm for living had been so cruelly cut short, and she was overwhelmed with grief. She dropped her face in her hands. Yet she could not bear to be seen weeping and she pushed back her chair violently, the tears spurting from her eyes, and rushed out of the room. For a moment she stood in the porch and gazed out into the compound, seeking to escape, but night had fallen and she was afraid to go out. It was Daniel, the red-haired white man, who came to her. He put his hand tentatively on her shoulder.

"I'm so sorry."

He turned her round to face him and put his arms round

her. She hid her face in her hands, trembling and crying, with deep, uncontrollable sobs, yet even while she cried, she was aware of the strength of his arms, of his touch on her back, and of his quiet, undemanding compassion.

After a while she disengaged herself, and apologised.

"What was it?" he asked quietly. "Someone you lost?"

"A brother," she whispered. "I... I lost a brother..."

"Ah... was he sick?"

"No... on the road. He was... shot."

Dan drew in his breath.

"Come on," he said firmly, taking charge. "That's enough for one night. Let me take you to your room."

"I cannot... I must not go out in the darkness with you," she said quietly.

Dan smiled. "Don't worry about that tonight," he said gently. "You'll be quite safe with me. And it's only to your room."

She capitulated. "Well, I must say goodnight to the bishop. I can't just..."

"Yes, you can. Presumably he doesn't know about this?"

"He does, actually... But there are so many of us who have lost family... I expect he has just forgotten."

"Then I wouldn't like to be in his shoes when he remembers! Come on," he urged her. "Where's your bag? Let's get you to your room."

He was glad to get out in the open air.

# CHAPTER 7

It was the third morning, and Dan was due at the Cathedral School. He had wanted to walk, since it was only ten minutes away, but was informed that a car had already been booked to arrive at half past eight. The compound was deserted and for a while he kicked his heels on the gravel, his eyes on the gate, but by nine the car had still not arrived. Luke was in the city and the porter did not speak English, so there was no one to tell him what to do. The heat was intense and he went back to his room for a hat. After a while, increasingly worried, he went to the kitchen to find Nathan. He discovered him busily chopping vegetables with a large cleaver.

"Yus, massa?" Nathan wiped his hands and turned to face him.

"Nathan, I was expecting a car to take me to the school."

"Yus, massa?"

"Well, it's late. It was supposed to come at half eight, but it's not arrived. Is there someone I can telephone?"

"The car is surely on its way, massa."

Dan was relieved. "Oh, well, that's okay, then. Sorry to have troubled you, Nathan."

Nathan wagged his head politely. "No trouble, massa."

Still the car did not come and, at ten o'clock, he returned to the kitchen but Nathan was nowhere to be seen. At that moment, the door to the corridor leading to the bishop's office opened, and a clergyman appeared. He looked at Dan enquiringly.

"Can I help you? I'm the bishop's secretary."

"Oh, good!" replied Dan thankfully. "Look here, I was expecting to be picked up at eight- thirty. I'm supposed to be at the Cathedral School."

The man frowned. "The car has not come?"

"No."

"It will, without a doubt, come very soon, and then you

can go to the school. All right?"

"Well, okay. But, when it comes," said Dan, turning to leave, "could you possibly get someone to fetch me? I'll be in my guest room."

"No problem. I'll send Nathan over."

Dan lay on his bed and tried to read. He kept looking at his watch. There was no view of the gates from his room and he was now very afraid of missing the car. Nathan did not come, so at eleven he made his way back to the house. Parked in front of the door was a battered car, its driver dozing at the wheel. Was this his lift? He knocked on the windscreen. The driver roused himself, and wound down the window.

"Yus, massa?"

"Are you here to take me to the school? I mean, did they send you to...?"

"Yus, massa. I have been waiting for you! Are you ready?"

Dan broke out in a sweat. He hated being late for anything, or letting people down, and he'd been stuck here when he could easily have walked, and over there, in the school, were children waiting for a white man who couldn't be bothered to turn up on time! What sort of impression did that give, for heaven's sake? He suspected the driver had not even inquired for him, that he hadn't even got out of his car.

When he arrived at the school it was mid-morning break. Some boys, dressed in pristine school uniforms, were kicking a ball against the wall on which was chalked a goalpost, and Dan asked them for directions to the reception office. They looked at him curiously and started to laugh. *"Bature,"* he heard. *"Bature!"* He took the stairs two at a time to the third landing, the children flattening themselves against the pockmarked walls to let him by. At the top he looked around breathlessly, found the headmaster's office, and knocked at the door.

*"Shigo!* Enter!"

It was a tiny box room with a large desk cluttered with papers, the walls lined with filing cabinets from which files protruded untidily. A grimy curtain hung from the dusty window. Sitting behind the desk was a small man and opposite was a distraught woman dressed in a flowered African robe. She had been wiping her eyes with her shawl, and her bloodshot eyes gazed at Dan in amazement.

The man looked up at him. "Can I help you?"

"I'm looking for the headmaster," said Dan "I'm Daniel Marsden and I'm a guest of the bishop. I'm here to teach maths."

"I am Mr Umgobe. I'm the headmaster here." His tone was cool. "But the mathematics class was this morning. Now the students have gone on a visit to the Peugeot factory. We expected you at start of school."

Dan wiped his forehead. "I'm sorry," he said. "The car didn't come."

"It's not really that far..." Umgobe murmured. "Never mind, you're here now. In fact, we'd be glad of your help. We have an English teacher missing. She has not returned to school after the disturbances last night, so, if you'd like to take her class...?"

"I'd be glad to."

"Then please wait for a moment. I must finish with this parent first, then I shall take you along."

For some minutes Dan sat outside the office on an upright chair watching the door, expecting it to open at any moment and the man emerge. After a while he started to look around. The landing was quiet. Hanging on the dingy walls were posters and charts, and a line of unframed photographs of students from previous years, some clad in sporting gear. Nearby were an empty trophy display case and a couple of broken bookcases filled with tattered books. From somewhere down a corridor he could hear the universal twittering sound of an ill-disciplined classroom.

\* \* \*

Dan was suddenly struck by the contrast between his own school and this one. Nothing in his experience had prepared him for it. As a child he had been precociously clever, with a natural aptitude for study that had both bewildered and awed his council house parents. Throughout his childhood they had poured all their energy into the realisation of a dream – university, a good job – that they had never achieved, relentlessly driving him through his school exams, giving him rewards they could little afford. Dan neither acknowledged nor resented them for this. Deep down, he hated his working class roots and couldn't wait to get away. A potentially rebellious adolescence was spent overtly cooperating with their dreams for him, for what they wanted, he also, uncritically, wanted for himself. Even in adulthood he was the last to acknowledge the part his parents had played in freeing him from the constraints of their own values and lifestyle, but he remained emotionally immature and socially inept. He had never learnt the language of the street.

In Cambridge, freed from the discipline of home life, he procrastinated, postponing even vital tasks, arguing whatever problems he encountered round and round in his head, but never taking action. As soon as he recognised this weakness he became, almost overnight, rampantly dogmatic, yet his opinions were never informed; he never tossed his ideas around in public and he never took advice. Except, perhaps, from Stephen. He became a good teacher but he wasn't naturally convivial; he avoided the false democracy of staffroom conversation, the gossip and the backbiting, preferring to spend his lunch hours doing extra tuition, or just sitting in the empty classroom marking books. He hardly ever read a newspaper, and until his arrival in Nigeria had no idea what was going on in the wider world.

Now he realised that he had trawled through life, picking up only those experiences that could serve his own purpose. That included his relationships. Since starting college he had found it difficult to reconcile the exclusive, hierarchical life of Trinity or the cold atmosphere of the school with the unconditional warmth of the welcome he received on his infrequent visits home. Even now, his parents were still inordinately proud of him and couldn't wait to tell the neighbours when he was coming. Tired, stressed by his work, he savoured the undemanding atmosphere they provided: home-cooked food, his old bedroom, his old books, and he basked in their genuine pride. Yet after a few hours their trite domestic habits exasperated him; he would be appalled by his mother's shy deference, irritated by his father's false bonhomie, and be relieved to get away.

He suddenly felt ashamed, almost impoverished. Such a profound contrast existed between what he had known in life and what these children would experience! Their circumstances rebuked and humbled him, and he was immeasurably saddened that a mere accident of birth and geography should make such a difference to a child's life. He thought of the boy with the goats on the airport runway, the stories the bishop had told about the Mothers' Union women, and the group of children on a country road smashed to oblivion by racial hatred. How on earth could a child of the West and a child of the bush even begin to communicate? At that moment, deep in his innermost being, unsure of his motives but already deeply embroiled, he opened himself to Africa and resolved to take whatever it threw at him.

\* \* \*

The noise of the school bell was deafening, imperious, and as it died away, Dan became aware of the ticking of the large clock above the headmaster's door. He got up and went to the window. Below, through the soiled glass, he could see a line of children crossing the playground. Even as he watched, they filed into the building and he heard loud instructions being given from the landing below. Somewhere a door banged, and once more there was silence. He wondered how much longer he would have to wait. It must be nearly lunchtime, if indeed, they had lunch. He suddenly realised that it was not, any longer, his responsibility. He sat down again and rested his head against the wall, his arms folded.

At last the door opened and the headmaster ushered the woman out. She smiled at him timidly, but they had reached the top of the stairs before Umgobe turned abruptly, as if only then remembering why Dan was there.

"Oh, you're still here! I thought you were doing English..."

"You said I was to wait..."

"Oh, did I? Well, come along, then. You can do the afternoon class."

Dan was taken down a corridor completely enclosed by glass. The heat was oppressive. The classroom doors were open to let in air, and a hubbub of sound issued from each room. One or two rooms were empty but Umgobe glanced into each one before he found the English class. The room was full of young teenagers who were behaving like any class without a teacher: some chatting, sitting on top of the desks, one was bouncing a ball against the wall, and others were leaning on the windowsills gazing out.

There was an immediate silence as they entered, and

81

everyone looked round. Those who had been sitting stood up, and desks banged and feet shuffled as they got themselves into some sort of order. They stared at Dan curiously, and again he heard the whispered word: "*Bature! Bature!*" Dan thought their behaviour was not unlike what he was used to in England, and he began to feel more confident.

"This is Mr Marsden from England," the headmaster announced. "He'll teach you today, so mind your manners and make him welcome. Say 'You are welcome' to him – one... two... three..."

"You are welcome, sah!"

It was a full-throated shout, almost military, and Dan was amused.

"Well, I'll leave you to it," said Umgobe. "Who'll take Mr Marsden to lunch?" Several hands shot up, and he waited before choosing someone, waiting too long, Dan thought, as he watched their eager, jerking outstretched arms. "Okay, you, Ibrahim, you, Musa, and, yes, okay, the twins. He's Sammi and she is Maria." Once more he turned to Dan. "Come up and see me after school, let me know how you got on."

After he had left Dan gestured to the children to sit down, which they did with a clatter of chairs, then they waited, scrutinising him, a sea of round black shiny faces and solemn tawny eyes.

"*Bature! Bature, yauwa! Bature!*" The whisper ran round the class; their faces creased, and they dissolved into giggles, covering their mouths.

Dan smiled. "*Bature?*" he asked. "What does that mean?"

They sparkled with mischief. "White man! White man...!"

"Well, I can't argue with that." He did not realise that it was a derogatory term.

\* \* \*

The rest of the morning passed quickly. He wrote their Hausa words on the blackboard together with the English translation, making them repeat his pronunciation. He learnt quite a little Hausa in the process. When the lunch bell pealed, he and his four stalwarts joined the rush to the canteen, where they

82

tucked in to packed lunches of bread, maize, or sugarcane. He
was given a thick yam broth doled out to him in a bowl, which
he ate with pieces of flatbread, feeling guilty at taking their food
– next time he would get Nathan to make him a sandwich.
Children crowded round him, watching him eat and showering
him with questions. With Sammi and Maria propped against
each shoulder, he spoke of rain, green fields and marshes, of tall
trees and flowering meadows, but when they asked about where
he lived or what he ate, or about films or clothes, he became
more reticent, unwilling to describe anything that they might
perceive as wealth or ostentation. He learnt the emphatic
affirmative, *Yauwa*! but he could not bring himself to use the
negative, *A'a;* to his ears, it sounded ludicrous. He told them
about water coming hot from the tap, and they were astonished
to hear about central heating, cinemas and English traffic laws.
He had to confess, wryly, and to their amazement, that he was
unmarried, and that, married or not, he had no children.

"But I want to hear about *you*," he said, and turned the
questions on them. He found them alert and perceptive. Several
of them were from bush villages, now boarding with relatives,
away from their families except for Christmas, some had single
parents, others orphaned by a mysterious disease, which he
suspected might be AIDS. Most of them lived in the shacks of
outlying townships such as Television and Nasarawa, and came
into Kaduna by school bus, but others walked to school, setting
out very early in the morning.

For the rest of the day he taught arithmetic to a different
class of older children, stabbing at the blackboard with strong
staccato movements of the chalk. Each time he asked a question
they stood up to answer, and though he soon wearied of this and
told them to stay sitting, it was not their custom. He also
discovered that many of them, even the most intelligent, were
almost illiterate, and from then on Dan abandoned the
blackboard.

All too soon the bell rang for end of school and they
scrambled for their bags. Like all school children, worldwide, the
girls went off arm-in-arm, while the boys prepared for football.
A few of them were reluctant to leave, and gathered around him,
holding on to his arms so that he couldn't move. Not until he
promised to return the next day did they finally let him go. He
went in search of the headmaster and found him shepherding the

children on to school buses, and he repeated his promise to return in the morning. He felt stimulated and renewed by his day in the school, and immensely humbled by what he had heard of their lifestyles. He felt a rush of love for them all and determined to be there early the next day. As for any danger on the streets, he'd take his chance.

* * *

Dan lay on his bed in the weak light from the overhead bulb writing down the Hausa words he had learnt that day and what he could recall about the children. Outside the wind had risen; he could hear leaves rustling and the occasional sharp yelp from one of the dogs. Here, in this room, he was mostly protected from the sounds of the city, but once he heard a car revving up the street, and then a siren, and someone far off, shouting. Later still, he heard the disconcerting and rather sinister rhythm of drums. He paused for a while, listening, then, tapping his pen against his teeth, he wrote:

*Nathan came with tea. Refused a chair – sat at my feet. Colonial sahib.*
*Can't remember how we got on to it, but he told me some of his story. My blood ran cold. Knelt upright with spread arms, eyes very wide. Tears. Lots of smiles, though – apologetic.*
Nathan :
*Worked in the kitchens of one of the big hotels in Kaduna, returning to his home compound at weekends. Grateful to have a well-paid job – but liked the nightlife too. Supported wife, two small boys, parents and himself, with still some to save. Bought a TV for his room, new clothes, ate well from the kitchen & life was good.*
*Early last year, the riots. Muslims attacking Christians, terrible wounds, shootings, burnings, killings. Christians avenging themselves – mosques burnt, attacks on innocents, army called in.*
*Vaguely aware of this on the news, but perhaps I switched radio off? (Incredible.)*
*Nathan out of Kaduna at that point. Wealthy guy from Abuja had invited him to Abuja for a week as valet. Promised rich wages. Nothing sinister about this (?) so Nathan gave up his*

84

*job and went. With the money he could maybe find similar work,
improve himself, maybe study, get some qualifications. Said it
was a dream he'd always cherished.*

*It was a Monday. Two hours down the road, the guy
switched the news on. Curfew in Kaduna, roadblocks in place.
No one allowed in or out but no details. Nathan panic-stricken.*

Dan tapped his teeth again, and began to write more
fully, as though he needed to make an accurate report.

*Every day the situation got worse. Massacres of
Christians by Muslims, and vice versa. Horrific stories of
mistaken identity, bestial killings, the innocent caught up with
the guilty, a complete cessation of law and order – telephones
down, public transport disrupted.*

*Thursday – Kaduna open again except for checkpoints.
(We passed one on the way up!) Nathan desperate to get home,
begged the man to let him go. The guy refused to pay him so he
hitched the 100-mile journey, sometimes walking for miles
beside the road.*

*What he saw in the city sickened him. Wrecked shops,
buildings and cars burnt out, etc. Used back alleys and climbed
over walls to get back to his home.*

*The gates were down and there was a terrible smell. He
said he hardly dared look. He said he fell to his knees and
covered his face. The whole area was littered with decomposing
bodies. fifteen families.*

*(Can't cope with this image. Can't write it down the way
he said it. All through it Nathan knelt on the floor, telling the
story with his arms flapping and his eyes wide.)*

*He began to search for his family... found his father,
then his wife, an aunt, then one of his children. All were dead,
lying on the open ground. The other boy lay dead in his bed. He
never found his mother. He said that he let out a great cry,
holding the dead child in his arms. God! God! God! He ran from
that place. He says, perhaps his mind was unhinged.*

*The hotel was boarded up, others using his room. Slept
in boxes, under walls, later in an oil drum beside the road. He
was broke and went thieving – common here, if people fall on*

*hard times. (In England too, I suppose.) Much to loot, much to sell, but after the first day he became afraid, he said, for his soul. (Unlike England!) He explained that there were always pickings to be had by the roadside, travellers caught up in stationary traffic, and that if he looked maimed in some way, a man could beg there, make a living. So he killed a rat and bloodied his clothes. He joined others, some genuinely maimed, some feigning. They beat him up for his profits.*

*He began to think how much money he'd wasted when he had a good job. (I suspect he drank or gambled it away.) One day he decided to find his pastor and ask his advice. The pastor listened to him, wept and prayed with him. Nathan promised to return the next Sunday, and this he did. In the meantime, the pastor met with the bishop about things to do with the Church, and the bishop told him he needed someone to cook for him as his wife was working in England, and a general house manager, to live on-site. (I must admit I had wondered where the wife was – there's been no sign of her in the house.) Nathan smartened up, was interviewed and got the job.*

*And this is where he works and lives. He's a happy soul, always smiling, always willing to do whatever is needed. The shout goes up from the bishop... Nathan! And Nathan responds, Yas, Baba! (Father [?] like Ghandi: Bapu.) He does whatever the bishop requires, bed-making, cleaning the Guest House, cooking, laying up & serving meals, shopping, doing the laundry, running to the photocopy shop, answering the telephone, gardening... He's transformed this garden by all accounts. He loves the bishop with a great devotion. He says he loves God, for rescuing him, for getting the bishop to rescue him. Whatever – he certainly feels loved and cared for again.*

*He said he was like the Prodigal Son.*

*What could I say to him? He'd seen my tears. I just gave him a hug. He was sweating and trembling, but he was smiling.*

*I mentioned all this to the bishop at supper. His reaction impressed me:*

*OUT OF THE VERY DEPTHS OF DEGRADATION AND MISERY, NATHAN HAS FOUND A PURPOSE IN HIS LIFE, BUT IT COULD ONLY HAPPEN ONCE HE TOOK HIS FIRST STEPS TOWARDS GOD – And a bit more about God's plan and needing to see things in the light of eternity.*

86

*Not sure about that. Seems to me Nathan paid a heavy price to learn God's plan.*

*What about all the deaths? Were they part of God's plan, too?*

\* \* \*

Dan was in the shower when he heard a knock at his door. He flung a towel around himself and glanced at his watch. It was after 11.30. Who could be calling so late? When he opened the door a wave of heat hit him and he could hear the sound of crickets in the darkness beyond. Luke was standing on the gravel below.

"Saw your light; thought I'd just check you're okay."

"I'm fine, come on in. I'll just find my slacks."

He hurried back to the shower room, snatched up his crumpled trousers and put them on. When he returned Luke was sitting on one of the cane chairs gazing into space. He looked exhausted and in the poor light his face seemed paler than usual.

"Sorry," said Dan, looking at the rumpled bed. "The room's a bit of a mess."

"Don't apologise. It's your room, and I'm intruding. Incidentally, I meant to mention – Nathan will do your laundry if you just give him the pile."

Dan was shocked. "I couldn't possibly! He's not my servant!"

Luke smiled at that. "It's part of his job and he'd be glad to, I assure you. He's proud to be of use. He likes us to look fairly smart. Reflects well on the bishop."

Was this an oblique way of saying that Dan was not smart enough?

"I wore my jacket all day in school," he said defensively.

"Come on, I didn't mean…"

"And it was bloody hot, I can tell you. Sweated like a pig; came home dripping."

They looked at each other and laughed.

"How did it go, the teaching?"

"It was great."

Luke looked at him closely. "Sure?"

Dan bristled. "Do you doubt me?"

"No, I don't doubt you," said Luke slowly. "I must

87

confess, though, I wondered how you'd get on. I thought, perhaps... Well, it's not exactly what you're used to, is it? I thought you might find it a bit overwhelming."

"Why should I find it overwhelming?" Dan knew he was sounding prickly.

"Look, let's leave it, shall we?" said Luke, tiredly. "I'm glad things went well. Are you going back tomorrow? Because I'm going to Kateri, and you said you'd like to come."

Dan hesitated, but he knew that nothing could now tear him away from the school. It had been a marvellous day, a wonderful experience, and in any case, he'd promised to be there. After this morning's debacle, he wasn't going to renege on it.

"I'll stick with the school, I think."

"Okay, then. That's all I came in to ask." Luke stood up wearily, putting a hand on his stomach. Dan tried to be more hospitable, and offered Luke a drink, but he refused, saying he just wanted his bed.

"How was your day?" Dan asked, as he opened the door for him. It sounded awkward, like a suburban housewife, and he flushed, but Luke seemed not to have noticed. "And your friend, how was he?"

Luke turned. "The newspaper office was interesting. I spent the whole of the morning at Nasarawa." He leant his forehead against the doorframe for a moment, a thin film of sweat on his forehead. "God, Dan, these people! They're hurting so much!"

Dan saw that he was holding himself slightly stooped.

"Are you all right?"

"I'm actually feeling a bit queasy. Just tired, I expect." He raised his face from which every vestige of colour had drained. "Dan, before I go, I'd like your opinion. Today I heard two opposing views, okay? One, from the journalist I met this afternoon, who'd had a letter saying that the religious identity of Nigeria was being compromised." He broke off. "Do you mind hearing this?"

"No, not at all. But you know I'm not into religion. Anyway, go on."

"Well, the reason given was that the Anglican schools, because they're church schools, ought to be abolished because they exclude a whole section of the community. Referring, naturally, to his Muslim neighbours and probably native religions, too."

"But Muslims don't want to go to Anglican schools, surely? Or vice versa?"

"Hear me out. He wants to see greater integration and he can't see it happening while there are faith schools of any sort. Of course he doesn't mention Muslim schools, only Christian ones. And he doesn't seem to mind how it happens so long as it happens. He speaks as a Christian wanting to affirm his own faith but also wanting more tolerance."

"Seems contradictory. He doesn't seem sure what he wants!"

"Hang on a minute. Here's the other view. In the morning, you see, I'd been with my friend Gibo. He told me that he's not sure he can be a priest any longer, and he's taking his family back to his wife's village, which is animist. His church has been burnt by the Muslims, and he's had death threats. He says they'd actually be safer if they stopped being practising Christians. So, given what you've seen since you've been here, and given the fragile nature of the political climate, how do you read that?"

"That religion's the cause of it all, that's how I read it. Given the choice I'd scrap it altogether!"

"Dan, you're in a religious country! You're *surrounded* by religion! It's the heart and soul of the place. It's not a matter of choice, and *you* don't have to live here! But let's say, for argument's sake, that you do. If you're born and bred here, and you don't have the choice, what would you think then?"

"I'd be conditioned to accept whatever was dished out, I expect."

"Oh, great!" Luke made a dismissive gesture. "Dan, you can sometimes be very shallow, you know! Why can't you *give* a little?"

"I'd actually rather prefer to go to bed!"

Luke stared at him angrily. Dan, his head bent, tried to quell the revulsion he always felt whenever the subject of religion raised its ugly head, and wondered what Luke meant by 'shallow'. Had Stephen been speaking to him? Then he remembered Hadissa's grief about her brother and his own terror on the road. He recalled Nathan's story, so lately told. He looked up.

"Well, what did you say to Gibo?"

"Oh, I don't know. Said he should talk it over with the bishop. But that's not the point. Two such opposing views, Dan!"

"Yes, but one's idealistic and theoretical, and the other's pragmatic."

"You think it's pragmatic for Gibo to consider stopping being a priest?"

"Well, as you said, I don't have to live here. I suppose some sort of integration ought to happen, but it probably matters *how* it happens. You can't impose it. Or can you? You asked me what I thought. I think they need to communicate more, ask questions of each other, get alongside, but I don't know how they'd do it. Maybe they could engage more with others on the opposite side of the fence, not just in the schools, but right across the board."

He swept his arm across his forehead, wiping away the sweat. "From what you tell me and from what I've seen and heard today, it seems to me that everyone is hurting. If they didn't exclude each other so much but actually spent time with each other, shared things they have in common, spoke about their own hurts and listened to the others... Well, then, perhaps they could then start doing things together while preserving their own identities. Actively blur the boundaries..."

Luke was intrigued. "You'd say that? Actively blur the boundaries?"

"Yes," replied Dan. "I think so. I think, perhaps, I would."

"When push comes to shove?"

"Look," said Dan, "you know much more about it than I do. But, from what you tell me about your friend Gibo, it sounds as if push *has* come to shove."

Luke turned to go. "Hmm...I'll sleep on that. Thank you. Kept you from your bed, too. Well, I'm off. I don't feel all that well."

He put a hand on Dan's shoulder. "Don't mind me saying this, Dan, but... well, I think Stephen would be proud of you. Only one day, and you've got your finger on the pulse."

\* \* \*

90

Dan came sharply awake. There it was again – the sound of bare feet scuffing against a dry wall, surreptitious, and slightly menacing. He sat up, listening, and edged the curtain aside. On top of the wall lay the huddled shape of a man, completely motionless, his clothes camouflaged by the shadows. Dan knew that if he could see him, he also could be seen. Their eyes almost met.

Dan became very afraid, and then furiously angry. He leapt out of bed and switched on the light. He knew it was dangerous, that if the man was armed he presented a very clear target, but at that moment he didn't care. He peered out of the window but the light had altered his vision and it was too dark to see anything. He switched off the light and sat on the side of the bed, breathing heavily. Outside all was now quiet. When, a few minutes later, he looked out again, the figure had gone.

For the rest of his life Dan would remember the intimacy of this silent, anonymous encounter in the darkness of an African compound – the black man on the wall at night, the white man raising himself from the clean sheets of his bed to gaze out, the electric light flowing onto darkness; the sense that, in spite of guards and guard dogs and high walls, nothing here was ever totally secure – and that it was utterly different from England.

# CHAPTER 8

When Dan returned from school next day he saw that the room that Hadissa had used was once more occupied; the shutters on the window were open and the door had been left ajar. His heart lifted. He encountered her as she was coming out of the bishop's front door. No longer in uniform, she wore instead a patterned, emerald green wrap-around skirt and bodice and a matching headdress that accentuated her glossy black skin and her almond shaped eyes. Dan thought he had never seen anything more beautiful. She saw him looking at her and her eyes dropped.

"Hadissa, *sannu!*"

"*Sannu kade*, Daniel."

She hadn't smiled. Perhaps, thought Dan, she was regretting her display of grief the other night, so he laid his hands reassuringly on her shoulders. She looked up, as startled as a bird, and he was conscious of the fragility of her bones, of the heat of them under his fingers.

"Are you well?" he asked, trying to look into her eyes.

"Very well, *na gode*," she answered quietly. "And you?"

He searched her face. "I'm well. But you, how are you?" he repeated. "How's the tiredness?"

She looked up at him then, and a flicker of amusement crossed her face.

"No tiredness," she said, using the Hausa formula but speaking in English. She stayed quite still under his hands, and again Dan thought how like a bird she was, a trapped bird, and he dropped his hands from her shoulders.

"Forgive me... How's your work?"

"Dan," she said with mock severity, but with a twinkle in her eyes, "these questions, this is how we, in Hausa, greet each other. It's a mere formality and we don't expect to be given accurate answers. And we don't expect strangers to ask quite so many questions!"

92

Dan was disconcerted, and he took her hands impulsively. "I wasn't being formal! I'm interested, for God's sake! I really want to know."

"And you shouldn't take the name of God." She paused, smiling. "And, excuse me, but you shouldn't touch me."

His hands dropped from hers as if they were live coals, and it was his turn to be confused. She turned the subject tactfully, and asked him how he had been occupying himself. The phrase rankled – to her I'm just a visitor, he thought; the real work is done by others, people like her. They began to walk together on the grass, side by side, but he was careful not to touch her again. He began to tell her about the school.

"And what of you?" he asked, finally, "Is there some way I can find out about you, without being too formal, and actually get some real answers?"

Hadissa laughed, and told him that she had been working in the hospital again, and that her consultant had been pleased with her report about the clinic at Kateri.

"I didn't know you'd written a report."

She told him how her consultant had instructed her to go to Kateri and examine the medical facilities there and discover what the situation was like in the bush. She did not tell him about her broken love affair, and he saw no reason to tell her about his, with Ellen. Thus they lost their first opportunity to confide.

Dan studied her face in the harsh light of the late afternoon sun. She looked straight ahead as she spoke, and he was able to examine her profile. He could see every mark on her face, including the three faint, diagonal scars of her tribal markings on each cheek. Her lips were full but finely shaped, and her nose, though it was wide at the nostrils, was retroussé. Her skull was strongly slanted from the base of her neck, and her body was slim, with high breasts and a virginal, flat stomach. He thought, again, how immensely dignified she was, graceful, like a young gazelle, and he felt his heart constrict.

"So, Harmattan," she was asking, "did you learn the children's names?"

"Not many! There're a couple of twins who are absolutely gorgeous, Sammi and Maria..."

"Twins *are* a couple." She smiled at him. "I should know. Go on."

He grinned. "I stand corrected. Well, they're easy to

remember, though if I met them separately I don't suppose I could identify them. Bright as buttons. They can't read, but they seem to understand the concepts perfectly well. There're quite a few like that."

"Some of them come straight from the bush," she said defensively, "and often there is no *makaranta*. English, you realise, is their second language, too."

"You said 'makaranta'?"

"Village school."

"Of course. They told me that word yesterday."

"Even some of the makaranta kids don't learn, especially if they're needed in the fields. Most don't start to read properly until they go to secondary school."

"Well," he said, after a moment, "tell me, what are you doing here tonight? If it's any of my business, which it's not. Are you here for the meal?"

"Yes, and a meeting. My consultant is talking with the bishop, and they want me present. Probably to add some details about the clinic."

They had done a full circle of the garden and were now back at the door of her guest room.

"Well, I'll say goodbye for the present," he said reluctantly. "I must go shower. How do you say 'goodbye' in Hausa?"

She smiled at him and her eyes gleamed. "You say *sannu*."

"Oh, I thought that was 'hello'."

"We do not have much in Nigeria," she remarked mischievously, "so we have to be economical with what we do have. It's the same word."

Smiling, he left her at the door and went in to change. He showered, towelling himself vigorously, thinking about her. He was immensely attracted to her, and wanted to know more about her. She had called him 'Harmattan' more than once, and he wondered what that signified, if anything. He discovered that he had completely put aside his thoughts of Ellen and that, in fact, he was no longer depressed. He had only been in Africa a couple of days, but already he felt renewed and stimulated. He attributed that to the teaching.

* * *

94

Dan had not seen Luke since the previous night, but on his way over to supper he found him walking back to the guest room, still holding his stomach.

"You'll take your meal in your room tonight," he announced as they drew near each other. "The bishop's got a meeting."

"Oh." Dan was disappointed not to be seeing more of Hadissa, but then he saw Luke's white face. "What about you?"

"I'm not eating. I've been in bed the whole day. Dicky tummy."

"My God, why didn't anyone tell me? Are you all right?"

"Not very..." Luke looked at him, unfocussed, and then suddenly leant forward and vomited, splashing Dan's sleeve. Dan caught him before he hit the ground. He was shivering and he seemed very weak.

"Sorry..."

"Let's get you back."

Dan half dragged him to his guest room, fumbling with the key that Luke handed to him. Once inside Luke managed to tear off his outer jacket before collapsing on to the bed, and Dan hauled the covers over him. He ran to the shower area and fetched the bucket, which he put by his bed. Immediately, Luke was sick again, then he fell back, panting, feverishly clutching the bedcovers. Another spasm shook him and he retched in his throat, swallowing convulsively, but did not vomit again.

Dan looked at him helplessly. "Where d'you keep your water?"

"Ran out. Nathan was going to get me some more, but he forgot, I think. Too busy." He lay back on the bed, his face as white as the pillow.

"Will you be okay if I go and fetch some? I've got some in my room. You ought to drink, you know."

"Thanks." Luke closed his eyes.

Dan spent the whole evening looking after Luke. He sat in his shirtsleeves on the chair by his side, watching him, sweating as the heat rose in the confined room. At last the sick man sank into a troubled sleep, and Dan picked up a book from the floor by the bed, and tried to read, but it was a Bible commentary and he couldn't concentrate. Luke had said it was

95

only a 'dicky tummy', but Dan felt he didn't know enough to be sure, and he didn't want to leave him. He was aware of cars arriving and later, departing. Once he went back to his room for more water and found a tray of congealed food on the table inside his room. He snatched a mouthful of bread but couldn't face the rest, so he grabbed a new bottle of water and returned to Luke. At about midnight, he began to worry, for he sensed that Luke was showing no sign of improvement. He suspected he was becoming delirious. He was mumbling incoherently, words and phrases reminiscent of the prayers Dan had heard in the past, in their college chapel.

He wondered what to do. He got up and went to the door. The night hung over the compound, heavy and oppressive, and except for the loud pulsing call of the crickets, the compound was completely silent. There were no lights to be seen and he could hear no sound from the city. He went back to the bed and put his hand gently on Luke's forehead. It was clammy and cold, but under his perspiration it was like a furnace.

Dan stood there a minute, acutely conscious of his isolation. Then he remembered Hadissa, asleep across the compound. She was a nurse, damn it; she would know what to do! Quickly he threw on his shoes and raced across to her guest room. Low clouds swept across the sky obscuring the stars, and a warm wind blew through his shirtsleeves. Hadissa's shutters were partly open but behind the silvery nets the room was in darkness. He went to the door and knocked, at first gently, then more insistently.

"Who is it?" Her voice sounded tremulous, fearful.

"Don't worry," he hissed. "It's me, Daniel."

She opened the door, clad only in her night shift, though she had pulled her shawl over her shoulders.

"Daniel, what on earth are you doing here? Is anything the matter?"

"It's Luke. He's sick. I'm afraid he's… He's very sick. Hadissa, can you come? I mean, are you allowed to?"

She regarded him for a moment, and then turned away.

"I'll just get my things."

He waited, shoving his hands in his pockets and fidgeting, but when she emerged she was dressed, and carrying her bag and a stack of water bottles.

"Take these, will you," she said. "I'm about to drop

96

them." He caught the bottles as they slipped from her grasp.

"What is it, do you think?" he asked, as they hurried across the drive.

"Don't know till I see him. Has he had malaria?"

"*Malaria?*"

"Don't worry. It's more likely something he ate, but we'll see." She laid her hand on his arm, and even though Dan was desperately worried about Luke, he was conscious of her touch. It was the first time she had voluntarily touched him.

"Has he been in the townships?" she asked.

"Yesterday. Nasarawa."

"In that case he's probably eaten something bad. Bush meat. Or drank bad water. Is this the door?"

She walked straight into Luke's room without knocking. She seemed very professional. She pulled back the covers and palpated Luke's stomach, rolled his eyelids back and peered into his eyes.

"Take his trousers off, please."

Embarrassed, Dan pulled off Luke's trousers and dropped them on the floor. Hadissa carefully pulled aside his underpants and felt in his groin. Dan found himself flushing as her fingers disappeared among the soft hairs of Luke's navel and he turned away. Hadissa felt in her bag for her thermometer and took his temperature anally, then glanced up, frowning.

"I don't think his glands are up, but he has a very high fever. Dangerously high, I'm afraid. This man needs the hospital, Daniel."

"What is it?" Dan's voice was high pitched, and she smiled.

"Well, I don't think it's malaria or yellow fever. I'd know from his complexion. I think it's what I said. But he's very dehydrated, so we need to get him to a hospital. I'll go and wake the bishop. We'll need Nathan to drive him."

She looked at him closely. "You're sweating, too. Do you feel okay?"

"I'm fine. It's probably just the anxiety and the running about." He gave her a weak smile, watching her adjust her shawl round her shoulders.

"It'll take a few minutes to organise things," she said at the door. "I have to ring the hospital, tell them we're coming. And someone needs to ring the police so we can bypass the curfew. Will you be all right?"

"Just *hurry*."

Dan sat and waited, watching the sick man, who for the most part lay quiet and motionless on the tumbled bed, though occasionally he moved restlessly, and muttered disjointed words, the flush on his face deepening as his fever rose still more. As the minutes went by, Dan became increasingly anxious. Luke had not moved or spoken again, and Dan feared he was unconscious. He felt tired and sweaty, his teeth furred up. He got up, went to the door and looked out.

Outside the sky was paling and the wind had dropped but he could hear the sound of a car starting up in the compound. He rubbed his eyes, which were pricking in the cool air, and waited while the car moved slowly across the gravel to where he was standing. The bishop was walking alongside, dressed in a linen dhoti over casual trousers and wearing his pectoral cross. He greeted Dan cheerily.

"Now, then, don't worry, he'll be in good hands."

Dan shook his head miserably and turned back into the room.

Nathan got out of the driver's seat, and together they wrapped Luke in blankets and lifted him into the back of the car, Hadissa squeezing in beside him with a bottle of water from which a knob of cotton wool protruded. Apparently the bishop himself was going to drive. Dan felt a moment's surprise, and then thought, *Well, why on earth not?*

"Can I come?" he said. "I'd like..."

"Get in beside me, Dan, if you want to come," said the bishop. "But there'll be nothing to do once we reach the hospital and you're teaching in the morning. Shouldn't you get some sleep?"

"I'll be okay. I'd like to go with him. I'll just grab my jacket."

To his amazement, as he climbed into the car, the bishop was praying out loud.

"... And we ask your blessing on Luke, and all of us in this vehicle, that we may pass safely to the hospital, and that Luke may be healed for your glory."

He finished, and turned on the engine, even while Hadissa was murmuring her 'amen'.

The road into the city was deserted. Piles of litter and

broken cartons were strewn around the pavements, where scavenging dogs slunk away at the sound of the car. The bishop drove quickly but efficiently, taking the corners gently, then he braked suddenly, muttering under his breath. Ahead of them, the road was blocked by a tank positioned across their lane. Orange lights were flashing, and armed soldiers moved forwards, training their rifles on them.

"Accident?"

"No, just surveillance. Leave it to me."

Slowly they edged forward, then stopped at the road-block. The bishop switched off the ignition and got out. Dan craned his head to see what was going on. It was too much the echo of his first journey and, fearfully, he wondered what would happen next. He could hear nothing, but eventually the soldier waved them on. The tank jerked forward loudly, its treads churning up the surface of the street, raising a red dust.

The bishop got back in and started the car. "Good. Soon be there now."

At the hospital everything happened very fast. As Hadissa was known in casualty they were able to bypass the form-filling. She and the bishop disappeared with Luke, now on a hospital trolley and covered with a thin hospital blanket, and Dan was left alone. The electric lights went out one by one, leaving a single blue bulb illuminating the waiting area. The corridor was lined with trolleys, and when he looked more closely he realised that each was occupied by a sleeping figure. Between them other people slept, curled up in blankets on the bare floor. He saw eyes gleaming in black faces, and he supposed they must be relatives.

He stretched out on the plastic chairs, making himself as comfortable as he could with his jacket and Hadissa's shawl, which she had left behind. He pressed it to his face, smelling the musk of her body, comforted. He dozed fitfully then fell into a troubled sleep. He dreamt of wide black eyes, flaming torches, and unaccountably, of russet leaves blown by the wind and a lane stretching away between the hills. It wasn't until he heard his name that he realised he had been sleeping. Hadissa was standing over him smiling, and he pulled himself upright, running his tongue round his teeth.

"Are you all right?" she asked.

"Yeah, I'm okay." He sat up awkwardly, looking

around. "God, what's that smell?"

"It's only the buckets," she said defensively. "I'm sorry."

"No, don't be!" he exclaimed. "It doesn't matter... I need a drink, though," he added, getting up and reaching for the half-empty bottle in her hand, but she shook her head.

"You shouldn't drink from this – it was Luke's. I'll go and fetch some..."

"No, don't go yet." He grabbed her sleeve. "How is he?"

"He's fine, but we're keeping him in for the day. We don't have a spare bed, but he'll be okay where he is for a few hours, then we'll send him back to you."

"What's the matter with him?"

"Not much. He's stopped being sick, so I think it was as I thought, just something he ate. Then, of course, he got dehydrated. That's what caused the fever. The fever itself was more dangerous, but now he's on an intravenous drip, so he'll be okay in a few hours. But you'll have to see that he rests for a day or two."

"I will. Thank you." He wanted to ask, "Was the needle clean?" However, he was too ashamed. "And I'm very, very grateful," he said fervently. "But what about you, Hadissa? I mean, are you on duty now?"

"No, I'm on nights, so I can go back with you. I need to pick up the rest of my things and then go to the Nurses' Home. I'll just have my shawl, if you don't mind."

He picked up the crumpled shawl and rather shamefacedly placed it around her shoulders.

She looked up at him gravely. "You were worried, weren't you?" she asked gently. "But I couldn't have come back to you sooner. There were things we had to do for Luke. And then others, who came in later."

"I *was* worried last night," he admitted, "but I stopped once you'd come. You probably saved his life." His voice caught. "I... I didn't know what to do."

She put her arm around his waist as though she was helping a patient. It was a light, almost sisterly touch and Dan felt the strain of the night dissipating. He reached behind him and grasped her wrist.

"Let's get out of here. Let's go home."

# CHAPTER 9

Outside the sun had risen and the light sparkled on the loose gravel of the street and reflected, dazzlingly, from the roofs of passing vehicles. Crowds of people thronged the pavements, dodging the dusty piles of litter and black plastic sacks bulging with refuse. Dan looked at his watch and discovered it was nearly seven.

"I've got school and I'm shattered. And I'll hardly have time to change."

Hadissa was used to sixteen-hour shifts and it didn't cross her mind that Dan might be too tired to teach that morning, so she did not make an issue of it. They walked on through the streets, Dan slightly ahead of her, and though he persisted in waiting for her, looking at her quizzically, she urged him to stay in front, saying that it would not be good for her to be seen walking alone with a man who was not her husband, especially a white man.

It was the first time Dan had been to the city centre. Smart concrete office blocks behind high wrought-iron gates were juxtaposed with low wooden shanties, and every possible space between was occupied by a ramshackle outbuilding of painted brick, or a lean-to, its sloping, corrugated iron roofs copper coloured with rust. On the older buildings the shade of the original paint had long since faded in the sun, but the colours were still vibrant, and Dan recalled the African love of bright colour. In the shop doorways were old paint cans stacked with red canna lilies or clusters of yellow maize, and through the barbed wire fencing surrounding the weed-clogged yards, the occasional vegetable plot. Rusted hulks of burnt out cars lay against the kerbs among tattered mattresses and unspeakable gutter garbage. In one place chickens ran freely among the pedestrians and in front of one shack, he saw partially-clad children squatting in the dust, their bottoms bared, teasing a heavy sow tied up by its nose. Running alongside the road and panning away from it was a street market, where traders were beginning to unload their produce from battered vans and trucks, which were double parked, dangerously close to the passing traffic. Strong purple shadows slanted across the street, and a miasma of traffic fumes and dust was rising in a hazy cloud to obscure the sky.

The tank had gone. Cars moved slowly along the road, bumper to bumper, hooting and honking as bikes got in their way or someone jaywalked. A truck full of factory workers edged through the traffic on its way to the Peugeot plant nearby, and Dan could see children in school uniform walking in twos and threes carrying their large school bags or bundles. They were all going in the same direction, all heading further into the city centre. At the same time, ahead of them, a school bus was passing up the street. On the corner was a mosque, a huge, imposing building built of concrete and mosaic tiles, and the bus paused in the traffic, waiting to turn. It was packed with school children and even at that distance Dan could recognise the bright blue uniforms of the Cathedral School. He stopped, glancing over his shoulder at Hadissa. "This is useless. I'll never get there and back in time. I'd better run. I'm not fit to be seen."

Hadissa looked at him in surprise. "No one will mind if you go as you are."

"No, but I ought to change my shirt, at least. Anyway, what are your plans...?"

He stopped abruptly and gripped her arm.

Afterwards he would say that there had been no warning, but at the time he felt a strong premonition that something was about to happen. It was as if all sounds had ceased, all his senses suddenly alert.

A man ran swiftly towards him, pushing his way through the crowd, the expression on his face a strange mixture of exultation and blind panic. He was dressed in a soiled white cotton tunic and he was so thin that he was almost cavernous. His face was gaunt, and he had an ugly scar on his cheek, extending from his ear to his chin.

Hadissa gasped, clutching Dan's hand fearfully. The sight of anyone running was unusual and always aroused suspicion, for the heat prohibited it. They clutched each other, watching as the man disappeared into the crowd.

Dan would never forget what he saw then. It was

branded on his mind forever.

There was a colossal explosion; the street rocked with it, as the whole of the front high wall of the mosque was ripped apart. It canted outwards, scattering chunks of concrete and twisted steel rods, pieces of polished wood and brightly patterned tiles across the street. Even as he watched, aghast, the whole wall seemed to land on the bus, flattening it like a crushed beetle. At the same moment, the back window of the bus disintegrated, and to his horror, Dan saw the small limp bodies of children catapulted through the air, together with shards of glass and fragments of clothing, which fluttered lazily down, like falling leaves caught in a gust of wind. Dan saw a man, thrown backwards by the aftershock, fall against a woman with a baby, knocking them both to the ground. The nearest cars slumped on flattened tyres, and other vehicles stopped haphazardly on the road, their brakes screeching. Out of nowhere, a motorbike mounted the pavement, its rider toppling headfirst into a pile of boxes outside a nearby shop front. For a brief moment, it was a tableau caught in time.

It became very dark. Then the screaming started. People lay where they had fallen, moaning, bleeding and struggling in vain to get up. Others ran from the scene as if demented, shouting and screaming. Those Muslims who had been at prayer in the mosque were pouring out of the ruins, a forest of waving arms and wild, streaming eyes. Bareheaded, barefooted, their clothes tattered and bloodstained, they carried the inert bodies of their friends, or limped alone, shrieking their anger with hoarse voices against the sky. Every one of them was covered in dust.

Dan tore his eyes away from the stricken bus, searching for Hadissa, and saw to his dismay that she lay hunched on the pavement. A piece of charred cloth landed on her hair, and he leapt towards her, slapping out the sparks.

"I'm all right…" Her voice was almost inaudible. "Oh, *God*…!"

It was a long drawn out moan, for she had seen what was left of the bus. She tried to get to her feet, but Dan stopped her.

"Wait. You might be hurt. Wait a minute…"

"*No*! Let me *up*! Let me *get* to them!" It was a scream of anguish, hard, primeval, and ugly, and Dan drew back. She began to totter down the street towards the wrecked bus. Her shift was torn and her knees bloody. Dan ran after her and

103

grabbed her by the arm.

"Hadissa, wait! *Wait*! It might blow up…"

"Let *go* of me!" It was almost a snarl, and he dropped her arm.

"In that case I'm coming with you!"

They fought their way through prone and bleeding bodies towards the wreck of the bus. Children lay where they had fallen, draped over the shattered window frames, their small bodies punctured by innumerable splinters of glass, and across the gaping emergency exit was a small boy, limp as sodden washing. Dan could see pieces of flesh spattered on the paintwork. To his horror, when he attempted to lift the child away from the lethal shards of glass, his arm came away in his hands. The sight of the red flesh against the smooth black skin made the bile rise in his throat. It seemed to light a fuse within him, and he discovered a depth of anger of which he had hardly known he was capable. He ran the length of the bus, like one possessed, peering in at battered child after battered child, swallowing convulsively, terrified that there would be another explosion or that the bus would combust. The door was twisted under a huge slab of concrete, so he returned to the back of the bus, ripped off his jacket, threw it hastily across the gaping window, grabbed the frame and hauled himself up.

Cowering back in the dusty darkness were a group of children, huddled together, keening, their eyes liquid with fright, their noses running with mucus. Thankfully, they recognised him, and stretched out their hands to him. It was an image that imprinted itself on his mind and remained with him for years.

One by one, he shepherded them to the rear window, and with his arms extended to the limit of his reach, lowered them to the road, where, shocked and bewildered, they immediately collapsed, clutching each other and wailing. Then he turned back to face the deeper interior, which he feared would be little more than a desolate pit of shattered concrete, twisted metal, and crushed limbs. There was little light from the windows, and heavy dust obscured what light there was. The further in he penetrated, the darker it seemed, and soon he had to stoop, for the roof of the bus had buckled and flattened itself on its occupants. The smell of spilled diesel penetrated everything and the heat was intense.

What he saw then seared his mind. Among the open

bundles and bags was the body of a young girl, her eyes closed as if asleep, her long eyelashes sealed over the glossy brown skin of her cheeks. His heart lifted in uncertain hope, but when he gently turned her head, he saw that half her face was missing and the white collar of her school shirt was stained a delicate pink, as if dyed.

The sweat poured off him as he worked his way along the dreadful innards of the bus, where, out of the bright morning, death had come so swiftly. Fragments of metal tore his knees and shins as he fought through the havoc to reach the shattered bodies of the children. Here were scattered books, open to reveal childish handwriting and squared-out sums; there, an untouched crate of water, the bottles completely intact. The backs of seats were ripped and torn, their stuffing protruding like entrails, and, all around, an incoherent jumble of blue-uniformed bodies lay on the buckled floor. The front of the bus had been completely compressed and in places, he could have reached down and touched the road. Vertigo assailed him and, for a moment, he was blinded by sweat and tears. Although he no longer expected that anyone else had survived, he edged forward, gently touching and stroking each face, hoping for a sign of life. Three were already dead; one, moaning at his touch, died under his hand. Mercifully, there was no fire, and at last, deep under the blackened interior of the slanting roof, he heard whimpering. His heart leapt. He had to fight through bodies to get to the sound, and only when he pushed aside the last shreds of clothing, did he see that it was the twins, Sammi and Maria, huddled together under the crushed frame of the front seat. Beyond he could just discern the contorted figure of the driver, head back, his eyes staring, empty, his white shirt bloodied and torn. His mouth was wide open in a silent scream and a trickle of dark blood stained his throat.

Maria had a huge gash right across her cheek and she was unconscious, lying partly on top of Sammi, both of them imprisoned under the weight of the crushed seats and smashed concrete. Sammi was groaning and gasping for breath. Dan touched his arm.

"Quietly, now." His tone was exquisitely tender. "It's okay. It's going to be okay. I'm going to get you out. Now, don't worry, but I am going to yell like a banshee."

He took a deep breath. "Here, in here!" he shouted.

"Help me! For God's sake, someone come and help me!"

His voice seemed harsh, even to himself, rough with his tears and the dust that had got into his throat, and Sammi shrieked in fright.

"Sammi!" he whispered urgently, "Sammi, listen! It's me, the Englishman – the *bature*. I taught you in school, remember? I'm going to get you out of here. Now tell me, does it hurt anywhere?"

"My legs... and... my back." Sammi's voice was almost inaudible, no more than a trace.

Dan looked around. The child should really not be moved; not, at least, by him. There should be paramedics and stretchers, anaesthetics and painkillers, a brace for the neck and another for the back and the legs. He knew it wouldn't happen. No one had come to help him. *This is Africa*, he thought bleakly, *where people are hurting all the time. I'm not in England now. I can't expect...*

He took hold of Sammi, but when he tugged gently the child screamed again, and he let go, fearful of causing more harm to the damaged limbs. Sammi was crying for his sister, "M'ia! M'ia!" and tears were coursing from his eyes, making transparent rivulets in the dust on his brown cheeks.

"Sammi, listen to me!" Dan said steadily. "*Listen*. We're going to get you out. Maria too. She's okay; she's alive. Now, don't scream again unless I hurt you, but if I do hurt you, then yell like mad. I want to be able to move you, but I can't move you if you scream all the time, because I'm afraid of hurting you. Sammi, try to understand," he pleaded. "Sammi, Sammi, do you understand?"

The child had fainted.

Once more Dan looked around for help but there was no sign that anyone was braving the deep interior of the bus, although the dust had settled, and he was aware that, outside, it was bright sunshine. Everything around him was silent, a nether region almost insulated from sound, but he could hear the sound of running feet and people shouting, and at last, a distant siren.

*Thank God*! he thought, and waited, cradling Sammi's head on his knee. With his free hand he tried to lift Maria's head away from the jagged metal of the back of the seat. The sun was beginning to penetrate the dust and darkness, illuminating the bodies with a sweet, diaphanous light, and dust motes danced obscenely in its slanting rays. He strained his eyes again to see if he could discern movement from the other children, but saw nothing that gave him hope. He waited, with mounting despair, resting his head against a piece of broken concrete, feeling his legs cramp under him and the sweat trickling down his face and his back. Again, feeling panic rise within him, threatening his equilibrium, he shouted again. He needed to move, to get out, but he knew that he couldn't possibly leave the twins in case they woke and found him gone. He couldn't have borne that – for them to wake in terror.

It seemed an age before he became aware that a figure had darkened the passageway behind him.

"Daniel?" It was Hadissa.

"Here!" he shouted. "I'm down here!"

He tried to twist round. She was covered in blood up to her arms, and a swathe of blood was smeared over one cheek.

"You *are* hurt..." he whispered.

She heard him. "No, I'm not – it's not my blood, Daniel."

He couldn't speak.

"I heard your voice," she said. "Are any alive?"

"Two. I don't know about the others. You must look, Hadissa," he said, his voice straining. "You must look. I can't... I don't know how..." Something snapped within him, and he began to sob.

She worked her way methodically down the bus towards him, gently feeling for a pulse in necks and wrists, her face impassive and concentrated now, once more professional.

There was no one else alive.

"Where the hell are the emergency services?" he growled, his voice muffled with emotion, and Hadissa looked at him, noticing the dust and blood and tears on his face.

"What emergency services?" She was scathingly angry, but not with him.

"I thought I heard a siren..."

"Police. The police are here. No medics, yet."

"But the hospital's just up the *street*!"

"No, it's up to you and me. Who've you got there?"

"The twins, Sammi and Maria. Sammi's hurt his legs and his back, and Maria... I don't know about Maria. She's unconscious. Sammi's drifting in and out."

107

"Let's have a look." She squirmed down into the gap. "They're lucky…"

"*Lucky*? My God…"

"The seats protected them a bit. We'll get them out."

"How?" He almost screamed the word at her. "They're trapped!"

She was panting, wrestling with a piece of metal. "We'll get cutting equipment. It's coming. It's on its way. We'll get them out."

"Why only them?"

The relief at seeing her, at seeing anyone, had broken him, and he was distraught. This experience was unlike anything he had ever known, and it unmanned him.

"Why only them? Why not the others?"

Hadissa suddenly reached down and stroked his cheek. It was a sweet gesture, and it calmed him. It seemed to go on for a long time, this stroking of his cheek. She wiped away the tears, and smoothed away the traces of blood.

"Hadissa…" It was a whisper.

"I know, I know," she crooned, and he became still.

"Now," she repeated, once more businesslike, "let's get us out of here, shall we? Look, I'm going to leave you for a minute, try to speed things up. The police will have a radio."

Others helped at last. It was a macabre task, and once more it reduced Dan to tears but Hadissa was grim-faced and indomitable. With the help of shopkeepers and an engineer from the Peugeot factory with a toolbox in his car, they finally released the twins from their confinement. There was another long delay while they waited for the ambulance to reach them, but at last it arrived and they were able to hand over their charges. Through all this Sammi's eyes were wide open, glazed with shock, and he was completely speechless. His wide, chestnut eyes searched for his sister, and only when they laid her next to him did he close his eyes, and drift into sleep.

Superfluous, Dan stood on the pavement and waited for Hadissa. He looked around, dazed. Someone from the market had covered the diminutive bodies of the children with lengths of brightly patterned cloth. It lifted slightly in the slight breeze, and then settled once more on the contours of their bodies – an almost obscene sight that brought more tears into his eyes. He was exhausted, but filled with admiration for Hadissa. She worked tirelessly, moving among the dead and wounded, until the last patient had been taken to hospital and the last body removed. Only then did she return to him. She sat down with him and leant against the wall, her hands dangling. He noticed that her nails were broken, her knuckles bruised, as though she had been in a fight.

By then it was late morning, and the traffic had begun to pass once more, though a noisy crowd of people had gathered, waving their arms and shouting for revenge, their eyes gleaming with hatred. Dan and Hadissa watched them soberly as the police sealed off the area with ribbons and began to disperse the crowd. A team of workmen appeared to shore up the remainder of the mosque with scaffolding and wooden planks.

"Is there anything more to do?" he asked tiredly.

Hadissa looked down at him. His eyes were red rimmed and she saw that under the reddish stubble on his cheeks and neck his face was ashen.

"No. You'd better go home. Will you be okay on your own?"

"Yeah. But what about you?" He choked in his throat. "Hadissa..."

"Yes?"

"Thank... thank God we were here!"

"Yes," she replied softly, "thank God."

They were silent for a moment, both of them trying to absorb what they had seen and done. Then he said, "It's strange, but..."

"What?"

"Oh, nothing," he replied. "It's just that, immediately before the explosion... What was it, a bomb?"

"Probably. We'll hear later. But, dear God, why on earth would they target little children?"

"What?" He looked at her, confused. "Who? The Muslims? They didn't. It was the mosque, Hadissa. The bomb was in the mosque."

"In the mosque? I thought the bus exploded."

"No, it didn't," Dan said. "If it had, we wouldn't... It was the mosque, Hadissa. It just came down on the bus. Don't you see?"

"You mean *we* did it?" she interrupted incredulously. "The Christians? Are you sure? Oh my God, that's even worse!"

109

"Remember the man, running? I think it was him. Oh," he sighed, "I don't know who did it, but I know the mosque went first. The bus just happened to be there. They were caught up in it, that's all." He recalled the first, sickening thump of the explosion, and felt a surge of disbelief, knowing himself to be truly a stranger in a strange land. He blinked furiously.

"What were you going to say?"

"When? Oh, nothing," he said, subsiding. He roused himself again, grasping at normality. "Just before the bomb, I was going to ask you what your plans were. I thought we might have met up later, if you'd have liked. Now it hardly seems…"

"My plans…" she said, smiling ruefully. "My plan was to have a girls' day, all on my own. Have a shower, wash my hair, do some food shopping… We had a long night, remember? Now, well, I shall go back to the hospital. They'll need everyone they can get. And you? What will you do? They'll shut the school."

"How can they shut the school? There'll be children who've come in from other areas. And the Head, he'll be devastated. No, I'll have to go there. Incidentally, what happened to the bishop? One minute he was there, the next I lost sight of him. In the hospital, I mean."

"Oh, he went home sometime in the night, while you were sleeping. I don't think he realised you were still in the waiting room."

"He forgets things, sometimes, doesn't he?" Dan got to his feet. "Anyway, you'll let me know about Sammi and Maria?"

"Of course. And Daniel…"

"Yeah?" He ran a hand through his hair.

"I'll come back tonight and see you. Before my night shift."

He met her eyes. "You will?"

"Yes."

*   *   *

It was a long walk. Dan's sweat had dried on him while he was waiting for Hadissa, but he was wet through again by the time he arrived back at the compound. Everything was quiet. He went to his room, grabbed a bottle of water and ripped the plastic cover off, downing it in one go. Then he showered, standing naked under the warm water and gazing into space. The blood from his cuts ran freely down his arms and legs, and he ran a basin of water and emptied the salt cellar into it, then bathed them with his wet towel and dressed them with clean handkerchiefs from a drawer.

The images of the morning would not leave his mind and he knew he would be in for a few rough nights. He found a clean shirt and looked around for his jacket, only then remembering that he had left it on the bus. Well, he could say goodbye to that, but what was he to do instead? He went in search of Nathan, dreading how the news of the bomb would have affected the already traumatised house servant. Nathan was in the kitchen preparing food for the evening, the tears running down his face. He flung down his knife and walked into Dan's outstretched arms.

"Oh, massa!"

"You know, of course."

"We got word, sah. His Lordship and all his staff went straight to the cathedral."

They stood there for a minute, then Dan released him. There was nothing he could say. Nathan wiped his eyes with his sleeve and looked up.

"Massa, how can I help you?"

"Nathan, it's stupid, but I need a jacket. Mine got lost this morning. Is there one around I could use?"

Nathan thought for a minute and then his eyes lit up.

"There is one. It was left behind, but..." His face fell. "I don't think it will fit you, massa, for you are tall and this man, he was short and, I am sorry, sah, rather fat."

"Let's have a look. I can always leave it flapping. On the scale of things it hardly matters, does it? But I suppose I ought to wear something."

"There's something else you can wear, just to look smart."

Nathan took him along the corridor to the bishop's private quarters. The bedroom was spartan: a single bed, a chest of drawers piled high with books, and a wooden utilitarian wardrobe. Two rugs partially covered the bare floorboards, and against the partially closed shutters was a single curtain, lank in the midday heat. A naked bulb hung from the ceiling. Nathan led him through to the dressing room, where vestments hung from hooks on the wall. He opened a deep wooden chest, and felt among the neat piles of clothing, laying some of them out carefully on the floor. Finally, he brought out a full-length, unbleached-cotton tunic, made of a single piece of homespun, with long wide sleeves and a plain square neck.

"You can use this while you're with us."

Dan held it up. "I can't wear this! It's a dress!"

Nathan laughed softly. "No, massa, it's not a dress. It's the tunic of a chief. It belongs to the bishop but he never uses it…"

"I'm not surprised."

"…I think, perhaps, it is not to His Lordship's taste. He prefers bright colours. But it's quite new. It was a gift from some women in one of the villages. Try it on."

There was no mirror but when Dan slipped the tunic on over his head and shook out the sleeves, even Nathan was impressed.

"Now you are Af-ri-can!" he smiled.

Dan was unconvinced. "It still looks like a dress, to me."

"Not to an African, massa!"

"Hadn't I better take the fat man's jacket instead?"

"No, massa." Nathan was firm. "You must wear this. Oh, massa, I heard what you did! You have deserved it."

\* \* \*

They walked back to the kitchen together.

"Is there anything else I can do for you, massa?" Nathan asked. "Some little thing? Any little thing?"

"No, Nathan, I'm fine. How's Luke, though? He's not back, is he?"

"We've heard nothing, sah. I'm sorry. You could visit him in the hospital."

Dan put a hand to his forehead and sighed. "I should have thought of that. I could have done it before I left. Now I've got to go to the school…"

"Yus, massa."

Dan was suddenly ravenously hungry, for he had had nothing to eat since the school lunch of the previous day, and that had only been flatbread and soup.

"Nathan, I know you don't serve lunch, but I'm…

desperately hungry."

God in heaven, he'd nearly said dying of hunger! How carelessly we use words, he thought, but not here. Not in Africa. No one would ever say they were dying of hunger unless they meant it.

"Peanut sandwich, sah?"

"...Great."

He took a bottle of water and munched the sandwich in the street, retracing his footsteps towards the school. He turned his eyes away from the half-demolished mosque and the wreck of the bus. The school building was silent and empty and he wondered where everyone was. The cathedral was situated behind the school. He had not yet been inside but now he made his way across the dirt yard to the main door.

To his amazement, as he approached he heard sounds of singing, which ceased as he climbed the steps. The doors were wide open and he could see rows of dark, rounded heads, and a flurry of movement as they sat down. The bishop, wearing his purple cassock, was standing at the front, though from this distance Dan could not hear what he was saying.

"You want to come in?"

Dan recognised one of the teachers, peering round at him from just inside the doorway.

"Come in. There's room. You are welcome."

"No... No, it's okay," Dan replied diffidently. His white face would stick out like a sore thumb, and he had no intention of intruding on their private grief. "I'll just stay out here for a bit, thanks."

After a short while the children stood up again, and once more they began to sing. It was a hymn that he recognised from his college days. The tune was *Finlandia*, and the words, like 'dying of hunger', had a deeper resonance in this place. At the sound of the high-pitched treble voices, he felt the slow tears once more rise into his eyes.

> *Be still, my soul: your God will undertake*
> *To guide the future as he has the past.*
> *Your hope, your confidence, let nothing shake,*
> *All, now mysterious, shall be clear at last.*
> *Be still, my soul; the tempests still obey his voice*
> *Who ruled them once before, on Galilee.*

113

*Be still my soul: the hour is hastening on*
*When we shall be forever with the Lord,*
*When disappointments, grief and fear are gone,*
*Sorrow forgotten, love's pure joy restored.*
*Be still my soul: when change and tears are past,*
*All safe and blessed, we shall meet at last.*

If Dan thought he had no tears left, he was mistaken. As he listened to the children blithely and courageously singing the hymn with their wide African accents, he lowered his face into his hands and wept bitterly. He turned away, stumbled down the steps and propped himself against the school wall, wiping his eyes on the soft linen of his tunic. He did not want, entirely, to leave, but he could not bear that either the children or their teachers should see him in tears. Then he heard the bishop's voice, sonorous and deep, the prolonged African cadences ringing out into the schoolyard:

"And now to God, who *alone* knows the secrets of men's hearts, and for whom *nothing* is impossible, keep your hearts and minds in the knowledge and love of God – and may the blessing of Almighty God, Father, Son and Holy Spirit, be with you all, and those whom you love and pray for, this day and always..."

The childish, trusting long-drawn-out chorus of "Amen".

There was a shuffle of feet and Dan moved away. He retraced his steps to the front of the school and climbed the staircase to the Head's office, intending to wait for him. He was already there, talking on the telephone. Dan stayed outside on the landing, where only two days before he had waited so impatiently. Ruefully he recalled how he had resolved to take whatever Africa had to throw at him.

He heard the headmaster's deep sigh as he put down the phone, and he tapped on the door and went in. Umgobe's face was buried in his hands, but as Dan entered he looked up, and Dan was struck by the greyness of the pallor beneath the darkness of his skin. His cheeks were wet. Dan held out his hand and Umgobe stood up, his eyes flickering over Dan's tunic, then he leant across the desk to grasp his hand.

"Oh, *Mars*den."

"Headmaster..."

"Marsden, what can I say to you? What a terrible, terrible day! What a tragedy!"

"Mr Umgobe, I..."

"Yet we're so, so grateful... so grateful for the ones who were saved. *Praise* God! And praise God you were there. We have all heard what you did. We will ne-vah, ne-vah forget...!"

Dan felt distinctly uncomfortable. This was not why he had come, and he turned the conversation as politely as he could.

"How many? Do you know how many were lost?"

Umgobe spread his hands sadly. "Man, they are still counting! Some were away sick, but others... Some families have lost *all* their children! A generation gone..." Suddenly angry, he raised one hand, one finger iconically pointing upwards. "Whoever did this wants to *annihilate* us! They are trying to *drain* the life-blood of our people! But they will *not* succeed! We will strangle them where they stand, for they have slain our children! It was... it was *butchery*...!"

His voice broke, and he tore his hair. Dan was repelled by this level of vitriol, understandable though it was, and he interrupted him.

"How did you hear?"

"*Ah*! We did not hear until after the bus had not arrived."

He sat down at the desk and motioned to Dan to join him.

"You know how it is," he said, mournfully, "times are hard at the moment. You never know what will happen next. So, you see, ev-ah-ry day we wait outside to count the children in. And that bus... that bus, it did not come down the street! It did *not* come down the street. So we wait. Then we go inside to telephone. But *who* do we telephone? The bus company, it knows nothing. The police, they know nothing. So we phone the hospital. *They* know nothing. What else is there to do? Only then do we hear. *Hours* later! Someone ran in from the street. They were bringing them in, he said. Into the hospital. Only *then* do we hear!"

Dan was silent.

"So, what next?" the Head asked. "We telephone the bishop and he comes. But we cannot do more. So we bring the children into the Cathedral and count them there. Now they have a service..."

"Yes, I went over."

"But the parents? How can we tell the parents? So many in townships or out in the bush – how can we inform them? With no telephones... *Still* they do not know!" He smacked his forehead with frustration. "A few will discover tonight, when their children do not come home from school. For others, I shall have to visit them... Out in the bush, where there is no post, it will be word of mouth only. Only *then* they will know. Word will get round, and only *then* they will know."

Dan was aghast. "This is terrible! Can't the police help?"

"Oh, *yes*," Umgobe said, in a sarcastic, singsong voice. "They'll send a letter to the Deanery... It won't arrive till next *week* – if it arrives at *all* – then the pastor has to visit all the parents..." He spread his hands, and spoke more normally. "It could be another week before some of them hear. I am... helpless... I am..." He exhaled, lost for words. "Well, the governors are coming in. That is why I did not go to the service... We need to decide what to do about this."

"What to do? What can you possibly do? *You* can't visit all the families!"

The Head suddenly became incandescent with rage. "Meester Marsden, you do not understand! I am not talking about the families. I am talking about the Muslims, what to do about *them*! These Muslims," he spat the word, "these men, whoever they were, who targeted this bus... they are evil! *Evil*, I tell you! They have... they have slaughtered our children! They have... they have launched them into eternity... with no thought for their sufferings!" He leant forward excitedly, pressing his index finger so violently on the desk that it bent upwards at the knuckle, the spittle flying from his mouth. "I tell you, Marsden, this will be the deathblow to any work for peace! We will contact the press! We will speak to the Imams! These men will be found and then, *then*... they will be made to... to face up to the consequences... of... of what they have done to us! We will *make* the Imams denounce them! Then... then... *then*..." he said passionately, "you will see what will happen! *Then* they will know our rage!"

Dan hesitated. It should not really be him, standing here, listening to all this. It should be the bishop. Again he felt like an intruder. But he could not leave him with the wrong impression. Who knew what acts of revenge might not be taken against the Muslims? After all, and whatever else they might have done in the past, he felt convinced that they were innocent, at least of this particular outrage. He had to tell him.

"Headmaster… it was not the Muslims. The bus… it wasn't the bus that was targeted. I was there. I saw everything. It wasn't the bus… It was… I'm afraid it was the mosque. The bus just happened to be there. Whoever it was, whoever did this… *they didn't target the bus*."

Umgobe looked at him. For a moment he remained expressionless as if he could hardly take in what was being said to him, then suddenly his mouth dropped open.

"You are telling me…?" he whispered. "What are you telling me?"

"I'm sorry." Dan stood up to leave. "I was there. I think you will find that it was… not the Muslims."

\*　\*　\*

Once more, he walked through the streets, oblivious of the traffic, astounded at how brisk and animated the place was, as though nothing had happened, or as though what had happened had been merely part of a normal day. The market, with its rampant and insistent colour, dominated the whole street. He could smell it, too, spicy and pungent, overlaid with something less wholesome. Nearby was a long trestle table of bush meat, the tiny animals slit open and pinned out to dry as if on the rack, black, shiny and covered in flies. What Dan had smelt was the stench of putrefaction, and he walked on quickly, narrowly avoiding an adolescent boy pushing a cart stacked with crates of live chickens, blowing through his lips with exertion.

The noise of the market stabbed the dusty atmosphere: the endlessly repeated "hi-hi-hi" beckoning call of the market traders, the chatter of the women, the squeals of animals, the shouts of children running between the stalls. When they saw Dan they sobered instantly, wide eyed, fingers to their mouths. It underlined his foreignness; it made him conscious of the colour of his skin, and he felt exposed and vulnerable. Didn't they know what had happened? How could they simply carry on, as if…

Nevertheless he looked around him avidly, at the stalls, draped with enormous swathes of patterned cloth, at stacks of basket ware interwoven with brightly-coloured ribbon, at shiny leather goods inlaid with decorative tool work hung from aluminium frames, at endless rows of rusty-looking tools and field implements: long-handled hoes, spades and wide, ugly-looking knives, at a group of men haggling over a set of spanners, their voices raucous and argumentative. Bemused, he stored the images in his mind, as if researching a book. He saw black cooking pots of every size, reflecting blue in the sun, and burnished hand painted trays and beakers. He saw pyramids of multi-coloured peppers, tomatoes, and green plantain. Under the striped awnings were more burnished skins of bush meat, the carcases cardboard-flat, dry and odourless; strings of onions and piles of yam, and blue plastic crates of canned drinks. Once more he stepped aside to avoid a pushbike and its tottering boxes of tomatoes and sweet potatoes, noticing how the lad negotiated the narrow spaces between the parked vans, ringing his bell and cursing under his breath. All was busy-ness, buying and selling; belligerent, strident, stunningly vibrant life.

Dan stood still, the hubbub around him fading into nothingness, for there, in the midst of the street and in harsh contrast, lay the silent wreck of the bus, battered and dismembered. Tattered remnants of cloth swung in the slight breeze and above it the ruined dome of the devastated mosque reared up towards the blue sky, monstrous and obscene, like an enormous decapitated egg.

Bewildered, he asked himself again, *Don't they know?*

* * *

Dan slowly became aware that he was not the only person standing immobile, staring across the street. A few yards away was the man he had seen that morning, the man with the scar. As he watched, the man began to walk slowly across the road between the cars, ignoring the angry hoots and shouts that punctuated his progress. For a moment his figure was obscured by a moving truck, and Dan lost sight of him. He scanned the road. The man was standing on the low wall of the central reservation, stooping slightly, and peering with great concentration at the devastation in front of him. Stealthily, for the distance between them had now reduced, Dan moved to join him in the middle of the road, careful not to attract his attention. For some minutes the traffic streamed past them in both directions, then, abruptly, the man was gone. Dan narrowed his eyes against the bright light and searched again, determined not to lose him. Then he saw him, for in the midst of all the activity, only the figure of the man was still. He was standing by the scene-of-crime ribbons that the police had put up that morning, and when Dan reached the opposite pavement he was no more than a few feet away from him.

He looked at him closely, observing once more the livid scar that disfigured his face. He seemed, if possible, even dirtier, his mouth distorted in anguish. He reached out and ran his hand over the back of the bus, fingering a shred of clothing that hung from the jagged windows, tears streaming from his eyes. Dan was now near enough to touch him. He laid his hand on the man's shoulder, and at the same time he leant forward and spoke softly in his ear.

"*You* did this. Why?"

The man jumped as if shot, swayed and lost his balance. He would have fallen, had not Dan grasped his arms. He was aware of the bones beneath his hands and the heat from his sweat. Dan held him firmly, almost with triumph, deeply conscious how his own sunburnt face under its shock of red hair, and the white African tunic, would appear like an apparition from another world. He was right; the man's eyes widened with terror, revealing their bloodshot whites, and he opened and shut his mouth convulsively. He was younger than Dan had first thought, and he had sores at the corners of his mouth and on the rough skin of his neck.

The man recovered quickly, and glanced around furtively, as if seeking to escape. Dan's anger surged, and he shook him violently.

"It was you, wasn't it!" he hissed. "Don't deny it – you were seen!"

The man's head drooped forwards and Dan was afraid he was going to pass out. He grasped his shoulders and marched him backwards at a run, shoving him hard up against the wall. No one intervened; it was as if they were alone on the street. Dan breathed heavily through his nostrils, then let his arms drop. He stepped back. The man propped himself against the wall, shaking and trembling.

"I was going to turn myself in..." It was the merest whisper, spoken from the side of his mouth, for the muscles of his damaged cheek had atrophied.

"Oh yes?" Dan was scathingly dubious.

"Yes... I didn't realise..."

"*What* didn't you realise, for God's sake?"

"So many people... the children..."

"Poor you! Got it wrong, didn't you?" Dan exhaled, then spoke more civilly. "You were aiming at the mosque?"

"Yes."

"*Why?* Tell me why!" The man was silent. "You're a Christian?"

"Yes. They killed my..." He slumped down against the wall, his arm across his face.

Dan looked around. The gateway to the mosque was open, and he took the man by the arm and hauled him to his feet. He walked him through into the courtyard and sat him down on a stone seat. Here were narrow pavements of white marble shaded by purple bougainvillea trees in full bloom, and the noise of the street had lessened so that, to Dan, it seemed an oasis of peace. The trees were full of birdsong, the first Dan had heard in Africa, and the rear of the mosque was entirely undamaged, its white concrete gleaming in the bright sunshine. Below the ornamental arch of the doorway was a line of tattered slippers, the only memorial to the terrible events of the morning. For each pair, a dead man.

The man gazed around him fearfully. "I cannot be in here..."

"You can. Sit still."

Yet the few words that the man had spoken hinted at tragedy, and Dan found that he could not, any longer, indulge his rage. He felt it dissolving, suddenly invalidated by those benign surroundings, and he sat down next to him. The man leant forwards with his hands dangling between his knees. He spoke hesitantly at first, stumbling over his words, then they rushed out of him, a torrent of harsh staccato phrases.

"I am from Nasarawa," he said in a low voice. "Two years my wife... my wife and my... my children are killed in the riots. They are... they are burnt... Our home is burnt. The Muslims, they do it." He raised his tear-filled eyes to Dan. "In those days our children *know* each other. Every day they play together. My wife give food to them, food of their own kind. Many times she do this. Now it is all gone... They are all gone. I am alone."

120

Dan was quiet.

"I had a business. I was mechanic for Nasarawa. When they burn I go live with my brother, but there is no room. So I come to the city but I... I have no money. No one will take me on, so I starve. I starve on the street." His voice rose, and he rounded on Dan, gesturing wildly. "Oh, I see what is around me!" he said sardonically. "Here the Muslims are rich! Many have large cars, big houses, where Christians work as servants. *I* cannot do this," he said savagely. "*I* cannot work for the Muslim. There are many Muslims in the city. My family burn, so... why should they live? Every day I see them come to pray. Five times a day they come to pray. Every day I ask myself, Why should they pray? *I* cannot pray! So I make a plan. Every day I plan what I will do, then, one day – I *strike*!"

He raised his hand and brought it down on his thigh, his heel jerking reflexively in the dust, and Dan saw that his nails were bitten and encrusted with dirt.

"How did you...?"

"I fill a milk carton full of petrol, and put it on top of their gas tank. Inside, in the storeroom, at the back. I cut the pipe near the pilot light and I soak a string in the petrol and run it to the pilot light... No one sees me." He bent over and covered his face with his hands, his back hunched and tense, leaning forwards over his knees, the bones of his spine and shoulder blades prominent under his soiled tunic.

"After two years? Why did you wait?"

"Because... because... in my heart I know it is a bad thing. My plan, it is a wrong thing. I want to kill him, but... I am a Christian... yet I cannot pray for mine enemy."

His voice was muffled and Dan was silent.

"How old are you?" he asked.

"...I don't... Twenty, I think."

"And now?"

The question was unanswerable, and silence descended between them once more. After a long time the man raised his eyes, and they were filled with agony.

"Will you give me up... to the police?" The tone was tremulous, pleading and fearful and Dan turned to him sternly.

"You were going to do that anyway, you said."

"Oh..." It was a groan, deep in his chest. "They will cut off my head..."

Dan looked up at the trees, to the invisible singing birds. He thought of his home in England, of its inherent peacefulness, of its systems of law and order, of its belief in free speech and its untrammelled freedom to worship, and he felt mortified. Who was he to judge this man, after what he had suffered? When push comes to shove... Might not he have reacted in the same way? Suddenly, he realised that neither Umgobe, nor this pathetic stranger, who had raged against God, had asked why? Unlike himself. When Hadissa had come to him on the bus, it had been his first question. The bishop was right – here, they did not ask why, for they were accustomed to misery and hardship and premature death and violence as part of their way of life. Thus, when it came, they did not question but simply endured.

He stood up. "I will tell you what you must do," he said sternly. "But you must obey my instructions."

The man looked up and nodded warily.

"You will go to your pastor and you will tell him what you have done."

The man looked his question.

"That's all," said Dan peaceably. "And... God be with you."

The bloodshot eyes of the man stared up at him, supplicating, his irises pale as cataracts, his lips loose and tremulous around the broken teeth.

"Will you do this?" Dan demanded. "Will you go to your pastor?"

"...I will."

"Is that a promise?" asked Dan, relentlessly.

"It is, in God's name."

"Then go in peace."

He reached down and gripped the grimy hand. Then he walked away.

* * *

It was early afternoon by the time Dan returned to the bishop's compound, and he didn't expect to see Hadissa again that day. Even if she was able to come back for an hour or two, she was due for a night shift and would need to sleep. He had no idea when he would see her next, but the certainty that he would see her eventually shone like a light in his mind.

It was Friday, a week, almost to the day, since his arrival in Kaduna. Another week, and they would leave. Part of him wanted to leave immediately, fly back to leafy, peaceful Cambridge, take up the reins of his life and forget all that had happened, as if it was nothing but a bad dream. Yet he knew he could not forget, and probably never would. The immediacy of the images would recede over time, but he would still be in possession of them. He might try to let them go, but they would never let him go. And although he might absorb himself in his own life again, life, as it was here in Nigeria, would go on much as before. What was it Luke had said on the plane about grass skirts and mud huts and cooking pots, that nothing had changed very much? No, and it wouldn't, either. It was a pattern engraved on the culture, like tribal markings on a face, a pattern set by years of use and abuse, an irreconcilable pattern carved in intractable stone.

He recalled what he had said to Luke – was it only the day before yesterday? – about the man who had written the letter to the newspaper about exclusion. What had the fellow said? Something about how he felt that his Christian identity was being compromised because a whole section of the community was being excluded? Something like that. And he, Dan, had given Luke some rubbish about sharing hurts and breaking down barriers! He could hardly believe his arrogance. What did he know, *then*, compared to what he now knew? His answer had been totally inadequate, at best superficial and at worst, banal, and it shamed him.

The compound was full of cars, including the bishop's, but there was no one about. Then Dan noticed a door at the side of the house, an arched door, as if to a small chapel. It was open and figures in clerical black could be seen moving within. He hesitated, thinking, *What now? I can't take much more of this –* but he had to pass the door to get to his guest room. As he drew near he heard once again the sound of singing, not from children this time, but from full-throated adult males. He glanced in furtively, and saw that the room was packed with clergy. They were singing in the rich, natural harmony peculiar to African voices, repeating the same words again and again, one simple tear-laden chorus, yet, incredibly, it sounded to Dan to be full of joy.

*Within our dark-est night, you kin-dle a fire that*
*nev-ah dies a-way,*
*Nev-ah dies a-way...*
*Within our dark-est night, you kin-dle a fire that*
*nev-ah dies a-way,*
*Nev-ah dies a-way...*
*Within our dark-est night, you kin-dle a fire that*
*nev-ah dies a-way,*
*Nev-ah dies a-way...*
*Within our dark-est night...*

As he listened, Dan became aware of a subtle change in himself. He was not the same man who had set out the week before, as if after a day of agony and uncertainty and fear there had been born in him a small seed of recognition, that if there was a God, and if indeed he cared, then this life of faith was both utterly real and completely right. What was more, the people who believed in him as these people did, or as Stephen and Luke did, or as Nathan did, *knew* that God existed and that he cared. This great God of human history, who was both worshipped for his omnipotence and revered as their personal Saviour and Lord – they believed He wept alongside them. And because he wept, they praised him and knew his presence and they did not fear. In spite of all the killings, even of little children, the massacres and the burning of churches and mosques, even their ongoing lives of poverty, hardship and deprivation, they did not fear. On the contrary, they met these calamities with indomitable courage, hoping and trusting even in the midst of their adversity. And, because of their faith, even while they wept and prayed and huddled together, they were somehow full of joy.

It was too much for Dan, and he fled.

# CHAPTER 10

Early on the morning of the bomb, John-Sunday, stripped to the waist, was on top of his mother's hut repairing the thatch when suddenly, and infinitesimally, the world tilted. He lurched sideways and snatched at the roof to save himself from falling. Grasping the rough, dried reeds with shaking hands, he looked frantically around. Everything seemed as usual. Across the terracotta fields he could see women carrying bundles of firewood on their heads for the cooking fires, and within the circle of huts children were playing in the dust or collecting the maize seeds from an enormous pile of cobs kept for pigs and chickens. The sky was an incandescent blue, and there was no evidence of what he now suspected had been a small earth tremor. The huts were not leaning more than was usual nor had any trees fallen. Then he heard the sound of his mother's voice, calling his name. He slid down the makeshift ladder, rasping his fingers and bare feet against the rough wood, and dashed into the hut. At first, dazzled by the outer brightness, he could see nothing, then he became aware of his mother's luminous eyes as she sat, reared up on the mattress.

He crouched down beside her. "Momi, are you all right?"

"There was a noise on the roof. Was it you?" Her voice was brittle and unsteady. She had felt nothing. He was bewildered. Had it been a moment's vertigo? He cast around in his mind, trying to recall if he had felt anything before the tilting of the world.

*Hadissa!*

He ran out of the hut, ignoring his mother's protests, and began to race down the hill to the pastor's house, fighting the tall yellow grasses that clung to his ankles, threatening to trip him up. It was nearly three miles and he did not falter or change his pace, but ran with the smooth fluid steps of his tribal ancestors, the rhythm of his breathing shallow and systematic, his head erect, his arms loosely swinging by his side, his brow furrowed with suspense.

*Hadissa!*

He ran between the high banks of adobe huts, through fields of bleached, yellow-ochre sorghum, and past the sunken waterhole where women were bent double, washing their clothes in the brown, turgid water. Every detail of their movements imprinted itself on his mind in intense and unwavering focus. He took the incline of the escarpment with long strides, skidding on the orange earth, scattering stones. At the bottom, he ran silently on, his bare feet lightly thudding the ground, hardly conscious of the steady thumping of his heart, his mind always a step ahead of him, the path ahead always accomplished. The sweat poured off him, pooling against the belt of his trousers. At the upper reaches of the village, where the huts crowded together on the bare earth, he took the main path that would eventually bring him out beside the road. Here the dense foliage created long shadows, which stretched across the path between patches of bright sunshine, and he rolled his eyes fearfully at the hidden darkness under the trees and in the reed bushes, expecting he knew not what. Approaching the village he passed a long crocodile of little children, their faces lit pale by the sun, clutching exercise books, on their way to the makaranta. They called to him with their high-pitched, singsong voices, mocking him, clutching at him with their bare, brown arms.

"*Sannu*, John-Sunday! Why do you run? Is a lion after you? A devil?"

They stood back to let him pass, giggling, but, hardly breaking his stride, he skirted them, plunging into the high yellow grass that bordered the path, the seeds floating upwards into the sunlight as his legs brushed through, and raced on down the track. He pushed rudely past women carrying heavy iron cooking pots, and did not stop to apologise. The women looked after him, shaking their heads; one called after him angrily, "Where yo' mannahs, John-Sunday?" He ignored them. All he could think of was Hadissa. At length, his chest heaving, he arrived at the road. Almost keeping pace with the thundering traffic, he ran alongside it for a while, the hot broken surface singeing his bare feet, then took the turning into the concrete dwellings where the pastor lived, and finally arrived at the door. It was shut.

"Pastor!" he roared, beating at the peeling, sun-scorched panels with his clenched fist. "Pastor! Open up!"

The door opened and the pastor stood there, half clad. His collarless shirt was open to the waist and he still wore the short wrap-around shift in which he slept.

"Why you knock so hard, John?" he asked icily. "Is there fire, that you clamour so rudely at my door?"

"I'm sorry, pastor." John-Sunday caught his breath. "But, can you tell me... Please tell me... have you had news? Has anything happened to Hadissa?"

"Hadissa? What news? Today? Are you mad! If I had news would I not bring it to you?"

He turned as if to go back into the house, and John-Sunday grasped him by the arm.

*"Has anything happened to Hadissa?"*

"No, not as far as I know!" The pastor looked at him sternly and shook him off. "John-Sunday, you ought to know better than this. You'll raise a panic." He paused, turning back, his expression slightly embarrassed. "But, now that you mention it, there has been a letter. Not, I think, from Hadissa. It's on official notepaper. It came last night, but very late. I was going to give it to you this morning," he added hurriedly, "if I saw you."

John-Sunday was grim. "Give it to me now."

The pastor fetched the letter and gave it to him, concern in his face for the first time. John-Sunday stumbled to the bench in front of the house, sat down and ripped open the envelope. Inside was a single typed sheet of headed notepaper from the bishop's office.

*In response to your letter of last week the bishop of Kaduna would be pleased to grant you an interview to discuss the matters therein. Please present yourself at the bishop's house on Thursday, 2nd August and be prepared to stay overnight.*

That was all. No mention of Hadissa. John-Sunday closed his eyes and drew in his breath, testing to see if what he felt was relief, but the sense of danger did not pass. He turned to the pastor.

"Forgive me, pastor, I must have made a mistake." But inside himself he did not believe it. Something was amiss, and it concerned Hadissa. Were they not twins? It had happened with them before, this strange prescience, and they would always respond to it. When they were still small, scarcely six years old, Hadissa had gone through a stage when she was afraid of snakes. Anything that pinched or bit, or moved in the grass or dropped from the low ceiling of their hut, or any indentation in the dark corners, became, for her, a curled up viper, waiting to strike. He did not know where this fear originated, but he did know that for her it was very real. He had tried, with her, to hide her dread from their parents and her teasing older brother, but one night she had been in the latrine when she heard rustling between her and the door, and this time it was no figment of her imagination. Half naked, her hands clutching her hair, she whispered, "John-Sunday!" and, totally inaudible though she was, he had 'heard' her from his sleep, and woken. He had not shouted for his father, but had come running, leaping with one bound over the poised and threatening head of the snake to gather the terrified, wide-eyed little girl into his tiny arms. Only then did they both scream for help, huddling together in the dark. By the time their father arrived the snake had slithered away. John-Sunday was beaten for being in the latrine with Hadissa, and though she stumblingly tried to placate their father – "It was the snake, the snake!" – she was not believed, for so many times before it had been a false alarm. John-Sunday bore the beating with a closed mouth. He would not speak further, either to reveal her neurosis or to defend himself.

This had not been the only occasion when their closeness, their profound and unquestioning love for each other, and the telepathy born into them as twins, had given them an insight into each other's nature and personality. For this reason, and for this reason alone, John-Sunday was convinced that he had made no mistake. Something was wrong with Hadissa. Hadissa was in Kaduna. Therefore he must go to Kaduna. Thursday was too long to wait. He had to know now. He resolved to go at once, as soon as he could get a lift. If there was no room for him in the bishop's house, he would seek out one of the city pastors and ask for a bed until Thursday. He left the pastor and ran back up the hill to his mother's hut to say his farewell.

"I am going to the city. I will come back when I can."

"*Aieee*," she cried, raising herself in alarm. "Why you

128

suddenly go to the city? Ah, you do not answer me! You have no respec'! You will go, anyway. You are now all gone," she mourned, turning herself on the bed and grasping with trembling fingers to find her shawl. "When will I see you again? Who will carry the firewood for me? None of you care for me! You are a bad son! You and Hadissa, you are both bad chil'ren..."

"You have the little cross she gave you. Pray for her!"

"Ah!" she wailed, lifting her shawl to cover her head. "You do not care what happens to me! You do not care! Ah! You only care for yourself! You..."

He tore himself away and, taking up his bundle, headed down the path once more through the village to the road. This time he did not run, but took the time to say his prayers. He went to his concrete house and changed into his western clothes and then left the house with his bundle, sliding over the dusty earth in his city shoes. He stood by the road for a long time before anyone stopped for him, and he rode beside the driver in almost complete silence, frowning with frustration at the slow speed of the battered vehicle, the man casting suspicious, sideways glances at him all the way. It was mid-afternoon when he arrived at Kaduna. He was dropped off in the city centre, and carrying his bundle on his head he went straight to the bishop's house, and knocked at the picket gate.

The bishop was in his office when John-Sunday arrived, taking calls from distressed and angry pastors whose own township children had been victims in the attack. Until the boy explained to him, he was astonished by how quickly John-Sunday had heard, living where he did. Regarding the 'tremor', he was less surprised.

"You are a Christian, John-Sunday. God moves in mysterious ways, his wonders to perform. Give thanks that you are open to the Spirit, and be grateful."

John-Sunday was grateful as much for his own instinct, that the tremor that he had at first perceived as taking place within the ground of the real world, had in fact taken place in the ground of his being. His ancestors were watching over him, and that awed him and gave him confidence to refer to his letter.

"Yes, I've read it," the bishop said. "What you desire is difficult, but not impossible. People do go abroad to study, and there *is* a need for properly trained nurses. We will talk further after I have consulted one or two people. I will share your request with one of the white men who are staying here. He comes from England, from a place called Coventry. That diocese has interests here, and he may be able to help. I am not making any promises, you understand, but, as I say, there is a certain need... not in casualty, but in general nursing."

"Yes... that's what she wants."

"Well, it may fit in rather well, but we'll see. I must have your promise that you will not mention it to Hadissa yet. Now, go away. Stay in the compound and make yourself useful to Nathan. There is work in the garden that you can do, or the field. And, John-Sunday, let us both pray about this. Believe me, I shall not take it lightly. I understand what it means to both of you. Now, the Spirit is alive in you, so pray about it, and we will try to discern what the Spirit is saying. Do not be troubled, all will come clear."

Rested from his journey and somewhat comforted, he wanted to see Hadissa at once, but was informed that young men, even brothers, were forbidden to visit the Nurses' Home. Her time off was restricted to early mornings and late evenings when, even if he could have dodged the curfew, it was unsafe to be out on the street. For the time being he had to be content with a telephone conversation with her, which was regularly interrupted by the bishop's secretary coming into the room, ostensibly to search for papers and files, but in reality, John-Sunday suspected, to check up on him. He didn't mind. It was enough for him to be within speaking distance of his twin and to look forward to the Tuesday evening when, the bishop informed him, she would be joining them for supper. That night, for the first time in his nineteen years, he slept in a real bed in a room with electric light and running water.

\* \* \*

On Saturday morning, when Dan first saw the figure of John-Sunday working in the garden, he merely dismissed him as the latest recruit to the household, and it wasn't until the boy turned his head that he noticed that his face seemed somehow familiar. His first thought was that maybe he had seen him at the school, and it was only when he heard his voice that he realised that he was older. John-Sunday, curious about this white man, but rather repelled by his complexion, returned his scrutiny, put down the fork with which he had been digging, and leapt over the box hedge to stand in front of him. They were of a similar height, but while Dan was tall and slim, John-Sunday was more compact, his neck thick, and the muscles on his shining, hairless chest, well-developed.

"You're visiting here, sah?"

"I'm staying here, yes." Dan's tone was cold, as if the conversation being initiated in this way by a black boy, his colonial ancestors had twitched in distaste.

"My name is John-Sunday. You are a guest of the bishop, from England, Coventry!" he stated eagerly. "You are the *malam*, the teacher!"

"I teach maths, yes."

"Math-ah-matics! When I was at school, sah, it was my favourite subject..."

"Really."

John-Sunday was not deterred by Dan's chilly tone, but eager to share his dream. "Yes, and now I want to learn engineering, for farming and for vehicles, and one day become a mechanic."

Dan raised his eyebrows superciliously. "But instead you work here, in the garden."

"Just for a few days, sah, helping Nathan. I am also a guest. I come from Kateri to see my sister."

Ah, Dan thought, kicking at the gravel, there's the resemblance. The little blighter is her twin brother!

"Great. Well, see you inside." He turned away and began to walk to his room, feeling somewhat guilty. He was aware that his reaction had been patronising, almost racist, but he excused himself – he'd been taken unawares, and the boy disturbed him in a way he did not care to examine. Given the difference in gender and height, he and Hadissa were very alike, but a male version of Hadissa, he thought ironically, was distinctly superfluous. He did not want a watchdog nosing about in his affairs, and with regard to his blossoming friendship with her, he very much feared that John-Sunday would do just that. Suddenly he knew himself to be at a grave disadvantage. He was white, English and transient; enough, surely, to raise the hackles of any little whelp determined to defend his territory. He turned and watched John-Sunday resume his work, and as he looked at him more closely, he discovered that there was something about his bland and open features which reproved his hostility, temporarily at least, and dissipated it. What was it, gracefulness, a sense of inner peace and harmony? Simplicity? Whatever it was, he had seen the same qualities in Hadissa's face.

Dan had not previously admitted to himself the strength of his feeling for Hadissa, but at that moment he knew he loved her. The fact that he'd only just met her and would be leaving within days seemed, at that moment, irrelevant, for they were shackled to each other with an indissoluble iron band, their shared experience of tragedy. Even though he knew he would leave her, it seemed to him, then, a stronger foundation for love than anything he had hitherto known. With that thought, the last traces of Ellen slipped from his mind and were blown away, like dried leaves on the wind.

*　*　*

Luke arrived back later in the morning, strolling unaccompanied into the compound as though he had never been away. He had recovered sufficiently to discharge himself from the hospital – telling Dan, with a laugh, that there was a shortage of trolleys – and taking a taxi he had found idling in the street. Even in his fever he had been aware of the sudden influx of the wounded into the hospital, but he had not realised that Dan had been involved with the rescue of the children until Hadissa had stopped by his bed and told him. It seemed to Luke rather heroic, that Dan had not only very efficiently got Luke to hospital, but had then risked life and limb to go to the aid of the children. "Hero" was Hadissa's word but Luke agreed with her. Dan, had he known, would have shrugged it off, albeit with pleasure that they thought so highly of him. His scratches had almost healed, except for one broad abrasion on his knee, which was constantly bleeding from the irritation of his slacks.

"Got more than you bargained for, coming on this trip," Luke joked, but his eyes were serious and he examined Dan anxiously for any sign of the depression about which Stephen had warned him. He saw none, but in reality Dan felt harried, and the night before, had woken sweating, calling out from a prolonged and intensely vivid nightmare. News had reached them, in a rushed telephone call from Hadissa, that while Maria was progressing well, Sammi had lost a leg. Indeed, what did "progressing well" mean, Dan asked himself, his mind churning, if the little girl was disfigured? There was no plastic surgery here. And, without prosthetics, would Sammi ever walk again? Would he now be condemned to a life on the streets, begging for his living? The two of them, so young, maimed for life.

What Luke did not realise was that Dan was taking immense care to conceal his feelings. He did this partly for his own sake, for his tears were still near the surface, and partly for Luke's, who was still weak. The deception worked. Luke was reassured that Dan seemed not only to have coped with his ordeal, but also, surprisingly, to have been energised by it. After all, hadn't he just broken up with someone, or someone broken up with him? To have left behind the turmoil of a broken relationship in England, only to be traumatised in Nigeria, was not, in Luke's opinion, the most obvious panacea, yet Dan seemed to have more than adjusted; there was a new quickness of movement about him, and a new light in his eye. Luke was puzzled. He wondered what had triggered it, what had made him so resilient, for he would not have been surprised if, after Friday's events, Dan had demanded an immediate flight out.

On Sunday Luke got his answer. He and Dan were crossing the compound together on their way back from Chapel when the picket gate opened and the tall figure of John-Sunday came into view, closely followed by his comparatively diminutive twin.

"That's Hadissa, isn't it?" Luke remarked, and Dan had to remind himself that Luke had only met her once. "Who's that with her, I wonder? Looks like a brother. But I thought she'd lost her brother…"

Dan scowled. "She has. This one's her twin."

His tone was surly and Luke glanced at him in surprise.

"What's the story there?"

"I have absolutely no idea!" Dan had not ameliorated his tone and his eyes gleamed. "He turned up yesterday. He probably got word about the bus and came to see if she was okay. Which she is."

Luke shrugged. "Well, that's natural enough. You want to go and say hello, or what?"

They walked over and Dan introduced them. "Hadissa, remember Luke? You met him last week. Luke, this is John-Sunday, Hadissa's brother."

133

It was cursory to the point of rudeness, and Luke was taken aback. Hadissa was standing very still, silent and rather wan, as if in some way she had transgressed. John-Sunday looked from one to another in bewilderment, sensing the atmosphere. Then his eyes became stern and his mouth tightened with animosity. They were like two circling bulls, Luke thought, fronting each other over a female.

"You have been ill, sah," said John-Sunday to Luke, casting a sideways roll of his eyes at Dan. "Are you well, now?"

"I'm quite well, thank you," returned Luke, smiling at him gravely.

"I am glad."

John-Sunday turned towards his sister and spoke in Hausa.

"You're staying here tonight?"

"You know I am. You are, too."

"I'm not sure. I may not come back to sleep," he said, reverting to English. "I'm going to walk back and visit with our old headmaster. I need to find out how he is after Friday. I may be too late for the curfew. If so, I'll stay with him."

"You'll come tomorrow?"

"In the morning. But you'll be at the hospital." His face was still stern, unsmiling.

"I'll see you in the evening, then?" said Hadissa, gently, placating him.

"*Yauwa, mad'allah.*"

"*Sei kadawo.*" She inclined her body towards him, as if for an embrace, and he softened.

"*Barka da deh…*" He took her in his arms and with a last, inscrutable glance at the two white men, he slipped out of the picket gate. At that moment, he seemed to Dan intensely African. Hadissa stood there for a minute, looking at the closed gate, then she turned to the two white men.

"John-Sunday is my twin," she said with dignity, "and we tend to know what the other is thinking. But I have no idea why he should have been rude. If, indeed, you think he was rude." She gave Dan a secretive grin. "I do know that boys are less mature than girls, at the same age. Don't you think that, in your experience, it's all a question of maturity?"

Which was how Luke got his answer.

"My brothers used to fight," Hadissa said. "When they were little, about ten and twelve, and still at the makaranta, it was terrible with them."

"'Makaranta': village school," said Dan.

"Quite right. You're learning Hausa. That's good."

It was later that evening, and he was lounging in the low cane chair outside his guest room, while Hadissa had perched herself on the wall that divided his room from the next. John-Sunday had not returned, and Dan was glad. The light was rapidly fading, but the glow from his room shone over the patio, and a multitude of small insects danced around his window. Dan hated them and feared for his skin; he already had inflamed lumps rising on his ankles and neck, although he had sprayed himself liberally with insect repellent. He should have gone in, but he valued Hadissa's company too much. She stimulated and intrigued him, and he was greedy for more. The days they had left were not so many that he could spin out the hours when they could be alone together. He refused to contemplate how he might feel when the time came to leave.

"I should not talk ill of the dead," she said quietly, "but Stanley was a bully. He used to tease John-Sunday, and it made him mad. There was a real barrier between them, to the day Stanley was killed. I don't know how they'd have been if... if he'd lived. My mother used to say that what begins with a barrier will end with a wall."

"Why are we suddenly talking about brothers?" Dan asked drowsily.

"We're not talking about brothers," replied Hadissa firmly. "We are talking about barriers. Remember the grace the bishop prayed tonight? About God helping us to break the dividing wall of hostility in our world? Did you pray it? Well, I can tell you a story of how a barrier broke down a wall."

Dan frowned. "A barrier broke down a wall? I don't get you."

"It was the wall around the mosque in our village. I will tell you about it, and maybe it will help you understand more about my brother."

"Which brother?"

"John-Sunday, of course."

She adjusted her robe more closely around her legs. During the day the delicate chestnut of her skin resonated with colour, but now she seemed so much part of the night itself that he could hardly make out her features, although when she moved he could see brief flashes of light reflecting on to her cheek. He wanted to run his fingers over its smoothness; to imprint forever on his memory the sensation of its texture. The moment passed and he began to listen to her again, for she was speaking in the singsong voice of the African storyteller, gathering a rapt audience around the night fires. It reminded him of Cletus, on the road.

"In the bush, families live together when the children are young. Then, at puberty, they have to make new arrangements. So my brothers used to share a hut, which my Dadda had built with his hands. Each of them had a plank bed and foam mattress, each his curtained alcove where he used to keep his things, but still they fought. You'd think, with a separate hut and so much space, they'd let each other alone. They should have tried what I'd got," she said, with sudden bitterness, "sleeping with my parents and only a plastic bread tray from the city to keep my skirts in. We all shared the toilet area, which was a mud brick hut like the others, but with no window. Still, we had plenty of candles and buckets to choose from. There are flush toilets in the concrete houses – John-Sunday has one – but they haven't worked for twenty years, since the mains leaked out. We use river water for all our needs, just as we did before the white man came."

She hesitated. "Daniel, I don't mean... I know you're white, too, but you are different."

"How, different?" he teased, shifting in his chair.

"Never mind... Well, I remember, once, and it was not so long ago, that the boys changed the buckets around in the dark so that it got so that you couldn't tell which was clean river water and which was... anything else. There was some evil in them in those days! There was no telling what they would get up to next. Sure, the seeds for disarray are sown long since in blinkered and defiant thinking." She laughed. "I am sounding just like my mother... Yet I must not call them evil, for was it not they who used to carry the mud bricks my mother had made? That was some hard work!"

Her voice suddenly sounded more African again, as if,

136

remembering those times, her inner eye rested on village scenes, and the intervening years had left her accent unrefined.

"Your *mother* made the bricks?"

"Yes, all the women did. Why not?"

"Seems heavy work for a woman."

She laughed again, a low, very feminine sound, deep in her throat.

"Women do all the heavy work, Daniel, even in the field. The men can't manage without them! One day I'll tell you how we make the bricks, but right now I'm trying to tell you the story of the wall, and mud bricks are not in the story."

He smiled. "So it wasn't a mud brick wall?"

"*Yes*, it was a mud brick wall!" For a moment she sounded exasperated. "Please, Daniel, if you tease me I cannot tell you this story, and it's important!"

"Sorry. Go on."

She was quiet a moment, recovering her humour, then she said, "Well, the church and the mosque were built side by side and it… it caused a lot of hate." Her voice broke and he saw the glint of tears in her eyes. He felt ashamed. Cletus had told him this, and how a hit and run driver had caused the death of four young boys. He should have remembered sooner. He realised again how different the scale of suffering was in Africa, and how a small spark could cause a conflagration. She wasn't talking about something trivial, here; she was describing a life changing event.

"Were they competing," he asked gently, "when they built the church and the mosque so close to each other? Which was built first?"

"Daniel, that doesn't matter." Her accent suddenly became more educated. "You don't understand. It wasn't a question of competing. They had simply rejected each other's creed. We Nigerians – we are who we are because we are both separate *and* connected. For example, in Kateri, some Christians are even related to some of the Muslims, but when a woman marries she goes to her husband's house and things get forgotten, even faith, if he forbids her to go to church. Which is one reason we keep ourselves apart. Our whole culture, the way we live, our schooling, our whole history as Christian and Muslim, even our food or how we cook it, teaches us to reject what is different. We keep the boundaries in good faith but they do make a barrier between us."

"And the wall round the mosque was a barrier?"

"Yes. A barrier to understanding. Every mosque has one, but it closes people's minds. They don't understand what goes on in a mosque and they don't want to. I'm the same. But the wall, if it shuts people out, it shuts people in, too; it underlines their difference."

"Ah! I begin to see," he said. "Sorry, I've been dense."

"No, not dense." Her voice was lighter now. "Just... English." She stood up and walked towards the edge of the patio. "There was a history to it, you see, to do with how we pray. You know that Muslims pray five times a day, or are supposed to?" She turned to face him. "I'm not saying they're all naturally devout – the elders even take truncheons to them, sometimes, to make them go to the mosque. But then, the Christians aren't devout either, though in Kateri the pastor wields a different sort of stick! He calls your name out in the church and then tells everyone to pray for you, and then you meet them coming home from the service and they say, 'We prayed for you by name, my dear'. Which is bad enough and no good thing, since we mostly know where we should be on Sunday mornings, and sitting around is not it. If God can be with us weekdays, we surely can be with him Sundays!"

"But people, generally, do go to church?"

"Yes, unless there's sickness. People come for miles to worship at Kateri. It's packed out and very noisy with praise and thanksgiving, and all day there's food cooking." She gave a deep sigh. "The noise and the food-smells – it annoys the Muslims very much. But, on weekdays, nothing much happens in the church, except for some women's groups in the afternoons, or John-Sunday does Bible study with the kids after their makaranta lessons. My father trained him to do this, before he... before Stanley got killed. We have a Hausa Bible, so if they can read, they read it, otherwise he reads out the bits he wants them to know, which were the bits he's learnt best, leaving out the bits he's never learnt, or never understood properly, I think. But mostly the church is quiet on weekdays. The mosque, on the other hand, is busy on weekdays and quiet on Sundays. Five times a day the leaders send out the call to prayer. They use a ram's horn trumpet. It's a lovely sound, and I used to think, that's the Muslim call to prayer, so why don't I pray too? It's all the one God. And I still think that, though I'm not saying I wait till the call, no ways, I pray very much and often... Well, I used to. For a time I stopped praying... I do not find it easy to pray..." She stopped, tongue-tied.

"About the wall," he said softly.

She looked away. "I am trying to tell you, but my mind keeps flitting to the behind-the-story things... to what happened later. One day," she added, "I will tell you why I stopped praying, but not now."

"Tell me tomorrow," he grinned, but she was shocked.

"Oh, no, this I cannot tell tomorrow! I hardly know you, Daniel. But if I got to know you, I might tell you."

"You hardly know me?" he repeated, leaning forward in his chair. "After all we've gone through together? You hardly know me?"

"Daniel," she said softly, "that was distressing for you, I know. But not so much for me. I see things like that every day..."

He hardly heard her. "Hadissa, Luke and I have to go soon. I may never see you again!"

"It is in God's hands, whether we shall meet again," she riposted. "For the present, I hardly know you."

Dan flung himself back in his chair. "Well, get to know me, then! I'm not stopping you!"

He thought, For God's sake, we only have five days! Hadissa ignored his outburst and sat down on the wall again, folding her hands demurely on her lap.

"Let me finish the story. There is a reason why I'm telling it to you... Well, what really upset the Muslims was that their wall was so low that you could see right into the mosque. And if there was anything to fight over in the village or on the market, or about land for a house, or whatever, be sure the men would walk past and gaze in, apparently by chance, but everyone knew it was not chance, but mocking. Occasionally someone would rush out and throw a punch and there'd be fighting, which would have to be settled in the Council. And everyone there pretended there was something to fight over, like a piece of land or the produce, or whatever, when really it was that the Christians would look over the wall in mockery. It really infuriated the men at prayer, though they shouldn't have noticed, given that they had to have their heads down for prayer."

139

Dan chuckled and Hadissa looked at him sharply.

"This is not a matter to laugh at," she said reprovingly. "There was a whole long time, when my mother forbade me to go past, even to the market. She didn't want me to get hurt. But that meant she had to walk three miles for her produce, there and back, and she isn't a strong woman, Daniel."

"Sorry, but it wasn't all the fault of the Christians, surely," said Dan, laughing openly now, "if the others were supposed to have their heads down?"

Hadissa smiled broadly and he could see her strong white teeth in the gloaming.

"No, but the Muslims said that looking over the wall, or even using the path next to the wall, was a blasphemy and a desecration on the name of Allah. So the Christians replied that if they *chanced* to tread that path, well, it was their way home to their huts, and if their eyes *chanced* to look that way, meaning no offence, that was not a problem, surely? So they quarrelled in the Council and there was much shouting, though they were only like small boys, like my brothers, choosing to fight, and pretending there was a real issue to fight over, and no one backing off and making space for free air to be breathed."

She reached up and pulled off a twig of bougainvillea, and began to shred the pink petals, which blazed brightly with colour as they fell at her feet.

"I am ashamed of telling you this," she muttered.

"No, don't be ashamed," he said gently.

"Well, I am, but I'll go on because the ending is really something... So it was decided that the problem could be solved if they just raised the wall, then no one could look over it, and the Muslims wouldn't know when the Christians were passing. But who should build it? The Christians said it should be the Muslims, for it was their wall. No, said the Muslims, it should be the

Christians, for they were the ones giving offence. It took some time for them to decide, and they couldn't decide, so then it was told them that both should do it, and that was agreed. Both sides provided men, and of course the payment had to be from both sides, and that meant something else to quarrel over, but that was settled, too, and the work was begun. They started to build it at the side of the mosque where the old wall began, otherwise it would be a different height to the front wall and not look very smart. Every day you would see the men working on the wall, and stopping for prayer, some of them, and then the others either wouldn't work because the Muslims weren't, or they would rush on with the building of it, and mock at how much better they could manage without them. Always quarrelling about something!"

"And your brother got involved in this?"

"Everyone was involved." She seemed surprised he should ask. "After school, when they were free, he and the other boys used to rush to help, and the girls, too. And the men of both sides were proud in teaching us what to do. And everyone, Muslim and Christian alike, got mixed up, so that whole families were working together, Muslim with Christian and Christian with Muslim. At the end of the day the women carried down the food and cooked it near the wall, and made a party for the builders, each group their own diet. Everyone settled down together, talking and eating, sitting about, and playing football." Her eyes had been intent on the petals, but now she lifted her head, and he saw how far away her mind was, in her memories.

"It took the men a while longer to reach the right conclusion," she resumed, recollecting herself. "At first they'd quarrelled still, then they'd begun to compete with each other, then they began to enjoy themselves, then they'd actually done things to help each other, and then, *then*, all the barriers came down. Finally, you couldn't have told who was who, there was that much fun to be had with the wall. I remember, we even prayed for it on Sundays!"

"Prayed for a wall?"

"Daniel, we pray for everything, haven't you noticed? Everything that affects us. This wall, it was important. So, yes, of course we prayed for it!"

"Dear Lord, we just ask you to bless this wall..." Dan murmured.

Hadissa giggled. "Yes! Something like that! So anyway, one day John-Sunday went to the men and said, "Why are we building this wall?"

Everyone was friends, he said, who was there left to shut out? He was very young to talk to the men like that, only fourteen at the time. But they saw the wisdom of his words. Then, of course, they all downed tools and went home, and the high front wall never did get built. The side wall was built, but

141

that was no use, it was only where the long grass grew, which they had to cut down to get at the wall, but then grew up again, anyway. But that was the time," she said proudly, "when they saw that John-Sunday was wise. And he is wise. He's mature beyond his years."

Abruptly the light went out in Dan's room, and he glanced round.

"Ah, the power has gone." Hadissa rose, and brushed the petals from her robe. "Well, that's a sign for us – darkness is for sleeping."

Above their heads the sky seemed suddenly closer and more luminous.

"But, just think a moment," she added, her voice coming at him, warm out of the night. "Who would have thought that building a wall would break down barriers? Sure, the Christians still look in, and sure, they still tread over that path, but memories are chosen, sometimes, and no one wants to remember fighting about it. They only want to remember working together, and what they'd shared. The barriers became bridges. John-Sunday was right; it can be achieved. They'd grown up, you see. And, for sure, God was in it, in the working out of it all."

She turned as if to leave. "You want me to dress your knee before I go?"

"No, there's no need, unless you actually want to."

"Why should I want to," she said lightly, "if there is no need? We've sat out long, Harmattan, and I must go in. I should not stay sitting with you here, like this, in the dark. My brother would be very angry."

"Then I'm glad he's not here to see it," growled Dan under his breath, but she heard, and her face snapped with surprise and anger.

"Daniel! You must not say such things! My brother, he is…"

He was instantly contrite. "I'm sorry! I was being…"

"He is the dearest thing, to me," she said simply, and he saw that her eyes were suddenly wet. Fool that he was! He had completely forgotten about her older brother. Idiot! And she had intimated another, even more private grief. What had she not suffered?

"I know he is. I'm really sorry. For a moment I was jealous. Stupid of me."

She made no reply, but stood there in dignified silence, then shook out her robe and wound her scarf around her head. He had never seen a motion as graceful, and he took her hand.

"Do you forgive me?"

She let her fingers rest in his. "You must not be jealous of John-Sunday," she said bluntly. "That was the whole point of telling you the story! He's my brother and you... you're my friend. Am I so small that you cannot share?"

"You're not small," he said softly, and then he said, "I'm not jealous," surprising himself, for it was suddenly true. The boy knew more of her than he, and was more to be trusted. He would be there when Dan had long gone. "I was, but I won't be again. I promise. Now, say you forgive me."

"...I forgive you."

He asked her, then. "Why do you call me Harmattan?" His voice was gentle. "I've been wanting to know."

She looked at her hand lying in his, then withdrew it, and he heard her laugh in her throat.

"You have just proved how appropriate it is! Harmattan is the wind, the red wind that blows in from the Sahara. Your hair, you see, and the way you... take control of everything. Like the way you rushed into the bus," she said hurriedly, taking the sting out of her words. "So brave." She hesitated. "But we learn to guard ourselves against the harmattan... The dust is... forceful. It gets into everything, all our secret places!"

"I don't mean to!" he protested.

"Ah, but you do, Daniel," she said gently. "You do mean to."

She stepped down softly on to the dry grass, her bare feet rustling among the dried petals of the bougainvillea tree. He could just discern her shape, and her voice, when it came, seemed disembodied.

"I'll say goodnight."

"Are you going?"

"I'm going."

"Go with God, then," he said tenderly. "That's what you say, isn't it? 'Go with God?'"

"Yes. And you, stay with God. Goodnight."

After she had gone the night seemed strangely empty, as if she had taken with her all sound and colour. Dan sat for a few minutes, his hands loose on the arms of the chair, overwhelmed by the sheer multitude of the sensations he had experienced in so few days. In his room he lay for a while on top of the bed, his arms clasped behind his neck in the darkness, the light bulb above his head sporadically blinking; on, off and on again.

# CHAPTER 11

"I dig your African robe, by the way."

It was Tuesday evening and Luke and Dan were making their way over to supper. Self-consciously, Dan smoothed down the wide folds of homespun fabric against his legs.

"It looks like a dress, but I lost my jacket…"

"Good for you."

"No, I really did. I left it at… at the scene of the crime."

"You never liked wearing it much anyway."

"It's not just that… I've sort of got used to this. It somehow makes me feel more in tune with… No, that's silly."

"Not at all. It's good you should want to. It means you've really arrived, in more than one sense."

"Yes," Dan said morosely, "just when we're about to leave."

"Oh, we're not leaving yet. There's still a coupla' days to go."

"Four, actually."

"Well, four, then."

Hadissa, John-Sunday and Cletus were already assembled in the bishop's dining room when Luke and Dan arrived. They stood while the bishop said his usual enigmatic grace.

"Lord Jesus, we pray that you will end the years of locusts in our lives and open the doors of blessing to us once more, in Jesus' name, a-men. Lord, help us to consider our ways so that your blessings can flow on us unhindered. Surplus and restoration are upon your government, Lord Christ. Gracious God, we ask for your blessing on this food, that it will give us strength to do your holy work, a-men."

"Now," said the bishop, as they all sat down. "It's not usually our custom to talk while we eat, and Cletus is here to make sure I do the right thing, but there'll be time later. Help yourselves to the dishes, or Nathan will serve you. Eat plenty, for

145

who knows what tomorrow will bring!"

He laughed, and they got on with the meal, each with their secret thoughts. Hadissa was reminded of the bishop's high spirits the first evening they had met, and his natural charm, and she smiled secretly to herself as she ate. Her initial awe of him had been replaced by a deep respect. On the day of the bomb he had put down his work and gone straight round to the children, had returned to minister to his clergy, and had fielded the press. He had also listened to Dan's report of his encounter with the bomber, but what still disturbed her was the general perception that the perpetrator of the attack was a Muslim, and unless the bishop could advocate restraint, it was certain that the Christians would take revenge. How would the bishop handle that, or reconcile to himself his secret knowledge?

As for Dan, all he cared about was whether the small seed of doubt he had sown in the mind of the headmaster would filter down through the parents and prevent more bloodshed. Yet, why should Umgobe believe him, a foreigner and a white man? However, if he chose to, it might just be enough to restrain him from infecting the parents or the press with his own hysteria, justified though it might have seemed at the time.

While he ate, John-Sunday cast furtive glances at Dan. When he had encountered the white man at the gate he had not realised how closely Dan had been involved with the rescue of the children. At first, his red hair and his white face had merely repelled him, but he knew that was only his own racial prejudice. More particularly, he was deeply offended by the intimacy Dan seemed to have established with Hadissa. John-Sunday could not approve and it deeply disturbed him. What right had he to meddle with his sister? Yet, he was a teacher, and a teacher of maths! He must be very clever... and he had shown such courage with the children... thrown himself into the bus without thought for his own safety. John-Sunday was young, and during the course of the evening as he listened to Dan he could easily have hero-worshipped him. Even so, his first duty was to his sister, and he remained suspicious. This man, whoever he was and however heroic, had no right to interfere!

Cletus was also looking at Dan. He saw a man who had greatly changed from the one he had met from the airport at Abuja, and with whom he had travelled on the road. For a start, he no longer seemed short-tempered but more confident and self-possessed. He was behaving like some-one who had been in Nigeria for a lot longer than one and a half weeks, and surely his experience with the bomb could not have given him such a degree of self-assurance. There was more to this, thought Cletus, observing him, than met the eye. And obviously Luke thought so, too. Watching Luke watching John-Sunday, and John-Sunday watching Dan, who in turn was watching Hadissa, he thought he could fathom the mystery, and he also became disturbed.

After the meal was cleared away they sat round in a circle in the main reception room and Nathan served tea. As the door closed behind him, the bishop began to speak, incisively, and with authority.

"I'd like us to speak as equals," he said, "so don't defer to me because I'm the bishop. It's a bad time for us, and we need all heads. Now, I've been considering the implications of this bomb for our two communities. The general perception, at the moment, is that what happened was a Muslim attack on a Christian bus, and it affected the mosque because of its proximity. However, I think it's indisputable, Daniel, that the man you saw was the perpetrator, and he's a Christian. Do you realise where that leaves us? If it gets out that it was a Christian attack the Muslims are bound to retaliate, and then more of our churches will be burnt, more deaths will occur, and more children will be maimed. So, either we take steps to denounce this man, which will be catastrophic for our community, or we protect him."

Dan was aghast. "What, a cover-up?" he interrupted rudely. Luke raised a hand, embarrassed at Dan's terminology, but equally troubled.

The bishop was unmoved. "Yes, Daniel, a cover-up. In the circumstances it would be entirely judicious. If you think that so reprehensible you have no idea how we live here! And just *think* of the alternative! A bomb in a mosque? Yes, if I have to, I'll do it. I'd do anything to protect my people," he added loftily.

"Forgive me, Bishop," said Luke deferentially, but as anxious as Dan to forestall what seemed to be a typical African plot, "but what would you say in public? You surely won't allow the blame to fall on the Muslims! I suppose you could say there were two events, happening simultaneously, a Christian attack on the mosque and a Muslim one on a Christian bus. People might take the view that they somehow cancel each other out, and be less inclined to... But could you do it, when we know quite well that it was the action of this one man? And would you be believed? I'm sorry," he said, raising his hands helplessly, "I don't see..."

"The point is how it will be *perceived*," replied the bishop, "and if we do it this way it may well be perceived as a *quid pro quo*, and there would certainly be less violence. Only *we* know that it was the action of this one man. But tell me, Cletus, what are your thoughts on this?"

Cletus had become increasingly agitated, and now he leant forward. "Bishop, without *question* we should do what's necessary for our own people! They must be our first concern, whatever... But with your permission, I'd like to hear more from Daniel." He turned towards him. "You were actually there. How do you read this situation?"

"It's obvious!" Dan had been chafing under this politicking, and he replied sharply. "A Christian was to blame, and that's that! But – and it's a big 'but' – the man lost his family in the riots, and for that the Muslims were responsible – if not for the riots themselves, I have no way of knowing. What he did, he says, was in revenge. So he sets the bomb and it goes off as the bus is passing. It's chicken and egg, so it depends how far back you want to go in apportioning blame. Whatever the *perception*," he said, with a sideways glance at the bishop, "the bus, plainly, was not targeted, and anyway, it was only a Christian bus in that it was from the Cathedral School. Am I right in thinking that even extremists wouldn't generally target children?"

"Oh, not directly," replied the bishop. "Collateral damage, perhaps. This case is most unusual."

"But they *didn't*, in this case!" Luke protested, under his breath.

It seemed that the bishop had convinced himself of the lie, and Dan was equally appalled. "No, they didn't! It was just an unfortunate coincidence, tragic, with tragic consequences. That man, he's devastated by what he did, not just because of the children, but because he knew that what he did was terribly wrong. He'll have to live with that and I don't envy him. He hasn't much of a life, anyway."

"Incidentally, did you give him any money?" asked Luke.

"It never crossed my mind. Perhaps I should have done. But things were too raw, and the conversation we were having was on a different level. It might even have done harm, if he ended up thinking I was doing the British colonial court thing."

"A British colonial court would have hanged him..." muttered Cletus, "...not given him money!"

"I mean," said Dan patiently, "if he had seen me as some sort of arbiter of justice."

"Well," sighed the bishop, sitting back in his chair. "We have to recognise that there'll be a great deal of anger from both communities, even if it doesn't get out that the perpetrator was a Christian. I must meet with the Muslim leaders, and very soon. I don't know what their reaction would be if they knew the whole story, and I'm not sure I want to take that risk. On the other hand, if they did know, they might be able to quieten things down. They do have some responsibility for this unhappy event. What's important is that they admit that both communities are scandalised, the Muslims by what they perceive as an attack on the mosque, and the Christians by what they perceive as an attack on the school bus. It's an extremely difficult and complex situation."

"There is one idea that may work," said Dan thoughtfully. "If you'll allow me, Bishop."

"Go on. You're one of us."

Dan stood up and began to pace the room, the long skirt of his robe hanging gracefully from his shoulders. He was an impressive figure although he was unaware of it. Standing up to speak reminded him of Jacob, from the school, who could only answer standing up, and momentarily his mouth twitched wryly.

"I haven't thought it through," he said. "But what if, with the press, you do ignore what you know, and talk about actions and consequences instead, you can stress how it's a cycle of violence, that when one faction acts, everyone suffers. Put out a general statement to that effect. But with the Muslim leaders, tell them the truth – apologise, whatever..."

"We'd never apologise to *Muslims*!" interrupted Cletus huffily, but Dan ignored him and rushed on.

"...but also suggest some other ways of dealing with conflict, so that the cycle can somehow be broken. The more people can get used to peace, surely, the more they'll want to hang on to it."

"Break the cycle?" The bishop frowned.

"Yes. Like, for instance, the Muslims could visit the Cathedral School. Or, I don't know, maybe the faith leaders could pray together. Surely if they pray together they could work together?"

Cletus shook his head. "Muslims would never…"

Dan raised his voice, speaking over him. "Or the children from the school could be involved in the rebuilding of the mosque; like, planting a garden or something." He shrugged. "Okay, it sounds outrageous, even to me. But, to do something together, share in some project or other? Get to understand where each of them is coming from? Not yet, perhaps; feelings are still raw, but sooner rather than later?" He stared at them for a moment, frowning, then his face cleared. "Or there's another way still," he said eagerly. "What would happen if you were completely open and truthful, and don't attempt to conceal anything?" His excitement mounted. "Yes, come straight out with it! Get it into the public eye and let people work it out for themselves! Let them see the *consequences* of violence! You know, the unacceptability of collateral damage. That might work in some situations, but you know better than I do. As you say, I don't have to live here." He sat down next to Hadissa, and artlessly laid his hand on hers.

"Are you all right?" he asked her quietly.

"Yes, I'm fine." She removed her hand gently, glancing at John-Sunday who was glowering at her.

"You mean, actually *tell* them about this man?" the bishop asked. "I've said I don't know we can go as far as that."

"Indirectly," replied Dan. "I mean indirectly. Let them know of his existence, but not, actually, name him. We can't do that anyway because I didn't ask him his name. But tell them the story, and while things are still sensitive, let them see how anger begets anger, and prejudice begets prejudice? And give them an exit strategy; show them how sharing can beget sharing. How barriers, in other words, could become bridges."

Hadissa drew in her breath.

"People are hurting," Dan continued. "Both sides have experienced terrible pain. I'm sorry, but the question I'd want to ask is, are they hurting *enough*? Enough to be able to really see each other's desperation? And desperate enough to be able to want to be in any other situation other than a hurting one. Which might mean, a healing one."

Dan paused and his eyes darted from one to another of his listeners. He was now sitting on the very edge of the two-seater sofa, leaning forwards with his arms resting on his spread knees, his back almost completely turned to Hadissa who was watching the expressive movements of his hands as he spoke, her eyes gleaming with something like pride.

"I know it sounds an awful thing to say," he continued, speaking more slowly, "but if they've fallen so low there's no place left to go... They might be ready to improve things. And then... then it's not just one more shattering event to add to a long list of other shattering events; it becomes... it's... Well, I'm probably naive, but, maybe it can become the first of many events that could put things back together again."

He sat back.

"This event," he said quietly, "the mosque and the bus, well, *quid pro quo* means it doesn't belong to either community, does it? Neither can appropriate it because in actual fact it affected both. Perhaps both can have a share in the reconstruction, I don't know. They all have to live in the same place, whether it's the city or the townships. How else are they going to learn to live with one another, if they don't collaborate? I don't see that there's any other option. Peace can't always be shoved into the future, surely? There's got to come a time when you seize the moment."

His voice trailed off, and he lowered his eyes. "It's the sort of thing that might appeal to people's imaginations," he said, almost pleadingly. "I must say, after what I've seen... I know I'm an outsider, and I've been here less than two weeks, but if I lived here, well, it's certainly something I'd like to be involved in." He closed his lips.

It had been a prolonged speech, and the bishop and Cletus had been silent throughout. Now they met each other's eyes interrogatively, and Cletus nodded imperceptibly. The bishop leant forward.

"What you say is very significant," he declared. "And I must say, as a church leader I've always felt we should talk to each other more..." Dan was astonished by this apparent hypocrisy, but even more so by the bishop's next words. "And, of course, I've encouraged our clergy to do the same. Perhaps," he mused, "we haven't done it enough. We must learn to celebrate the inter-connectedness of the two faiths, instead of forever excluding each other. I think that people on the ground are beginning to think this way, too." He waved his fingers at Luke. "Did you read that letter in the *Post* today, about people no longer wanting to leave it to the politicians? They want to get involved, and the church should take a lead, not just from our ivory towers, as we used to say at Oxford, but out there in the street! And this really may be the moment, as Daniel says. The time is ripe, and God forgive us, there have been so many moments…"

He stood up. "It could be a revolution!" he said excitedly, punching his fist into the other hand. "As you say, Daniel, we could start with the children, which are especially important, given what's happened. The children are our future! It would benefit both communities, and not only in our respective faiths, but socially as well. Something like this would be completely different. It would be like the river of God!" He seemed genuinely moved, and Dan relaxed for the first time since coming into the room.

"Do you have the resources for this kind of work?" asked Luke. "Because, if you don't, we could help. I mean Coventry could find some funds. It's very close to what Coventry's about. If you wish, I could make some inquiries next week…" As he said to Dan, later, he was determined to get it in writing before anyone changed their minds.

"We do have some resources, but not much, as you know. Most of our money is tied up with repairing the world we live in rather than initiating new projects…"

"But Daniel has said it, Bishop," interposed Cletus. "Projects such as this would *be* repairing the world! But one of the questions we'd need to ask," he continued, "both as Christians or Muslims, would be how our own way of believing has made us exclude others. It's a difficult question and it will be hard to face up to…"

Dan interrupted rudely. "Hold on, we don't want to get all theological over this. We need to be practical…"

"My dear chap, we also need to know *why* we're doing it!" murmured Luke.

"Okay, but don't bring in the creeds, otherwise you're right back where you started. The religious side has got to be kept separate, surely? Otherwise, aren't there situations where to exclude somebody might be right? I mean, is it always wrong? You talk about it as though it's always wrong."

Cletus took up this challenge. "Certainly there are situations when we have to say, beyond this line I will not go... That won't change," he added complacently.

Hadissa interposed, for the first time. "But if you draw a line, Brother Cletus, there's always someone who'll be shut out..."

"I agree with Cletus," interrupted the bishop sternly, "and Hadissa, you must let us men decide these things..."

Hadissa's eyes widened with shock and Dan was incredulous. All this talk about inclusion, and yet the first time she spoke they bit her head off?

"What about your Mothers' Union, then?" he said mildly. "Women take the lead there, don't they? And the children will make leaders in their own right." He glanced at John-Sunday as he spoke, thinking about the wall, but the bishop was in full flow.

"In terms of our two creeds, what we have to acknowledge is where lines have already been drawn, and where they must continue to be drawn. I don't think it need stop us doing all we can on a practical level. Maybe there are just too many lines! People have learnt to say 'no' for the wrong reasons, not just out of integrity but out of longstanding fear, and they make religion the excuse. It's a long story of outrage, counter-outrage, and point scoring. It's become a way of life. Even we, as Christians, are not entirely innocent of this."

He turned to Hadissa, whose head was still down. "Don't worry, Hadissa. We're not talking about creeds, here, but about faith. To do what Daniel is suggesting will take faith. And faith is another matter! Believing in impossible things – that is faith! Someone has got to break the pattern, and only Christ can do it. And we are his hands on this earth, so we must do it in his name! I think we should pray about it," he announced firmly. "I suggest we stand."

All except John-Sunday got to their feet. He remained where he was, an expression of utter bewilderment on his face, his eyes staring ahead, looking somehow lost and rather forlorn. *Miles away*, thought Dan. Hadissa was embarrassed for him, but she was too far away from him to nudge him. Then the bishop caught her eye. He shook his head at her, indicating that she

153

ignore him, and she tried to smile, then shut her eyes.

Prayer, again, thought Dan, sighing inwardly as he got to his feet. Oh well, in another time and another place, I'd be fretting to leave at this point, but here, it seems right. They do it all the time, anyway. I'm sort of getting used to it. Through half-closed eyes he stole a look at Hadissa, standing immobile, her head bowed and her eyes closed, her sinuous fingers clasped together. He saw her lips move.

The bishop prayed aloud, as he had at the grace.

"Lord Jesus, be the ruler of our hearts, touch us with your hand of blessing, spew out from us all un-forgiveness, and let love take root in our hearts. Lord, we enter on this project with your pow-ah, determined not to lay it down until it is completed. Put a new heart within us, and make us faithful citizens of your country. Amen."

*Does he mean it?* Dan wondered. *Have we actually won?* The thought that his and Luke's presence might have swung things, was staggering. *He believes in his God, though, that's for sure. Well, they've got to believe in something, I suppose. But this project they've just taken on – they must realise the risks involved. God, I hope it works! Did I just pray? Was that a prayer? I wonder why John-Sunday isn't joining us. Is he upset for Hadissa, too? These guys, how they suffer at the hands of authority! The bomber, too – I bet no one was around to help him when it was needed. Well, I can maybe sow a seed or two.*

"Um, this chap, the bomber," he said slowly. "Just a thought, but is there any chance we could do something for this chap, if he's found? Get him out of the city, help him set up somewhere, find him a new home, I mean?"

Luke touched his arm. "He's only one of very many in the same plight, Dan. You can't help them all, you know."

Into the silence that followed, Cletus said, "I've just realised that I can find out his name. Stupid of me not to think of it before, but... well, while we were praying, I had an image of this man going to see his pastor. Well, if he was a mechanic in Nasarawa, his pastor will know him. There'll only have been one mechanic..."

"Of course," said the bishop. "Find out what you can, Cletus, and let me know. Well, friends," he added, "I think we can call it a night."

John-Sunday had not moved, and Hadissa crossed the

154

room to him and bent over him, whispering softly. He leant forward, and to their surprise and dismay, he clutched her around her legs, and buried his face in her skirt, muttering inaudibly. She took him by the shoulders and pushed him backwards so that she could see his face, but he hung his head, refusing to look at her.

"*What*?" she hissed. "What did you say? Get up!"

"I said, I killed him!"

"Who?" she breathed. "What are you talking about?"

"Stanley. I killed Stanley..."

"Now then, young man," said the bishop, coming forward. "It's very late and emotions have been running high. What you need is your bed..."

"But it's true!" he wailed hoarsely, refusing to look at him.

The bishop spoke in a voice that was both businesslike and, to the boy, calming. "John-Sunday, you need to explain what you mean. Do you want to talk about it? Do you want everyone to go away, and talk to me, or talk to Hadissa? What do you want?"

John-Sunday, who by this time was kneeling at Hadissa's feet, pushed himself back into the chair, wiping his eyes on his sleeve. "I'm sorry. No, I will say..."

They sat down again, their eyes riveted on John-Sunday. When he spoke it was in a tone that made him seem much younger than his nineteen years.

"Dadda... Dadda came to Kaduna... looking for parts for the tractor... and then the riots started... and we didn't know where he was... so Stanley, he came after him, to look for him. And Stanley was killed, on the road."

"This much we know," said the bishop gently. "Go on."

"Oh," the boy cried despairingly. "But there was a mechanic at Kateri all the time! On the... the other side of the road! I knew he was there, but I... I didn't say anything! Only, this man... he was a Muslim... Dadda didn't need to go to Kaduna! If I'd told him, he wouldn't have gone! But I didn't tell him! I didn't tell him! That's why Stanley was killed. It was all my fault!"

"That's not true, John-Sunday." Hadissa's voice was firm. "Even if Dadda had known, he wouldn't have gone to a Muslim."

155

"But it's why he *left* us!" he shrieked. "When I told him there had been a mechanic there all the time, he... he couldn't bear it. He blamed me! That's why he left."

Luke leant forward. "John-Sunday, surely your father knew of this mechanic."

"No! Dadda *hated* the other side of the road. He *hated* the Muslims!"

"So even if your father had known he was there, he wouldn't have gone to him for parts?"

The boy did not reply.

"John-Sunday, answer me!" Luke demanded, his voice very quiet, but insistent. "If your father had known he was there, would he have gone to him for parts?"

"No."

"John-Sunday," said Luke, "the reason your father left was not because he blamed you for Stanley's death. He was an adult, John-Sunday, and you were a boy. He almost certainly knew there was a mechanic on the other side of the road. If he blamed you, it was because he, himself, felt guilty."

John-Sunday raised his head and looked at Luke through eyes that were rimmed with red.

"I'm sure of this," Luke said robustly. "It was nothing to do with you."

"It was..."

"It was nothing to do with you," Luke was firm. "You don't need to feel this burden."

John-Sunday was quiet, then he raised his eyes to the bishop.

"Bishop, Dan is right. If you find this man, will you send him to Kateri? We'll look after him there, and he can teach me what he knows about engineering. I would... I would like to look after him. We can give him a home. He can start a new life..."

"Then perhaps," said Hadissa, stroking his hair, "we can look for our father again..."

The bishop rose to his feet, looking as exhausted as they all felt.

"There are pastors in Abuja, too," he said quietly. "We will contact them. This is also a project for peace. Don't worry, John-Sunday. We'll find your father."

# CHAPTER 12

The atmosphere in the school was sombre, and Dan was acutely conscious of the gaps in the long rows of seats in his classroom. However, little by little, as he struggled to find imaginative ways to teach the children, the mood changed and they became more animated.

On his first day back they gathered round him, fingering his African robe, eagerly clamouring to be told how he had rescued Sammi and Maria. He refused to talk about it, and instead, on the first day, got those who could write to compose little stories about friendship and family, or about how, in the past, they had been taught to deal with racial issues. The others he put in groups to talk about the same subject. The silence, then, was profound; those in groups either couldn't discuss the subject, or refused to, and later, when he read the written work, he felt he had completely misjudged the situation and was mortified. Without exception their contributions were uncritical, phonetically spelt summaries of what they had been told by their parents. *Abrahim, hem gan to de Lord; Mano, hem place empty. Amaka, hem with God. Jesus woch ober Chukwu* – and more of the same. Looking at the stained, screwed up, badly-written and blotted scripts – pages he had torn from the school secretary's notebook – he realised he couldn't just treat them as an exercise in composition. In the end he simply wrote 'Thank you' above his signature at the bottom of each page.

On reflection, Dan realised this parental influence would have been just the same in England, but he was still startled by the complete absence of any real grief, at least overtly. All of them knew people who had disappeared, or families where someone had been killed or maimed, but there was no tradition of dealing with it, no capacity to engage with the issues. He thought it was hardly surprising, therefore, that the violence was perpetuated.

*Tomorrow*, he thought, *we'll all do something orally.*

157

Yet, the next day, when he tried to discuss their work with them, and engage with the larger political and religious issues, he found no points of reference from which to start, and no common ground. They avoided his eyes and would not answer his questions. He felt more of a stranger than he had on his first day. Their answers were stilted and unemotional, and he realised that it was already too late; they were now merely regurgitating what they had heard from their elders, which they were reluctant to deviate from, or connect, with their own feelings. He realised that, once again, he had trespassed where he had no right to go, and he gave up. Otherwise, what demons might he evoke? What night-time terrors might he initiate? He felt that if he'd been able to live with them for a while, become a more acceptable face among them, he might have made more headway. But he was leaving them soon, and they knew it.

*　*　*

He was counting the hours that remained to him to be with Hadissa, but each day she worked her shift at the hospital and he did not see her until the Thursday when Boseh, her consultant in the casualty department, had been invited for supper. Nathan, having ransacked his store-cupboard for every ingredient, was in his element.

The bishop held court at the top of the table with Boseh on his right. Luke and Dan were on either side of Hadissa, while John-Sunday was allowed a place at the foot of the table, by the kitchen door. During the meal they kept silent, and even Dan, now more acclimatised to the African way, did not find it too oppressive. He had no idea why Boseh had been invited to this supper, but he knew he was an honoured guest, and therefore it was all the more surprising when, once they had finished the meal, the bishop immediately deferred to John-Sunday.

"Now then," he said to the boy, "it's time to tell Hadissa what you've been doing."

All through the meal, John-Sunday had been on edge, his eyes dating from one to another, alive with hope, for Boseh would hardly have been invited on this particular occasion were it not to discuss his plan for Hadissa.

"Hadissa," he said, gravely, "you remember, when you left Kateri last week, I asked you to deliver a letter to the bishop?"

She nodded, frowning curiously, her hands hidden in her lap.

"Well," he said, quietly, "in that letter I asked the bishop if you could go abroad to study nursing – *general* nursing, Hadissa – and to qualify there."

"But I can qualify here!" she exclaimed, her eyes darting to Boseh. "If I'm good enough, and if Mr. Boseh allows me to."

"My dear," said Boseh, smiling at her, "of course you're good enough. But am I given to understand that your preference would not be in 'A and E'? And you've proved yourself so efficient preparing the report on the clinic that I'd already decided that you ought to change course. But let's listen to what the bishop has to say. It is he who acted on your brother's letter."

"But I don't understand," she said, turning to her brother. "Why did you write such a letter, John-Sunday? Why didn't you discuss it with me, first?"

"We did discuss it, sister. It was how I knew you were unhappy."

She looked at him quickly, shaking her head. "But a *letter*, John!" she murmured, "and without telling me!"

It was difficult enough for her to sit at table with Boseh, a remote, authoritarian figure whom she usually hoped to avoid, without having her unhappiness revealed for everyone to examine, like some impersonal body on an operating table.

"I *was* unhappy," she confessed, looking down and then raising her head quickly. "But not with the hospital itself, or the people there, or anything. It wasn't just the work. I was already... in my personal life..." A hot flush mounted in her face and she was silent.

She could not confess the personal affairs of her heart, even to the bishop. While it had left her shamed, there was much about her love affair that she did not regret. The experience had taught her that she need not always feel soiled, as she had with her father, although those feelings had returned later. Most importantly, she had also discovered in herself a capacity for passion and for long-term commitment, which she determined that next time would not be illicit. That had been one reason why she had avoided seeing her mother, whose dark imaginings raised a knowing gleam in her eyes whenever she contemplated her daughter, woman to woman. As for John-Sunday, she knew instinctively, and with a natural prescience born of Eve, that in order to keep his respect, she must never confide in him. He was perceptive and compassionate, but he was also a man and the head of the family. As such, he could be very stern.

Were it not that Hadissa's discomfiture was painfully evident, Dan would have been intrigued and delighted to see how roseate her dark skin had become. As it was, he tried to deflect everybody's attention by making a remark himself.

"Do many people go abroad to study?"

"I would have loved to have done general nursing."

He spoke loudly, Hadissa in a whisper, and they spoke together. The bishop chose to ignore Dan for the present. He had been studying Hadissa carefully, and now he leant forward and said, "What attracts you about it?"

"Yes," said Boseh, placing his elbows on the table and clasping his hands, "I, too, would like to hear the answer to that."

Hadissa took time to recover and to think. For some reason unknown to herself, it was not her past that was under discussion, but her future. There was a hidden agenda, initiated originally and unaccountably by John-Sunday, and she suspected that what she next said could determine the future pattern of her life. The issue, she mistakenly thought, was whether she wanted to change her course to general nursing, and she roused herself to address it.

"As a child, and growing up," she said quietly, addressing Boseh, "we lived in Kateri. John-Sunday lives there still, with my mother... We lived out back of Kateri, in the bush. But the school was nearer the road, and almost every day, there'd be an accident."

"You mean a road accident?" Boseh frowned and then his face cleared. "Yes, that road's notorious..."

"We used to hear the screech of brakes and then the crash..."

She paused. "It made me want... Seeing the victims made me feel..."

She shrugged helplessly. "I was very young, but..."

She floundered, then spoke directly to Dan.

"You have to understand," she said to him, "there's no hospital for fifty miles. And people don't have cars. So, when there's an accident, and the ambulance doesn't come, and the police don't come, what do you do? If you can find a truck or

160

something to get the victim to hospital, well, then the hospital is very expensive and there is no money to pay for it. And where shall the driver stay if he can't get back the same day? You can't be on the road at night! Luke knows this already. It is why they are building the clinic at Kateri."

Luke leant forward and touched her hand. "We understand. Go on."

"Like in the bus – how many could we have saved, if only they had come?" She had tears in her eyes. "All these delays," she said, unconsciously clutching his hand, "and people dying where they lay, dying for want of medical attention... It made me so... so angry. In my heart," she added, touching her breast. "It was the same in the village. It made me want to *do* something! It made me want to be a nurse."

She picked up her glass and took a long drink of water, catching the drops on her lips with her forefinger.

"You have to realise that I was very young. In Kateri people were dying from all sorts of things but I... I never realised. I didn't see. There've always been things like... like abscesses or peritonitis or food poisoning or accidents at work or on the market. Or still-births or women dying in childbirth. I just didn't *see* these things – they were just part of life. So, when I finished school and they accepted me on a nursing course, I began to train in casualty." She glanced at Boseh deferentially. "You taught my first module, Mr Boseh."

"About two years ago."

"Yes, just before our brother was killed."

Dan drew in his breath sharply, beginning to make the connection.

"But even before our brother was killed," she continued earnestly, "I knew it was wrong. What am I saying? Not wrong... but wrong for *me*. When the disturbances started, the riots and everything, and people began coming in off the streets with... with terrible wounds, I used to dread going into work. It all seemed so... It was just never-ending!"

Hadissa hiccupped and began to sob quietly, covering her mouth, her words almost intelligible, so that they leant closer to hear. She seemed to sense this and put her hand back on the table.

"And... and my job was to patch them up, and then just send them away again..."

161

She made a huge effort to control herself, swallowing hard, but the recollection of all she had seen and experienced in the overloaded casualty department overwhelmed her. It lit a flame within her and fuelled the indignation, which had been simmering for so long.

"And to what?" she said angrily, thumping the table sharply with her clenched fist. "To a life which was maimed forever! Some of them had lost whole families, and were scarred emotionally as well. And the machete wounds and the burns! Some of the patients went away terribly disfigured, terribly crippled, and there was no after-care, no medicines... We didn't give them painkillers or send anyone to check on them and see how they were doing. We just discharged them," she said bitterly, "and for many that meant throwing them out again on the very streets where... from which they had come to us for... for... for help."

Hadissa was weeping openly now, the tears running unchecked down her face, and Dan wanted to take her in his arms. *In two days' time*, he thought, *we fly out. I shall never see her again! How will I bear it?* He was filled with compassion and tenderness. He yearned to touch her and stroke away her tears. It was like a physical pain, but instead he took out his handkerchief and handed it to her. She took it gratefully, and mopped her face with it, unopened, and handed it back, like a child.

"Then my brother was killed..." She choked in her throat, and was silent.

"I began to think about changing course," she continued with an effort, "but I knew it was... Oh, it was impossible! We're terribly understaffed and under-resourced. I'm sorry, Mr Boseh, but we are."

"Oh yes," he said, "that's quite true. It's common knowledge. But we do what we can."

"I know... But I began to think about a different sort of nursing. Preventative medicine, post-operative care, dealing with people whose lives might be changed by a little extra knowledge, so they don't die of silly things, like infected cuts. Like dealing with things like cataracts or helping them with diet so their kids can survive, even trivial things where a simple operation in a day ward would transform their lives. Or teaching them prenatal care, or helping the women in childbirth. So *many* of our women die in childbirth!"

She was eager now, turning quickly to Boseh. "When you sent me back to Kateri I saw a man lying under a tree on a mattress. I hardly recognised him, but ten years ago he'd been my teacher. For the last five years he has been paralysed from the waist down. He is totally dependent on the goodwill of others. You know what his trouble is?"

She looked around the room almost triumphantly. "Piles! I am sorry to bring this out in public, but that's what it was."

Dan drew in his breath. Piles, the sort of thing that people in his own culture, unless they were sufferers, sniggered about. The bishop leant back and sighed, resting his elbows on the arms of his chair with his hands in front of him, his fingertips touching.

"You paint a vivid picture, Hadissa. Of neglect and inattention." He was quiet, then he said, "Well, gentlemen, now you've heard her, I'd like to know what you think."

Boseh smiled. "Hadissa," he said, "you've always been an exceptional nurse. I am sorry that you've not been happy in the work. I'm sorry, too, that I didn't notice. I'm afraid being too busy is not an adequate excuse. I feel I have failed you. And there's not much I can do about it. We just don't have the resources for people to change track in the middle of a course. Afterwards, well…"

Luke leant forward.

"Forgive me, Boseh, just give me a minute." He turned to the girl. "Hadissa, what you have been telling us is very important. You see, your brother thinks it would be a good idea if you were to finish your training abroad. Change courses there, move over to general nursing. That's really why Mr Boseh is here tonight. And why John-Sunday is here."

Hadissa surveyed him incredulously, her eyes wide, then turned to her brother.

"Abroad? But…"

"Let me just finish, my dear," Luke interrupted. "There are places you can go, but could you cope with the different culture? To be honest, you could go anywhere; America, France, England, but if you came to England my diocese could probably help you with funding. Not all of it, but certainly with part, especially if you came back and worked at the clinic." He glanced at the bishop, who nodded. "It's a project where we're already heavily involved..."

"And there are funds here," interjected the bishop. "I've had a word with the state governor, and he says it would be an investment."

"And," Luke continued, "...the British High Commission in Abuja has a special fund for the training of indigenous Nigerians who will train abroad and then return to work in this country. But there's one thing..." He hesitated. "Hadissa, you do need to realise it's a very different culture, and take a bit of time to think." He looked at her, and nodded emphatically. "Take time to *think*, Hadissa."

He turned towards Mr Boseh. "If she's to go, I'd like to know about timing, and whether what she's already done will go towards her final assessment. She'll need that to qualify for the course in England, if she decides to come."

Hadissa began to tremble. John-Sunday stood up and went to stand behind her, pressing her shoulders, and she lifted her hands and laid them over his. Dan got up quickly, relinquishing his chair so that John-Sunday could be next to her, and went to sit in the chair that John-Sunday had been using. As he sat down he caught Luke's appreciative grin. Yes, there was no denying he would have liked to be in John-Sunday's shoes. Yet his mood was changing. Suddenly there was hope on the horizon, not just for her but for him, too – and for them.

"Yes, let your brother comfort you," said Mr Boseh. "He has been your guardian angel in all this. And I was going to add, I think I can make it up to you. You'll have no trouble with your final exams. If we could advance them a little, say, a few weeks, then you'd already be a qualified nurse. I'm keen to get on with this," he added. "You see, Hadissa, we need someone at Kateri. The area is huge and we need someone who knows it, someone the people would accept, someone who would live there and be one of them. Someone who could come and go in the bush without fear."

Hadissa was bemused. "You are talking about me?" she asked, gazing at him intently. "You want me to nurse – at Kateri?"

"My dear child," he said, tapping the table with his forefinger. "Do this, and I will put you in charge of the clinic."

\* \* \*

164

Luke left the table to go and telephone England. There was a man he knew, he said, a priest in the Anglican church who might be able to help. They would have to find the right college and sort out accommodation, and this priest, Stephen, would know how to proceed. Privately, Luke feared for Hadissa. It was all very well sending the girl to England, but how would a bush village girl cope on her own, and in a strange land? If only he could persuade Stephen and Verity, a mere ten miles away in Ely, to keep a watchful eye on her! She would stand a better chance of survival if she could relate to them.

Luke was absent a long time and returned to the table disgruntled.

"Telephone lines are down again, so I can't get through. It'll have to wait till morning."

"We can try again later tonight," replied the bishop. "You know how it is, we do not always have power." He looked around and smiled. "But tonight that is not the case, eh, Boseh? Tonight, we have Power!"

Boseh slapped the table. "We have the Pow-ah!"

"It's cutting things a bit fine," said Dan anxiously. "For heaven's sake, we fly out on Saturday. And the flight's early so in effect we lose a whole day. That means we only have one day left to sort things out."

"Harmattan..." The voice was a whisper, and it was full of laughter. "If God means me to go, I shall go. Why the rush? I've told you, you are so like the wind..."

"Well, there is a certain urgency," said Luke, smiling at her. "I think Dan's right." He glanced at him slyly. "Wind or no wind. Unless you want to wait a year..."

Her laughter vanished abruptly. "No... Oh no... I..."

"In that case, we need to move quickly. The academic year starts in October, September in some places, and that's only a few weeks away. We can get the paperwork done, but if we are to get you on a course and find you somewhere to live as well, *and* get you over there, we need to move fast. I'll stay up tonight, I think, and telephone if I can."

"It's like a dream," she said, wonderingly, her hands to her mouth. She looked at John-Sunday, and there were tears in her eyes. "It's like a dream, isn't it John-Sunday?"

He put his arms around her. "It has been your dream for

165

a long time. My dream too, being a mechanic. Now, thanks be to God, it looks like becoming reality."

* * *

Two days left, thought Dan, as he walked across the dark compound to his room. It was one of those nights when the world seemed to resonate with added depth and colour. The sky streamed with stars and the full moon cast strong horizontal shadows across the garden. Above the dark protecting curtain of the oleander and the bougainvillea trees he was dimly aware of the noise of the city, distant and otherworldly, while below was silence, the heady scent of blossom, the white gravel and his white homespun robe, redolent of everything African. He paused, enjoying the sensation of being alone after the intensity of the evening's discussion. This minute he was separate from her, but the future was now leaping towards him and he felt a lightness of spirit that he had not known for a very long time. *Two days*, he thought jubilantly, and then its only weeks, weeks, and I'll see her again!

Unexpectedly he was deliriously happy. He bounded high off the ground, punching the air with his fist, his robe swirling round his legs. He did not see the figure of Nathan, standing like a sentinel outside his kitchen door, as dark and motionless as the trunks of the trees, observing him with suspicious, wide, white eyes.

166

# PART 2
*England*

# CHAPTER 1

Abuja Airport was deserted, the next flight to Heathrow due out at midnight. In the departure lounge John-Sunday and Hadissa sat very close, holding hands like lovers. It was a long wait. For fear of the road they had arrived in the late afternoon, and John-Sunday had arranged to spend the night in the Christian hostel nearby. What he had not told her was that he intended to take an extra day in Abuja, and that, armed with the names of the pastors that Cletus had given him, he intended to initiate a preliminary search for his father.

Why should the prospect fill him with such dread? During the two and a half years of his absence John-Sunday had attained a measure of peace, and it had been some time since he had attempted to conjure up his father's image. The likeness of his father's face had become subsumed in the memory of his dead brother, as if both were dead, and as if they had died at the same time and in the same manner. John-Sunday now realised that this was a projection of his own guilt; a burden he had hardly known he carried until the conversation in the bishop's house had revealed it to him. He would have welcomed the opportunity to talk more about his childhood, in simple terms, and holding nothing back, yet there had been no time. He knew what he would have said for he had gone over and over it in his mind for months, if not years, and he yearned to be liberated from it. He would have described, unemotionally but in detail, how Stanley's perpetual bullying had diminished him, adolescent as he was, and left him unacknowledged as someone worthy of respect. He would have described how his father had seemed to sanction the older boy's behaviour, as if this domination of the younger sibling was, for both his sons, a test of manhood like the abandoned initiation rituals of pre-Christian days. During the long-drawn-out years of his turbulent adolescence, John-Sunday felt that his father had treated his growing mental anguish with

169

an indifference bordering on contempt. That he had instinctively sought refuge with his twin sister only confirmed him, in his father's mind, as an object of derision.

Yet his feelings were complicated by an ambivalence that he found hard to reconcile. He genuinely missed his father's wisdom in the fields, his authority in village affairs, even, childishly, his presence at the storytelling around the cooking fires at night. This, by itself, would have been enough to root John-Sunday in his village but since his father had gone he had no one to advise him about the practical problems of his daily life. He needed a father's solidarity. He would have liked his father to have known him now, when he might have treated him as an equal; perhaps, at times, deferred to him, or at least to have included him in decision-making. The episode of the tractor epitomised all that he felt – the fact that it was now sunk in long grass on flattened tyres was in itself a rebuke. He had done nothing about it, and he felt that somehow his father would have done *something*, that they would not have had to manage without it all this time. John-Holiness had been right; a tractor could do in one afternoon what it would take a week for a man to do, working on his own. He could almost hear the echo of his father's raucous, contemptuous laugh.

Finding his father implied a meeting, and it was this meeting that John-Sunday most feared, for it would tell him much about that fateful day when his brother had been killed. The fact of the matter was plain. Indirectly, his brother had met his death because they had deliberately rejected the help of a mechanic from a despised and hated creed. For that reason and that reason alone his father had gone to Kaduna. And then Stanley had followed him, to look for him.

That was their sin. John-Sunday had been brought face to face with his own prejudice, but his father's state of mind was still a mystery. John-Sunday now suspected that it was the consciousness of this sin which had driven his father from their village and probably into the hands of the drink-dealers of Abuja. He told himself that he longed to bring his father home, drink-sodden and maudlin though he might be, that they could be a complete family again, that it would be for his mother a recovery of respectability, of life itself, that they would surround each other with love, that somehow what they had done wrong would be redeemed, and that it would allow him to decide his

170

own destiny for a change, that he would be free.

Deep within him, John-Sunday could not believe it. It was a phantom hope as elusive as the person his father had become. He already had one doomed parent to look after. To take on another would test his scant resources infinitely. He would be ensnared forever. He would have liked to have had more faith. He would have liked to believe that somehow it was, as the bishop had said, an answer to prayer, but it was not, sincerely, his prayer at all. He would have liked even to have approached and undertaken the task dispassionately, an experiment capable of either success or failure, but all he could actually feel was blind panic and the resounding echoes of his childhood fears. In the meantime the shadowy figure of a skeletal shambling father loomed over his daylight hours and figured in his dreams like an image of the waking dead.

\*　\*　\*

Hadissa was glad to have been allocated a window seat, primarily because she did not want to sit between strangers, but also because they would be arriving over England in daylight and she wanted a good view of the country that was going to be her home for the next year. She was unprepared for the chill of the bulkhead against her thigh, which, as the flight progressed, seemed to penetrate her whole body. Neither had she foreseen the ignominy of having to excuse herself to visit the toilet. Her face flaming, she climbed awkwardly across the two seats, apologising profusely to the two male passengers who had to stand up for her, while trying at the same time to keep her wrap-around skirt from bunching up to reveal her knees. There was no separate facility for men and women, and this dismayed her, for she had not shared a toilet area with a male since puberty. She took refuge for more time than was polite in the dubious privacy of the narrow cubicle, unaware that a queue was forming. Waiting impassively outside was a burly black-bearded Muslim cleric, and as she squeezed past him, avoiding his eyes, she inadvertently let the door close against his hand. Once again she had to disturb her fellow passengers, one of whom had fallen asleep during her absence. She resolved that on no account would she move from her seat again until the flight was over.

Weepy with cold and with a mounting sense of isolation

she leant her head against the cold bulkhead and tried to sleep. Her courage all but extinguished, she pulled her pashmina over her face, taking deep shuddering breaths to camouflage her distress, and squeezed her eyes tightly shut. To an onlooker she appeared to be sleeping, while under the pashmina, she was overwhelmed by loneliness, a dark tense knot of misery around her heart.

In the past it was at times like this, when her morale was low, that Hadissa turned to John-Sunday for succour. Already she felt his absence like a physical pain – as if he was dead, like Stanley, or as if *she* were dead, moving inexorably to another world, not by her own volition, but because she was being punished for something – she knew not what, except that it was what she had always expected of life. She could not foresee her future but she refused to distract herself by thinking about what awaited her in England. Enough to know that she was being met, for Luke had promised to meet her with his friend Stephen, the priest from Ely, who, with his wife, Verity, had offered to house her for the summer vacation. After that, they said, she would be at the college, Homerton, or perhaps take lodgings in Cambridge. The names seemed awkward and unwieldy; they sat clumsily on her mental tongue. There was so much to learn, not least about her hosts. Apprehensively, Hadissa wondered what Verity would think of her, a bush village girl from Nigeria. Would she be treated like a servant? Another anxious little sob caught in her throat.

Suddenly Hadissa remembered the tiny cross of nails that she had found only a few weeks before in the clinic at Kateri. The cross that she had given to her mother in lieu of a shared meal, the cross that, as she had made her final farewells to John-Sunday at the airport, he had pressed into her hand.

"It is from our mother."

"She returns my gift?" Hadissa's voice was bleak.

"It was all she had to give you. Take it. It will keep you safe, God willing."

"It was your thought," Hadissa said, mulishly. "She would not think of it."

"Hadissa! Don't blame her so!"

His reproof was fierce and immediate, and the ready tears sprang into her eyes.

"John... John..." she stammered, "don't... don't be

angry with me…"

John-Sunday took her hands in his, clasping them to his warm chest.

"Hey, don't cry…" he said gently. "But try to understand her, please. It would help me so much if you would. She is a frightened woman, Hadissa." He raised his head and indicated the vast waiting area of the departure lounge. "Look around you…" His tone was tender but still stern. "Look! Electricity, miles of carpets, tables, chairs, glass windows!" He shook her gently. "Hadissa, our mother lives in a dark mud hut on the bare earth and her life's mate has deserted her. She's lonely. She lives in darkness. She's lost her husband and her elder son. She feels she is losing you."

"John-Sunday!" She gasped his name. "I'm sorry! I'm sorry… for everything!"

"It would help," he said diffidently, "if you were to marry, and one of our own kind. Perhaps a man from the village."

"Not yet," she pleaded. "I have work to do."

"Well, try not to forget… either of us."

She promised, uttering inarticulate phrases, whimpering against his shoulder, breathing his smell deeply into her nostrils.

The cross was still without a chain. Her mother had tied it to her bodice with a scrap of cotton, but Hadissa, fearful of losing it again – though she had not lost it but given it away without generosity – had exchanged the cotton for a safety pin from her medical bag and pinned it to her bodice. She unfastened it and clasped it in her hand.

It gave her such immense comfort that she was as calmed as if it had been the benevolent hand of God on her head, and she was thrilled to the very heart of her being. *This* was the God who had answered her prayers in the days when she used to pray! Despite her apostasy, the same God who had set forth the momentum of the world in all its many forms had purposed and guided *her*! *This* was the plan for which she had unwittingly prayed on the night her lover had deserted her. *This* was acceptance and forgiveness, though she had not asked for forgiveness and did not know that she was acceptable. He had called her name in the waking darkness of the night; as she had sat vigil by a child's bed in casualty, and on her reluctant journey to Kateri next day. Summoning her, though she had not expected any summons. Redeeming her, though she had not sought redemption. Using her exhaustion to give full rein to the compassion of John-Sunday, to work through Boseh's clear eye for opportunity, to evoke the kindness of Luke and others. Daniel, too. She must not forget Daniel, who had treated her as an equal. Was she not surrounded by love? In her heart, therefore, should there not be only joy? Comforted, she slept.

\* \* \*

"God, she looks cold!"

Stephen and Luke, both in clerical dress that occasioned some curious glances, waited among a small crowd of people by the barrier in the arrivals lounge. Luke was holding a placard that Verity had prepared with Hadissa's Christian name written on it in large felt-tip letters.

"She's smaller than I remember," replied Luke. "I do hope we're doing the right thing..."

"What, bringing her to England? A bit late to worry about that now!"

"It's worried me all along."

"Well, stop. We'll look after her... Only one suitcase?"

Introductions were made and they walked across the road to the car park. It was still early in the morning and Hadissa was shivering again. Stephen took off his jacket and draped it around her shoulders.

"Wrap yourself up in this. We'll put the heater on and you'll be as snug as a bug in a rug."

"I'm sorry?"

"Snug... you'll get warmer. Look, here's the car."

The two men sat in the front and Hadissa curled up on the back seat under Stephen's jacket. They set off, Stephen driving, and after they had negotiated the roundabouts and the worst of the traffic she began to relax and to gaze around. Everything seemed ordered and controlled. The traffic was heavy but the road was in better condition than anything she had seen in Kaduna, and all the cars seemed clean. There were no signs of any accidents, no vehicles burnt out on the hard shoulder, and no pedestrians walking beside the road putting themselves in danger. At first the high banks of the motorway obscured her vision of what was beyond, but soon she was able

174

to observe villages nestling in the valleys of gently rolling hills, and small houses clustered around tall church towers. Stately trees in the full mature leaf of late summer dotted the fields and bordered the side roads, which were not dirt tracks but tarmac. Cattle and sheep roamed freely on wide pastures enclosed by hedges, and in the fields the crops seemed to have already been harvested. Road signs proliferated, especially on the motorway, where exits were indicated several times before the slip road swung away and disappeared over the top of the motorway. As they went under the bridges Hadissa ducked. She could not imagine how they stayed up.

Luke turned his head to look at her. "All right so far?"

"Everything's so... tidy and clean!" she exclaimed. "And so many greens! And the fences around the fields and the trees and the hedges! And the cars, they all go between white lines, and they're all so shiny, even the lorries...!"

"Did you see much from the air?" Stephen asked, cocking his head to look at her in the mirror.

"Oh yes! Lots of houses like little boxes in patterns, and a lot of water, rivers and lakes and blue squares..."

"Blue squares? Oh, swimming pools! Yes, you'll see plenty of those round here, fewer as we go north. We don't have one, I'm afraid. Disappointed?"

"Well, I can't swim anyway...."

"There's lots of water around us, though." he continued, amused. She was as excited as a child. "We live in the Fen country. Wide ditches and boggy fields... marshes reclaimed from the sea."

"Is the sea near, Mr. Ashcroft?" she asked shyly, using his surname in deference to his age.

"Call me Stephen. Yes, not far. We'll take you there if the weather holds."

As the car hummed its way towards Ely, Hadissa drifted off to sleep. It was a three-hour journey, and after a while they stopped for refreshments in a motorway service station. To Hadissa it was luxurious, and there seemed to be unlimited food. She contented herself with French bread and jam and a cup of coffee, and watched with amazement as Luke worked his way through a full English breakfast. Stephen saw her expression, and grinned.

"He's a growing lad!"

175

"And we had an early start," added Luke, through a mouthful of food.

She laughed, hiding her mouth behind her hand. Stephen was much older than she had envisaged, older than any of the elders in her village, but unlike them he was warm and attentive. How could she be lonely anymore? Everything was going to be all right.

"Where are we now?" she asked as they walked back to the car.

"Outside Cambridge," replied Stephen. "You'll see it soon. Not today, because we'll bypass it. All in good time. Your college is near here."

"Hom-ah-ton?"

"Well done! Yes, Homerton. Here we are," he said, opening the passenger door. "Get in the front, you'll see better. I want you to have a good view of the cathedral when we get to Ely."

"Verity will take you over to the college before the start of term," said Luke, getting in the back of the car and leaning forward, "so you'll see it then. You know Stephen's wife is called Verity?"

"I remember. Will she...? Will I...?"

She stopped, confused. It was not that she would mind being a servant, for it was the least she could offer in return for their kindness, but she needed to know. So far nothing had been said about her status in Stephen's house, only that she would remain there until the start of term.

"Can you tell me, please, what my house duties will be?" she asked in a low voice.

"*House* duties?" Stephen glanced sideways at her in surprise, raising his eyebrows. He would have laughed had he not realised that she was perfectly serious. She must be feeling very insecure, he thought. How young she is.

"I mean, will Mrs Ashcroft wish me to clean the house and cook?"

"My dear girl, not at all! Not remotely! You're our honoured guest. We're pleased to have you, and just want you to be happy. Verity feels the same, I assure you, and you must call her Verity, my dear. She can't wait to take you shopping, show you the town and the countryside. She loves the cathedral and the Fens."

176

"She has someone to look after the house and the meals?"

"Well, no, she does it herself, and I'm supposed to help! I'm retired, but as busy as ever. She'll mother you a bit, I expect. Our own daughter, Joanna, has left home."

"I'm sorry she's left you," Hadissa remembered her own filial inadequacy and was embarrassed for him. "I'm sure she'll come back to you one day."

"Hadissa," interjected Luke carefully. "She hasn't actually *abandoned* her parents. In this country we... Children usually leave home about your age and move away. Some of them make a home for themselves and others go away to college, like Joanna and you are doing. It's okay, parents expect it, and they'd be upset if we didn't!"

"You don't live with your parents, look after them?"

"They wouldn't want me to, not as such."

"It's a different system, Hadissa," Stephen said lamely. He reflected that he could hardly tell Hadissa that he still supported his daughter financially and would do so for some years to come. "It doesn't mean they don't care. At any rate," he added brightly, "you'll soon meet Jo. She's a nurse, too."

"Oh!" Hadissa was delighted. "What branch of nursing is she doing?"

"Right now? Geriatrics. Old people, mostly in hospital, but some in the community. Old people's homes, warden accommodation, that sort of thing."

Stephen became aware of Luke, smothering his laughter, and he suddenly heard the echo of what he had said.

"You're quite right, Hadissa, it's a crazy system. Now, let's change the subject. Look out of the window, and tell me when you see our cathedral."

*   *   *

The child, which was how Verity first thought of Hadissa, had almost fallen asleep over the evening meal. Later, when Verity went up and peered through the bedroom door, she discovered her lying sound asleep under the duvet, fully dressed, her cloak wrapped around her head. Verity stood watching her for a moment, noting the high cheekbones and the full, evenly sculptured lips and the delicate flush on her ebony cheeks and

177

forehead. Over the large domes of her sleeping eyes her eyelashes were glutinous as if she had been weeping. Verity felt a rush of compassion for her, so very far away from her bush village in Africa.

The heat of the day was trapped under the eaves, and it was as if the whole room was cradling the girl in warmth, gentling her against the shock of separation. Outside it was quiet, for the dense foliage of the tall beeches in front of the house muffled all sound of passing traffic. Verity could hear a blackbird singing somewhere and the chattering of squirrels. She looked around. On the floor was Hadissa's suitcase, still strapped up. Quietly she closed the curtains to shut out the encroaching night, and switched on the lamp. The small sound woke Hadissa, who raised herself up in the bed, blinking, but when she saw who it was she got out of bed stiffly, draped her cloak around her shoulders, and began to fumble with the strap.

"I meant to unpack..."

"Here, let me help you." Verity put her hand on her shoulder. "Poor love, you're dead on your feet."

Hadissa looked disconcerted, and Verity reflected that she was going to have to be a little more careful what she said. She got down on her knees and opened the lid of the suitcase. Inside was a neatly folded uniform, some flimsy-looking underwear, two un-hemmed pieces of brightly-patterned cloth and a pair of worn leather shoes. Underneath was a pile of medical books.

"Hadissa, is this all you've got with you?"

"Oh, I only brought the ones I'm currently studying. I know I'll need more when the course starts. I thought, perhaps, I could borrow some."

Verity did not reply. To give herself time she shook out the uniform and hung it on the back of the door.

"And let's hang your cloak up, get the creases out of it. I'll give you an extra blanket instead. But there's an electric blanket on the bed as well. Look, here's the switch. When you want to go to bed, you just press it once, like this. It stays on all night."

"It won't hurt me?"

"No, no, it's quite safe. Just switch it off in the morning." She stood there for a moment, deliberating, then she said tentatively, "Hadissa, dear, would you mind awfully if I took you shopping in the morning? For clothes, I mean. Would you be offended?"

"I haven't brought many clothes, I know," said Hadissa hesitantly. "I brought what I have. I did think I would have to buy something. The bishop, he gave me some pounds, so I can spend some of them if you think I should…"

"But I'd be glad to…"

"No, really, you've already been so kind." Hadissa stood by the bed, her head down, an expression of such misery on her face that Verity's heart went out to her. She took her hand, and sat down with her on the bed.

"Hadissa, we don't need to spend very many pounds. And I would be delighted if you'd let me…"

Hadissa raised her head with quiet dignity. "Will they be very expensive?"

"Depends where we go. We could try the cha…" Verity hesitated. "Well, I don't know how to say this, but we have sort of… recycling shops. Charities run them. It's a very good system. People give them their old… any clothes that they've finished with. Some of them are quite new…!"

She stopped. Hadissa was looking completely incredulous.

Verity rushed on. "Or perhaps they've grown out of them and they're too good to throw away. Often they're in very good condition. In fact, most of what I wear comes from charity shops. That's what they're called, charity shops. I've used them for years. They only charge two or three pounds, and you could buy a new coat and some warmer skirts for the winter, and a couple of pairs of shoes…"

"And people have so much they can just give these things away?" Hadissa looked close to tears.

"I know it's… Well, yes."

Hadissa looked down at her lap. "It's true, I'd like some warmer clothes. And if I don't have to buy them new… England is so cold!"

"You poor dear, you must be frozen!" exclaimed Verity. "Look, I'll show you the bathroom, and you can have a nice hot bath. There's plenty of warm water. I'll run it the first time, and then you can do it yourself other nights. Just pull out the plug when you've finished. And here's the extra blanket. Why, child, what's the matter? Did I upset you?" Hadissa had put her face in

179

her hands.

"You're so... so kind," she said, her voice muffled. "And everything's so strange, and I'm..." She rubbed her eyes with the palm of her hand.

"Far from home. I know." Verity put her arm round the fragile shoulders. "And you're very, very tired. Don't worry, my dear, we'll look after you. This can be your second home."

She went downstairs to where Luke and Stephen were sitting laughing over their coffee.

"Poor kid, she's exhausted. I expect she'll sleep the clock round. She's cold, too. I found her wrapped up in her coat..."

"She will find it cold, after Africa," Luke said. "Especially the Fens."

"Yes, well, she's come with absolutely nothing to wear. I said I'd take her shopping in the morning. When she balked I told her about charity shops. She found the whole concept incredible – she was nearly in tears about it."

Luke looked anxious. "If there's one thing that really worries me about this whole project, it's that. The sheer difference in culture, and how she'll cope."

Stephen raised his hand. "I promise you, Luke, we'll do our very best with her. And don't forget, Jo's based in Cambridge. I'll have a quiet word with her, see if she can't take her under her wing for a bit."

Verity poured out a mug of coffee and sat down next to Stephen on the sofa. "Well, that relieves my mind a bit. Anyway, what were you two laughing about as I came down?"

"Luke was telling me about his hat," said Stephen, putting his hand on her knee.

"His hat?"

"Yes," said Luke. "On the way down to Abuja I lost my hat. Blew out of the car window. Well, it was only an old straw hat, but..."

"He had his old college tie round the brim," laughed Stephen. "A talisman..."

"So, the driver said he'd stop," continued Luke. "The car was full of clergy going to Abuja. And Dan and me, and our suitcases. The driver said, 'Hey, man you've lost your hat.' I said it wasn't important, but he must have seen something in my eyes. And I must admit I'd have been rather sorry to lose that old thing! Stupid, but there we are. The Diocesan Secretary told the driver to turn round and go back for it. So he did. He just did a three-point turn on the road."

"What sort of road?" asked Verity.

"Oh, the dual carriageway. The main road between Kaduna and Abuja. So this guy, the driver, he just does a three point turn across the road and heads back the way we'd come in the fast lane."

"In the fast lane? You mean there was traffic?"

"A great wall of the stuff heading towards us. So when the secretary says he can see the hat sitting in the road the driver begins to slow down, still in the fast lane and still facing in the wrong direction."

"My God, I bet you prayed!"

"Well, no, I didn't, actually," Luke confessed wryly. "I thought, I've got myself into this mess and I can hardly expect God to get me out of it. It was a damn silly thing to do."

"Anyway, you were quite safe or you wouldn't be here."

"Oh yes, the driver stopped right across the two lanes, got out, went round, picked up the hat, gave it to me through my window, bowed, went round to his door, got back in, turned the car on the hard shoulder, such as it was, and we drove on."

Verity raised her eyebrows. "So what about this wall of traffic?"

"Well, there was more hooting and shouting than usual, and swerving, but, anyway, it missed us."

"You must all have been terrified!"

"You can't tell with Nigerians, but I felt quite white with it." Luke leant across the table and helped himself to more coffee. "But it was a doddle compared to what happened later."

Stephen glanced at Verity and smiled. "What was that? You haven't told me this one."

"Well, outside Abuja there's a crossroads and everything was queuing because the cops had stopped the traffic. Obasanjo – that's the President, Verity – was coming through with his convoy, so they stopped everything else in all four directions. People knew there was something afoot and they all wanted to have a look, so do you know what they did? You won't believe this but it's true. By this time the road was three lanes, so they stacked up on all three lanes and the hard shoulder. When they'd done that, they drove across the central reservation and stacked

181

up the other three lanes, which by that time were empty because all the traffic going in that direction had, of course, been stopped." Luke took a breath. "And *naturally* the same thing was happening the other side of the crossroads. So after the President had passed there was a kind of free for all. Six lanes of traffic fighting for three lanes of road plus all the traffic doing the same thing at the intersection, plus the other lot coming from the other direction. Talk about a traffic jam!"

"Unbelievable," murmured Verity.

"You've never seen anything like it, Verity – utter chaos! Quite a lot of cars got hit. No one seemed to mind very much, though, but there was an awful lot of shouting. There was a guy with a herd of goats by the road and he was watching all this and laughing. I didn't blame him, though I must say I didn't feel like laughing at the time. Makes a good story, though, doesn't it?" he smiled. "I shall dine out on it for weeks."

"And the hat story…"

"Well, perhaps not the hat story…"

Verity began to clear away the cups. "That just about sums it up, doesn't it?" she said. "It's just a very different culture. And, somehow, we've just got to see that Hadissa survives it!"

# CHAPTER 2

The following day Verity took Hadissa to the station to meet Joanna. As the train approached, rocking slightly on the rails, Hadissa held back fearfully until it stopped, the engine ticking and pulsing. As the doors slammed and the tannoy blared, Verity looked at Hadissa curiously. The girl's eyes were once more gleaming with excitement, but she made no comment. This is also a new experience, thought Verity. She probably hasn't seen a train before, or heard a tannoy.

There was no mistaking Joanna. Of a similar height to Verity, they were both a head taller than Hadissa, both slim, with the same long straight hair and fringe, though Verity's was grey and tied back on the nape of her neck, while Joanna's was a chestnut brown and loose. The greeting she gave her mother was restrained, a mere peck on the cheek, but Hadissa could sense real affection between them. Joanna shook hands with Hadissa, and then hefted her bag over her shoulders.

"Have you had lunch? I'm starving."

\*   \*   \*

With Joanna's help, Hadissa soon began to know her way around the little town and occasionally Stephen and Verity drove her into the Fens or round the brown-stoned villages. The landscape of wide flat fields, stunted trees, and a plethora of dykes and hidden pools enthralled her. There seemed no distinct seasons; at times a heavy mist hung over the fields and she would see the silhouettes of trees emerging from pastel cloud, or cattle moving noiselessly in the sodden pasture. At other times the day would be radiant with light, the sky full of shifting clouds, creating dark shadows that flowed across the contours of the land. Always, when she turned, there would be the cathedral, either rising out of the mist, ethereal and unsubstantial, or else, in bright sunshine, dominating the vista with its weighty presence, every stone delineated, and around each pinnacle, an aura of flickering incandescent light.

On Sundays Verity and Hadissa attended Stephen's church and although Hadissa found the service itself familiar, she was disturbed by how few people were there, and how undemonstrative they were about their faith, as if they took no joy in it. When she asked Stephen about this, he seemed discountenanced and asked her to describe a typical Sunday service in Kaduna.

"Well," she said, thinking hard, "there's always lots of music and chanting, and what they call thanksgivings. People offer thanks, oh, for all sorts of things, for crops, for employment, for healing, for... for mission, things like that. Everyone puts a little money in a bucket and all the time the drums are beating and people are dancing and stamping and singing. It can go on for hours."

"I thought people didn't have much money," said Verity. "How can they afford to do it so many times?"

Hadissa gave a mischievous smile. "Oh well, the *naira* – that's our currency – breaks down into very small coins, and the people know there are going to be lots of thanksgivings so they only give the very small coins each time. But sometimes they give a chicken or a piece of woven cloth instead. Or even a goat..." Her expression was pensive, remembering. "But the church is always full. If people don't come to church for a week or two everyone would think they'd lost their faith, or maybe there'd been an accident or someone killed. If they'd just sort of stayed away, they'd end up feeling very ashamed."

"Sounds a good system to me," said Stephen ruefully. "I wish I could make people feel like that!"

"Oh, but mostly they want to come to church," said Hadissa earnestly. "They take faith very seriously. They believe God is everywhere, and they need to pray and ask him things. There's nothing else to do on a Sunday, anyway, and it's the time when everyone can exchange news. They eat at the church, too – for some it's the best meal of the week. Church services can last all day, especially in the bush, because people travel huge distances to get there. They set off early in the morning, whole villages walking in a long line carrying parcels of food, even the children, the elderly pushed on carts. They meet under a canopy and stay until sunset. In the city I expect they go home

184

earlier…"

She says "they" all the time, not "we", Stephen reflected
– she doesn't identify with them, but why? He looked at her
more closely, wondering what was happening in her life of faith.
He also wondered why, when it came to the daily tribal conflict
that so beset the peoples of that area, such a patently efficient
structure was so powerless to prevent bloodshed. He suspected
that the answer lay in the structures themselves. They might be
too paternalistic, too deficient in real teaching, to allow the
selflessness and compassion so obviously prevalent on Sundays
to influence the rest of the week – but then he rebuked himself.
That was just as true here.

*   *   *

One day they drove out to Sherringham so that Hadissa
could see the sea and walk on the sand dunes. The weather was
mild and she kicked off her shoes and paddled in the shallows,
uttering shrill, little cries of pleasure, then stood for a long time
gazing out over the vastness of the water to the misty horizon.

"Which way is Africa?"

"Not this way, I'm afraid," smiled Verity. "You'd need
to be on the south coast to be able to look in the right direction."

"But it's the same sea?"

"It has another name, but yes, it's the same water."

Hadissa pointed out to the horizon, the cloth of her
cotton blouse fluttering on her slim bare arm. "Then my
brother's over there?"

"Many hundreds of miles away, yes, I suppose he is.
You miss him very much, don't you?"

"…Yes. Yes, I do. He is crying for me, I think."

*   *   *

The cathedral drew her like a magnet. She would sit for
hours in any patch of sunlight, huddled in her charity shop coat,
watching the dust motes dance upwards towards the lofty ceiling
to disappear among the towering arches. Although it was
completely different from the cathedral in Kaduna she felt close
to John-Sunday there, and closer, also, to God. There, at last, she
began to pray, and afterwards she prayed each night by her bed.

185

Her prayers were a chaotic jumble of inarticulate thoughts and half-spoken words. She prayed about the year of study that she faced. For the first time she let herself think of her ex-lover, and prayed that they might be forgiven for the harm they had caused each other. She still felt soiled. It was a feeling that she recognised from her childhood but she felt unable to explore it in more depth. Despite John-Sunday's plea that she marry, she realised, bleakly, that any man who married her would soon discover that she was not a virgin and would be entitled to reject her. She had no idea how she would deal with that eventuality. John-Sunday's anger would be immense, intolerable, and she felt a frisson of fear at the prospect. Yet, in spite of that, she clung to her hope that what she was now doing was part of God's greater plan. If she let herself, she could be surrounded by grace, the slate wiped clean, and somehow be given a new beginning.

\*     \*     \*

*Dear Luke,*

*Calvary greetings from Kaduna! I am writing to tell you that the Muslim and Christian leaders have met with the governor of Kaduna State and the British High Commissioner in Abuja, and have come up with a wonderful proposal, thanks to the name. They have not only agreed to give the Muslims* a piece of land *to rebuild, but also to buy the land where the original mosque stood, on condition that we work together to help the* children *of both communities. They plan to build an advice centre for nutrition and other issues of childcare, and to encircle it with a Garden of Reconciliation. The Peugeot factory has offered to donate funds for a play area on the ground floor and, above, a small conference centre.*

Work has already started in clearing the land, and soon we shall be able to arrange for some of the children to visit the site so that they can help to design the garden. (You never know, the man who planted the bomb might return and see what is going on. Who he is might then emerge.)

*Also, some of our local manufacturing firms want to invest money in the* education of children, *both Christian and Muslim, through work experience. The governor has stipulated that we select firms that already serve the needs of the state, but*

*I think an important by-product will be how this improves conditions socially. It will allow children* from both communities *to work together in constructive ways, as well as being a good resource for industries.*

*So, you see we have not been idle. When you next come to Kaduna I will have great pleasure in showing you how matters have advanced. In the meantime, dear colleague, please give my greetings in Christ to your kind friends and to Hadissa. Please let me know if she has any needs that we can supply, for she is our great investment for the clinic at Kateri.*

*This is all* mission – *and with God's help, we will not* fail.

*Yours in the Peace of Jesus,*
*Cletus.*
*(Area Dean of Kaduna)*

\* \* \*

Daniel telephoned, and Hadissa took the call in the study. It was the first time she had been in and she was awed by its atmosphere of peace and tranquillity. This was where Stephen prayed, prepared his sermons, read his Bible and answered the telephone. The lingering scent of Verity's lavender polish was overlaid with a slight musty smell of antiquated books, and hanging on the door was his cassock, redolent of burning candles and damp stone. On the leather topped desk was a neat pile of papers held down by a glass paperweight, a small brass crucifix and a black figurine which Hadissa recognised as Nigerian. On the window sill was a framed photograph of Joanna and, catching the sun, a small glass vase filled with yellow flowers. Pushed neatly under the desk was a pedestal chair; the crazed surface of its leather gleaming dully in the sunlight, and next to the desk an easy chair, on which lay a flat blue cushion. This would be where his visitors sat, pouring out their troubles. The window was partially open, and a light breeze fluttered the papers on the desk.

"The phone, Hadissa!" Verity's voice, from the hall. "Pick up the phone! And close the door, will you, dear. The papers'll fly everywhere!"

Hadissa sprang to the door and shut it, then back to the

desk to pick up the receiver.

"Hallo, I am Hadissa," she said tentatively.

"Hadissa, *sannu!*" His voice seemed as close as if he were in the next room, and she jumped. "How are you? Have you settled in?"

"Thank you, I am very happy here." She was unused to the telephone, and spoke formally. "Are you well?"

"Hadissa, I'm ringing because your course starts soon and I... I'd very much like to see you before then. Would that be possible?"

Hadissa was silent. The sound of his voice evoked his presence, his sunburnt face and his red hair. It also reminded her of their conversations in the bishop's house and on his patio outside his guest room.

"Hadissa, are you there? What do you say?"

"...I'll ask permission..."

"You don't need *permission*..." he expostulated, his voice rising.

"Daniel, I'm a guest here," she relied simply. "I need to ask Verity." She carefully laid the receiver back in its cradle, and went down the passage to the kitchen.

"Verity, it's Dan... He'd like to visit with me..."

Verity turned from the sink. "Do you want him to?"

"Yes, I think so... Yes, it would be nice..."

"Well, let him come then. We'll get Luke, too, if he's free. What d'you think? You could have a reunion."

Hadissa's eyes lit up. "Oh yes, it would be very good to see Luke again!"

"Well, shall I speak to Dan, fix a date? Wait, I'll just grab the diary..."

When Verity went to the study she realised that Hadissa had hung up the phone. She was amused, wondering how Daniel had reacted. She retrieved the number and then dialled it afresh.

"Daniel? This is Verity. I think you got cut off..."

"She hung up on me!"

"She didn't mean to, dear, I don't think she realised... She says you'd like to meet up with her again. Where're you living now? I've forgotten."

"In Cambridge... I thought I'd pick her up from the station..."

"Oh, in Cambridge, quite near then, that's good."

188

Verity's mind was racing. Was Dan going to prove a complication? "Why not come here?" she suggested quickly. "I'm sure she'd like to show you where she's staying. We could invite Luke – have a reunion. What d'you think? Next Sunday lunch, if you can manage it?"

"Why, thank you," said Dan politely, "but..."

"Our daughter will be home, too. They've an awful lot in common, Daniel, it's really nice. She's a nurse, too, you see. It means Hadissa will already know someone when she gets to Cambridge. Isn't that lucky?"

"But I thought..."

"I can't wait to tell Stephen. He'll be so pleased."

\* \* \*

Dan stood for a moment by the telephone, running his hands through his hair in frustration, then he went through to his small kitchen for a coffee. The sound of Hadissa's voice, brief and inconclusive though their conversation had been, echoed in his head. What a pity he'd agreed to go to Ely! What he'd intended to do was to invite her out, but hanging up on him like that, she'd pulled the rug out from under his feet.

The kettle was boiling and he spooned coffee into a mug and took it into the next room, standing in the doorway and sipping the scalding brew. His flat was very rudimentary – the rent was exorbitant – but as he looked at the untidy room, trying to see it through her eyes, he made a resolution to clean up a bit before she came. At least it was better than a mud hut.

His flat was three flights up in a high Victorian tenement that stood on a wide sweep of the Chesterton road opposite the river, in walking distance of the city centre. The rooms he inhabited had previously been servant's quarters, now refurbished as flats. He seldom saw his landlord, nor the other occupants of the house, except for a woman in a downstairs flat who sometimes brought up his milk. She did not always render this service; more often he would find the bottle standing amid the dust and accumulated junk mail on the empty chest of drawers in the hallway.

The weeks that had elapsed since Hadissa's arrival in England had put him on tenterhooks, but although he had an aversion to ringing the house in Ely, the start of term was drawing near, and he felt that he could not concentrate on his work unless he had at least the prospect of seeing her. He stretched out on top of the bed in his shoes, his hands behind his head, and stared up at the ceiling. Okay then, he'd go to bloody Ely and meet the bloody folks! He must think positively, simply work out another plan to see her on his own. He must be affable and courteous, perhaps even slightly donnish. That would give the right impression. Stephen would never suspect his motives, but Verity, she was *another matter*, he thought, aping the African cadences. He scowled. Fancy taking over the phone like that, like a mother hen! Hadissa was perfectly capable of handling her own telephone call! Except, she did hang up on me, he reflected ruefully, smiling to himself, but then, she hasn't much experience of telephones.

Or anything else, he ruminated, imagining them both walking hand in hand through the shopping precinct or going to a concert or sitting in a teashop. He'd fetch her from Homerton or wherever she'd be living, spend the day in the city and then come back to the flat in the evening. Or she might prefer countryside. They could go out in his car, and then come back for the evening. Or they could hire a couple of bikes and go down the tow path, have a pub lunch, go for a walk in the meadows or by the river – she'd like that, he thought, she'll like the water – and then come back for the evening. How will she cope with all that? For the first time he began to wonder what it must be like for a bush village girl who had grown up in a mud hut in darkest Africa, having to adapt to life in a city like Cambridge. Would she have got herself some Western clothes? Surely Verity would have seen to that. Or the daughter.

It didn't matter what they did the first time, he thought, discounting Ely, which would only be a preliminary to whatever else they would do together. In any case, they'd be dependent on the weather. If it was wet, he thought, he could take her to Kettle's Yard and see the pottery. It was nearby, and then they could come back here afterwards. Or the Museum, the Africa Room, perhaps. Or the Black Mambazo concert that was being advertised. He was less sure of that. He didn't want to remind her too forcibly of Africa. He wanted her to forget all that, concentrate on Cambridge, on settling down, on having *him* in her life. Perhaps the Africa Room was not such a good idea either. He didn't know how it would make her feel.

That was the trouble, really, he didn't know how she felt about anything, least of all about him. He knew what *he* wanted. He wanted to make love to her. He wanted her to make love to him. If he made himself indispensable maybe she'd stay in England. Then he could decide their future. After a while, he could find a little house for her and the child. What child? The brown-white child she would have. His child.

# CHAPTER 3

Luke sat in the drawing room while Verity prepared lunch, hunched over the Sunday newspapers spread out at his feet. Occasionally he called out to ask if he could help and then sat back gratefully when the answer was always negative.

"I've got two other cooks in the house, if I want any help. You can tell me what the papers say, later, when I'm asleep after lunch."

Joanna and Hadissa were upstairs deciding what Hadissa should wear. Joanna suggested the newly-laundered emerald wrap-around skirt in which she had travelled, but Hadissa demurred, preferring Western dress. She did not know what to expect from this visit. She strongly suspected that she had been the inspiration for some of the ideas he had shared with the others in Kaduna, but other than that she had no idea what was on his mind. She knew that she was attracted to him, that she was flattered that he wanted to visit her, that she was excited and disturbed by the fact that he was coming, but beyond that she could not see.

Joanna watched her undress, noting the slim black burnished legs, the flat stomach, the high breasts and the long slender neck. She's a beauty, she thought; my, she's going to break some hearts! She looked at her watch.

"He'll be here, soon, Haddy. How're you feeling?"

Hadissa paused in her dressing and looked at this girl who, over the few weeks she had known her, had become more to her than just Verity and Stephen's daughter.

"Why should I be *feeling* anything?" she said artlessly. "He's Luke's friend, or your father's friend. I just know him from Kaduna. I expect they'll want to talk business."

"Oh, come on, there's more to it than that, or why call you up?" said Joanna shrewdly. "Why not just call Dad? And why're you bothering about your clothes?"

Hadissa sat down on the bed, holding the jumper in her hands. "But it's not what you think, really. Things happened in Kaduna, Jo. First Luke was ill, then the bomb – well, you've heard about that. Daniel and I, well, we helped rescue some of the children, but he was marvellous, Jo, really brave. It brought us close to each other. And afterwards we talked a lot..."

"The meaning of life?"

Hadissa refused to be teased. "Yes, if you like! Or death. About life in the bush, and about breaking down barriers. Faith issues, things like that. And he met my brother...."

"That's John, isn't it?"

"John-Sunday, yes. He met him when he came to the bishop's house. It's because of John-Sunday that I'm here now. Without him..."

"How did they get on, Daniel and your brother?"

She was astute, was Jo, and remembering the uneasy meeting by the gate, Hadissa evaded her eyes.

"I don't think they liked each other at first," she admitted. "But later, when Daniel was talking it all over with the bishop and Luke, he came to admire him very much. We all did." She pulled the jumper over her head and turned to the mirror. "You'll see," she added, running her comb through her wiry hair. "They'll talk business."

There was the sound of a car pulling up in front of the house, and the two girls went to the window and peered down into the drive. Dan was getting out of the car. He glanced up at the windows of the house and they drew back.

"Hmm," said Joanna, "tall... Quite good looking. Well, I'm glad it's only business," she added, taking Hadissa's arm and going with her to the door. There was a wicked glint in her eyes, and Hadissa laughed lightly.

"Only business."

\*　\*　\*

Was she different in some way? Dan wondered. She seemed more fragile than in Kaduna, as if the delicate bones of her neck, half obscured by the high collar of her jumper, were hardly sufficient to bear the weight of that sleek little head. Her hair had grown and though it seemed more lustrous, it was slightly red at the ends, or maybe that was only the effect of the light. Inexplicably, he felt critical of her clothes. The black skirt with its narrow waistband emphasised the smallness of her waist and was obviously more sophisticated, but he missed the other

193

elegance of the intricately patterned wrap-around skirt that she had habitually worn in Nigeria. The jumper, too, seemed fraudulent in a way; it cooled the russet tones of her skin too much, and made her seem darker than he remembered, more glossy. In fact he was surprised just how very black she was. This disconcerted him more than he liked. It was the first thing he had noticed when she entered the room, arm in arm with Joanna, how very black she looked in the blue jumper. The older girl held her protectively – against what or whom Dan could only guess.

In this he was not far off the mark. To Joanna, the two vertical marks of what seemed a permanent frown on Dan's forehead revealed a sullen temper. He couldn't take his eyes off Hadissa, yet, at the same time, seemed not best pleased with what he saw. Joanna took an immediate dislike to him.

"Sit here, Haddy," she murmured, indicating an armchair well away from where he was sitting.

*Haddy?*

Joanna took the seat next to him on the end of the sofa, placing herself between them, but regretted it immediately as he leant forward, obscuring her own view of the others. Luke was speaking.

"Remind me to show you the letter I've had from Cletus," he was saying to Dan. "Great things are happening at the mosque. I'm sure you'll be interested, given it was your idea to do some bridge-building."

Joanna looked at Hadissa and grinned. Business.

"Bridges, in Kaduna?" Hadissa said, quizzically. "Oh, you mean *bridges*."

Luke and Dan both laughed, exchanging glances, and Dan relaxed. The mere mention of those eventful days in Kaduna brought back in vivid detail the whole context of his meeting with Hadissa, and he smiled at her gently. Joanna watched him. He looks okay when he smiles, she thought grudgingly.

"Yes, your kind of bridge," Luke said, turning to Hadissa. "Inter-faith bridges, reconciliation."

"Big word," Joanna muttered. "What's it mean?"

"Which reminds me," Luke continued, "I meant to ask you if you'd like to come over to Coventry and see what we've been doing there. Do you know anything about the history of our cathedral?"

"The old one was bombed, wasn't it?" replied Dan. "I've never seen the new one."

"It's worth seeing," said Luke. "It has a unique vision, you see, which I think you'll find is very close to what your vision was for Kaduna. Since the war Coventry has become one of the word's foremost centres of reconciliation and inter-faith understanding. It's a place where both faith leaders and politicians can explore critical issues together without pressure, and they're aiming for the same positive outcomes that we're looking for in Kaduna." He turned to Stephen, his manner earnest and slightly ingratiating. "Religion has all too often been the cause of conflict around the world, hasn't it, Stephen? So it's crucial that it should be central to the healing process."

Joanna groaned. How incredibly pompous, she thought, but her father didn't seem to notice.

"Absolutely," he replied. "It's what I always say. Faith should be a blessing, not a curse. Anything else," he added gravely, "is an abuse of the name of God."

"Oh, for goodness' sake, you guys!" protested Joanna. "Leave it out, will you?"

Stephen grinned at her and then glanced at Hadissa who had been listening intently.

"Okay, but it's relevant in Nigeria, isn't it, Hadissa?"

Hadissa hesitated. "Religion *is* dangerous, Jo," she said softly. "Not faith, but religion. So if we can, we should do what you say, we should leave it out. The work needs to be done, though, and if it can answer people's needs on a practical level, then it keeps the doors open for real healing between all the faiths. Like in the clinic, and whatever Cletus told you about their plans for the mosque. They were all Daniel's idea."

"No, it wasn't!" Dan replied self-effacingly. "The whole reason why Luke was there in the first place was to help with this kind of thing."

Stephen made a gesture. "My dear chap," he said effusively, "don't underestimate yourself! We heard great things about your stay in Kaduna. I was most impressed, especially with what you did for the children."

"So, you'll come to Coventry, Dan?" Luke repeated. "I'd really like to show you the cathedral."

"Sounds great," Dan replied. "I'll bring Hadissa, too, if she'd like to go."

195

Hadissa nodded. Good! He could pick her up from college and then they'd have a nice long journey together, there and back. No one could quarrel with that.

They sat down for the meal and Stephen said Grace, spreading his hands wide.

"Lord, bless this food to our use and us to your service. Amen." He rose to his feet and began to carve the meat, and Dan smiled inwardly, comparing this cursory grace with the more fulsome ones he had heard in the bishop's house. He stole a conspiratorial glance at Luke, but he was already speaking to Hadissa and he restrained himself. Verity helped them all to vegetables, and they began to eat.

"I see you're wearing a Coventry cross," Luke was saying to Hadissa. She reached up and touched it with her fingers. "It's a Cross of Nails. Did you know?"

Hadissa, remembering how she had found it under the mattress in the clinic compound at Kateri, was baffled. How could her cross be from Coventry? And were they really nails?

"Did someone give it to you?" he asked innocently.

"No, I found it when I was staying at the clinic in Kateri. The chain was broken, so I bought a new one in a charity shop."

"Ah, so that's where it was..."

"Have *you* been to Kateri?" She was incredulous.

"Yes. I slept in that same compound..."

"...in a little room off to one side..."

"So that's where it was – the 'Bed and Bucket Hotel,'" he said, with rare humour. "I wondered where I'd lost it!"

Sadly, she started to take it off, but he stopped her.

"Oh no," he said, gently. "It's yours, now. You must keep it."

"Oh, but I couldn't!"

"Yes, you can." He pointed to the lapel of his jacket on which a little cross was fixed, identical to hers except that it was smaller and not set in glass. "See, I've replaced it. It would give me great pleasure to know that you wear it. It's a woman's cross, anyway."

"I didn't realise they were nails," she said. "It seems... hard. Are they supposed to be the nails that fastened Christ to the cross?"

"Sort of, but it's actually more complicated than that, and you have to go back a bit. You see, as Dan said, in Coventry there're actually two cathedrals. The first was pretty well destroyed in the Second World War – only ruins left now. Afterwards, a choice had to be made, either to forgive and look forward, or give in to hatred, and retaliate. Same as your own situation. Well, the story goes that, the morning after the bombing, a workman found some of the old nails from the roof beams lying in the smoking ashes, and he fashioned them into a cross, and gave it to the Provost. That's a sort of Dean of Cathedral, and *he* persuaded the local community not to think in terms of revenge, but about reconciliation. During the years that followed he travelled all over the world telling people about it and preaching, and that's why you find crosses of nails overseas. That's really the origin of this particular cross, so you must keep it, you see, and when people ask you about it, you can tell them where it came from. And you'll come to Coventry?"

"Gladly," she said, "if Daniel can bring me."

Dan heard his name and raised his eyes to her. She smiled at him briefly then lowered her eyes and carried on with her meal. Verity saw the look and tried to distract him, asking him when his term began.

"Are you looking forward to it?" she asked. "You're Head of Year, now, aren't you?"

Joanna looked up, surprised, and everyone waited for him to answer. When he did, through a mouthful of food, it was to launch into a monologue. He thought, This will demonstrate my involvement with the serious things of life! He described the school and its problems with bullying, and the necessity to exclude some of the more difficult children; he described the catchment area and its racial mix, and he even described the reorganization of the timetable. He talked for a long time; even when Verity cleared away the main dishes and served the dessert, he was still in full flow, sitting with his elbows on the table and frowning slightly each time she broke in to ask how much people wanted. He couldn't converse and became impatient when anyone else tried to speak. He dominated the conversation and gradually an atmosphere of unease began to develop, which did not dissipate until Stephen announced that he, for one, was not going to sit over the dinner table while the sun shone over the garden. Daniel and Luke went with him, leaving the women to clear the table and wash up.

"They're all as sexist as each other, aren't they?"

grumbled Joanna, drying the carving dish and looking out of the kitchen window. The men seemed deep in conversation, but at that moment Dan glanced up, and she waved the tea towel at him defiantly.

"Oh, I expect they've got lots to talk about," said Verity comfortably. She was stacking plates and glasses in the dishwasher, while Hadissa was washing up the saucepans.

"If Dan gives them the chance," Joanna muttered, still vigorously drying the carving dish. "Talks a lot, doesn't he?"

"He's a teacher... Do leave the pattern on it, dear."

"Doesn't listen though..."

"Jo," said Hadissa, giving a sideways look at Verity, "what is 'sexist'?"

"It's where the women do the domestic work while the men..." Joanna had put down the carving dish and was picking up a dripping saucepan. "Hey, Hadds, this is gravy."

"Oh, sorry, give it back. It's the same in Africa, Jo..."

"They don't even *offer* to help," continued Joanna. "They eat the meal and then just bog off."

"What's 'bog off'?" asked Hadissa, innocently, suppressing a giggle.

"Oh, Haddy! It means getting out while the going is good. If there's two things you need to know about men, it's 'sexist' and 'bogging off'! It's what they do best!"

"Jo, that's not quite fair," protested Verity, smiling. "Luke offered to help several times before the meal..."

"Bet he didn't actually help, though, did he?" said Joanna, undaunted by this remark. "And I bet Dan bogs off regularly. I bet his flat is full of dirty washing and cobwebs and piled up dirty plates... I bet he's the kind of guy," she said, vigorously attacking the surfaces, "who puts his feet up until the job's done, then looks up and asks if he can help."

They were still laughing, when Dan appeared at the kitchen door.

"Still at it?" he asked. "You should be outside in the sun. Is there much more to do? I can't help, can I?"

Joanna snorted, and Hadissa gave him a smile in which, he felt, there was a hint of condescension. He looked from one to another and then around the spotless kitchen.

"Oh, you've finished," he said lamely.

*  *  *

On their last evening Hadissa and Joanna went to the cinema and saw *Schindler's List*, and that night Verity woke to the sound of her shrieks. She and Joanna sat on the bed with their arms around the shaking girl, and, for the first time, heard about the death of her brother. Hadissa had never heard of Second World War, and was aghast to think that Christian countries could fight each other. Neither had she heard of the Jewish Holocaust and had imagined that the film was fictional. She found it shaming to discover that six million Jews of her grandfather's generation had perished in gas chambers without her ever hearing about it. She became increasingly confused. On the one hand she felt her own country was only now emerging from primitive darkness, but on the other hand, war on such a scale was even more appalling than the sufferings of her own people. She felt a new resolve forming within her, and a renewed desire to work to the bush. She was eager to start her course, for a letter had arrived from Kaduna informing her that she had qualified. It seemed to Hadissa that God's plan for her was working out very well, and for the last time she walked up to the Cathedral to give thanks. Shortly afterwards, Verity helped her to pack her bags and, with a heavy heart, put her on the train for Cambridge. It did not help to know that Daniel would be meeting her off the train.

# CHAPTER 4

If Dan had not visited her each day after school Hadissa would have found it easier to settle in her new life but, as it was, the time she could have spent sociably with her fellow-students after lectures were, instead, occupied with him. She found his attentions flattering and even took a mild satisfaction in having what was generally perceived as a boyfriend. She did not think of him as such but, in some intangible way, he was a bridge between her old life in Kaduna, and her new, culturally challenging life in England. He, alone, was aware of her roots, and because of their shared experiences she felt comfortable with him. When she had questions about her work or had difficulty with the language of the textbooks he helped her interpret what she was reading. He guided her in her essays and helped her to plan and present her work. She began to get very good marks, but although this increased her self-confidence it also increased her dependency. However, the umbilical cord of her mother Africa had been cut, and she felt adrift in a world that, although it was there to serve her needs and ultimately the needs of her country, it could in no way satisfy her deeper appetite for stability. She was merely a sojourner, and in a matter of months would be on her way home. Yet 'home' inevitably meant her work at Kateri, and although her innermost being craved something deeper, she could not conceive of being, anywhere, more than an outsider and a transient.

Dan frequently collected her from Halls, courteously opening the car door for her with a light touch to the small of her back. Sometimes he took her out for a meal, although usually he bought something to eat on his way over, to consume in her rooms. By half term he still had not taken her to his flat. As the reality of her had sharpened he had become more content to let matters take their course. When he arrived he would give her a brief hug, and after a while she reciprocated, putting her slim arms around his neck. If he felt disturbed by this physical contact he did not show it, but it encouraged him to find even more ways of making himself indispensable to her. Increasingly he rendered her little services, such as collecting text books that she had ordered from the booksellers or finding a second-hand bike for her use on the campus. It was a strange, passionless wooing, calculated not to frighten her. He kept himself firmly in hand, casting the bread of altruism upon the waters and trusting that his sheer proximity, and her reliance on him, would eventually repay it to him a hundred-fold.

That situation was bound to change, and it did so the day he found her in tears. She had received a letter from Verity with an enclosure from John-Sunday. She had opened it eagerly, in full confidence that she would read words of love and affirmation. She was shattered by what it contained. There was no affectionate greeting at all; instead a tirade of blame and censure. He accused her of being too wrapped up in her new lifestyle to consider those she had left behind, of being ungrateful for his efforts, of forgetting that it was he, in the first place, who had suggested that she came to England. The letter was written on a sheet of paper torn from one of his school exercise books, on the back of which were the inky stains of his younger fingerprints. It was the sight of these fingerprints, rather than his stern reproaches, that had reduced her to tears. She could almost smell the earth of her home. She wanted to run away, to disappear. She wanted to go back to Africa. The weather did not help her mood; the dark days of autumn had arrived, and the rain was incessant; a cold, chill rain, which bore no resemblance to the splendid, if infrequent, tumultuous rains of her own country. She felt cut off from John-Sunday and all that he represented.

When Dan knocked at the door of her room she threw herself into his arms, weeping bitterly. He dropped his wet coat on the floor and gripped her, deeply thankful for the contact for which he had for so long yearned. He bent his cheek to touch hers and ran his hands down her back, trying to disguise his mounting passion. Gradually she became aware of him and drew back, but this time he did not intend to let her go.

"What's the matter?" he asked, keeping a grip on her hands. "Here, come and sit with me in the window. Now, what is it?"

"I've had a letter from my brother... He's angry with

me..."

She spoke in such a woeful, childlike voice that he almost laughed. "What on earth for?"

She did not reply immediately, but got up and stood with her back to him, gazing out across the bleak landscape. These days she hated to go outside at all, and frequently missed lectures, lying huddled in bed instead. The heat of the hospital wards were in stark contrast to the frigid street, where the wind funnelled up the road towards her bus stop, and she would return drenched, riven with cold. The central heating had not yet been turned on in the college, and her room was often chilly. Every day she found herself longing more and more for heat and light of Africa. Predicting this, Dan had bought an electric fire for her and it was now fully turned on, laden with her morning's washing, steaming up the windows and forming puddles of condensation on the windowsill.

Dan stood up and ran his hand over the windowpane, and then wiped it on his trousers. Outside the sky was restless with clouds and the stately trees in the college grounds were swaying in the wind, their leaves fluttering in profusion to settle in russet pools on the wet, overgrown grass and on the paths that bordered the lawns. Beyond, the mist transformed the distant buildings into dreary, dismal and graceless silhouettes. Somewhere a window was banging, a rhythmic, desolate sound, echoing down the corridors.

Hadissa turned and gazed at him with an expression of utter misery.

"Oh, come here!" he said at last, and pulled her on to his lap. "Now, what's the matter? It can't just be John-Sunday's letter."

"It is! Well, it's everything. Oh, you don't understand!" If Dan had been a Christian, she might have been able to say more; to express, for instance, the serious doubts she felt in relation to her faith. He knew nothing about her, she thought bitterly; he rarely asked about her childhood, or about her village, but then, she had told him very little. She could not tell him how she sometimes dreamed about her Igbo lover, or how humiliated she had been by his rejection. She felt that Dan's lack of a Christian faith, which made him unable to discern how vulnerable she was, precluded it. Perhaps, she thought despairingly, there is no one on this earth who has the understanding and patience to listen to me. I've damaged myself, she mourned, and only someone as damaged as I am would understand, and even then, she realised, his own needs might still get in the way.

She had been sitting awkwardly on his knee, rocking slightly with the distress of her thoughts, and he pulled her closer. She resisted him and disengaged herself, standing up.

"I can't sit here like this."

"Then sit opposite me, but sit close."

There was a little table by the window and she sat down on one side of it, on an upright chair. She sat with a very straight back, her hands clasped on the table, and he reached out and took them.

"I'm sorry he's made you unhappy..." he began. He looked down at her slim hands disappearing into his, unconsciously stroking her narrow wrists with his thumb. She withdrew her hands gently, and composed them on her lap. Her eyes glistened with unshed tears.

"He didn't mean to," she said loyally. "And it's not just his letter. I get lonely sometimes, that's all. It's all right most of the time, but sometimes I feel... I don't know, as though my roots have been torn up. This isn't my country, Daniel. I admit it doesn't feel good to get a letter like this, but I think he's the one who's most unhappy. He's missing me, I expect. I sent a parcel – a shirt, and a blouse for my mother, and I don't think he can have received it."

"When did you post it?"

"Over three weeks ago."

Dan frowned. "I'd have thought he'd have had it by now. Where did you send it?"

"I addressed it to the bishop," she replied, "thinking he'd send it on. There's no international post to Kateri. But things still get lost. It could be anywhere."

"'Lost'. You mean stolen."

"Yes, I suppose so." She sighed heavily. "I'll just have to hope he gets it soon."

"You could send him a chaser," Daniel suggested. "Just a postcard, maybe. Then you'll at least have a clear conscience."

She brightened. "Oh, why didn't I think of that?" she said eagerly, sounding more optimistic. "They've got some in the stationery office downstairs! I could find a view of the river.

He'll be amazed to see so much water in the middle of a town!" She laid her hand over his. "Daniel, you're so good to think of that!"

He hesitated. "I think of *you…*" he said awkwardly. He remembered, then how in Kaduna she had seemed like a bird, quivering in his clutches. If he pressed her too hard she might escape him for ever. "I do try to think of you," he said gently. "What you need, what you'd like."

"I know you do," she responded. "I feel it, here.…" She touched her breast. The movement galvanised him, and he seized her hands in a stronger grip and half rose from the table.

"Do you? Do you really feel it?"

"No, Daniel, sit back in your chair. You shouldn't…"

"What? Love you?" He reached across the table, wanting to encompass the whole of her body in his arms. He grasped her by the shoulders, feeling the tense muscles of her shoulders. He closed his eyes. "Oh, God, Hadissa, if only you…"

"*Don't*, Daniel!" She squirmed away from him. "Don't hold me like that!"

"Why, don't you like it?" He tightened his grip. "Don't you like it?" he repeated softly, meeting her eyes. He stroked her arms, feeling the beat of her pulse in her wrists.

She looked down, confused, her cheeks flaming to a ruddy glow.

"Why shouldn't we love each other?" he whispered.

"*Love*?" she repeated quickly, her eyes flashing. "You don't know me, Daniel! You don't know anything about me, or what's… happened to me! You don't know my… my past! I've had… I'm not…"

"What? You've had, what?"

She subsided. Even now she could not tell him about her broken love affair, and took refuge in the obvious. "I am… another country…"

"Yes!" he said fervently. "You certainly are! That's what you are to me, another country! And you're all the country I want!"

"Oh, I'm not just talking about Nigeria, Daniel. I meant…"

"What, then?"

"We're different, Daniel. For one thing, I'm… I'm black…"

Dan released her and threw back his head and laughed. He got up from his chair and came round to her side.

"Yes, you're black. So what? You think I don't like it? Well, you're wrong! You're my black, black..."

She was taken off guard, and she did not resist when he took her into his arms. He picked her up, still chanting, "You're my black, black, black..." He carried her to the bed and lay down with her, gripping her tightly and cradling her head against his chest.

"My black, black *beauty*!"

"Daniel, we mustn't..."

"Hush, my beauty, hush. Lie still..."

He began to caress her. He smoothed down her coarse hair and trailed his fingertips across her high cheekbones and her lips, then he cupped her head in one hand, letting his fingers explore the delicate bones of her neck. With the other hand, he began to stroke her hips, pressing her hard against him. He carefully parted her blouse, and ducked his head to kiss her small breasts. He felt the nipples harden under his mouth, and he raised his head and looked into her face. Her eyes were half closed, as if in a reverie, and between her lips he could glimpse her pink moist tongue. The sight was irresistible, and he began to kiss her lips, at first gently, almost chastely, then, as she wound her arms around his neck, with increasing passion. He reached up under her blouse and found her breast again, kneading the firm flesh, and squeezing the protuberant nipple. As he took it into his mouth, sucking and licking it, Hadissa came alive, and gasped with pleasure. The sound inflamed his senses and he could bear it no longer. He wrenched at the zip on her waistband.

"Please. Oh, please, Hadissa."

She stiffened suddenly and he raised his head.

"Are you all right?"

"Yes," she breathed. "Oh *yes*... But what if...?"

It was enough. He heaved himself up, fumbling with his trousers, and shoved them down over his knees until he was free of them. He tugged down her skirt, took the fabric of her panties in his fist and scraped them down over her bottom. Whatever Hadissa was going to ask seemed forgotten, for she kicked her legs free, helping him, her hands clutching at his thighs, and at last he entered her. He felt the slippery slide of his erection meet the wet, infinitely welcoming, warmth of her body, and he heard

205

her cry out – with anguish or delight, he did not wait to discover – and his own muffled groans. He wound his arms round her, smothering her cries with his mouth, aware of the deep beating of her heart against his, and they began to move rhythmically on the soft mattress, his mouth open, panting against her ear. The air around him seemed to vibrate, and the heat rose in his head. He felt the sweat break out on his body and, as he climaxed, her body arched under him and he felt the repeated pulse of her coming.

Spent, she lay quietly in his arms, and for a long time he lay with his head buried in the pillow, his heart thumping, then he dropped into a shallow sleep.

"Daniel, what if…?"

He did not stir.

"Daniel… you're so heavy," she whispered. "Let me breathe a little.…"

He roused himself and lifted his head, groaning, shifting the weight of his body until they were lying side by side.

"Daniel…"

"Wait. Wait a minute. Not just yet."

His arms were round her, imprisoning her, unwilling to let her go. He'd hold her a while longer, he thought. There'd be time for talk later – later, when their bodies had separated, in the cold, cruel light of day.

# CHAPTER 5

In the immediacy of Dan's lovemaking Hadissa's conscience slept, and she was now too emotionally involved with him to discuss whatever qualms she might once have felt. According to her tradition, sexual intercourse outside the confines of marriage was forbidden, so she no longer asked herself if their relationship was part of God's plan for her. Deep in her heart she knew what the answer would be, but over that she drew a convenient veil.

The day they drove to Coventry marked the first time that Hadissa had been out of Cambridge since the start of her course, and she was glad to be once again motoring through the countryside. They sat very close to each other, his hand clasped over hers, lifting it in his to change gear or to point something out, their fingers tightly entwined. They felt free and happy.

Once in the city, they found a parking place and set off across the road in the direction of the cathedral, Hadissa curiously observing the crowded streets. Here were more black and Asian faces than in Cambridge, where the foreign students tended to be of oriental extraction. She saw bearded Asians, clad in white *burnous*, the women in elegant saris or totally muffled in the *jilbab*. At first she was shocked to see how they moved through the streets with such easy familiarity, and then she was merely envious of their freedom. Under a wide canopy covering a tall statue of a horse and rider was a group of young people of mixed race, smoking and drinking. She looked more closely at the statue and grasped Dan's arm.

"Look, Daniel, it's a woman, and she's... *naked*!"

He laughed, tucking her hand into his pocket.

"Old story. That's Godiva, so-called saviour of the city. A long time ago."

A cobbled street led down towards the cathedral precincts, where a long line of taxis were parked, the mostly Asian drivers chatting to one another or absorbed in newspapers spread over their steering wheels. Hadissa dropped Dan's hand self-consciously, but far from giving rise to curiosity, they were ignored, as if a black girl and a white man walking together hand in hand was unremarkable – unlike in Kaduna, she reflected, where it would have caused outrage, if not a riot.

She was stunned by her first glimpse of the cathedral ruins. Ahead, the immense tower of the old St Michael's rose up above them into the sky, and below it lay a little garden surrounded by cobbled paths, lined with railings and filled with trees. It was a very bright morning, and the sun-drenched stone glowed with intense light. Through the main arch they could see the interior of the old church, open to the sky, and at right angles to it, the new cathedral. Hadissa noticed a group of Japanese tourists taking photographs, and it gave her an idea. She broke free of his arm.

"Daniel, take a photo of me and I'll send it to John-Sunday."

Dan unfastened his camera and squinted at her through the viewfinder, but at that moment one of the Japanese touched him on the shoulder, indicating that he had a Polaroid and would photograph them both.

Dan positioned himself next to her, under the arch.

"Look a bit happy, then," he said, nudging her, "otherwise he'll worry even more!"

Hadissa gave a shy grin, and at the last moment held out her arms towards the camera.

"He'll think I'm wanting to hug him."

The Japanese looked nonplussed, then handed them the print and quickly walked away.

Dan grinned. "I think that tourist thought so! Now come on," he added, glancing at his watch, "we've got a bit of time before we meet Luke. Want to look around?"

They passed under the tower and into the ruined nave. At their feet ancient paving stones glistened in the bright sun, and the arches cast strong violet shadows across the ground. At the far end, within the apse, hung a huge charred cross.

"The body's gone," Hadissa murmured. "The fire would have charred it…" She began to shiver with distress, holding her coat tightly around her. Recollecting her background, Dan was concerned for her.

"Oh, I don't suppose this one ever *had* a figure on it," he remarked dismissively. "Luke said it was made out of beams after the bombing. The original one will have fallen to pieces ages ago."

To one side of them a flight of steps fell steeply away to the lower level, and under a high canopy they could see the sheer glass wall that housed the entrance of the new cathedral. Within the building, far back but at eye level, Hadissa could just discern the monochrome image of a huge face, the eyes wide and penetrating. They seemed to look directly at her and the mouth seemed about to speak. She knew instinctively who it portrayed.

"Look, Daniel," she said, taking his arm again. "He's staring right at us!"

"Who is? Luke? Where?"

Hadissa laughed shrilly, and he looked at her closely. Her eyes were lit up with an intense excitement and her lips were parted. "Not Luke, Daniel. Jesus. There, behind the glass. Come on, I want to get closer." She began to run down the steps.

Dan peered at the window. At first, all he could see were figures, incised into the glass; then, between them, far down the nave, he saw an immense green tapestry depicting the risen Christ, its oval face dominated by wide compelling eyes. It crossed his mind, then, how differently he and Hadissa perceived the world. She always seemed to see through things, or beyond, or more profoundly, as if to a distant horizon – like in Kaduna, the way she'd told that story about the wall to help him understand her brother – while his vision was more parochial. But it's not a personality thing, he thought, silencing his uneasy conscience, merely an accident of birth. Both her upbringing and the nature of her countryside necessitated a distant view.

He caught up with her at the door. In front of them the nave streamed away into the distance towards the high altar, untrammelled by the usual thick columns and arches, and behind it hung the tapestry. Even at that distance it seemed overtly triumphalist, almost pagan, and he turned away in distaste. Hadissa, on the other hand, was staring at it in wonder.

Dan touched her arm. "Time to find Luke. Look, there he is, hard at prayer."

"I can't take my eyes off that tapestry!"

"Come *on*," he said, his tone so brittle that she was taken aback. Luke must have heard their voices for he glanced up. He bent, and replaced the hassock on which he had been kneeling, then he got up and came towards them with a smile of welcome.

"We shouldn't have disturbed him..." Hadissa murmured.

Dan scowled. "Oh, it's only for effect. Luke, you old hypocrite, you knew we were here!"

"I only just saw you!" Luke said defensively. "I'm taking a brief service in the Chapel of Unity at midday, and I was getting ready for it. Want to come? Well," he said when they didn't reply, "in that case you look around, and I'll see you afterwards. I'll meet you back here and we'll get a bite to eat, okay?"

He walked away, leaving Hadissa feeling rather embarrassed. Dan took her arm.

"Oh dear, I think we've upset him! Well, we'd better do as we're told, hadn't we? Where d'you want to start?" He indicated a large rough hewn boulder that was situated below a huge stained glass window. "What about here? Looks as good a place as any...."

Hadissa stood back, tilting her head to look at the lofty window, which reared up above her head, her dusky skin lit to a roseate glow from the light that streamed through its coloured panes, and an expression on her face of childlike wonder. A moment later, she drifted away as if lost in thought. Dan stood still, watching her as she wandered down the south aisle, her eyes occasionally travelling to the tapestry as if drawn there by a magnet. He stifled his impatience and followed, making little effort to engage with what he was seeing. He knew the whole ethos of the cathedral was to do with reconciliation, but he blotted it from his mind, his inherent obstinacy repudiating any consideration of his own spiritual state. What was it about his personality, he wondered, that made him so averse to religion? Why did it irritate him so much, this universal yet vulgar obsession with God?

Neither was it as quiet as he had first thought. The whole place was echoing with the murmurs of visitors, and somewhere a door banged, reverberating in the silence. As if on cue came the metallic sound of the tower clock striking the quarter hour and the noise of a car accelerating along the road outside. He looked around angrily. A church should be quiet, people able to pray in peace, if that's their bent. It was too cluttered; that was the trouble. Around him were statues in wood and stone, stained glass, calligraphy, wall hangings, metal sculptures, but to him it was more like an art gallery, and even on those terms, he found it hard to relate to it. The place was surreal. It was bizarre.

Hadissa was unaware of what was going through his mind. From the moment she had spotted the naked charred cross and the penetrating gaze of the distant tapestry, all her senses seemed heightened, her inner eye more acute. She realised, with some reluctance, that this was the sort of place that might compel her to examine the fundamental questions of her life, not necessarily with words, but in silence. This was risky, but it was something that she recognised instinctively, just as she knew where water could be found in the bush, and it filled her with awe. She was insensible to the fact that her single-minded absorption in the place irritated Dan; she was merely aware that he was there, roaming quietly behind her.

Exasperated, and inwardly cursing, Dan followed her once more until suddenly he found himself at the foot of the tapestry, its great expanse stretching far above him, and he stopped and craned his neck to look up at it.

What a monstrosity! The image embodied all that he most loathed about the idea of God, as inaccessible and as pitiless as a pagan image. The naked man, imprisoned between the gigantic feet like a human sacrifice, seemed to him the personification of blind, unreasoning acceptance. He could not take it seriously; it alienated him, and he almost laughed aloud. Yet, as he focussed on the eyes, he saw there was something about them that demanded his attention. Their expression seemed almost accusing, as if, somehow, they *knew* his innermost thoughts, and were challenging him to face up to them, as though his love for Hadissa was nothing more than a wild striving after sensation. It was like a rebuke, and immediately he knew it was true. Yet, he asked himself, wasn't he just interiorising the effect of the tapestry? Or did this recognition come from some supernatural outside force? Was it *God*? He refused to contemplate the possibility; he couldn't *realise* it, or let it come near him.

What he did realise, painfully and very grudgingly, was that he had never taken into account Hadissa's deep sense of purpose, her determination, her sheer *otherness*. He thought back to how their relationship had evolved out of chaos and tragedy, and defiantly he repeated to himself the mantra of his dream: a life together, a house for them both, and a child. Surely what he wanted was innocent enough; it had integrity. Yet, under the gaze of the tapestry, its compelling, quiet authority, he suddenly realised how shallow, pointless and unrealistic this was. It was like a punch in the stomach. He would never get what he wanted! Apart from anything else, their roots and culture were so different – how could she settle in England? It was a pipe dream. Futile even to have imagined it. Yet what was the alternative?

At that moment the thought was born in his mind that he might go back with her to Africa. He had enjoyed his time in the Cathedral School. He had felt drawn towards the children, and the work had involved his whole being in a way that nothing else had, before or since. It had been a good experience, good for his teaching and good for his soul. It was not Dan's habit to reflect on his soul, but he realised now that if he went to Nigeria his life would not only be less self-centred and less materialistic, it would have purpose and direction. But what about the language? he thought uneasily, and not just the Hausa, but their language of faith – he could hardly declare his atheism outright, when all around him people were praying fervently for every issue under the sun. And he was still loath to relinquish the idea that she might settle in England.

And what had God ever done for him, that he should throw his hat in the ring? What, for that matter, had he done for Hadissa? Indirectly their faith had shattered the whole family! Or the man who had planted the bomb, who now faced a life of loneliness and starvation? All because of his religion. As for the children who were killed or maimed on the bus, where was God then?

These were the questions that Dan always asked when he considered issues of faith. They were precisely the questions that he and Stephen had tussled with, and he had not been convinced then, either. Something prevented him. Was it the whole *idea* of God, a God who ought to have intervened, but chose not to? Surely, to anyone of any intelligence, belief in such a God was untenable.

\* \* \*

The light changed abruptly as the sun went in, making everything monochrome, and Dan breathed a sigh of relief. The colours of the tapestry faded in front of his eyes, and the figure of Christ became suddenly less immediate, its scrutiny less direct. So, he thought ironically, the battle for my soul has been lost, has it? God's given up on me, turned his mind to other things. Indeed, the eyes seemed no longer to pursue him, but seemed to be looking away down the church, as if in search of others more amenable to his message. Dan turned away, but as he did so, the sun came out again and shone through the stained glass. It sent bright rays of lustrous colour across the tapestry and on to the receptive concrete, creating a vivid, intricate pattern of rust-coloured green, royal red and celestial blue, obscuring the matted texture of the walls, as a receding tide obliterates ripples in the sand.

* * *

"When I was very young I thought that God was like the sky. In Kateri you're constantly looking at the sky because the land around is so flat. To me, as a child, it seemed like a hand over the earth, warm and kindly. Then, when I got a bit older, I thought God was more like the road. If you weren't very careful, terrible things happened and you got punished. I almost stopped thinking about him entirely. I certainly found it hard to pray! Then, when I first left home, all I could think of was Stanley – you know, the one who was killed, and God just seemed far away. I stopped praying altogether. Then I found that I... I minded... About not praying, I mean."

"Is it tomorrow?" he asked gently.

She looked at him, bemused.

"In Kaduna, when I asked you to tell me about this, I said, 'Tell me tomorrow'. Remember? You said you didn't know me well enough. So, is it tomorrow?"

"Yes, I think so," she said gravely. "I think I can tell you now. I've started to think he's like John-Sunday, you see – God, I mean – only bigger and better. John-Sunday... he was always there for me. He took care of me always and he cared about who I was and what I did." She hung her head, her hands deep in the pockets of her coat. "I do think God is stern, like John-Sunday, but also I think he knows me very well..." She lifted her face, her eyes candid, but troubled. "I think he knows the mistakes I've made in my life. I don't think he wants to... to punish me,

213

or anything. I think he wants to hold me in his hand... but I'm not sure. Maybe he wants me to... to change. But maybe I'll only find the answer when I go home – I'm not sure he recognises me here," she added wistfully.

Dan indicated the tapestry. "But you find this figure compassionate, welcoming?" he asked curiously. She gazed upwards, contemplating the expression of the face and the raised hands of the seated figure.

"Not exactly. I feel unable to approach, as if I'm unworthy in some way. I feel the hands and the eyes... they're calling me, but I'm not ready. I'm still holding back. I need more time..."

"Time to...? To do what?"

"Not to *do*, Daniel. To be. To become."

Dan did not know what to say. He felt totally mystified, so akin was her faith to that which he had repudiated. Nearby someone began to tune the organ, but coming at that moment it was an intrusion and they moved quickly away down the north aisle towards the carved glass screen, its incised figures flickering in the light. Beyond they could see the walls of the ruins silhouetted in the bright sun, and Dan thought, that's where we started, the ruins, and I admit I know more now than when we came in. But how insidious it all is!

\* \* \*

Luke was waiting for them under the screen. His eyes had not been deceived; there was more between these two than just friendship. He felt a mixture of emotions that he could not begin to analyse. Partly, he envied them. The austerity of the life he had chosen had not, as yet, left room for close relationships and he longed to feel something similar. Yet he still felt protective of Hadissa. He should have known what would happen when she got to England. He couldn't turn a blind eye to it any longer. The time had come when he must say something, warn Dan off. But not in front of Hadissa.

He managed a strained smile. "Now you see why I let you do it by yourselves? You've got to do it that way, otherwise it's like being shown round an art gallery. You've got to pray it."

Dan was mute, knowing full well how it had felt.

"I haven't finished," smiled Hadissa, edging away. "I

want to look in there." She pointed to the Chapel of Unity, where the candles lit for the service still burnt. "I'll go by myself, if you don't mind."

"Go on, then," said Luke. "But don't be long – they'll be serving lunch in a few minutes." He watched her go, and then turned back to Dan.

"Dan," he said awkwardly, "I must speak to you about this girl. I didn't think it was appropriate to say anything in Kaduna but I simply must, now. I feel a certain responsibility for her, you know. After all, it's largely owing to me that she's in England at all."

Dan looked at him in amazement. "Rubbish!" he said irritably, and then averted his eyes. avoided his eyes. "You take too much on yourself. You always do. If it was anyone's *idea*, it was John-Sunday's. In any case, I don't know what you're talking about!"

"I'm talking about you and Hadissa."

"None of your business," Dan growled, flashing him an angry glance.

"It *is* my business. *She* is my business."

"Hardly, I'd have thought. Anyway, I don't see what possible objections you can have."

"Oh, for goodness' sake!" Luke expostulated. "I would have thought that was obvious! The difference in culture, for one! She's a bush village girl, and she'll have to go back to a bush village! There are certain questions one might ask!"

"If so, it's not for you to ask them," said Dan stiffly, meeting his eyes.

"And I'm telling you that it is! I can assure you, it gives me no pleasure..."

"No?" Dan looked at him with dislike. He'd had about enough of Luke. He was far too self-important and sanctimonious. Yet it wouldn't do to antagonise him; it might backfire.

"Okay, I admit you have an interest here. So, what do you want to ask? Fire away! I'll answer if I can."

"Well, to start with... Are you just playing games here, or are you serious? You can't compromise this girl. She's falling in love with you. You do realise that, don't you?"

"Yes. And as a matter of fact it's mutual."

"Have you told her?"

215

"Not for you to ask."

"But you want to marry her?"

"Again, not for you to ask."

"For goodness' sake, can you really imagine yourself living in Africa? Because, don't you see, nothing else will do? Not if you are going to avoid ruining her whole life."

"Now, just a minute!" Dan said angrily. "I want us to be together. I want her to make her life with me! How we do it is our own affair!"

"Oh, Dan," Luke said wearily. "I can't believe you're that dense. She can't possibly stay in England. She belongs in Africa. If you know anything about her, surely you know that! It would kill her. Okay," he amended, sensing another denial. "Maybe that's a bit melodramatic. But it would stifle her. She belongs in *Africa*," he insisted. "She has work to do there, important work; work that she quite desperately wants to do. It's the whole purpose of her coming here. You can't possibly want to stand in the way of that! Think how you would feel if the boot was on the other foot. How would you feel about moving there?"

This was so close to what Dan had been contemplating that he was taken aback, and he didn't answer. He found he'd been staring down at an engraved inscription under his feet, set in the paving. At that moment the huge brass letters came together as words.

'TO THE GLORY OF GOD + THIS CATHEDRAL BURNT'

"What *is* this?" he asked irritably.

"This? What it says. 'To the glory of God this Cathedral, burnt November 14 AD 1940, is now rebuilt.' It's a commemorative plaque. But you're changing the subject...."

"That's not what it says," said Dan pedantically. "There's no comma after 'cathedral'. It says 'to the glory of God this cathedral burnt'. That's what it says. What sort of God is that, to take glory in a holocaust?"

He looked up, angry and hostile, and found that Luke was now regarding him intently, an expression on his face that was not entirely lacking in sympathy.

"It's about renewal, Dan," he said quietly. "You ought to read the Psalms sometimes. A holocaust is the last thing God wants. No, but 'a broken and contrite spirit he will not despise.' Oh," he said, turning away, "I blame myself..."

216

"Well, don't," said Dan absently. "You had nothing to do with it."

Luke turned back, his eyes steely. "One way or another, Dan, you're going to have to make a sacrifice. Your interests for Hadissa's. You must know that. I'm sorry, but I really think you ought to give her up."

*　*　*

The chapel was small, star-shaped. At each point of the star was a deep concrete recess blocked by tall narrow windows of thick, brightly coloured glass. Hadissa chose one of the recesses at random, and stretched out her arms to touch the walls on either side. With delight she saw that the primitive designs of lit glass were strangely familiar, like sunlight glimpsed through a crack in the wall of a mud hut. If she had found the vastness of the cathedral awe-inspiring, breathtaking in its beauty and meaning, here she simply felt enclosed, not repressively, but as if within the hollow of an almighty hand. She stayed there a long time, her palms spread on the smooth concrete. The uncertainty and strangeness of the last weeks and months slowly receded, and she began to weep. Tears ran down her cheeks, but they were not, as they might have been, tears of sorrow and remorse, but of longing.

# CHAPTER 6

Three months later Hadissa had successfully completed the first part of her course and was working long hours in the hospital. The weather had not improved, and as her next residential module would not begin until the spring, she accepted Joanna's offer of a room in her house. In any case, it was convenient to Dan's flat, and she continued to see a great deal of him.

Stephen and Verity paid her a visit, and left disturbed by what they saw of her. Although the girl appeared to have put on a little weight, there was an expression in her eyes almost of desperation. Verity guessed she was simply exhausted and probably homesick as well, but Hadissa promised to go to Ely over the Christmas period and with that she had to be content. Talking it over with her daughter later, Verity was upset to discover that Hadissa was spending very little time with Joanna. Since the two girls had been such good friends in Ely she wondered what could have happened between them.

Joanna, herself, was puzzled. She still felt intensely protective of Hadissa, and couldn't understand why she was not more sociable. She regularly excused herself from Joanna's circle of friends, saying she didn't want to party. She didn't say how much she disliked the smoky atmosphere or the loud music with its explicit sexual lyrics, or the binge drinking, for Joanna seemed to be able to tolerate it, even if she didn't actively participate in it. It made Hadissa feel uncomfortable, prudish, an outsider. It was too wet to explore the town, and films and concerts were of little interest to her. When Joanna brought friends to the house, Hadissa would sometimes join them, sitting on the carpet and drinking coffee and exchanging hospital gossip, but would soon excuse herself and seek refuge in her room.

Hadissa knew that Joanna thought she being unreasonable. Her excuse was that she felt easier keeping something of a distance from the other students. She said that the other black girls on the course were English, and therefore more sophisticated; they made her feel backward, she said, or at least badly educated, so it was hardly surprising if she didn't want to mix with them after hours.

This was true enough. For those of Afro-Caribbean origin, the fact that Hadissa was from a primitive bush village made a significant difference to how they perceived each other, making them uncomfortably conscious of their race, when they had not been before, and they avoided her. Nor had she actively sought their friendship for she was unused to social contact for its own sake. In Kaduna it was not on anyone's agenda; work dominated everything, and afterwards the women would be too exhausted to do anything other than sleep. Here, it was different, but Hadissa did not have the language of the bars and common rooms, and she refused to take part in anything Joanna tried to persuade her to do.

Joanna was aware, however, that when Hadissa did go out she would often not return for a very long time and then be evasive as to where she had been. Not that she wanted the girl to think that she was checking up on her, but inevitably, as time went by, she began to feel suspicious. What was Hadissa up to? Where did she go, these cold winter nights? Had she been wrong to invite her to share the house?

Hadissa's life, therefore, when she was not working or studying, was spent waiting for Dan to telephone, waiting for Dan to pick her up, waiting for Dan to decide what they were going to do, and then being with him. He had taken her to his flat and she had seen the state in which he lived. It horrified her, that with so many material advantages he could live in such squalor, but after her initial disgust, she simply cleaned up after him and made no comment. Preoccupied with this, her vision in the cathedral was soon forgotten.

*   *   *

Early one morning, Joanna found Dan in the kitchen making a hot drink. It was obvious that he'd stayed the night, and all the sense of guardianship that she'd always felt for Hadissa rose to the surface. She propped herself against the kitchen door and folded her arms aggressively.

219

"What are *you* doing here?" she asked coldly.

Intensely wary of her, and against his better judgement, Dan felt an unwilling admiration for the loyalty of this girl and a certain pricking of conscience.

"Making a cup of coffee," he said, implying that it was not her concern.

"You stayed in Haddy's room last night, didn't you?"

He pointed the spoon at her. "Her name's Hadissa, okay? And what I do is my own affair."

"Not in *my* house!" she retorted angrily. "So you can get the hell out! For God's sake, you're just messing about with her, aren't you? I'd like to know what the hell gives you the right, because..."

Dan felt his anger mounting. "Our relationship is none of your business!"

Joanna ignored him "...Because that's what you're doing, isn't it? You won't be going back with her, will you? I can see that happening, I *don't* think! Oh no, you'll just get out from under! You'll just bog off!"

"I'm sorry, Joanna, but I don't care what you think, and I don't suppose Hadissa does, either! It's her life and she's old enough to make her own choices. It's not up to you to bloody well stick your nose in...!"

"Oh, God, you men!" She turned around in disgust. "You make me weep!"

"Well, don't interfere, then."

"*Someone's* got to interfere!" she snapped. "*Someone's* got to look after her interests, because you certainly aren't. Oh no, you've just got your eye on the main chance, haven't you? You've turned her head, that's all. All that money, a car...."

"What money, for heaven's sake?"

"You're earning, aren't you, which is more than we are! And who's got a bloody car, in Nigeria? No, you're just out to impress her. I think you're a bloody fraud, a fraud and a scheming bastard! What do you think my father's going to say when he hears about this? My God, what a kick in the teeth...! And what about her brother?"

"What about her fucking brother?"

They glared at each other, not realizing that Hadissa, disturbed by the sound of their raised voices, had come to the door. She was just in time to hear Dan's last words, and she

220

gasped in dismay, putting her hands to her mouth. Dan swung round. Her face was a picture of anguish. He knew she'd heard what he'd said, but as he reached out to her, she turned and fled down the passage. The front door slammed shut, and there was silence.

Dan glared at Joanna. "Now look what you've done!" he snarled, but she turned away, refusing to meet his eyes. He flung down the spoon that he'd been holding, and strode past her, shoving her hard against the wall with his elbow. Again the front door opened and before she could collect herself, he'd gone.

Half-heartedly, Joanna began to tidy up the mess in the kitchen. It wasn't until she had smashed a mug on the floor that she realised that she was shaking uncontrollably. She began to cry. She picked up the pieces, bundled them into a sheet of newspaper and threw the whole lot into the bin. Then she ran a sink of water and piled into it all the dirty plates, mugs and saucepans that had accumulated during the previous day. She poured in some washing-up liquid and swished the brush angrily around in the water. This caused bubbles to rise and to float upwards, making her sneeze.

"Oh, heck," she muttered, "heck, heck, *heck!*"

She bent over the sink, sneezing and weeping, then wiped her eyes and her nose on a damp tea towel before flinging that, too, into the soapy water. She cleaned everything in sight, meticulously and slowly, as if by doing so she could wash the argument out of her mind. She had no idea where Hadissa could have gone, or where Dan would start looking for her. She very much hoped that she wasn't just walking about in the pouring rain.

After a while she climbed the stairs to her room and sat on the bed. Should she phone her mother? What Daniel had said about Hadissa being a grown woman was true. They were not her keepers. There was nothing any of them could do except pick up the pieces. This could not possibly be a permanent relationship. Daniel would never agree to live in the African bush! Joanna found herself wondering whether they had used contraception. She sat immobile on the bed for ages, the thoughts churning in her mind, wondering where Hadissa was. She could only speculate about her state of mind.

The hours dragged by and neither Daniel nor Hadissa returned. Perhaps they were making love somewhere – no doubt his place, she thought, with renewed anger. By mid-morning the weather had improved and a watery sunlight was beginning stream weakly through the window. At least Hadissa wouldn't be rained on any more. Joanna looked at her watch. She'd had no appetite for breakfast but she was due at the hospital for her next shift and she hadn't even changed into her uniform.

She began to get dressed, occasionally peering down into the street for any sign of Hadissa, and when she was in the bathroom she left the door open so that she could listen for the sound of the front door. When she was ready, she sat down on her bed and scribbled a hasty note.

*Dear Haddy,*

*I'm sorry you heard us rowing, but I wish you'd told me about you and Daniel. I've got a late shift but I'll be home just after midnight. I'll pop in and see you if you're awake.*

*Love,*
*Jo*

\*   \*   \*

Joanna munched a whole packet of ginger biscuits on the bus, but for hours afterwards she could not concentrate and by the end of her shift she was tired, hungry and very worried. It was raining again and very late. The buses had stopped running, and she had to wait a long time for a taxi. By the time she reached home she was exhausted. As she opened the front door and switched on the light, she noticed a letter lying on the mat, and on it the footprint of a man's shoe.

So Daniel had returned. What about Hadissa, then? She picked up the letter and saw her mother's handwriting. Inside was a small blue envelope addressed to Hadissa, postmarked Kaduna State. It was not an educated hand. Joanna knew that Hadissa's mother couldn't write, and that she was expecting a letter from her brother. She walked slowly along the passage reading Verity's note and stopped outside Hadissa's room, stooping to slide the envelope under the door. Then she paused, listening. From inside the room she could hear Hadissa's voice. It sounded as though she was crying, or perhaps calling out in her sleep. Joanna looked through the keyhole to see if there was any light in the room. Framed in the small space was an image that Joanna was never to forget. Lit by the dim light of the bedside lamp was the back view of Hadissa's naked body, and under it the pink hairy legs and squeezed hairy buttocks of the man she had come to despise.

A sense of impending doom came over her, and she drew back, her hand to her mouth, at the same time fully aware that if it had been anyone other than Hadissa she would not have reacted so strongly. She felt she was in the presence of tragedy, a tragedy that at all costs must be averted. She ran back to the front door, wanting to escape, to remain uninvolved, to turn back the clock, to not know. She felt breathless and not from exertion.

She opened it the front door quietly, and then slammed it, calling out again, pitching her voice as though she had just arrived.

"Hadissa? You there, Haddy?"

After a moment Hadissa's door opened, and she stood there, clutching her dressing gown around her body. She came out, closing the door behind her.

"What is it? Is something the matter?" Her face was open and bland, but the expression in her eyes was shifty and she did not look directly at Joanna. "Sorry, I didn't hear you. I was asleep..."

"Sorry to disturb you, then," said Joanna. Her voice was shaky and she couldn't help but sound a little brusque. She was accustomed to greet Hadissa with a hug, but this time she kept her distance. "I was worried about you."

"I'm fine. What's that in your hand?"

"Oh... It's for you." She handed the letter to her. "Your brother, I expect."

*   *   *

That night Joanna was too exhausted to spend any more time with Hadissa, and in any case Dan's presence in the house precluded further discussion. The next morning she got up early and went to church. She was not a regular churchgoer, but she did go when she was troubled. After the service the parish priest came up to her, a young woman at his side.

"Jo, this is Ellen. She'd like a word, if that's okay."

He left them to it, and the two women stood facing each other. Joanna saw a woman about her own age with auburn hair and a strong jaw.

"Hi, have me met before?"

"No, but we have a mutual acquaintance, I think. Dan Marsden? Tall, redheaded, a teacher. You know who I mean, don't you?"

"I know *of* him." Joanna shrugged with distaste. "What's this about?"

Ellen hesitated and looked around.

"Can we go somewhere a little more private? I don't want anyone to hear...."

They settled themselves in a pew in one of the side aisles, and Ellen adjusted her skirt over her legs. Now that she had Joanna's attention she seemed lost for words. Joanna waited politely, wondering what was on her mind.

Avoiding Joanna's eyes, Ellen said, "It's just that... I used to know him and I've seen him around... with a black girl."

"It bothers you that she's black?"

"This isn't to do with her being black!"

Joanna looked at her appraisingly.

"No? Then why mention it? And this guy Daniel, he hurt you? Is that what you're saying?"

"No, of course not!" The response was immediate, and in spite of the contempt with which it was uttered, Joanna knew it was a lie. She was silent, waiting.

Then she said, "I don't understand what you're getting at. Who're you bothered about, this girl, or Daniel? And what makes you think I'm involved in any way?"

"The girl's a nurse. I've seen her in uniform. And you are, too, aren't you? The vicar here says you are. I thought, perhaps, if you worked at the same hospital, you'd know her. If so..."

"If so, what?" asked Joanna patiently. "She's a friend of mine, actually," she added, wondering if this was true anymore. She shifted in her seat and pushed her hands into her pockets. "Come on, why don't you say want you want to say? Behind Hadissa's back, of course." she added unkindly.

Ellen ignored this. "Hadissa?" she said quickly. "That's her name, is it?"

Joanna looked at her watch. "Let's get to the point shall

we??"

"Just that... if she's a friend of yours, you'd do well to put a stop to it, if you can, while the going's good." Ellen spoke quietly, leaning forward intently to look at Joanna's face. "I wouldn't want her to get hurt, that's all. He's an interesting person, is Dan," she added unexpectedly, sitting back again, "but he's... he's not very deep. Oh, that sounds like a contradiction and I suppose it is. What I mean is..."

"Go on, you've got my attention. Not that I think it's my role to put a stop to anything, as you put it, even if I should. In what way is he not very deep?"

"Well, you start off thinking he is. You think, he's good looking, he's got a good job, he's earning, he's interested in the things I'm interested in, let's give it a whirl. Then you discover he's not like that at all. He lives like a pig, for one thing. He's sexist, selfish, extremely cussed, and very self-opinionated..."

Joanna grinned. "My, what a list of imperfections! I feel quite sorry for him! I take it you cooled off?"

"Yes, I couldn't stand it. It wasn't entirely his fault," she admitted. "We argued too much... One minute he was, I don't know, loving and generous, and the next he'd be really horrible. I shouldn't have got involved with him in the first place. He's a redhead like me, and we set each other off. We used to have terrible fights – not real violence, I don't mean that, just shouting. He's got quite a temper... So have I, I suppose. I think he really wanted to fall in love, but... well, obviously I wasn't the right person. Perhaps this black girl is. Perhaps he's different with her. Or perhaps he's changed. If not..."

"I'm sorry, but I don't understand why you're telling me this."

Ellen looked at her carefully.

"If he's changed..." she said, "...if he really is in love, and she with him, well, maybe it's all right. I don't think he's capable of it, but never mind. But if he's not, she could be very badly hurt. You could stop it, if you tried. All you'd need to do would be... well, to tell her about me, what I've said... She ought at least to take warning."

"So this is some sort of, what? Solidarity?"

"Yes, if you like." Ellen stood up, preparing to go, then looked down at Joanna. "I don't really know *why* I am telling you all this. What happened to us only happened last year. I don't know if he could manage a real relationship. He tries to give, but he's not really a giver. You see, I *was* hurt. I expect you've guessed that. When I told you I wasn't, well... He didn't make room for me, you see. He didn't care tuppence what *I* was feeling or thinking. He left me feeling, sort of out of count. He made me feel... nothing, as if I was nothing." She turned away.

"You feel better now?"

"Oh, God, yes! Leaving him was the best thing I ever did!"

*   *   *

*Dear Hadissa,*

*Greetings to you in the Lord's Name from your loving bother,* John-Sunday. *I hope you are well and happy in your new life and working* hard.

*The days seem long since you left Africa.*

*I look for your face in the clouds and your face is not there, you are far away.*

*Please forgive me for* my angry letter. *Your parcel arrived the day after I sent my angry letter, and then I was angry with myself. The shirt is too big but I like it very much.*

*A man has come from Nasarawa. He is the bomber. His name is* Zacarias Ibrahim Umkole. *He is called Zac, and he is a mechanic. We are working together. He lives in the other room in my concrete house. Our mother likes him and he cuts her wood, I fetch the water and cut her thatch. Our mother is well.*

*Another man came. He is the mechanic from Kateri on the other side of the road. He is the Muslim mechanic* who we would not let him help us *with the tractor, why Stanley got killed. There was an accident on the road and he came suddenly and he said, "My name is Hassan." He is that same man. So we are working together. We are building a concrete workshop next to the clinic.*

*I have looked for our father but I cannot find him. The bishop says* pray *and he will tell the pastors to carry on looking. If we find him I will tell you.*

*We have lost three chickens. I think it was rats. I am mending the chicken hut. I liked the picture of Cambridge. Is that your building it is very big.*

*PLEASE* write again because there is nothing in my heart *to tell me how you are.*

Your loving brother,
John-Sunday

*  *  *

Hadissa was making a futile attempt at study when she heard the front door close and Joanna's footsteps in the hall. She glanced quickly around her room. Dan had gone home and she had cleared away all traces of his visit. She had showered and changed her clothes and she now sat with a towel wrapped round her wet hair. She had left her door ajar, hoping that when Joanna arrived back she would see it as an invitation, but then she heard her feet on the stairs. She put down her medical notes and went to the door.

"Jo?"

Joanna turned, her hand on the banister.

"Hi."

"You want to come in?" said Hadissa, helplessly. "You want a cup of coffee? Have you just come back from hospital?"

"Church."

"Oh. Yes... Well, you want some coffee?"

"...Okay. I'll just go and dump my coat."

Hadissa made the coffees and took them back to her room, where she stood quite still, thinking. The events of the previous twenty-four hours had left her feeling empty and confused. She realised that she had probably lost Joanna's good opinion of her, and she felt deeply ashamed that she had lied about being asleep when in fact she and Daniel had been making love. It shouldn't have happened here, in Joanna's house, beholden as she was to Joanna's parents. The whole episode had left her, once again, with the pervading sense of having in some way defiled herself. God had forgiven her once, and what did she do, but go right out and get embroiled in another dishonest relationship. And it *was* dishonest, not because the man was married, this time, but because she and Daniel were not. Also, she had another even more insistent worry. She had missed two periods. The first occasion she could attribute to the change in her diet or emotional turmoil, but not two months in succession.

227

Hadissa's mother had taught her nothing about contraception. It would be considered totally irrelevant for an unmarried virgin to have need of such knowledge, and Daniel had never mentioned it. In Nigeria her work in casualty had led her to examine pregnant women, but she had never connected it to herself. Even now, the thought that she might be pregnant had hardly begun to cross her mind. The reality of it had not yet touched her.

"We need to talk, you know."

Joanna had come in and had settled herself on the bed, but Hadissa had been too preoccupied with her thoughts to notice. She did not reply, but smiled wanly and sat down next to her.

"Jo, I am sorry about last night. I…"

Joanna glanced sideways at her. "You two made it up, then?"

"He didn't mean what he said. He was just angry. I'm sorry he…"

"Doesn't matter… Your letter – is John-Sunday all right?"

"He's well. Joanna, I want to…" She paused, for Joanna had abruptly got to her feet and walked to the window. The rain was once again beating down on to the pavement outside and the gutters were running with water. On the opposite side of the street a man was struggling to unload two small children from his car, tucking his open umbrella under his armpit. As she watched, it fell from his grasp on to the wet pavement, and Joanna heard the sound of raised voices. He kicked the door of the car shut, grasped each child by the arm, and hurried through the open door of the house. The door slammed shut behind him, leaving the umbrella to roll into the gutter.

Why am I so angry with Daniel, Joanna thought? After all, it was Hadissa who'd lied to her, not him. He'd been straightforward enough, if his behaviour with Hadissa could be called straightforward. Ever since she'd met Hadissa, she'd felt protective of her – not, she hoped, in a patronising way, but to safeguard her interests. Oh, God, that *was* patronising, and pompous, too! What the hell did it mean anyway, and who was she to take it upon herself? Because, she reasoned, Hadissa was a child of the African bush, and would be going back to the African bush. Joanna had thought she'd make friends of her own, but it hadn't happened. Instead, she'd got herself involved with a man who couldn't possibly offer her anything but grief. This could blight her life. Daniel was a troublemaker, Joanna reflected angrily, nothing but a parasite, and the more it went on the more likely it would end in disaster. She obviously couldn't reason with him – his attitude in the kitchen had taught her that – but shouldn't she at least try to talk to Hadissa, wake her up a bit to the consequences of what she was doing?

Except that, as she'd said to Ellen, it was none of her business. Daniel had been quite right when he threw that comment at her. But she'd show him Hadissa was not without friends! Her parents would be up in arms if they knew what was happening. If she confronted Hadissa she risked losing her friendship, then the girl would be really alone. But she must at least attempt to bring her to her senses. It was a forlorn hope, but she had to try. She sighed heavily. What a menace the man was!

Joanna turned round and regarded Hadissa solemnly. She had no idea how her prolonged silence had terrified Hadissa, or how vulnerable she was feeling. She was sitting on the bed with her knees together and her bare feet arranged symmetrically on the carpet, simply waiting. Joanna was surprised by her apparent tranquillity, and thought what a quiet dignity the girl possessed. She was clutching her mug as if drawing its warmth to her, but her back was as upright as usual and her face was composed. Even her eyes, which had seemed so deceitful the previous night, were wide and guileless. Joanna felt a rush of pity for her – she'd no idea what she'd got herself into.

"Oh, *Haddy,*" she said, "what are we to do with you?" She tried to make her tone light and affectionate. "Well! Are you in love with him?"

"…I think so. I'm sorry if…"

"And he with you?"

"Yes. Yes, he is. Ever since we met in Kaduna, I think. But Joanna, I…"

"And is he going to marry you, Haddy?"

"I… we… We haven't talked about it. At least, he says… He talks about getting a little house…"

"But will he *marry* you? What about when you finish the course? Will he go back with you?"

Hadissa shook her head. "I don't know. We haven't…"

"Bloody *hell,* Hadissa!" Joanna kicked the skirting board

sharply with her heel, and Hadissa jumped. "There seems to be quite a lot you haven't talked about! You've obviously been too busy doing something else! A bit putting the cart before the horse, isn't it?"

This was one of the few times when Hadissa actually understood any of Joanna's clichés, and she hung her head in shame. She drooped, clutching her stomach.

"I feel sick," she murmured.

She *looked* sick and there were tears in her eyes. Under the dark hue of her skin she had a grey, unhealthy pallor, and Joanna realised for the first time the strain she was under. And *she* had put herself over her as judge and jury! Quickly she moved from the window and went and sat down again on the bed, at Hadissa's side.

"Oh God, I'm sorry!" She put her arms around her shoulders, and drew her head down onto her shoulder. "I shouldn't lecture you! It's not up to me what you do with your life. There, have a good cry..."

"I really do feel sick..." Hadissa whispered, swallowing convulsively.

"You're just worn out."

"Jo, I think I'm... I think I might be... pregnant." A dying fall to her voice.

Joanna felt as if a cold hand had squeezed her heart, and she dropped her arm. She peered round into Hadissa's face, aghast.

"You're joking!"

"No, I've... I think I've missed a period. Perhaps two."

"*Shit*! It only needed that! Does Daniel know?"

"No, he..."

"*Bastard*."

Hadissa looked at her fearfully. "You won't tell him, will you?"

Joanna stood up. "He'll have to know soon, anyway. You'll show. Here, get up. Get on the bed properly. Lie down..."

"What...?"

"I'm going to take a look at you."

She pulled up Hadissa's jumper and loosened her skirt, then bent over her and gently palpated the brown stomach. Hadissa watched her apprehensively. Then Joanna sat down on the bed beside her and took her hand.

"I'm not an obstetrician, but…" She nodded significantly.

Hadissa let go her hand and rolled away from her on the bed.

"Oh," she wailed. "What am I going to do?"

Joanna was silent. The options were simple, either to abort the baby or to keep it, and she said so.

Hadissa reeled with shock. "How can you say that? Abortion is… murder! How can you even *suggest* it? I thought you were my friend!"

"I'm telling you the options, Haddy. I'm not advising you."

"I can't have an *abortion!*"

Joanna felt completely out of her depth. She knew a number of people who had got themselves into this kind of predicament, nurses among them, and all had chosen to have an abortion, with the exception of one, who had disappeared into the ether. By this time Hadissa was sobbing bitterly, tearing at her clothes and her hair, and Joanna was afraid that she was becoming hysterical. She would lose the baby if she weren't careful. Wryly, Joanna reflected that that would be no bad thing. She'd had it anyway, poor little sod. Fancy talking home an illegitimate child! As if she had heard this thought Hadissa began to shriek. Joanna took hold of her arms and shook her.

"Hadissa, stop this! Stop crying! You'll make yourself ill! Come on, stop it, stop crying."

Hadissa gradually became quiet, but stayed facing the wall, her arm covering her face. Joanna began to stroke her back.

"There now, that's better. Now you're feeling better. Come on, turn round, and look at me. You'll be okay. Now, why don't you get up and go and wash your face. I'll be back in a minute."

"Where…?"

"I am going to telephone my parents. Is that okay? I must, I'm afraid. Haddy, look at me. I've got to talk to them. You understand? I need to talk to my mother."

# CHAPTER 7

Verity went into the study and waited for Stephen to notice her. He did not like to be interrupted, especially when he was struggling over a sermon, as he was now, and she usually left him in peace. He turned to face her at last, frowning, his pencil poised in the air.

"Something the matter? I heard the phone."

"Joanna," she replied. "I'm sorry, but there's no way of breaking this gently. I'm afraid Hadissa's pregnant. By Daniel."

"*Daniel*? Good *God*! But... there's not been time!"

"How long does it take?" Verity faced him, her arms folded across her chest. "Luke says it started even before she came here, in Nigeria," she said bitterly.

He looked confused. "The baby?"

"No, silly!" She gave a dry laugh. "Their affair, or whatever."

"But Luke knows?"

"Not about this latest development. He said something in passing when he was here that time, but I'm afraid I didn't take it seriously."

"I wish I'd known..."

"What could you have done about it?" she demanded. "Nothing. Apparently, he's taken up with her again since she went to Cambridge. We should have foreseen that, the way he was when... Anyway, there it is. Now she's pregnant."

"The silly, silly girl!" he exclaimed sorrowfully. "What on earth is she going to do? She can't possibly..."

"...get rid of it. No, I agree."

His mouth dropped open. "Get *rid* of it? That's an appalling suggestion! No, I was going to say, finish the course."

"Oh, I think she can finish the course," Verity said robustly. "Jo reckons she's about two and a half months gone. That means it'll be a June baby, or even May. She can finish her modules, if she keeps healthy, but she'll be very big by then."

Stephen was not listening, and now he interrupted her.

"That man! We put so much trust in him! I never dreamt…"

"No, well, I did, actually, but there we are. They've got to live their own lives, haven't they? But he's kept very quiet about it. Jo says she's suspected something for quite a long while. She didn't think it was Daniel, though. I don't think she knew until recently that Hadissa was even seeing him."

"This will really upset Luke, you know."

"For heaven's sake, Stephen, what you or I think, or what Luke thinks, is irrelevant! The point is, what are you going to do about Hadissa?"

"*Me?* What can *I* do? Does Daniel know she's pregnant?"

"Jo doesn't think so, not yet."

"Well, someone's going to have to tell him. Hadissa, herself, presumably. Is she in love with him?"

Verity shrugged. "Who knows? Not necessarily."

"They'll have to marry…" he mused.

"Stephen," Verity said patiently, "this isn't the Middle Ages! They don't *have* to marry! Whether they marry or not is quite a different matter, and it's none of our business. It's Hadissa we must think of; her health and her peace of mind, and the health of the baby. I could go and see her," she mused. "If she wants me to, that is. She's a grown woman, Stephen. We can't do anything unless we're invited."

"Well, whether it's our business or not," he said, grimly, "I shall certainly have a word with Daniel. In fact, I shall get on to him right away. And whether he likes it or not, I'm also going to tell Luke. They were at college together, and anyway, he's a priest. We're all going to have to pull together in this. Daniel has got to be made to realise the consequences of his actions."

He rubbed his hands through his hair vigorously. "What a despicable thing for the man to do! So cowardly, so… so un-thinking! I shall certainly send for him."

"You can't just *send* for him, Stephen. You're not his tutor anymore. Why don't you just go and see him in Cambridge?"

"No, I shall see him here," said Stephen firmly. "I want my desk between us, not see him in some dreadful pub or other. I shall be tactful, but… I shall make sure he comes!"

He turned away, shaking his head despondently and began to finger the thin pages of his Bible.

"Before you came in," he said, "I was looking at the readings for next Sunday. They're amazingly apposite. Advent Sunday, Psalm 25..."

"Stephen, is this rel...?"

"Yes, it *is* relevant! Here, I'll read it to you. It says: 'Let them be ashamed who are wantonly treacherous.' Well, I shall make sure he *is* ashamed," he muttered. "And it *is* treachery!" He looked up at her. "I know it's an old-fashioned word, Verity, but that's just what it is, treacherous. The Church has a high ideal of marriage, and for very good reason! Daniel's betrayed my trust. Luke's, too."

Verity was silent and Stephen continued to thumb the pages of his Bible.

"How I've prayed for that man! I almost wish I'd never sent him to Africa! Then none of this would have happened."

"You can't blame yourself..." she protested.

"Well, I do," he groaned. "What on earth was I thinking about? I suppose I thought I was doing good. I did think it would do him good. Good heavens, he was just getting over a broken love affair! What on earth is the man playing at?"

"Perhaps he's not playing," said Verity, soberly. "As far as we know, this might even be good news..."

He looked at her. "How on earth can it be good news?"

"Well, it might help him make up his mind."

"And what if he decides against her, hey? What then? Well, I shall find out. Good heavens, have you thought of her brother, when *he* finds out? Oh, what a disgrace!"

"You wouldn't refuse to marry them, though?"

"Of course not, if they want me to. And the sooner the better!"

"They could marry from here..." Verity suggested. "This is where the letters come. I can see to all the arrangements... She's already supposed to be coming for Christmas. If he really wants to marry her, well, they can both come, and we can discuss it."

"Oh, I shall see him before then!"

"Yes, of course," said Verity, going to the door. "But if he agrees, it'll be an opportunity to talk things over. Joanna will be here. She's very upset about this, but she'll come round if she sees they're in earnest. She'll have to. We all will."

Stephen groaned. "I suppose so. But, *Christmas*! It'll ruin our day! And I've got three services to take."

\* \* \*

Hadissa stood in the narrow doorway of Dan's flat in the pouring rain waiting for him to arrive home from school. It was very cold and a dismal blanket of grey river mist hung over the street, which was almost entirely empty of traffic. For an hour or more no one had passed in front of the house where she waited, shivering and increasingly tearful. He was very late. Surely he'd not be much longer? She was due at the hospital by mid-evening.

Anxiously she looked at her watch and then searched the street for his figure, for he usually parked the car in the service road behind the row of houses where he lived and would then walk round to the front door. There was nothing. Across the road the pewter-coloured river ran turbulently between sodden banks, and beyond was endless, unrelenting mist. The rain splashed pitilessly down, stabbing the air under the street lamp and disappearing into the darkness beneath, and a shallow stream of water ran across the pavement below the steps where she was standing. Hadissa pressed herself as far back as she could against the hard wood of the door. The wind was rising, chilling her whole body, and she clutched her arms protectively over her stomach.

For days she had been agonising about how Dan would react when she told him she was pregnant. Would he would blame her, refuse to have anything more to do with her, or did he love her enough for them to deal with it together? Although how they might deal with it, she did not even begin to speculate. He had repeatedly spoken about having a child, and for them all to be together forever, yet he would hardly be thrilled that she had pre-empted his purpose, which, being African and a woman, she thought she had done. She repeatedly asked herself if she loved him, and came up with no answer at all.

He was certainly occupying a prominent place in her life, and she had come to depend on him. She was drawn to him. She enjoyed his lovemaking, even though it was less inhibited than was the custom in Africa, and the little attentions that he showered on her inevitably attracted her very much. She liked the glow of intellect that shone out of him at times, and she respected his decisiveness. She knew it derived from a self-assurance that she herself lacked, and she had been grateful and incredulous that he had wanted to spend so much time with her. Basically, he represented security, and though she scarcely knew what this meant, and had no idea what it implied, she knew it was something for which she hankered.

Yet was all that enough to commit herself to him for the rest of her life? And where would they live? She could never expect him to make his home in the African bush, nor, if she was to oversee the clinic, could they live in Kaduna. She would never be able to venture into the street, let alone brave the wrath of the religious leaders by flaunting her mixed-race child. As for her mother, she would feel that all her previous condemnation of her daughter had been justified. It would be a vindication of all her fears and prejudices. And how would John-Sunday react? The answer to that question was obvious. He would be furious, scandalised, ashamed, and that was an understatement. He was not sophisticated enough for it to be otherwise. Sophisticated? Was it sophisticated, what she had done? A hard ball of misery formed in her stomach.

Daniel was here, and she had not even heard his step. He was standing in front of her, peering out at her from under his umbrella, his key in his hand. Seeing her there, wet and forlorn, he looked guilty and disturbed, but he let them both into the house quickly, and she followed him up the stairs to his flat. The words poured out of him like a torrent; short, sharp, staccato questions that did little to mask his state of mind.

"Did we have a date? How long have you been waiting? Hadissa, for heaven's sake, you're drenched! Here, I'll put the fire on. Take off your things, for goodness' sake! Just drop them there, and come and sit by the fire. You'll catch your death of cold! It's just as well I was no later. I had a meeting after school, but we cut it short. There's a flood warning on the river and people wanted to get home. Come on, sit down and get yourself warm. Do you want a hot drink? I've got to look after you, now that you're..." He flushed suddenly, and went silent.

"You know, then."

How did he know? Surely Joanna wouldn't have told him. How then? There was no telltale swelling in her belly, and it was a few days since she'd last seen him. She'd been on night

236

duty, and they'd had little opportunity to meet. Jo had told her parents – it must have been one of them.

Part of her felt grateful, and the burden lifted a little. At least she did not have to break the news herself, and see his reaction. Yet, if she had, at least she would have known the truth. His face always revealed his mood. He was never able, entirely, to dissemble; she could read him like a book. Had he been embarrassed, repelled, sickened by her simplicity, her naive attitude to sexual intercourse that did not include taking precautions? Did he feel trapped? Hadissa did not delude herself, but she had reckoned without his anger.

"I had to hear if from Stephen, didn't I? God in heaven, Hadissa, how on earth could you do this to me?"

"*I*, do it to *you*?"

She reared back with all the innate majesty of her race. Whatever her private thoughts might have been, or that she blamed herself, it was not for *him* to blame her! She looked as her slave forbears might have looked when abused by a master, and she responded in like manner. On her face was an expression of disdain. Her black eyes flared, hot with fury, and her full, slightly reddened lips curled with fury and contempt. She had extended her hands to him, but now she withdrew them, laying her slim, ring-less hand delicately upon her lap. It was the absence of any ring, and its implications, which brought Dan to his senses. His anger abated as abruptly as it had risen. He had been watching her, at once furiously resentful and yet spellbound by her beauty and dignity. She was splendid! He lowered his gaze, ashamed of his outburst, totally confused and miserable.

When Stephen had rung him it was entirely out of the blue, and he had been pleased to be invited to Ely again. After all, Stephen had said, they were old friends, weren't they? Wasn't it time that they caught up with each other? He had suggested two weeks on Saturday and Dan had accepted gladly. Then Stephen remarked that he'd heard there'd been a bit of trouble.

"Trouble?"

"Yes, old chap. It appears you're both in a bit of a mess."

So Luke had blabbed, had he, and told Stephen about their relationship. Well, it wasn't the end of the world – he'd have to know sometime. He'd have preferred, however, to break

237

the news himself, and said so.

"Oh, what news is that?" Stephen had said quickly. Yes, he'd been very clever!

"Well, about Hadissa and me..."

"Daniel," Stephen had said firmly, "I'm sorry, but I think we're talking at cross-purposes. I'm talking about the pregnancy. Now," he had added before Dan could recover, "we do really need to talk things over, you know. Of course, Verity and I will do whatever we can to help, anything at all, but I think you and I ought to discuss it first. I must say, I think you've taken it like a man. I knew we could trust you to do the right thing! But, of course you will! I expect you love her very much, and from what Luke says, she's absolutely head over heels about you. Now then, we have this date in the diary, and it's not too far away, so we'll leave it there for the moment... Take care, dear boy, and we'll see you soon."

On that note, he had rung off, leaving Dan completely stunned. But how clever Stephen was, how crafty, how... manipulative!

"I need a towel," Hadissa said, getting up. "My hair is wet."

"I'll get one."

He ran to the bathroom, came back with a towel, and handed it to her. She rubbed her hair vigorously until it rose up above her head in a black frizz, and wiped her eyes, obliterating her momentary tears. Dan had been watching, but now he bent down and, taking the towel from her, removed her sodden shoes and began tenderly to dry her feet.

"Oh, Daniel," she said mournfully, "what have we done?"

"Oh *God*!" he said, anguish and regret in his voice. "I'm so sorry. I'm so very, very sorry..." His head drooped and he hid his face in her lap. For Hadissa, it was the unmistakable voice of love, and she began to stroke his hair. The action, barely forgotten but now newly recalled, was the same with which she had comforted him in the darkness of the bus on that memorable day in Kaduna. It had the same effect, which was to simplify his motives.

"Will you let me look after you?" he said.

The stroking ceased as she withdrew her hands, then she took his head and raised it to see his eyes.

"What does that mean, Daniel? I need to know what you mean."

"Hadissa," he said helplessly, "I want to… I wish I could save you from all this. And I will! Let me…"

"Let you, what? What more do you want from me, Daniel?"

It was a cool challenge. The moment when he could have told her that he loved her had come and gone in the blink of an eye, or the passing of a single tear, and he sat back.

"Stephen knows," he mumbled.

"*He* told you, then?"

He scowled. "Yes, that girl must have said something, damn her!"

"Joanna? You should not speak of her like that. She was right to tell them. They are my only friends, they and Luke." She smoothed down her uniform and met his eyes with her usual direct gaze. "Well? What did he say?"

"He's persuaded me to go to Ely. He bludgeoned me into it, the devious bastard."

"Neither should you speak of him like that. He's a good man, and he and Verity care about me."

"I expect he'll be furious… and it's none of his damn business!"

"Daniel," she said patiently. "I'm not entirely without common sense. Except for Stephen and Verity I'm alone in this country, and I'm pregnant. Don't you see? I've had time to think. I've no idea how the college authorities will react, whether I can stay on the course, or whether they'll throw me out. I must make arrangements for having the baby. Maybe they'll send me back to Kateri. Everything is outside my control now. Stephen and Verity, Luke as well, they're the only ones I can ask for help. And Jo, of course. You do yourself no good to malign them."

Dan felt his life slipping out of control. She had not mentioned him in this little list. She was talking as though she was unconnected to him in any way. Already, she had distanced herself from him, and was sitting there, contained, small and utterly composed, her hands gently smoothing her belly as if to reassure the quiescent child – calmly speculating a life without him.

"Go to Ely, but only if you want to. Don't feel you have to go." She tried to smile. "I don't expect it will be a very comfortable experience!"

He was not listening. His mind had moved ahead. The foetus must still be very small. Surely she knew people who could help her... Okay, say the damn word, have an abortion... and then they could start again. They could test their love, and then after she qualified and if they still wanted to, they could marry, and have a child at a time of their own choosing. Not, for goodness' sake, have it thrust upon them now, when they had nowhere to live and he was halfway through his academic year! He forgot how desperately he had wanted her. He forgot his exaltation. All he could think of was that he'd only known her a few months, and he wasn't ready, yet, to write off his life for her.

"Hadissa, do you want to keep this baby?" He spoke in a rush. "Because, it's not really the right time for us, is it? Maybe I could find someone..."

"Adopt, you mean? I couldn't give my child away, Daniel."

"Not... adopt..."

She stared at him, then bent down to hide her eyes. She reached for her shoes and put them on, fastening the laces tightly. She got to her feet and quietly picked up her coat.

"It's stopped raining," she said, peering out of the window. "I think I'll carry this. It's really too wet to put on."

"Hadissa..."

"Yes?" She turned to face him, her eyes closed, long-suffering.

"I... I didn't mean..." He spread his hands helplessly.

She looked at him calmly. "I know what you meant," she said quietly. "I'll go now, if you don't mind. I have to get to the hospital and it's a long walk. Don't see me out."

She turned, and began to walk to the door.

"Stay a minute," he pleaded. "I'll run you up in the car... Hadissa, I..."

Hadissa shook her head slightly, the expression in her eyes more heartrending than he could ever have imagined. "Daniel, I don't think we have anything more to say to each other."

She stood, as if waiting for his rebuttal, then shook her head again sadly, went out of the door, and closed it softly behind her. He stood in the middle of the room, his hands still outspread. He heard her go down the stairs, and then the front door opened. A moment later, it shut again and he heard her feet on the pavement. He went to the window and peered down. She was walking purposefully away, hugging her coat in front of her, her head bent as if deep in thought.

*　*　*

It was Saturday morning. Dan had woken early and, unable to get back to sleep and miserable with himself, had got up, made himself a mug of tea, pushed an upright chair close to the window and sat looking out, sipping the hot brew. The rain had stopped and a watery sunlight clothed the street. The last leaves had vanished from the trees, blown down by heavy gusts of wind and the occasional sharp frost, so that now every branch and twig was silhouetted against the bright sky, lit to crystal clarity, sending dark shadows across the road. His flat was dirty and he, himself, unkempt. It was the story of his life, he thought, that in those areas where he had to be professional, he should be able to impose order, while in trivial things he remained chaotic, and inside, full of turmoil.

The question facing him was whether, after his quarrel with Hadissa, he would go to Ely at all. Bloody Stephen, he thought, resentfully, I know what he'll say! He'll call me a cad or a bounder – that's his sort of language, damn him. He'll sit me down and lay into me for all he's worth. And, having done that, it'll give him the greatest pleasure to boot me out of the house. So why on earth should I submit to that?

Dan knew he had behaved badly, but his reasoning was simple. Hadissa was loveable, so he'd loved her – that's all there was to it. Was he to blame if she had got herself into trouble? Hadn't she played a part in it, too? And to come to him like that, out of the blue, with such news! No wonder he'd reacted poorly.

No, hang on, it was Stephen who'd told him, not Hadissa. By the time she'd arrived he'd known for days. He went cold at the realisation of how near he'd come to deluding himself. Suggesting an abortion was a bit tactless, perhaps, but come on, it wasn't totally irrelevant. Didn't they have abortion in the bush, leaves or roots or something? And if he chose not to want a child at this stage who could blame him? Surely he had some rights in the matter? He tried to pull himself together. I'm just panicking, he thought, casting his mind back to the days in

241

Kaduna when he had first met her, remembering the rapture of their first meetings and the ecstasy of anticipated delights. What dreams of conjugal bliss he had nurtured! Yet, he admitted, what conceit, that he should imagine that when she came to England she would just capitulate.

There was a movement below him, in the street, and he leant forward. His elderly neighbour was emptying a bucket full of garden rubbish into Dan's dustbin. As he watched, the man looked around furtively, and disappeared into his own back yard.

Bloody cheek, thought Dan; has the man no self-respect? Skulking around like that in full view, as if he couldn't care less?

He sat down again, then rose abruptly and went into the bedroom to pack his bag. Stephen could be very unnerving and he was apprehensive about meeting him. But *he* wouldn't skulk! He may have been negligent, even rash, but he wasn't completely immoral.

# CHAPTER 8

*En route* to Ely, Dan realised that the previous ten days constituted the longest period of time that he and Hadissa had been apart since her arrival in Cambridge, and he missed her acutely. He had thrown himself into his schoolwork like a man possessed, but was impatient and irritable with the children, punishing one of them for some misdemeanour more harshly than was actually warranted. Normally he would merely have elicited an apology of sorts, but now it would take him days to restore the child's confidence.

I can cope with disobedient kids, he thought wryly, but I'm ill equipped to deal with this sort of crisis; weeping women – it's not my scene. It's not that I'm tired of Hadissa; on the contrary, there's no one to match her. She's beautiful and deep. She's unique, and she's given me, unquestioningly, this beauty and this deepness and this uniqueness. Then why, oh why, didn't I just take her in my arms? Something prevented me – was it panic, fear, or just my own inadequacies? Was it racial? No, of course it wasn't bloody racial! Was I frightened of losing control? What was it? There must be some flaw in my character, which, time and time again, keeps me from committing myself.

The thoughts churned round and round in his head. He recalled that the morning after she'd left, when he had started to shave, the face that greeted him in the mirror seemed almost unrecognisable, and he'd shrunk back in dismay. Later he'd found no distortion, and thought he must have imagined the whole thing. Yet the days after her departure had been miserable, his nights bereft. For there was no doubt that she had gone. She had gathered together the remnants of her dignity and slipped out of his life – and I can't bear it, he thought, gripping the wheel as the car ate up the miles to Ely. Occasionally he cast sideways glances at the seat beside him, where she'd sat so happily on their way to Coventry.

Yet what was to be done? He thought of going to see

243

her, pleading with her, but rejected the idea immediately, knowing that they'd be back where they'd started, for nothing had changed. It was still the child that was the issue. And if he was half-hearted about the child, she would know. She'd shut the door in my face, he thought ruefully, and she'd be justified. As for Stephen, how much of an inquisition could he stand?

* * *

Verity greeted him with forced politeness, her grey eyes unreadable.

"Coffee okay? I've got a tray all ready."

He'd have preferred a beer, but he nodded and took the tray and went and knocked on Stephen's door. He found the old man bent over his desk, an open Bible at his elbow.

"Ah, Daniel, and bearing gifts," he said cheerily, sweeping aside some papers. "Put it here. And take that chair, if you don't mind."

The chair was cavernous, and Dan sank into it gratefully.

"Good journey?"

"Not too bad. The roads…"

"Good. Good."

"There was silence while Stephen poured himself a cup and drank from it noisily.

"Now then," he said, dabbing at his lips with a pristine white handkerchief, "there's only one question I need ask you. Could have asked it over the phone, of course. Sorry to have brought you all this way, but there we are."

"So what's the question?" murmured Dan uneasily.

Stephen eyes twinkled. "Philosophically, or pragmatically?" he asked, but Dan didn't rise to the bait.

"Whatever."

"Yes, well…" Stephen said musingly. "What *is* the real question here, I wonder? Well, I suppose it's whether or not you really love Hadissa. That's about it. Yes, I think, maybe, everything depends on that, don't you think?"

The voice was quiet, slightly donnish but uncompromising, and Dan was immediately irritated, recalling all too well this pedantic manner of Stephen's, which on the surface appeared affable enough, even vague, but underneath could be extremely hard-hitting. He tried to contain his

244

resentment. It wouldn't do him any good to get angry. Anger, he thought balefully, would be the last card that he would play, but he would play it if necessary. He'd predicted this; Stephen at his desk like a headmaster confronting a recalcitrant schoolboy, himself in the lower chair.

"Stephen, I didn't need to come here," he said tightly. "I've come out of respect for you and because I know you have an interest in Hadissa, but that's as far as it goes. I'm afraid, contrary to what you may think, you don't have any jurisdiction over me."

"No, I know," said Stephen unexpectedly. He smiled sweetly. Dan had forgotten the sweetness of Stephen's smile but he didn't return it. He scowled instead and shifted impatiently in his chair.

"But, you see, my dear chap, I'm a priest. Like it or not, that gives me authority over souls, and I believe you have one? As for having 'an interest in Hadissa', isn't that a strange way of putting it? I'm concerned about her, as I am about you."

"About *me*?"

"Daniel, I've always been concerned about you. If I weren't a priest it wouldn't be relevant. Considering the unfortunate circumstances with which we're faced, that might actually please me very much. But, whether I like it or not, you're part of the equation. There are certain things I'd like to say, and there are certain things I'd like to know, but it really all comes down to that one question." He smiled. "Answer that, and we're home and dry, one way or t'other!"

Dan leant back in the chair. "You've no right to ask me about my relationship with Hadissa," he said quietly.

"I can still ask! You can refuse to answer, if you like, and that's *your* right! But that horrible word 'relationship', Daniel! Why can't you say 'love'? Why's it so difficult? Either you love her, in which case no doubt you'll want to marry her, or you don't. 'Love, cherish, in sickness and in health', etc – know what I mean? Either you see her for who she is, an innocent, unpretentious girl from the bush..."

"Not that innocent..." Dan growled.

"From the *bush*, Daniel," he repeated, prodding the desk with a forefinger. "She's hardly someone who's sophisticated, in our terms, or particularly experienced, except where it really matters, in matters of life and death. Or you don't. And if you don't, then you've acted very wrongly; you've ignored the *fact* of who she is and blinded yourself to everything but her sex. And I'm afraid I must say that, even if you love her, you've behaved with a singular disregard for the consequences."

He paused, watching Dan's face. "Now, I can't believe you're really like that, Daniel. I really can't believe that the man who was so compassionate and, yes, well, I'll say it, prophetic, in Kaduna, could be so... um, how shall I put it? Cold-hearted."

Dan grimaced. "No, I'm not cold-hearted."

Stephen shook his head sadly. "Don't you think, Daniel, that there's something significant about the fact that *that* was the only word you picked up on, out of all that I've just said to you? You didn't pick up on anything I said about Hadissa, and after all, she's the reason you're here."

"Is it? You just said you were concerned about *me*."

"Isn't it the same thing?"

Dan was silent. He rubbed the stubble on his chin, unable to meet Stephen's eyes. The old man was just too shrewd and he was finding it increasingly difficult to cope with his excruciatingly direct manner. He eyed his empty cup, which lay, as yet untouched, on the desk.

"As I see it," Stephen continued. "And God knows, I hope I'm not mistaken – it's a question of pride. You're a proud man, Daniel, but it makes you rather inclined to dismiss what you don't understand, or what makes you uncomfortable. I think that's what's happening at the moment. You see the truth of something, but if it's inconvenient or demanding, you rule it out of court. Sooner or later, my dear chap, the court catches up with us, and then all we can do is pray that God doesn't treat us in the way that we've *ill*-treated him!"

"I haven't..."

Stephen interrupted him. "You haven't ill-treated him? That's what you were going to say, isn't it? What d'you think you have been doing with Hadissa? It *is* the same thing, don't you see? 'Whatsoever you do to one of the least of my little ones, you do unto me.' Remember?"

"Oh, for God's sake, Stephen...!"

"Precisely."

"...Do you *have* to bring in the Bible?"

"Hmm, yes. I'm rather out of my depth, you see, and it's the only guide I've got."

246

They looked at each other in silence, and Dan remembered the fencing matches he'd endured in tutorials.

"You mind if I have a cup of coffee? I haven't had any breakfast."

"Oh, my dear chap, what a selfish old blankety-blank I am…!" Stephen swung round in his swivel chair, reached out for the jug of coffee and poured out a cup for him, spilling some into the saucer. "I do hope it's not cold! Milk and sugar? I'm sorry, I get carried away." He chuckled. "We want to make an impact on you, don't we, but we don't want to absolutely crush you, no, no!"

Dan met his eyes, and his mouth twitched slightly at this attempt to be avuncular. "You're not going to lynch me, then?"

Stephen smiled. "Not at all! Never crossed my mind!" He chuckled. "I won't answer for Verity, but… Should I, though?" he asked, raising his eyebrows, his eyes a piercing blue.

Dan looked at him doubtfully. "…Perhaps."

"Well, we'll see," said Stephen comfortably. "Now, sit back in your chair and relax, and we'll deal with chapter two."

"Chapter two?"

"Chapter one was pride. We'll come back to that." His eyes gleamed and Dan breathed a sigh of relief. The old man was incredibly devious, but he wouldn't mind if he could really help him see his way. What he minded was being put in the dock. I bet this is what it'll be like, he thought irreverently, when I get to heaven… but Stephen was speaking again and he didn't have time to finish the thought.

"You see, you've neglected to see her as a real person. You've only seen her through your own eyes. That's not…"

"How else can I see her except through my own eyes?"

Stephen pounced on that. "God doesn't see her through your eyes, so why should you?"

"I'm not God."

"I'm glad you've realised that…"

"Oh, come on, Stephen, that's unfair!"

"Is it? You *act* as if you've the power over life and death – isn't that playing God?"

"Not in my book!"

"No, perhaps not, but it is in mine!" Stephen thumped his Bible sharply. They were quiet, then Stephen said softly,

"But if you love someone, Daniel…" He hesitated, and then looked at Dan as if suddenly making up his mind. He put on his thick glasses, picked up the Bible, and began to leaf through the pages. Dan groaned to himself.

"Oh, don't sigh like that, Daniel… and don't frown, either! I know you hate all this, but bear with me, there's a good chap! I'm only a fuddy-duddy old clergyman doing his thing. Now, where are we, yes…" He paused, looking at Dan over his spectacles. "D'you know, Daniel, when couples get married, this is often their favourite reading. Goes hand in hand with *I'll Do It My Way* – which you, no doubt, can relate to! Of course it's not exactly unknown," he rumbled, "but when you're preparing people for marriage and you show them this passage, it's sometimes as if they've never seen it before. Some of them haven't, of course, especially these days. People don't really know their Bibles anymore, do they?" He was squinting at the words through his pebble lenses and muttering, almost to himself. "But even those who know it see it with new eyes. It takes on a new, very relevant, meaning. As I hope it will for you. Yes, here we are. Here's what it says about love. Are you sitting comfortably?"

He did not wait for Dan's reply, but began to recite.

"'If I speak in the tongues of men and of angels, but have not love, I am a noisy gong or a clanging cymbal…'" He interrupted himself. "This isn't about sex, Daniel, or even infatuation. It's about caring. Now, where was I? '…And if I have prophetic powers…' That's you, old chap, in Kaduna… 'and understand all mysteries…' which you don't, and neither do I, thank God! Dum- de-dum, 'but have not love, I am nothing…' Caring, remember. 'If I give away all that I have, and if I deliver my body to be burnt, but have not love, I gain nothing. Love is patient and kind…' dum-de-dum… yes, here: 'Love bears all things, believes all things, hopes all things, endures all things.'

Hear that, Daniel? *Endures*. That's your task. It means to bear the burden. 'Love never ends…' Dum-de-dum-de-dum… 'When I was a child I spoke like a child, I thought like a child, I reasoned like a child, but when I became a man I put away childish things. For now we see but a dim reflection in a mirror, but then face to face…'" He closed the book and looked at Dan through eyes that were very bright.

"Fancy a walk in the garden? By the time we come in,

Verity'll have got lunch ready. You stay, can't you, old chap? It would please us both very much. Come and see our vegetable plot. Verity handles most of the growing. I just do the spadework. The story of our life."

*   *   *

The back door opened on to a gravelled path which led towards an arch of stripped willow, and beyond, Dan could see the remains of courgette and cabbage plants, their leaves dry and yellow, flattened on the earth. The sun was shining, and the fruit trees, some with shrivelled apples on their topmost twigs, cast heavy shadows across the long grass.

"This is a very special place to us," Stephen commented. "We get a good harvest from it, and that's important, not just for us, but for the parish. We run it on the basis of 'pick-your-own'. We own; they pick."

Dan nodded politely. Stephen's habit of leaping from one subject to another was one that he remembered from college. It had discouraged him then, for it made him lose his train of thought, and it had the same effect now. Stephen, however, had read his mind.

"Ah, sublime to the ridiculous, eh? Well, you may be right. But when the subject under discussion is oneself a taste of the ridiculous is sometimes salutary, don't you think? Helps you to see things in proportion. We mustn't be too serious, must we? Except, of course, where Hadissa is concerned, and then, I'm afraid, we must be very serious indeed. Especially with regard to intent, eh, Daniel? Come and sit down on the bench, it's quite dry."

This was another ploy, thought Dan. It made him uneasy to have to sit so close to Stephen that he couldn't see his face, and he was even leaning forward slightly, crafty devil, just like that bomber in Kaduna.

"You think I intended to hurt her? Or that I didn't care? You do, don't you?"

Stephen hunched his shoulders, an infinitesimal shrug, and gazed out across the garden. "You've certainly behaved with a marked lack of caution," he replied dryly. "But then, both of you have." He spread his hands. "Just think, Daniel! A foreign country, a very challenging course of training, and then allowing

249

herself to get involved with *you*? *Well*! One does rather think of frying pans, you know. And, for goodness' sake, if you must have intercourse, surely you take precautions!"

"I thought *she* did..."

"That old turnip?" Stephen shook his head sadly. "My dear boy, what does she know of it? Still, she'll be chastened now. We just have to ensure she doesn't go under."

Dan was alarmed. "You think she might... What?"

"Daniel, I've no idea what a young girl in her position might do, let alone an African bush village girl. She mustn't do anything precipitous, poor little waif. You see, that's why we must know where you stand," he added mildly. "After all, you're the father of this child." He turned and faced him. "Have you thought of that, Daniel? You're going to be a father! Howzat grab you? Excited? Afraid? You should be! You won't say whether you love her, but you must at least see you've certain duties and obligations. As you said, you're not cold-hearted, and you're not a coward."

"No, I'm not, and I haven't said I don't love her."

"You haven't said you do, either!"

"Why should I?"

"My dear man, this is mere sophistry!" For the first time, Stephen showed his exasperation. "At least tell me how you left things..."

"She walked out on me," said Dan mulishly.

Stephen was astonished. "*She* walked out on *you*? I thought..."

"Well, you thought wrong." Dan's triumph was short-lived. "We were in my flat. I admit I didn't behave very well, and... she left."

Stephen laughed quietly to himself. "Oh, well done, Hadissa! Well, no doubt she has her pride, too. So what did you say to her to make her walk out?"

"I... the question of the baby came up, and..."

"The question of the baby? There's surely no question... She *is* pregnant?"

"I mean... I'm afraid I... not in so many words of course, but I sort of... suggested it might be a good idea if she... Well, if she saw someone..."

"Why not come right out with it, Daniel? You mean have an abortion. And what did she say to that nice idea? I expect she jumped at the chance!"

"No, she just left," he said miserably. "She didn't give me a chance to explain…"

"What was there to explain? Seems explicit enough to me!"

They were quiet for long moments. Stephen could have nothing left to say, thought Dan.

"So it's not just me you need to blame," he said reasserting himself.

"No?"

"No. It was her choice, to walk out. I couldn't have stopped her if I'd tried."

"Really."

Dan was silent. Slowly, as he inhaled the cool air though his nostrils, he discerned something not entirely fresh and wholesome – rotting cabbage leaves, perhaps. He felt bleak and very much alone. He got to his feet. Suddenly he wanted to leave; now, even before lunch. He'd had enough of Stephen. He had survived his onslaught, his frigid passionless morality, and now all he wanted was to get back into his car, turn the heat right up, and make for the nearest pub.

"Don't lose heart."

Stephen had spoken to his back, almost in a whisper, and Dan suddenly found himself overwhelmed with emotion. He rubbed his eyes with fingers that felt stiff and cold.

"I didn't mean to hurt her!" he said, his voice muffled. "I do want us to make some sort of life together. I can't let her go, I really can't! The baby… it's just come at a bad time, that's all. I couldn't see my way… And there're so many unanswered questions! Like," he said ironically, turning to face his accuser, "whether we love each other enough… It's not been long, after all! I thought that, if we could finish this year, and find somewhere to live and settle down together…"

"Not marry her, Daniel?"

Dan rushed on, "*Yes*, but only if it seems right! And *then* have a child! Not now, not right in the middle of the school year! She's no idea of the pressures I'm under!"

"Perhaps you should tell her."

"Oh, she wouldn't understand," he said tiredly.

"How can she, if you don't share?"

"Stephen, it's not her world. Anyway, she's put me on

251

some sort of pedestal... She relies on me for everything... thinks I'm a pillar of strength."

"Well, who made her like that? Anyway, now she knows you're not. So *talk* to her."

"How *can* I? I haven't seen her for days!"

"Hmm..." Stephen said. "Well, I think she's actually behaved very well, all things considered. She could have bent your arm a bit, you know."

"I know." Dan groaned, and sat down again. "God, I feel like chucking myself in the river!"

Stephen did not touch him or move to put his arm around him, but sat there on the cold bench silently listening. Then he said, "'A humble and contrite spirit', Daniel, not a defeated one, and not some sort of burnt offering, either."

Dan snorted. "God, you do talk such rubbish, sometimes..." He sat down again.

"Seems that way, does it?"

"'Burnt offering' – honestly, it's archaic. At least, it is to me. I don't know about your flock. Maybe they like it."

"I meant it literally. It's not a guilt trip, Daniel. God doesn't want to see you defeated by this."

"But, 'burnt offering', Stephen! What's that got to do with love? If someone cares about you, how could they want...? I just can't grasp it. It seems cock-eyed to me... extremely one-sided, too..." He floundered.

"It's an image, that's all. It's not meant to be taken literally, though there were enough martyrs in the early church for it to have been literal then! It's using extreme language to describe extreme love; the ultimate sacrifice to preserve something or someone greater than yourself. You know, Daniel, this question of who's to blame: if one finger points accusingly, well, three point back at yourself."

"Well, what have *you* been doing, if not accusing *me*?"

"Have I accused?" asked Stephen mildly. "Or have I just mirrored your own thoughts? No, truly to love means truthful loving. Just turn it round, as you *must*, whenever you start to question. Turn towards what's really true, and you'll find it's the presence of God."

This was changing the goalposts and Dan became quite desperate to get away. But he couldn't leave yet. Stephen was still talking.

"Now you see yourself as you really are, and you don't like what you see, do you? I'm not surprised; it's a very common experience. I wonder how I can look myself in the mirror sometimes! And you know why? Because it's not accusing, but judging. Accusations without moral judgement are destructive; they create anger, and anger blurs the real picture; you take refuge behind it and don't deal with the issues. No, Daniel, it's God we see in the mirror, and, although in a way it *is* judgement, it's a judgement of mercy, and it's entirely loving and forgiving. The questions you're finding it so difficult to answer are his questions. Didn't you find you were asking uncomfortable questions?"

Dan was silent.

"I take it that's a 'yes'? Well, where did you imagine they came from, out of the blue? You pride yourself on being intelligent, Daniel, or at last reasonable. But you're more emotional than you think. We're made in the image of God, and so your questions, my questions, Hadissa's questions, they're *his* questions, prompting us to take a good look at ourselves and then *move on*, for heaven's sake! Not to stagnate, and not to delude ourselves! You're in a prison of your own making, you know. Well, let's get you free!"

They got up, and began to walk back through the garden.

Stephen smiled. "I'm a tenacious old fool," he said. "I don't give up easily, and I'm really sorry, old chap, if you think I'm accusing you. You must trust that some of the things I say to you are the truth. My whole sad experience of life tells me so, and my own sins and failings. You went to Coventry, didn't you? Well, you know, the burning of Coventry Cathedral was a great evil in itself, and that's indisputable, but out of it came restoration and renewal, one joined vision, a vision of moving on. That was what you said in Kaduna, and that's what I say to you." He punched his knuckles together. "*That's* what love is all about, and *that's* what you have to do with Hadissa. I think you truly love her, Daniel, but you're panicking. More than that, I think you need her as much as she needs you. But how you work it out is your own concern. If you stay with her you'll face an enormous uphill task, and if you don't, it may be your ruin. But whatever you decide to do, for God's sake do it for the right reasons! Either way you must say to her what God would have you say, the plain, unadulterated truth, whatever it may be.

Rather than thinking you're God, which is what she might be thinking you're thinking!"

He chuckled. "Work that one out, mate."

*　　*　　*

Verity met them on the path, her face anxious. "Stephen, I've just had Joanna on the phone. It seems Hadissa's gone off somewhere. Jo's worried. She hasn't seen her for two whole days!"

"But she must have!" Dan protested. "She's living in her house!"

Verity looked at him neutrally. "Dan, you know as well as I do that if they do different shifts they don't see very much of each other. That's what Jo thought must have happened this time, but now she's scared…"

Dan moved quickly towards the back door. "Is Joanna still there? Can I talk to her?"

"She rang off…"

Dan turned, and Verity was struck by his expression. He had paled and his eyes looked haunted, but he spoke firmly.

"Then I'll ring her back!"

Verity and Stephen hovered nearby while he dialled, then they heard Joanna's voice answering. Her voice was clearly audible, excited and angry, and in spite of her anxiety Verity suppressed a smile. She knew what Joanna was like when she was roused, and she was roused now.

Dan interrupted the flow. "Joanna, just tell me what you told your mother…. Well, it *is* my business! I'd have thought you, of all people, would realise that! …Yes. …Yes, I see. …No, we haven't seen each other… Yes, I know it's my fault… Joanna, I'm saying I *know* it's my fault… Well, now I want to put things right! Is there anywhere you can think of where she might be? Well, did she have any money? …What for? …*Christmas* presents?" He turned impatiently, his head lowered, his fist clenched on his hip. "Okay, but did she actually *go* shopping, or…? Oh, all right, don't bite my head off! Okay, let's go back a bit. Who might she go to? *Luke*? Why Luke? …Yes, miles away, somewhere in Warwickshire… No, probably by bus. Okay," he said, decisively. "Leave it with me. I'll contact him and see whether he's heard from her…"

Dan was silent, then, for what seemed to Verity a very long time, his eyes gleaming like slits in his white face.

"Well, you're mistaken," he said flatly, "I know I gave you that impression... I've already said it's my fault, you stupid girl! Now give me a chance to put things right! ...No!" He suddenly shouted. "You're wrong! I do love her, and I want to marry her! Now get off the phone and let me do something about making it happen!"

# CHAPTER 9

During the days that followed her abrupt departure from Daniel's flat, Hadissa lived in a perpetual state of anxiety. She did not know what to do, where to go, or what would become of her. Her module had come to an end but it was some days before she was due in Ely for Christmas, and the thought of spending long hours cooped up in Joanna's house, under her eye, was distasteful in the extreme. Yet there seemed no obvious alternative. She felt that her world had turned upside down, that what had been reliable points of reference had shifted; the minutiae of her life; the necessity to work and study, her sporadic encounters with Joanna, even her relationship with Daniel, which had consumed so many hours of her time – all this was gone. Daniel's rejection of the child in her womb had made her feel more vulnerable than at any time in her life. It was worse than when she lived at home. It was worse than when her Igbo lover had left her.

The imperatives to eat, to sleep and to get up again in the morning remained the same, but their exact significance eluded her. She knew they had to be done if her world was not to descend entirely into chaos, and she was aware that she must try to remain healthy, if not for her own sake, then for the sake of her unborn child. Beyond that nothing was clear.

For the first few days, she occupied herself with putting her notes in order, doing some washing and, when Joanna was in the house, feigning absence or sleep. One evening, she made her way through the maze of roads to stand outside Daniel's house, but the door was closed and the windows seemed bland and inhospitable. In any case, even if she had seen him, what could she have said to him? As she returned timorously through the deserted, frosty streets, she felt a sensation of being pursued by some stern and relentless being, and she became afraid and quickened her pace; glad, when she got home, to shut the door behind her. Yet, after a few days, she realised that, if she stayed indoors any longer, her spirit would turn inwards upon itself and she would be completely lost. Another night, oppressed by the sheer weight of her loneliness, and fearing she was becoming anonymous, she walked down into the more populated area of the city centre, and wandered through the shopping precinct, huddled in her coat against the freezing rain, her fists gripping the fabric inside her pockets. She thought if she could walk again amongst people of her own age she might regain a sense of perspective, but it was the Christmas vacation, and all trace of student life had disappeared. Those who remained passed her by, seemingly oblivious to her shadowy presence, as if cancelling her out, a nameless wraith. It was so much the reverse of what she needed that she had to use all her will power not to turn and flee.

Once she caught sight of her reflection in an unlit shop window. It seemed to her that her dark figure in its dark coat, with its black face and short black hair, was of a unity with the darkness and blackness within, as if that was the world where she now belonged, and only there. The two largest omens in her life, the slow growth of the, as yet, quiescent child, and the unexpected void left by Daniel, appeared to be converging on each other, and she was terrified of what the future might bring. Possessed of the one, but bereft of the other, life seemed to have taken on a new and unwelcome clarity, yet, nevertheless, she felt out of focus, a nobody, cut off from the living. When she looked at herself in the mirror she was full of self-loathing. What had become of the revelation of God in the cathedral, of that strong sense of his protecting arms, of her renewed decision to embrace the tasks he had set before her? Once again, and this time irremediably, she had failed, and this time her deficiencies would be exposed to an observing and judgemental world. With fear and trembling she saw her life laid out behind and before her as one great, unbroken sequence of faults and imperfections, empty of meaning and completely barren of purpose.

One day she woke early. The thin curtains over her window were closed, but a diffused, watery light penetrated her room and fell across her pillow. She had been dreaming, and although the images quickly became elusive, she was left with a strange residual impression of a voice calling her name from a great distance. It was a whisper, no more than a dying fall, but it gave her hope and a thought began to form in her mind. At first it seemed no more than the first stirrings of an idea, as nebulous and undefined as she felt herself to be, but then, as it took root, it began to burn within her and to weigh on her with the force of a command. Abruptly, she knew that she must search once more for the inner resources of spiritual strength, for, in that way, she might find wholeness and healing for her troubled mind.

All that was necessary was for the thought to occur and she immediately felt a resurgence of energy and vigour. Now she knew what to do and where she would go. 'Underneath are the everlasting arms...' – the biblical words suddenly held a new and comforting resonance. She would place herself once more within the wellsprings of God. She would go back to the cathedral in Coventry. She would enter once more the mysterious concrete recess in the Chapel of Unity where she had glimpsed his presence. There, in that hollow aperture of stone, which so resembled the mud hut of her childhood, and in the shelter of his arms, she would lay the remnants of her dreams. She would take her hopes and desires back to their very source. Would not her going in and her coming out somehow be sanctified, and while she stayed there, would she not be guarded from all ill?

*  *  *

Nothing was familiar, for Hadissa had not been in this part of the city before. Inside the bus station was a map, but she was unable to get her bearings. 'You Are Here', the text read – almost like an affirmation of life – and below it, 'Pool Meadow Bus Station'. She returned to the door, but instead of a pool or a meadow she was surrounded by high office blocks draped in scaffolding, and nearby a bypass roared overhead.

"I'm sorry, but can you tell me, please? Where is the cathedral?"

The third person she asked pointed across the road.

"It's through there, isn't it, love?" he said, indicating the arch of a hotel that spanned the road. "You can't miss it."

As she walked up the road towards the cathedral the sun came out, creating a welcoming roseate glow on its looming walls, and her spirits rose. A wide flight of steps led between the porch and the brown, war-damaged arches of the ruins beyond, and she climbed them and then stood, irresolute. The door to the cathedral was on her right, but the ruins beckoned compellingly. She decided to stand once more under the charred cross, and begin her vigil there. As she approached the apse, she noticed that in the empty windows were tiny fragments of coloured glass, bright blues and reds, redolent of how these windows might once have looked, and the place seemed suddenly less formidable. Below, on a wooden board, a prayer had been inscribed, the 'Coventry Litany', but as the words, 'envy', 'pride' and 'lust' leapt out at her, she turned away unhappily. Not yet, she thought shakily; I've only just arrived. I'm judging myself enough as it is.

Below the steps she found washrooms, and this pleased her; at least she could remain clean and fill up her water bottle. She did not intend to buy any food, and in any case, her bus ride had consumed most of the money that she had borrowed from Joanna, and she must save some for her return journey, whenever that would be. She would drink plenty of water but, apart from that, she would fast and pray, and wait for God. In that way, she thought, I can at least hope to stand within his mercy. What happens then remains to be seen.

Hadissa ignored the tourists, confident that they would move on rapidly, but she stood among them for a minute in front of the intensely bright baptistery window, once more diverted by the immensity of it, entranced by the strong colours that reminded her so much of her own country. She avoided looking at the tapestry at the far end, afraid to meet the expression in the eyes, but her breath caught in her throat like a sob, for when she had come with Daniel, she had been happy, and had not known she was pregnant.

The Chapel of Unity was empty and silent, although she could still hear the patter of feet and the murmur of visitors in the nave, and the occasional lifted voice. She saw with distaste that one of the alcoves in this star-shaped chapel was filled with stacked chairs and piles of books, and in another, a lectern, and that yet another was completely blocked by a black upright piano. Her own chosen recess was resonant with light and colour, but on the side of the chapel away from the sun they were merely cavities of dismal, monochrome concrete, although she knew that, as the sun moved round, her own narrow space would be equally dull.

Satisfied that that she had reacquainted herself with the

place, she turned back into her own small secluded space and knelt down on the cold marble floor, bowing her head and making herself go still. She needed to find that interior quietness within which God might come, as she believed he had come to her while she, unmindful, had grown from child to woman, and in the chaos and disorder of the hospital ward. He had called her name, there, and on her journey next day to Kateri, and while out in the bush – surely he would come now, in his own place. Surely he would recognise her and call her by name, for she was defenceless now, no longer seeking to raise deceitful barriers against his word. All that, she felt, was finally done with.

The hours passed quickly and it seemed nothing would disturb her, but towards the middle of the afternoon a hand touched her gently on the shoulder. It startled her, and she swung round. A man was standing by her, holding a woven hassock.

"I saw you kneeling here," he said diffidently, "so I've brought you this." He indicated the hassock. "You shouldn't kneel so long on the bare floor, you know. It's bad for your knees."

Hadissa marvelled that anyone should feel such concern for her, and she looked at him closely. He was dressed in a light brown cassock and his sandy hair and moustache was so much the exact opposite to her own sultry darkness that she almost smiled. Then she saw that behind the thick lenses of his spectacles his eyes were examining her closely.

"There's a cafeteria downstairs," he said. "Thought you might like to know. Get a hot drink sometime, eh? And there's a Eucharist at midday, if you're interested, or evensong at five-thirty."

"Can I just listen from here?" she asked. "I need to be by myself."

"Why, are you here for the whole day?"

"...Yes."

"Well, of course you can, but actually the Eucharist takes place in here. If you don't want to take part just sit quietly at the back. And, I must warn you, after evensong we close up and then the doors are locked for the night. I'll make sure you aren't shut in," he added, turning to leave her alone.

"Are you a priest?" she asked.

"Yes. I'm on duty here today."

He seemed so approachable that she took her courage in

her hands. "Can I ask you something?"

"Of course. Go ahead."

"I just..." Her voice was tremulous and she hardly knew how to form the words. "Do you believe... Do you believe that, if you pray, God comes?" He looked at her silently for a moment, appraising her, and then he indicated the circle of chairs.

"We could sit here, if you like, and talk for a while. We can ignore any interruptions."

Hadissa got to her feet obediently, surprised at how stiff and chilled she already felt, and sat down one of the chairs. He took another, and turned it round so that he could face her, and settled himself with his arms folded across his chest.

"You want to know whether God comes, if you pray."

She nodded.

"The answer is: God has already come," he said quietly. "There is nowhere and nothing that doesn't have the presence of God in it, for he's in every created thing. You know this already, don't you? You're a Christian?"

"Yes... but I seek him here... for a reason."

"Do you want to talk about it?"

"Not... not yet. But I would be glad if you... if you'd speak about... about God to me."

"Well, you know, the fact that you're in this place at all means that you're searching for God, and if you sincerely search, you will find. But, you know, he's also where you came from today."

She lowered her head. "I've not found him there."

"But you're the same person there as you are here! Everything is connected, you see. Let me give you an example. If you create something, a building like this, for instance, or even a child, you're in that creation, yes?"

Hadissa wondered if he had noticed her pregnancy. She gave a slight nod, sitting very still and listening intently.

"Well, we are what we do and we are what we make, and it's the same with God. You and I, we believe that God made the whole world and therefore everything is connected to God. You came here, for whatever reason, but wanting to pray, yes? Well, when you do that, you're seeking to become one with God, and, because you're seeking, you're already no longer separate from Him. If you continue to pray, there'll come a moment when it will no longer be possible to know where you end or he begins. Then you'll find that you've been in the presence of God all along."

Hadissa was quiet. "I've not been good," she said, her head drooping. "I don't... deserve... that he should come."

"My dear child, none of us is good, and none of us *deserves* that he should come, yet he does! It's not, in any case, a question of deserving. Whatever people say, he's not in the punishment-reward business! And largely, how we feel about what we've done or not done is its own punishment or reward. No, he comes with forgiveness. He comes with terrible, terrible compassion and he comes with love. And all that's required of *you* is to love, and you're already on the road."

While he had been speaking, Hadissa had become increasingly distressed. She tried to hide it from him, but the effort caused her to tremble inside her coat so that she could hardly speak.

"...I understand. I have seen... something of this... Thank you."

"Tell me," he said, "you're using the alcove for prayer, aren't you?"

She nodded, her eyes black and wide and rimmed with unshed tears. Was he going to forbid her?

"Have you been right in?" he asked, getting to his feet. "There's a triangle of glass there. It's not until you go right up to it that you realise it's a mirror. Come and see."

They turned back to her alcove and he gestured to her to go in. She looked down. It was true, there was a mirror there, and in it she could see the tower of glass above her, all thirty feet of it, reflected downwards, vertiginous, like an abyss, and she drew back.

"It is so deep! It looks as though I'm right down there!"

"Only a mirror, my dear!" His voice came from nearby. "It's like a deep pit, isn't it? And a bit of a riddle, to discover him in the pit with us, as well."

He turned to go. "Well, I'll leave you to your prayers. If you want to talk more, well, I'll be here until we close and I'll be back tomorrow. If you want me, just ask for David. That's my name. Anyone here will tell you where I am."

He reached the doorway, then, as an afterthought, he said, "Remember the Eucharist here at midday. Just so you don't get alarmed when people begin to come in. Perhaps I'll see you then?"

"…Yes," she replied, guardedly. "If I'm still here."

\* \* \*

Hadissa slipped out just before evensong and wandered around the ruins, waiting for the service to finish and people to leave. She knew what she had to do. They would be locking the doors for the night, but she anticipated that if she could creep back into the chapel and find somewhere to hide, they would assume she had left with them, and then she could stay there all night. In the morning, she would go out and wash, and then wander in again as though she was simply resuming her visit.

Back in the chapel she looked round for a likely spot. Her eyes fell on the piano. She picked up her bag and the hassock, tiptoed across and gently pushed it aside, squeezed into the gap behind it and huddled down in her coat. Now she resembled nothing more than a dark heap of abandoned clothing. Apart from the odd settling sounds of a building at night, the cathedral was quiet, and the lights were off. A clock ticked somewhere and the heating droned, far underground. Outside she could hear people talking and she wondered if one of them was her kindly priest. It did not matter. No one would disturb her now. Outside darkness was falling, but somewhere nearby the faint glow of a streetlamp lit the narrow window, a pale imitation of sunlight, but enough to give it colour.

She cast her mind back over the preceding months and years and, one by one, began to summon up the events that had led her so far astray from the plan that God had intended for her. A hard knot formed in her throat, the tightness of unshed tears. She hugged her stomach where the baby slept and peered into the faintly gleaming mirror at the apex of her recess. Down there was the pit, into which she might throw everything that was wrong and ill intentioned and remiss. Yet she knew it was only an illusion – the pit was inside her. That was the reality. She had turned her back on God, and gone her own way. Again and again it had ended in disaster, and this time was worse then any other, for this time she carried within her belly the misbegotten fruits of what she knew to be her dishonest and immoral relationship with Daniel. Dishonest, for she realised she did not truly love him.

She did not accuse him, but her guilt at her own part in it, and her remorse, were acute, and she felt full of despair. Her tears burst from her and she began to sob; hard, rending sobs, which shook her whole body. Still her thoughts gave her no respite. Life, she felt, had defeated and broken her. On her heart was the leaden weight of anxiety about the future, and the shame she must carry for the rest of her life. From now on she would be an outcast. She knew that she would never find a husband to love her and protect her.

The night threatened to be very cold, and the long evening passed slowly. Once she was roused from her contemplation by the sound of running feet outside, followed by raucous laughter, but eventually the sounds faded and the silence returned. It was what she had wanted. She had no fear of the night and no qualms about staying illicitly inside the cathedral. To her it was a safe haven, a sanctuary, but the hours of the night passed more slowly than she had anticipated. After a long while she began to feel very cold, her legs and ankles chilled by the marble floor, and she had cramp in her thighs.

She became desperate to find something with which to warm herself. Placing her hands squarely on the floor in front of her, she moved slowly forward on to all fours, and then got to her feet, stretching her aching back. She took a long icy drink from her water bottle, and left the shadowy chapel, feeling her way in the darkness. The orange glow of the city sky shone through the huge glass wall of the west end, the light stretching down through the nave to reveal tables on which pamphlets and papers lay in neat piles. Every chair had its own woven hassock hanging from it, and she took two, laying them alongside the one David had given her, and with that added warmth the rest of the night passed more comfortably. She struggled to keep awake, but it was a vain attempt. Eventually she slid sideways in her narrow alcove, leant against the wall and slept.

# CHAPTER 10

"What on *earth* do you think you're doing here? Get up *immediately*! Come on, get *up*!"

The voice was female, elderly and peremptory, and it woke Hadissa from a deep sleep. For a moment she did not know where she was and she looked up fearfully. It was early on the second morning of her vigil. Having successfully hidden herself for two nights, she had been lulled into a false sense of security and, deeply tired, had fallen into a profound slumber, so that not even the advancing light had wakened her. In fact it seemed earlier than it actually was, for the weather had worsened overnight and now a light snow was falling, making the narrow window of her alcove dim and featureless.

"This is outrageous! Have you been here all *night*?"

Mustering what dignity she had left, Hadissa raised herself into a sitting position, gathering the folds of her coat protectively around her. She watched the woman nervously, wondering what would happen next. She made an effort to tidy the hassocks on which she had been sleeping, piling them neatly against the wall, but it was a futile gesture, and she knew it. She stood up, clutching her bag in front of her, mutely gazing at the floor. Was there to be no end to her sufferings?

"You just wait here! I'm going to fetch someone. *Then* you'll see! Don't you *dare* move!"

It was David who came, hurrying up the nave from his office in response to the woman's call. From where Hadissa now stood, silent and trembling at the top of the steps, she could hear the officiously complaining voice as they approached. She shivered, and it was not entirely from fear. She was cold, colder than she had ever been in her life, chilled through to the bone.

She thought, irrelevantly, he must have just arrived; his coat is wet. He was looking at her quizzically, the woman frowning by his side.

"Oh, it's you!" he said gently. "And have you really

265

been here all night? What a good idea!"

The woman was incensed. "*David*!"

He took her arm gently. "Well now, Mildred, don't you think that shows some spunk? I can't think of anyone who's done that before, except, of course, at Easter. But it's not a new custom. The saints of old used to stay up all night fasting and praying. A pity, in a way, that it's gone out of fashion."

He winked slyly at Hadissa, and steered the woman away.

"Mildred, my dear, leave this with me. I'm sure you're very busy..."

The woman left, darting a glance of animosity at Hadissa, who looked around, seeking some way of escape, and only then became aware that the pavement and steps outside were covered in snow. It lay, undisturbed by any wind, on the steps, and clung to the delicate stonework of the arches. Above she could see more flakes falling gently down under the high porch.

"It's snowing!" Her voice was filled with wonder and David looked at her curiously.

"Have you never seen snow before?"

"No, never! It's... beautiful!"

"May I ask you now," he said courteously, "to tell me your name."

"...Hadissa."

"You live in Coventry?"

"No, in Cambridge," she replied cautiously. "I'm studying there. I'm Nigerian, from Kaduna State."

"Kaduna? What a coincidence! Our cathedral has links there."

"I know... the clinic in Kateri village."

"You know Kateri?"

"I... I'm to work there. I'm... from there."

She faltered. Part of her was still reacting to the shock of having been discovered, but she was also becoming increasingly aware of how cold and hungry she now was. Tears sprang to her eyes.

"Can I go?" she asked timidly. "I must find a hot drink. I'm very cold."

His eyes sharpened. "You really *have* been fasting and praying? Waiting for God, you said. So, did he come?"

266

Her reply was inaudible and she held herself tightly. She was on the edge of breaking down, and he saw it.

"Come with me," he commanded. "You're quite right, what you need now is food and drink. We can get that downstairs. And then, if you want to, we can talk."

He took her down a flight of steps, which led to the undercroft. Halfway down she stopped, mesmerised by the sight of a crude charcoal drawing of a pregnant woman, mounted on the wall.

"You like that?" he asked, observing her. "It's the Leningrad Madonna. A soldier did it on the eve of war."

"Is she black?" she whispered, transfixed.

"It's charcoal, but probably not. She'd have been Russian, you see."

"*I'm* carrying a child..."

"My dear girl!" he expostulated. "What can you have been thinking of?"

She looked at him, bewildered.

*"You could have caught your death of cold!" he exclaimed. "For heaven's sake, let's get some food inside you!"*

He led her through the undercroft to a small cafeteria where women were laying cloths on the tables, then he deposited her near the radiator, and went up to the counter. She waited passively, hugging the radiator for warmth and thinking how like Luke he was in his grave formality. The thought brought her back to herself for the first time since she had woken, and when David returned and laid the food in front of her, she asked him if he knew Luke.

"Do you know his surname?"

"No, I don't think I ever heard it. But he came to Nigeria last summer..."

"Ah, that Luke! Yes, indeed, he's a curate in Long Compton, in the south of the diocese."

"Many miles away," she said sorrowfully.

"Nowhere in our diocese is very far away. About an hour's drive. Why? D'you want to contact him?"

"There's no one else..."

"Well," he said, getting up again, "eat up and I'll go and telephone him. Someone should be looking after you, that's for sure."

Under the inquisitive eyes of the waitresses Hadissa

slowly ate her toast and drank her tea, thankful for the warmth and comfort it gave her. When David returned he saw that she had stopped shaking, and he was glad. He hadn't liked the look of her standing up there under Mildred's hostile eyes. She'd looked almost grey, although with her colour it was difficult to tell. She was sitting hunched up in her chair and her head still drooped with weariness, but she looked better, and there was some warmth in her cheeks.

"He was already in the city and he's on his way. He says he'll take you home with him. Is that okay? Seemed to me the best thing..." She nodded listlessly. "But Luke's not your only friend, you know. He tells me there're quite a few people who're worried about you. Apparently you didn't tell anyone where you were going."

She hung her head still further.

"Do you want to talk about it?" he asked gently.

Hadissa hesitated, then shook her head. "Not really," she said shyly. "It's all so complicated. But I liked what you said before. I'd like to listen to you."

He grinned at her. "I don't need much encouragement." He leant forward, resting his elbows on the table, marshalling his thoughts. "To continue, then... He's a bit elusive sometimes, is God. Have you found that?" She nodded imperceptibly. "Well, you have to look for him where he may be found. He's not always found in big, dramatic acts, like the storm and the whirlwind, you know. He comes afterwards, in the 'still, small voice.' Ah, you know about that." He had seen her eyes light up.

"Yes, I've heard that before! When I was a child I heard it."

"It's a bit of a riddle but it's the truth."

Hadissa gazed at him intently for a long time, and then she broke down completely. She leant her elbows on the table and covered her face with her hands. Behind them, he could see the tears coursing down her cheeks. She made no effort to wipe them away. When she spoke her voice was a muted wail of despair and frustration, and she couldn't meet his eyes.

"He didn't come!" she sobbed. "If he knows I'm here, why didn't he come? He came to me in Africa, so why not here? I thought perhaps he... didn't recognise me. He came in the hospital – it was a terrible time, many wounded people – he called my name! And next day... he called my name again! He

268

called my *name*!" She swallowed convulsively, trying to control her voice. "And, later," she whispered, "there was a bomb... Many children hurt, many killed. He was there, then. But I've not listened to him and I've done bad things... Maybe it's too late, and *that's* why he hasn't come!"

"Have you family?" he asked, wondering why this waif of a girl seemed so unprotected.

"Yes. Some. But my father... he was..." She took a breath. "Long ago he was not... good to me, and I think I've been bad since then. Now I think, maybe I've been so bad that God has forgotten me or... turned his back on me... And I tried so hard to keep awake," she wailed, so plaintively that David would have smiled had he not been so moved by her story. "But I couldn't! It was so cold..."

He touched her arm. "You're too hard on yourself," he said gently. "'All have sinned and fallen short of the glory of God,' – that's in our Litany, you know. You might have seen it. It's written up under the charred cross in the Ruins."

"I saw... other words," she whispered, her voice falling, "I didn't see that bit."

"We see what we need to see," he said dryly, getting up. "Come on, my lass, we need to find out if Luke's arrived."

They began to mount the steps that led to the main body of the cathedral.

"And the prayer below the words," said David, looking at her intently, "you saw that? 'Father forgive'. Not 'Father, forgive *them*', but 'Father forgive'. We've all fallen short, you see, and we need to admit it, and start over. Admitting it is the first stage of coming to terms with it, and only by coming to terms with it will we learn to forgive – starting with ourselves. If you can't forgive yourself, then you won't be able to forgive other people. It's like a road – if you don't go down it yourself how will you know where it leads? But a word of warning, Hadissa. If you genuinely pray that prayer, there are consequences, as there are for everything. Once prayed, you see, it can't be un-prayed. We have to be prepared to change our way of life and even how we regard the people who've done us harm. You must move on if you can, my dear, and put some of these things behind you. And those things that seem attractive on the surface, but which are doing you harm; well, you must try to let go of them."

269

He added, more sternly, "And don't let anyone tell you otherwise, Hadissa. You must walk away from them." He touched her gently on her shoulder. "I don't deny it's a hard road, my dear, but if you trust in God, he won't let you down."

# CHAPTER 11

It had been snowing steadily for several hours and the roads were covered with a brown sludge of snow and grit, but by the time Dan reached the dual carriageway south of Northampton the roads were clear. Traffic was light, and he was soon able to put on speed. He drove like an automaton, and later remembered nothing of the journey.

He'd set off in a spirit of grim determination, but careering along the wet and slippery side roads of north Warwickshire, his mood had changed. What a farce that conversation with Stephen had been! How absurd, to let himself get into such a position where he, a grown man, had nearly burst into tears. He could hardly believe it of himself. Stephen's values were simply anachronistic, but, even now, he was forced to admit that what the old man had said about love was strangely compelling. That Bible reading about the dim reflection in a mirror had resonated with him strongly, given that it was so close to what he had experienced. That, too, was typical of the man, quoting scripture like there was no tomorrow.

Of course, he'd predicted much of what Stephen had said, and by delivering himself into his hands, he'd left himself wide open. Not like Verity, guileless and open, who couldn't have hidden her hostility if she'd tried. Nevertheless, he hadn't foreseen that they'd have completely swung him round in their favour. He decided that it was his very public declaration of love for Hadissa that had swung it – not that it had been premeditated. Far from it. It had been absolutely spontaneous, yet afterwards Stephen had been almost complacent, obviously convinced that it was all his doing. As for the pregnancy… No, nothing had changed there. His frustration mounted and he fisted the wheel, snaking the car on the slippery road.

It was the whole conspiracy – Stephen, certainly, but Luke and Joanna as well, which had brought him to this pass. He didn't deny that he loved Hadissa, and he did want to marry her.

271

If it had to be sooner rather than later, well, he'd just have to get on with it. This was what he'd said to Stephen as they parted – well, not quite those exact words, but that's what he'd meant. He'd said he was ready to do whatever was necessary. And Stephen, blinking slightly in the porch light, had chosen to interpret it as a change of heart.

"Well, you must do what you think fit," he replied, "but do *listen* to her, won't you, Daniel? Don't just... And I hope you're not going away under the impression that we've forced this decision upon you." He took Dan's arm and conducted him to his car. "I just hope you'll find talking it through has been helpful."

"Have I talked it through?" he'd asked lightly. "I thought you did most of the talking!"

"Well, but you do see things more clearly now, don't you?" He was almost pleading, almost – wonders would never cease – unsure of himself for a moment.

"I see something," he'd said obliquely, drained of talking. "I see that Hadissa has run away. I see I have to do something about it! Someone's got to find her, and it had better be me!"

Something had crystallised in his mind, however, caused not by what Stephen had said about love or mirrors and all that other nonsense, but much more the dread that had come on him when Joanna told them Hadissa had disappeared. He still felt it. How desperate and lonely she must have been! He came close to genuine panic, thinking of her wandering about in the depths of winter.

Yet he was awed, too, by her utter determination to put distance between them, a distance as profound as their previous intimacy. Even if Stephen *had* applied duress, or even if he unconsciously colluded with Stephen's values, he realised that he'd always sensed a difference between this love affair and others. In Africa it had seemed to have something of a dreamlike quality about it, as if they were actors on a stage, and as he recalled the headiness of those violent times, he realised that with Hadissa there was the potential for a great partnership and an almost magnificent love. She hadn't encouraged him then, in Africa. She'd been, if anything, rather remote, with an elusive quality about her that he found both immensely beguiling and challenging, an invitation that he'd have been a fool to ignore.

He knew the elusiveness hadn't been deliberate or calculated, but totally guileless – more, he supposed, an involuntary characteristic of her race and gender. Yet she had hinted at secrets...

Since then his love for her had grown and, not only that, it had been passionate – until, that is, she'd got herself pregnant. Looking back, it astounded him that he should have been party to such passion, for, until he'd met her, he'd thought such a thing was unattainable. It was incredible that they had come together so fully, so soon after her arrival in England. He knew he'd manipulated that, but even so, their love had been equal.

Ahead of him his lights lit up a signpost, and he drew into the side of the road to look at his map. He was nearly there, and he still didn't know what he was going to say to her. The whole situation seemed so much more serious then it had before. He decided to wait a bit before driving on, and try to sort out his thoughts. He had switched on the interior light to look at his map, and now he turned it off again, and sat looking through the windscreen at the pointing arm of the signpost.

Face it – once he'd known about the pregnancy, he hadn't managed things at all well. That's why she'd run away. If he'd shown delight, or at least a willingness to commit, she wouldn't have gone, so he supposed it was mostly his fault. It was Stephen's deviousness that he found so hard to stomach. And Luke's interference. And Joanna's hostility. And Verity's coolness. John-Sunday – well, he'd been unfriendly, from the first. Was there no end to the list of people ganging up on him? Even that meddlesome prat at the cathedral, whoever it was, who'd contacted Luke. But perhaps he ought to feel grateful to him, at least. The whole business was a maelstrom of his own mismanagement and the interference of people who reckoned they had a say in the matter. Well, he thought mulishly, they haven't. Whatever happens is up to me and Hadissa, and I'm not going to be forced into doing what I don't want to do by a bunch of manipulating do-gooders. I'm sorry she's taken it into her head to run off, but that's not entirely my fault. I can't be held to blame, and I won't be!

His anger and resentment mounted. Fancy taking herself off like that! It was nothing more than emotional blackmail. But no, when she had so politely and coldly walked out of his flat, she had walked away from that sort of casuistry. She had genuinely made herself independent of him.

Abruptly, Dan realised his resentment against Stephen and the others was in danger of distorting his whole attitude towards Hadissa. He must concentrate on what he was going to do and what he would say to her. Stephen had called her a waif, a poor waif, but he rejected this, for he knew her inner strength. It was part of what attracted him. And another thing. If she'd been truly a waif she'd never have left him. She'd have wept and clung to him, and he'd have been trapped.

The truth was that she'd left him because she was proud. Even as she had closed the door he'd been captivated afresh by her quiet, serene beauty and her innate dignity, which refused to plead with him. She'd left him free, and he realised now how unaffectedly selfless that was. But maybe she'd just felt lost. Lost? The truth was he'd made her feel rejected, abandoned.

Their love hadn't been equal at all, he reflected miserably, his mood swinging. He'd brought to their liaison a casual, mediocre and conditional loving, and it was entirely because of his failure to commit that he'd ended up being so panic-stricken. It was almost laughable, if he could have laughed. She'd trusted him but, when push came to shove, he'd let her down. Compared to her, he was a poor weak thing.

She'd penetrated all his defences, and whatever happened next, she'd got to the very heart of his being. Whatever her motivation, her love for him legitimated all her actions, and he found that he was no longer aggrieved or resentful. Stephen and Verity were right, after all. Even Joanna's belligerence had a certain justice about it. Because of the total ineptitude of his reaction, Hadissa was entitled to think and feel and do whatever she wanted. How, then, having let her down so badly, was he to find entry into her life again? Was there still time to make amends?

Dan did not delude himself over this. He recognised that he had probably lost Hadissa forever, and the contrast between his behaviour and hers, so forcibly brought home to him by Stephen, now reared up before him in all its ugliness. Somehow, somehow, he had to persuade her that he wasn't just an ignorant and insensitive fool who'd panicked and made a terrible mistake, but that he really loved her, that he was genuinely sorry, entirely trustworthy, and that he was ready to do anything in the world and make any sacrifice, to make her happy.

Except… Panic surged within him. Except, of course, to move permanently to Kaduna, or worse, Kateri, where she'd be working. Luke had never described the place, but he could imagine it. Dilapidated thatched huts on littered ground far from civilisation; scrawny, half-clothed women cooking in the open with their naked children squalling for food; the smells of latrines and other unmentionables, and over all an atmosphere of dirt, poverty and deprivation. Somehow, sitting in the darkness of the car on an English country lane in winter, Dan didn't really think he could cope with all that.

If he went along with her wishes he'd be deprived of any real choice in the matter. But what *did* she wish? She had made herself independent of him now. If he pleaded with her to return to him, he must prove that he loved her, that he understood her and accepted her for who she was, an African bush girl who desperately needed, and fully proposed, to return to her own country. Their relationship must lift itself above the realm of either simple seduction or blame or making amends, so that whatever he decided would be of his choosing. Was that what he wanted? Still he hesitated. Live in Kateri? Impossible!

\* \* \*

By the time Dan arrived at Luke's house in Long Compton it was very dark and a light snow was falling. He was anxious to collect Hadissa before the roads iced up, and he was reluctant to spend more time than was necessary with Luke. He couldn't stand it if Luke said, "Well I warned you, didn't I? And you took no notice." Or his critical, condemnatory silence. Or, worse, his pious, non-judgemental silence. *There* would have to be some explanations or Luke might not let her go, and also, he thought hungrily, not having eaten since breakfast, he might have prepared a meal. Yet he wondered whether he could keep his temper long enough to endure either the superficial conversation of a shared meal, or worse, Luke's self-righteous finger pointing inquisition. He'd rather stay hungry.

Luke took him straight to the room he had given her on the ground floor. He was expecting a guest, and before leaving for the city that morning he had opened the window to air it for a few hours. As a bachelor living alone, Luke was wary of having a young girl in his house, however innocently, so on their return from Coventry he had showed Hadissa in, made her the hot drink that was all that she seemed to want, closed the window and left her to herself. She had now been there some hours. Dan found her huddled on top of the bed in her coat, her feet drawn up under her, and in the dim light of the bedside lamp he immediately noticed that she had been crying. She must have heard the car but her eyes were wide open and staring, as if she was absolutely terrified of meeting him.

Immediately, all his uncertainties vanished and he was filled with dismay. This was worse than he'd imagined. He went to her quickly and, kneeling beside the bed, took her hands in both of his. They were like ice.

"Hadissa, I'm so glad you're safe!" Vigorously he rubbed her fingers to get some warmth into them. "And I'm so sorry about everything, and for taking so long to get here. I came as fast as I could, but the weather..."

She broke in with a whisper, "There's a rat..."

"What?"

"A *rat*. Under the bed."

"Surely not!"

"Do you think I don't know what a rat sounds like?" she said impatiently, jerking her feet more tightly under her. "I can hear it moving about! Not all the time, but... I didn't dare tell Luke. I think it's gone, and then it moves again. Or maybe it's a *snake*! Daniel, do you think it's a *snake*?"

She spoke as though there had been no quarrel between them, and he nearly laughed, partly out of sheer relief, but also at the implausibility of her suggestion.

"Impossible! Not in winter, anyway."

"Hear that? It moved...!"

Fearfully, she cocked her head on one side to listen, but Dan could hear nothing.

"Oh!" she cried desperately. "I wish I was at home! I wish John-Sunday was here!"

It was a plaintive and heart-rending cry, and it galvanised Dan into action.

"Stay where you are, then, and I'll have a quick look."

"Don't tell Luke! He's been so kind! And I think he's gone to bed."

"He hasn't gone to bed. He's in the other room. Have you been sitting here like this for hours?"

"I was waiting," she said mournfully. "I was waiting for you."

He felt as reprieved as a man under sentence of death who had been given the good news. "Oh, I do love you!" he said, joyfully, gripping her hands.

"Please look," she implored him. "Look for the... the thing!"

Indulging her, Dan got down on his stomach and peered under the low bed, but the area was in such deep shadow that he could see nothing but balls of dust and a few bits of screwed up paper.

"Someone's been eating sweets in here, I think." He stood up and reached for the lamp. "Hang on a mo'. I'll just shine this under..."

It was hopeless. The bed dipped in the middle, the base of it nearly touching the carpet, and he knew it would be futile to ask Hadissa to move.

"I'll have to pull the bed out. Don't move, I can do it with you on it."

He heaved the bed a few inches away from the wall and immediately there was the sound of small rustling feet and scuffling.

"*There*! You heard that? I told you..."

"There is something there," he conceded. "Let's see what it is."

Lying across the bed next to her, he peered down into the gap, and then he chuckled softly.

"Oh!" she cried. "What is it? What is it?"

"It's okay. It's a bird, a pigeon, I think. I can just... reach it." There was a fluttering of feathers. "There!"

He shuffled backwards on the bed on his elbows, his hands clasped around it, its pink claws dangling and its head back, quiescent now. He balanced it carefully on his lap and examined it.

"Oh!" she cried again, shrinking back against the pillow. "Kill it! Kill it!"

He looked at her, surprised.

"There's no need to *kill* it, Hadissa. It won't harm you. Was the window open? It must have flown in and been in here for hours. Look at its feathers; they're quite dry. Aren't they delicate? See the white collar round its neck? That means it's a

277

wood pigeon. Look, Hadissa..." She was still shuffling away from him on the bed. "Look at its pink little beak. And such bright eyes, Hadissa. It's not going to harm you. It's just come in to get warm. Ah, I thought so... Look, it's got a damaged wing. Must have hurt it on the window frame."

He held it out to her, but she recoiled.

"No, no, I don't want to touch it!"

"It won't hurt you. It's not a bird of prey, or anything. Look, give me your hand..."

She bent forward hesitantly, and fearfully stretched out her hand.

"There!" said Dan softly. "Just run your fingers over his head. Gently now, see how smooth it is?"

"It is smooth," she said tentatively. "It won't peck at me?"

"No, no... Do you want to hold it while I look at its wing?"

"...All right."

She took the bird into her own hands, and clasped it to her chest, unconsciously sitting so close to Dan that their foreheads were almost touching. He stretched out the broken wing and the pigeon quivered slightly, then was still.

"So soft!" she whispered. She was completely captivated. "I can feel its heart beating."

"Can you hold it while I go and get Luke? I want to find something to splint it. I'll come straight back."

She held it timidly while he left her and went in search of Luke. They came back together, Luke holding a large box of matches and an elderly cotton reel.

"My fault, I think, " he said to Dan. "I had the window open earlier."

"Yeah, we thought something like that."

Hadissa held out the wing so that it was straight, watching Dan's long fingers gently positioning the bit of matchwood and tying it in place with the cotton.

"Difficult," he murmured. "Got to watch the small bones. There," he said eventually. "I think that'll do. Now all we want is a box."

"A shoe box?" ventured Luke who had been standing helplessly by.

"That'll do. We'll put some paper in it. Won't be a

minute, Hadissa."

He took the bird and went into the kitchen. Luke reappeared with the box, and shredded some newspaper and fashioned a nest, then Dan placed the bird in it. Then he took a kitchen knife and punctured the lid, and sealed it with sticky tape.

"You'll take it home with you?" Luke asked. "I'm afraid I can't possibly look after it here, and I've got a friend coming tonight."

"…And I've got school tomorrow…"

They looked at each other. "Maybe *she* can look after it?" Dan suggested.

"Good idea, then she can let it fly. Take her mind off things. I'll ask her."

"No," said Dan. "I will, if you don't mind."

He returned to the bedroom. Hadissa had curled up on the bed and was fast asleep. For a moment he stood there watching her, then he sighed to himself. Now they wouldn't get home tonight – unless she could sleep in the car. He went out softly, back down the passage to the kitchen.

"Luke, can I borrow some blankets? She's pretty sound asleep, and I must get her home tonight. She can carry on sleeping in the car."

"But she hasn't had a meal! I've got a casserole in the oven – it can easily stretch…"

Dan hesitated, conscious of the hours dragging by. "A sandwich?"

"I'll make you some."

Later he fetched blankets and they made up a bed in the back of the car, then Dan went back into the house to fetch Hadissa, who was still fast asleep. When he bent and lifted her in her arms, she hardly stirred.

"Oh, where are we going?" she murmured. "I just want to sleep. Oh, I am so tired!"

"I'm taking you home to Joanna's. Are you hungry? Luke's made us sandwiches to eat on the way."

"…Not hungry."

"Well, don't wake up anymore, then. Go back to sleep."

He carried her out to the car and they settled her in and closed the door. The night was bright with stars, the snow underfoot crisp and sparkling. Dan stretched, and then turned to

Luke to make his farewells.

"That's it, then…"

"Thanks for coming," said Luke awkwardly.

"No, thank *you* for rescuing her…"

"And you'll let *her* fly, as well?"

Dan was exasperated, but amused, too. "Oh, for God's sake! Don't be so bloody sentimental!"

# CHAPTER 12

He got her home. Joanna opened the door and he half-carried Hadissa, still draped in Luke's blanket, into her room and on to the bed, where she immediately pulled up the bedclothes over her face. Dan gazed down at her wordlessly, mechanically folding the blanket into a neat rectangle. Where it had rested against her face it was damp. It had been a long journey back from Long Compton to Cambridge, and he had tried to tell her how sorry he was, how much he loved her – all the things he'd determined to tell her on the way over. She hadn't replied, and much of the time appeared to be sleeping. Had she really been awake all that time, crying silently into her blanket?

"Hadissa," he said softly. "Hadissa, say something. Speak to me. Are you all right? I… I do love you, you know."

There was no answer from the huddled figure on the bed and Dan glanced at Joanna anxiously. In her expression there was little sign of the animosity that she had previously shown towards him, and he concluded, gratefully, that her parents had told her what had been going on.

"Hadissa…"

He bent over her and tried to uncover her face but she resisted him with surprising strength, her fists clutching the blanket to her head.

"Hadissa… At least give me some sign… I've been driving for hours and I'm shattered. I've got to teach tomorrow. I must go home, but I…" He sighed. "Look, if you want me to stay, I'll stay. School doesn't…"

"No. Thank you for bringing me home, but… Please go away now."

"But I love you, Hadissa!" he said desperately, suddenly so overwhelmed with fatigue and despair that he was dizzy with it. "I'd do anything for you!" he pleaded, getting down on his knees by the bed. "I'd… I'd go through fire for you! *Please*…!"

Hadissa opened her eyes and nudged the blanket lower.

281

She looked at him bleakly, almost dispassionately.

"Daniel, I have let you go. You cannot be in my life. Please, *please,* do not talk to me anymore."

* * *

"You were hard on Daniel last night."

"Was I? What did I say? I don't remember."

It was the late morning of the following day, and the two girls were sitting at the little breakfast table in the kitchen, Joanna buttering a piece of toast, the small room filled with the comforting smells of coffee and burnt toast, the windows steamed up.

"He said that at Luke's you were okay, but when you got home, you know, you pretty well told him to get lost."

"Lost?" She was leaning her elbows on the table, hugging a mug of coffee in both hands. Joanna was wearing her uniform as she was due at the hospital, but now that term was finished for Hadissa, she had no obligations that day, and she was still not dressed.

For once Joanna did not elucidate. "You do have to consider your situation, you know, what you're going to do."

"If I was hard..." Hadissa's voice was sombre. "I *have* to be hard. On myself, too, for... for my own sake."

"I don't understand," replied Joanna. "You'd better be careful, Haddy. If Daniel really does love you, and if he wants to... You are carrying his child, after all."

"So, you're on his side, suddenly?"

"Not entirely, though I think he's probably genuine enough. No, honestly, I'm thinking of you. Whatever you're going to do, you'd better not hang about. But it's good to have you back, anyway. Glad you're in one piece." Joanna stood up and bent and gave Hadissa a quick hug. "Well, I must go. I'll see you later. Don't forget to feed the bird."

"...Bird?"

"Yes, you know; the bird at Luke's. It came back with you, for some reason. Oh, never mind! Anyway, it's on the chair by the front door. Apparently you agreed to look after it. Look, I must go..."

"I said *what*?"

Hadissa followed her to the door. She had little memory

282

of the previous night, but she did vaguely remember touching and stroking the bird. And that it had a damaged wing. It came back to her, how Daniel had splinted it with a matchstick. Nervously, she lifted the punctured lid of the shoebox, and peered inside. The pigeon, its head sunk sideways on its neck, crouched passively in its nest, the torn newspaper spattered with droppings. Hadissa reached in and stroked it briefly, then replaced the lid and took it to the kitchen, where she mixed up some bread and milk to a thick paste. But how to feed it? She would have to pick it up... Would it peck her, like the chickens did at home?

Later, the bird fed and safely back in its box, Hadissa washed up the few breakfast things, dressed herself and threw on her coat. She wanted air. She would go for a long walk into the town and end up by the Cam.

As she entered the crowded pedestrian precinct, Hadissa remembered that it was only a week until Christmas. The shops were brimming with goods and frippery and plastic Father Christmases of every size. Sacred music, blared from overhead loudspeakers, clashed with sentimental Christmas jingles from open shop fronts; the religious message, she thought distastefully, distorted and polluted. Like the air, she noticed, catching an unpleasant whiff of stale cigarette smoke. It was mostly women here, and many were overweight; their faces pinched and prematurely old, their drooping children fretting in their pushchairs.

Hadissa moved slowly among them, conscious of her colour. She had hoped to go un-remarked, to blend in with the crowd, to stay within the solitude of her own thoughts, but the shoppers, laden with huge carrier bags, dodging each other on the pavement, oblivious to each other and intent on their own business, simply made her feel excluded. She turned and looked intently at the nearest shop window, as though speculating what to buy, though her pockets were empty. After a while she realised she was looking at shelf after shelf of chocolates arranged in open trays, and the sight of them was so at odds with her mood that she moved away quickly, uncertain what to do or where to go. She began to walk in the direction of the river, stepping cautiously on the slippery cobbles, utterly oppressed by the noise and the clamour. She felt a deep bewilderment mounting within her and an almost puritanical tightening of her cheek muscles. Rather than festive, the atmosphere seemed exaggerated and superficial, suffocating.

As if desperate to root herself in what she understood best, Hadissa found herself thinking about Kaduna, where even now they would be decorating the hospital wards with coloured paper ribbons, the churches thronged with people cleaning up in preparation for the festivities. Choirs would be rehearsing amidst much laughter and endless singing of choruses, and over all would be the interminable, rhythmic, pulsating throb of the drums. Among them, the pastor would sit, his eyes misty with anxiety and pride. In Kateri, chickens would be rounded up against the day; stores of peanut butter, maize, yams and spices would be accumulating on the shelves of the huts, scenting the air; pyramids of baskets, piled high with tomatoes and peppers, placed beside the road, the vendor sheltering under newly-cut thatched canopies, and the market stalls would be heaped with leather goods, trinkets and baubles, lengths of brightly coloured cloths, dried bush meat, salted fish, and newly baked flatbreads.

Suddenly Hadissa was so full of longing for the smells and sights of her home that it was like a physical pain. She found herself stooping in order to ease it, gasping, clutching her stomach where the baby lay, tears springing into her eyes. Even at this moment John-Sunday might be stacking extra wood for the fires against the side of his mother's hut, or sweeping out his own house. How she yearned for the feel of him, or even for her mother's rough embrace. Even now, as she walked on the littered cobbled streets of cold Cambridge, Hadissa could almost feel the sweaty warmth of those fleshy arms, grimy from infrequent washing, and could see the particles of grit in her hair, the scars on her legs of splashed cooking oil, the dirt ingrained in the wrinkled folds of her neck and bosom. The habitual grime, and the smell of stale bedding and cooking fat that commonly hung around her mother's person used to repel her beyond imagining, but now she felt all that was infinitely more forgivable compared to what she, herself, had become.

Hadissa found that she had left the shopping precinct behind her and was now walking down a narrow alleyway towards the main road. Opposite was the entrance to King's College, and as she took the narrow path that ran down towards the stream, the old-world atmosphere of silence and repose embraced her like a beneficent draught of warm air. On her right was the college chapel, its stones creamy in the warm sunlight, and she could hear the faint sound of the organ. Near the water was a wooden bench and she sat down, the sun at her back. The only sounds were of the river, running musically between high banks, and the occasional mocking chatter of ducks or the staccato bark of a moorhen. However, the silence only served to turn her mind inwards again, and to rouse the questions that had been lying dormant at the back of her mind. They now crowded round her, as elusive and inconsequential as wraiths, as cold as the snow at her feet.

What could possibly be her child's future, without a father? She knew that the numerous illegitimate children born in the village each year were absorbed into its life as warmly as if they were trueborn, except in areas where religious leaders forced the mother into public displays of penitence, or, in the case of the Muslims, even stoned her to death. In Kateri, any lack of a father tended to be glossed over, the woman supported by the extended family in which she lived. But Hadissa no longer lived there, and had not done so for years. She had not only rejected the material poverty of the village, but she had openly despised the equally bankrupt attitudes of both sexes towards women. It was still considered inappropriate for a girl to pursue a career, or to educate herself or her children, for, apart from gender issues, it meant moving the whole family to the city, and there was no money for that. She had been the exception; John-Sunday had enthusiastically supported her ambition, and even her mother had reluctantly become reconciled to the scheme. And yet now she must return in shame and with a mixed-race child, and be obliged once more to submit to a life of dependence. It was intolerable, unthinkable. She felt nauseated by the very idea.

Suddenly she knew that the main reason why she had longed to leave Kateri had nothing to do with education or career, poverty or deprivation, or women's roles, or even the antipathy that existed between her and her mother. There was something else, a partially submerged memory, a memory that had dogged her every footstep and coloured all her perceptions of herself. Without a doubt, it had influenced all her wrong choices, both past and present. Whatever it was, it was subversive, like a primitive and very malign clay god standing in the darkness of her mind; a pestilence; a witchdoctor's screaming curse, echoing down the years.

Now, perhaps, it was time to face up to it.

Hadissa drew the folds of her coat more closely around her and huddled into the corner of the damp bench. She let her mind go back over the distance of miles and years until she could conjure up the stifling heat of her parents' hut, the hut in which she spent the nights of her childhood. She focussed her thoughts, and sadly, for the first time in a year and with a quiet resignation, she let the memories come.

...It's night and the hut is completely dark. The whole family sleep crowded together, Stanley and John-Sunday against one wall, then her grandmother, her parents, and finally she herself, against the opposite wall. A loose dividing curtain gives her privacy, for she is near puberty.

Her father is between her and the door. He is a big man, strongly muscled, and under his blanket he is naked except for a loincloth. His hair is long, reddish-brown, as if the sun lived in it even at night, for she can see the slight glow of it in the dark. In sleep his arms are thrown back, the skin of his armpits pale and coarse, like a plucked chicken. There is the sound of even breathing, the familiar smell of warm bodies, and the all-pervading smell of stale alcohol. Her father snores, but not all the time. Sometimes he is silent. Sometimes his breath changes and becomes irregular as if he is panting. It wakes her from her sleep, so close is he to her own head. She feels his hand, reaching up under the curtain, worming its way under her blanket like a snake, touching her. *Please, Hadissa, please...* His nails are broken, sharp where he touches her...

...It had started one day when he had beaten John-Sunday for some misdemeanour and she had flown at him in a rage, clutching his raised arm with both her hands, squealing with fury and sinking her small teeth into his arm. He had shaken her off, laughing, but his eyes had gleamed as if gratified by the contact of her small body and after that he began to touch her at night. During the day she avoided him, but when the family gathered again in the evening it would start all over again.

"Come and stand here," he would say, pointing to the ground at his feet as they sat around the cooking fires. "No, here, nearer."

He would push his hand up under her skirt and she would stand there, squirming.

286

"No, Dadda, no…"

"No? You say 'no' to me?"

She wanted to please him, but she could not restrain herself. "Don't… I don't like it, Dadda."

"She doesn't like it," he would say softly, to no one in particular, but her brothers seemed oblivious and her mother merely averted her eyes.

…At night the snake curled into her, pressing hard against her back while she slept. She came to abhor all living, creeping things; things that rustled in the grass and watched her with their gleaming eyes. Frequently, after he had touched her and then fallen deeply asleep in his drunken stupor, she would been unable to rest, and would get up, creep out of the hut, aware of her mother's luminous, serpentine eyes, for she was also awake. Slowly and tearfully she would walk away from the hut, pent-up with some strong emotion and feeling very much alone. Eventually, afraid to stay out in the dark, she would steal back, wrap herself in her blanket, and lie down again. She never told anyone of these disturbed nights and the fearful thing that came to her in the person of her father. She felt soiled, somehow, dirty, stained, as she was, with a guilt that was not her own. She stopped praying, for her prayers were never answered. She developed a slight stammer and became timid and introverted with everyone except John-Sunday, yet she did not confide in him – how could she? He was too young, too immature, and as for her mother, *she* knew already – she had seen her slitted eyes. That was the great betrayal, that her mother knew and did nothing, said nothing. It was their shared and agonizing secret, which they did not even discuss with each other, but it drove her from Kateri as soon as she was old enough to make up her mind and gather her courage…

*　*　*

Had John-Sunday known? Impossible! He was an innocent.

Hadissa sat on the cold bench, warm runnels of tears coursing down her cold cheeks. The effort of recalling those memories had been to no avail; they had merely added to the torment already in her soul. Her whole body ached. The burden seemed intolerable, and she longed to be free of it. Was there no

287

one in whom she could confide? She might have confided in Daniel, but that was impossible now, if it ever had been possible. Joanna? No, it was all too late, she thought, watching the Cam slowly moving beneath her like time stretched out, its hidden depths chill and dark.

Hadissa stood up restlessly and began to walk slowly along the gravel path, her hands deep in the pockets of her coat. Dimly, she was aware of the sun shining blithely down, creating dark pools of shadow on the water, and she could feel its warmth penetrating her hair to caress her scalp. At her side the stream murmured sibilantly, winding its tranquil way between the steep green banks. It was an idyllic scene and she felt the darkness of her thoughts to be almost blasphemous. The ducks had vanished.

Given Daniel's attempt at propitiation the previous night, and her unspoken acceptance of it in Luke's house, she knew he would think she was behaving unreasonably, but she was well aware when her mind had changed. It had changed on their long journey home. In the dark intimacy of the speeding car, Daniel, now obviously deeply ashamed of himself, had repeated over and over again that he loved her, almost stammering as he entreated her to give him another chance. His hand, stretched out backwards towards her, had felt and groped at her face while she shrunk away from him. "Please," he had said, "*please*, Hadissa." Stephen would marry them willingly, he said, and she could live with him in his flat. "*Please?*" His remorse had been palpable. It filled the car.

Silent and inert, ostensibly asleep in the back of the car, she had resisted him. His pleading and increasingly tearful voice, his searching hand, the flash of red hair as he occasionally turned his head look at her, served only to remind her of her father, his creeping fingers and his beseeching, maudlin tears.

\* \* \*

And yet, even if I could set aside my memories of my father, do I really want to commit my whole life to Daniel? He's generous, attentive, he thinks of my needs. He was wonderful in September when I first came to England. He's very clever and he can speak about anything. He's impulsive, but that, in itself, is not a fault – after all, he rescued those children off the bus. I shall never forget that, even if it's all that's left over, and all we'll ever have. But, is it enough? I fear...

What do I fear? I fear I don't love him. I fear that if we were finally to live together he'd soon tire of me. He'd guess I don't love him. Love might grow, but who am I, that I could hold on to him? Yet if it had been a man of my own race, would it have been any different? Soiled as I am, how could it be otherwise? Yes, surely he'd seek someone else, someone of his own culture and his own race, and I'd be left alone again, and this time it would be worse than ever before, because of the baby. I'd be ostracised. And what have I achieved, resurrecting these memories? Nothing! Nothing! All is as it was before – the harm that was done to me, and the harm I have done. Will it never end?

In the cathedral, David told me I must walk away from what is doing me harm. Shall I walk away from Daniel? David told me to trust in God, but how can I when he doesn't come? Shall I really walk away? I shall walk away! As for the memories, I shall put them behind me – walk away from them, too! And I shall come through this, somehow. This will not overwhelm me!

It was a brave thought, but where, when, and with whom her destiny lay, were questions for which the answers lay silent. Their love ought to have been a mark of greater things to come, she thought, not end in a cheerless walk along a riverbank.

* * *

That evening, when Dan came to the house and rang the bell, Hadissa persuaded Joanna to say that she had gone to bed early. She listened at the crack in the door and heard their brief conversation. Dan sounded mutinous, Joanna, conciliatory.

"But her light's on!"

"Yes, well... she often sleeps with the light on."

"Okay, if she doesn't want to see me, then I'll go!"

"Give it time, Daniel. She may come round."

"Yeah, pigs might fly."

The following night he came again and this time Joanna was not there to stand between them. Hadissa felt she could not just dismiss him out of hand, but she refused to let him into the house. Instead, she stood shivering on the doorstep with the door half closed behind her.

289

"Daniel, I can't talk about it yet."

"When will you?"

She shook her head. "I don't know… I'm sorry."

"Hadissa," he muttered, lifting his hands as if to take her arms, but she warded him off.

"Not now… Not yet…"

"When, then?"

"I don't *know*," she repeated. "After Christmas, maybe."

"I thought we were spending Christmas together!"

"No, I'm going to Ely with Jo…"

He brightened. "I'm invited, too! When I was there, they said…"

Hadissa hesitated. "Well, I won't go, then."

"No, you go," he said almost angrily. "I didn't want to, anyway! But what do you mean to do?"

She gritted her teeth. "I need some space, Daniel. Perhaps, after Christmas…"

He was quiet for a moment, then he said, "Okay, I suppose I understand…" He sounded resigned, as though prepared to accept a token delay, and turned away. "Anyway," he added, sneaking a glance at her. "How's the bird?"

"It's fine," she said, attempting to smile. "I've fed it several times. But it doesn't move. Is it dying?"

"It won't die if you feed it. It doesn't try to get out?" he asked. "Perhaps I should have tied its wings."

"Oh no, you mustn't tie its wings," she protested. "Anyway, it's not trying to get out."

"Not like you, then," he said bitterly. "No, never mind," he said, seeing her expression. "But you love it, now, don't you? I can see it in your face. I'm glad I didn't kill it. You wanted me to, remember?" His eyes gleamed at her.

"Like you wanted me to kill my baby," she spat back at him.

"*Our* baby…"

"No, Daniel," she said firmly, folding her arms protectively across her belly. "My baby. You wanted me to get rid of it… You'd save a bird, wouldn't you, but not my unborn child!"

"Oh, Hadissa," he sighed. "That was a mistake, can't you see? I feel differently now. At the time, well, it was a shock. And I could only see it doing us harm.…"

"Well, you have done *me* harm!"

He lifted his chin, appraising her, his lips compressed, then he touched her shoulder, his fingers on her bare neck.

"Can't we…?" he began.

She shrugged him off angrily. "Don't touch me, Daniel! And no, we can't."

"You're cruel, aren't you? I didn't know that."

She turned away. "I have let you go, Daniel. Please do not talk to me anymore, and don't come here again."

# CHAPTER 13

A letter came from Cletus:

*Dear Stephen,*

*Christmas Greetings from Kaduna and the blessed Christ child.*

*News of* Hadissa's village. *In only a few months she will be at Kateri. Then our clinic will really begin to* work!

*First, John-Sunday has taken on our bomber friend as his workmate. His name is Zac, and he is a good man. He knows more about mechanics than J-S and he is also a good son to J-S's mother. Every night, J-S says, he comes to the hut and says* I am Zac. This must be of some recompense to her, *praise be to the* Name, *for we have not found her husband, though we have looked mightily. I am very much afraid he may be dead. We can only pray that, wherever he is, he is* in God's hands.

*The Muslim mechanic from the other side of the road comes every day to work with Zac and J-S. His name is Hassan. I think they may get a government grant since it this is truly a* project for peace *such as the bishop and Daniel Marsden spoke of. The church will help also. Here is a list of things J-S wants for the clinic:*

*No. 1 tractor parts – to release J-S from the field*

*No. 2 water pump – repair of, and purchase of a second* one

*No. 3 generator*

*No. 4 radio-telephone link! J-S got lots of practise with this when he went to visit Nasarawa with Zac, and now wants one for the clinic*

*No. 5 an ambulance*

The walls of the new workshop are built and work is coming from all around. Hassan knows a good man in Abuja, and they go to him for all their needs. They employed men from the village but this did not work well until J-S put Zac in charge, he understands them and will stand in front of them, for J-S is still very young.

*Because of the wind, there was dust in the workshop. It was a real problem, but J-S visited the Peugeot factory in Kaduna and they gave him rubber sheeting for curtains plus overalls for the men, so with God's help he will overcome this. They also need some for the clinic to keep things clean when there are wounds.* All things are possible for God as we know full well of his mighty power. *Tell Hadissa all this from her brother who does not get letters from her now. Why is this, Stephen?*

> *Your brother in Christ,*
> *Cletus*
> (*Area Dean of Kaduna*)

\*　　\*　　\*

"Mary wasn't married?"

Verity and Hadissa stood arm in arm in front of the Christmas crib, where, under a roof freshly thatched with reeds collected from the marshes, the faded plaster figures of Mary and Joseph knelt in perpetual homage to their chipped blonde infant.

"In some cultures," replied Verity, "betrothal is as good as being married. It was like that in Mary's day."

"But Joseph could have 'put her away'. That's what it said in the reading this morning. He could have sent her back to her family."

"Yes, or denounced her to the religious leaders, and then she might have been stoned to death."

"They still do that, in my country, under Shariah law." Her tone was bleak and Verity looked at her closely. What was she feeling? She seemed almost resigned to being alone and having the baby alone. No, not resigned, but accepting. Yet surely she must be apprehensive; so much lay in front of her that was still unknown and unresolved, not least her family's reaction to her child.

"Have you told your brother about the baby?"

Hadissa looked away, hanging her head, which was answer enough.

293

"You won't get it adopted?"

Hadissa swung round. "No! I'm going to keep it. I'll find a way. But I'd hoped for better things," she said mournfully, "another sort of life, away from Kateri, and all that poverty. I blinded my eyes to it before, and now I shall have to blind my eyes to it again. When the baby grows up, he'll have to find his own way out." She met Verity's eyes. "I feel I've set us back a generation, and it's all to do again. What sort of future can I give him? And it's a poor sort of world I'm bringing him into, that's for sure! Fighting, every minute of the way!" She sighed heavily. "But, if it's a boy, it'll be easier for him…"

Verity drew her closer to the crib. "What about this one? Wasn't that stable poverty enough? But Mary pulled him through. She loved him and took care of him and told him all the old stories of his faith…"

Hadissa smiled wryly. "Yes, and look what happened to him! Anyway…" She muttered something inaudible.

"What did you say, my love?"

"I said, Mary was… pure. God was with her, and she didn't carry my guilt."

"Perhaps not. But he did, later."

"It's still… such a burden. I can't get free of it."

"Then, for heaven's sake, give it away!" Verity took her arms and held her firmly. "Talk to Stephen about it! It's time!"

\*　\*　\*

Hadissa and Stephen were closeted in his study. They sat in the full glare of the winter light, and he had adjusted her chair so that she would not feel too exposed when she told her story. Hadissa had reached the point where her inner resources were utterly exhausted, and she hardly knew where to begin. She felt as though she was living on the edge of a precipice, beneath which was an abyss where the darkness seemed as infinite as the gleaming brightness of an African noon. The thought of completely losing her balance unnerved her. Verity was right; Stephen was the only person in the world who would be objective enough to give her the kind of exceptional help that she knew she now needed. Perhaps he could look beneath the surface of what had happened and see that she was striving, now, to do the right thing.

Hadissa knew she must not rely too much on Stephen's affection for her. She must not deceive him, or play the victim. Dry-eyed, she spoke as simply and unemotionally as she could, quietly recounting the events that had led up to her departure from Daniel's flat, her journey to Coventry and her long vigil in the chapel. She gave him the bare facts of her relationship with Daniel, describing their meeting in Kaduna, their shared involvement in the episode of the school bus, and how their friendship had grown and developed during their subsequent evening talks. For the first time she acknowledged how apprehensive, even frightened, she had been about coming to England, but that Daniel's presence had comforted her so much that she had come to depend on him for everything.

"He treated me as a real person," she explained. "Someone in my own right. And everything seemed all right until John-Sunday's letter. It was... He was angry because he hadn't heard from me, but I had written. I'd sent a parcel, but it hadn't arrived..."

"Your brother thought you were neglecting him?"

"Yes. His letter was awful. He sounded just like my father, full of complaints and..."

"But you haven't, actually, written much, have you? Cletus' letter referred to that..."

She lowered her head. "No."

"Well, go on."

"Well, when Daniel came I was crying. That was the first time we..." she flushed and looked down.

"And by then you were in love with him?"

She hesitated. "In Africa we do not speak of love so easily. We don't expect it. Marriages are arranged... But, knowing he was here made coming to England much easier. We didn't plan it but we knew we'd live in the same town. And in England he was the only one who..."

"...knew you. Knew where you came from. Your roots."

"Yes, but it was more than that. I already admired him. On the bus, he was so brave! And later, in the bishop's house, I was so proud of him. His ideas... The bishop said he was like a prophet."

"But he's not a prophet, is he, Hadissa? From what Cletus says Daniel got most of his ideas from you. No, he's no prophet. He's a frail human being who perhaps took advantage

295

of you when you were vulnerable, and then, when it came to the test, let you down."

"I know," she said, despondently. "It was a terrible shock to me, Stephen, when he asked about the baby, whether I wanted to keep it or not. It... it broke something in me. I thought he cared about me... And he did care... but not enough." She sighed. "Not nearly enough. I didn't know what he'd say when he heard about the baby. I thought he might be angry, even make fun of me for not knowing enough about ... about preventing it, but I hadn't expected that he'd want me to have an abortion."

She paused, lost in her own thoughts, and Stephen did not interrupt them.

"I felt, I don't know... I was absolutely crushed. The life went out of me... That's when I left him. But I was very frightened. I couldn't even pray about it. I was too ashamed."

Hadissa began to cry softly and, looking at her, Stephen guessed that her tears were less because she was ashamed of herself, but more because Daniel had, with one stroke, shattered her image of him. It was a false image, and he hoped that Daniel realised it. Even so, he was outraged. I could find it in my heart, he thought, to be really furious with this man! What did he think he was up to? Yet of course it was more complicated than that, and with an effort he masked his anger, and quietly handed Hadissa his handkerchief. She wiped her eyes with it, sniffing slightly.

"Are you all right?" he asked. "We could do this later."

"No... I'm all right. I want to do it now. Give me a minute..."

After a pause she described how Joanna had confirmed her pregnancy, and how she had hesitated about telling Daniel.

"So you weren't seeing him regularly?"

"He... he was very busy at school and I was on nights. I didn't want to burden him."

"It was his burden, too."

"Yes, I suppose so."

"And unfortunately this delay paved the way for misunderstanding. Because," he said gently, "I'd let the cat out of the bag. I mean, he already knew. And then he mentioned abortion."

"Yes. I didn't know what to do. And then I realised that I really had to try to pray again... to find out... what it was I had to do... That's why I went to the cathedral, to find God again. But he... he didn't come, and now I am so confused. I still feel really guilty about the baby, but I feel guilty about Daniel, too. I think he's sorry and is trying to make it up with me, but David, at the cathedral, said I must walk away, and..."

"Walk away?"

"*Yes*, from what is doing me harm! He said, if I wanted to find God again I had to walk away. But no matter where I go or what I do, he doesn't come! And I feel... I feel so... dirty! I didn't, until Daniel showed me that he didn't care. Oh, it's a terrible, terrible burden to me," she said desperately, "I can't break free of it...!"

She fell silent, watching Stephen's face apprehensively for any sign of disapproval, but there was none. He had been sitting absolutely immobile in his swivel chair, completely focussed on what she had been saying, but now he shifted slightly, and bent forward, clasping both hands together on his knees, meeting her eyes.

"Hadissa," he said slowly, "let me say some things here..." he paused. "First of all, let me say thank you to you for telling me all this. It can't have been easy for you."

She shrugged. "I didn't know what else to do, who else to turn to... Verity told me to..."

"Ah, it was Verity's idea, was it?" He did not wait for an answer, but continued, "Well, we'll do what we can together, you and I, and see if we can find a way through this muddle."

He leant back, folding his arms.

"Well now, first off, Hadissa, you've got to realise something about God. You have to realise that he's no more pleased with you when you're good than he is now, when you call yourself bad. He accepts and delights in you as you are. It may sound ridiculous to you in your present state of mind, but that's how it is. It may not have been like that with your own father but that's how it is with your Father in heaven."

"My father..." she said hesitantly. How much could she tell him about her father? She was ashamed to speak of it, and decided to say very little. "It *wasn't* like that with my father. He always seemed to be judging us – he was the same with John-Sunday as well. He had very high standards but he always seemed to hold them just out of reach, no matter how hard we tried. He seemed to take pleasure in it... My mother's like that too."

"I wonder."

Her mouth dropped. "What do you mean?" she exclaimed. "I'm telling you the truth! Don't you believe me?"

He held up his hand. "It's not that, but parents usually want their children to do better than they've done, and not make the same mistakes, so they tend to work out in them their own unfulfilled dreams."

"Her dreams are not my dreams," Hadissa said mulishly, her eyes flashing.

"No, I expect not. But you're not free of them, are you? What we're actually talking about here is God, and with him it's the other way round. He only wants what's best for us, not as extensions of our parents, but as individuals. That's very hard to grasp when you've only known human parents who can be – well, always are – very fallible, but it's only when we've grasped it that we can begin to trust ourselves and our own separate, very distinctive nature. But fear makes us draw back, you see; it's the natural human response to anything we think threatens us. It's what Daniel did when he discovered you were pregnant – he drew back. But, Hadissa, it seems to me that it's also what you've done with him. Maybe because he didn't live up to your expectations. Perhaps you're like your father in this."

She was horrified and put a hand to her mouth.

"Me?" she breathed. "Like my father?"

"Only in what you expected from Daniel..." He broke off, scrutinising her. She still looked horrified, and he thought, Oh, no, the old story; why does it always have to rear its ugly head?

"He hurt you, your father?"

She looked down. "...Yes."

"Do you want to talk about it?"

"It's all in the past." She made a sweeping gesture with her hand. "I have put it completely behind me."

"I wonder..." said Stephen gravely, "...if you can ever, really, put something like that completely behind you."

"But I have. It won't touch me anymore. He's gone. I mean, really gone. He disappeared when my brother died. How else could I work at Kateri?"

"But your feelings about it haven't gone."

Hadissa wondered how he knew. "No," she replied

softly, her eyes suddenly brimming with tears.

"Because of how Daniel... made love to you? It reminded you...?"

"Not when we made love..." She stopped, confused. How could she discuss her sexual life with this, or any, man? "It was at other times..."

"Yes. Precisely. You made him into a prophet, an authoritarian figure; you gave him control, and he exercised it." Stephen couldn't tell her what he was thinking, that she had been a victim of her father's authoritarianism and now she had made herself a victim of Daniel's. Or that she had colluded in her own downfall. He might have been able to discuss it with his own students but it was far too complicated, psychologically, and far too cerebral, to discuss with her. But he could go some way to suggest it.

"Hadissa," he said, after a pause, "don't you think you might be punishing Daniel for what your father did, as well as for what he, himself, has done? And don't you see that while you're concentrating on his failings you can't ask forgiveness for your own? You're carrying your anger and hurt from the past, from what your father did to you, into your present relationship with Daniel. His behaviour has only compounded it. You understand?" He didn't wait for an answer but continued, "As a child you assumed that you were inviolate, didn't you?"

She looked at him in question and he spelled it out.

"Safe and secure. And you found out that you weren't. And by refusing to talk to Daniel you think you can go back to being safe and secure. But it's lonely, isn't it?"

"Yes."

"And not very secure at all."

"No."

"It's Daniel I feel sorry for," Stephen said unexpectedly. "Poor chap, he's bearing the guilt of your father's sins as well as his own. That's how I read it, anyway. An impossible burden! Presumably he doesn't know about your father?"

"No, I haven't told him..."

Her voice was almost inaudible, and Stephen leant forward again.

"You haven't told him?"

"No, I couldn't..."

"Well, that's natural, but the result is that he doesn't

know what's helped to make you who you are. He can neither rescue you nor redeem you – not that he should have to," he mused. "A relationship should be more egalitarian than that..." She was looking bewildered and he realised he was becoming too academic. "And now you've put a wall round yourself..." Her eyes widened and he looked at her closely. "That means something to you? Something significant?"

"A wall," she said pensively, "so that I cannot see him looking in, and he cannot see me looking out."

"Exactly! It's natural to protect yourself, but it needn't become a prison. It needn't do you harm."

"But David said I must walk away from what is doing me harm!"

"Well, how do you know what *is* doing you harm? Your feelings have been hurt at the very root of you, I grant you that, and your hopes for the future turned wrong side up. And, with regard to Daniel, your pride's been hurt too, of course. But what does he say for himself? Have you seen him since you got back? If I know him at all, I'd say he's begging your forgiveness on his knees!"

She gave a weak smile. "I suppose so, yes. And he's full of promises..."

"Has he asked you to forgive him?"

"Yes, he has, but..."

"Well, you can't ask more than that," Stephen said briskly. "Forgiveness is the key, you see, the clue to the riddle, and he needs it just as much as you do, or anyone else. He's had a shock as well, and I'm not talking just about your pregnancy. No, you walked out on him, you see, and then refused to talk to him – that's what's shocked him." He chuckled slightly, and folded his arms. "You see, my dear, Daniel's a person who likes to be in control – why, I've never discovered, and perhaps that's his story, anyway." Hmm, he thought, two frail and very bruised people... what a combination! Not unusual, of course, that the victim becomes the perpetrator. He looked at her shrewdly. "You're copying his behaviour in a way. You do see that, don't you?"

She was shaken. "How do you mean?"

"Well, you're using the same measures against him as he used against you. You felt he shut you out, the real 'you', and it felt like utter rejection. So now you're shutting *him* out, and you're rejecting *him*. Hadissa," he said quietly, "even if you don't go back to him, even if you never see each other as long as you live – and that may be right if you don't love him - no, you don't need to respond to that… " For she was about to protest. " – you do have to forgive each other, otherwise the hurt will just fester. You must see that. He may recover to fight another day, but you're different, and you're carrying a baby. For you it might become a memory that, because it was never healed, would always threaten to disturb you. And a memory that isn't healed is like… like polluted water, Hadissa. You think it can't do you harm but it is actually full of disease. You must forgive yourself, you really must. You've got your life to lead, and it's only if you can love yourself that you're able to love others."

"I can't love myself," she cried. "I *hate* myself! And he did me such harm!"

"Yes, he did you harm, but what's doing you harm now? Isn't it your own refusal to accept him as he really is? Or is it your picture of yourself that's been tarnished? Accepting the truth about yourself may bring pain, Hadissa – it's almost inevitable, simply because it makes you vulnerable. You can play safe and walk away from it, if you like, if you think it's too risky. But truth doesn't come by playing safe, Hadissa. Truth is invasive. It demands everything we have."

Hadissa frowned and pursed her lips rebelliously. But I haven't harmed Daniel, she thought, or John-Sunday, or my parents. What's wrong with me, that they've found fault with me so much? If that's the truth, I'm better off without it!

There was silence in the room for some minutes, but when Stephen next spoke it was to answer her unspoken thoughts.

"You can't always run away, my dear," he said quietly.

She looked at him. "You mean the village? The hospital? You think I ran away?"

*"Up to a point. You were escaping, weren't you, and you obviously needed to. But you can't go back, Hadissa…"*

She reared her head in alarm.

"I don't mean you can't go back to Kateri," he said quickly. "That's entirely up to you, Hadissa; no one will make you. What I meant was, you can't turn back the clock. You can't relive your life as though all this hasn't happened. But you can choose to go *on*, in spite of what's happened, or because of what's happened. Rediscover your village, your roots, even, God help you, your parents. That goes for Daniel, too. If you can find it in your heart to forgive him, I think you'll discover he's prepared to act responsibly. He's upset with himself, isn't he? Tell me, has he talked of going back with you to Africa?"

"Not as such, not right out. He's still saying he wants us to be together, but I couldn't live in England. I *have* to go and work in Kateri."

"Because you promised or because you really want to?"

"I *never* wanted to!" she cried. "I've always thought I'd *never* go back! By the time I left I hated the place! When I was training, I just thanked God I'd escaped!"

"But your brother's still there, isn't he, and your mother…?"

Hadissa's mouth twisted in distaste. "My mother…"

"You need to face the truth about your mother, Hadissa, not only how she relates to you, but to herself, and not only what she's suffered, but who she is now and what her hopes are. People never stop hoping and dreaming, you know. If you can find it in your heart to be tender towards her, instead of blaming her, you'll find you can be tender towards yourself."

Hadissa pondered. She recalled John-Sunday pleading with her to give her mother space, to sympathise with her a bit more. She wondered, then, for the first time, what her mother's dreams had once been, and what it must have been like for her, knowing how her husband was behaving with his daughter. What could she have done about it? Where could she have gone? *Ah, Momi!* she thought, and tears of longing came into her eyes. Then she realised that Stephen was still talking.

"You're a grown woman now, Hadissa, expecting your own child. If you're always seeking someone else's approval you'll never really grow up. You'll always be looking away from the business in hand to see whether someone approves of you or not. But real life's not like that. It's the same with your village. It would be no good, would it, if they felt they always had to watch themselves in case you disapproved of them. And you won't be happy working there unless you accept and love them as they are. Forget their shortcomings and relate to the truth of them, not only as sick and needy people you need to help, but as individuals in their own right, struggling to stand on their own two feet. Then their truth will meet your truth, as an intelligent, reflective, trained nurse, who left as a child and returned as an equal."

"It wasn't my plan, to return," she said bleakly. "But, somehow, I did think it was God's plan..."

"Independent of your wishes? Surely not! Surely God's plan is that you're happy and fulfilled. He doesn't impose his will on us. No, he gives us free will, and he treads lightly. Leaving the village, training to become a nurse, and coming to England – all that was an answer to prayer, wasn't it?"

"I thought it was."

"Well, I'm sure you weren't mistaken. You see, God has given you certain gifts. Gifts that gave you the courage to leave Kateri in the first place. I'm sure John-Sunday saw this. According to Luke, your brother's a person of great insight, and he loves you dearly. You're only looking one way at the moment, Hadissa, and that's inwards. Try looking the other way for a minute, towards your village. You know every detail of that landscape, and you know it with a degree of intimacy and familiarity that is incomparable. Look outwards," he insisted. "God is working out his purpose just as much with them, as he is with you."

He hesitated. "I'm not saying you shouldn't look inwards at all. That's all part of the riddle, Hadissa, and the answers are not always obvious. Right now you have to look within, because that's where you are at the moment. As you were rightly doing in the Chapel of Unity. Luke told me that David found you in one of the alcoves there?"

"Yes, but God didn't come..."

"Didn't he? He sent you David, and *he* sent for Luke, and *he* sent for me, and *I* sent Daniel... Well, I couldn't have stopped him – he rushed away without having any of Verity's delicious lunch... but you see what I'm getting at. God talks to us in words but rarely, Hadissa. Very often his presence is in the people he gives us. Even Daniel, perhaps, the father of your child. But that's for you to work out. But he's got to be somewhere towards the top of your agenda, at least for a little while."

Tears welled in Hadissa's eyes. Stephen sounded so sure of God – how could she tell him she had lost her faith?

"You're so wise, Stephen," she merely said.

"Oh, my dear, I'm not wise!" he said, shuffling the

papers on his desk. "Or if I am, it's from a lifetime of making mistakes!" He glanced at her affectionately. "Just because I'm a priest, you know, doesn't make me faultless. No, if I know a thing or two, it's accumulated from years of agonizing over my own mistakes. In my ministry, my parenting, my marriage..."

"Your marriage? But I thought..."

He laughed. "My dear child," he said dryly. "Nothing comes free in this life except one thing, and that's turning away. We're always free to do that, Hadissa. You've got to *choose* life."

# CHAPTER 14

Hadissa lay on her bed in the attic room that Verity had given her on her arrival in England. The house was completely quiet around her, for it was Christmas Eve and the family had gone to the midnight service and would not be home until the early hours. Outside there was no sound except the hiss of rain among the branches of the trees and its light patter against the windowpanes.

Hadissa ran her hands slowly across her belly, as if to caress the tiny undeveloped form that lay within. How different she now was from that naive and vulnerable youngster who had lain here just five months previously, how reluctantly acquainted with, and saddened by, her own complex nature! As a child, life had not threatened to become so complicated. She could still see herself clutching her school books, her face set and determined, racing through the bush up to the makaranta with John-Sunday. And later, huddled in the darkness of the family hut, listening to Stanley teasing his younger brother, weeping with rage and impotence because John-Sunday was hurting. Yet there were lighter memories too: John-Sunday parading his first pair of real boots, handed on from Stanley who'd grown out of them; her father's rough tenderness as he'd swung both his twins up by the arms on to his shoulder – she could still remember how it felt, that stupendous view from such a height, and the warm touch of his enormous palm. She wanted to push that memory away, to deny it. It did not fit with her later picture of her father, but how she had adored him, then! So it wasn't always bad, then, her relationship with her father?

Maybe not, but what he'd done had shattered her confidence. Was this why she had found it impossible to pray, that, in spite of all she had been taught about the mercy of God, life had shown her only hardship? Or that whatever punishment was meted out to her was deserved? She remembered telling Daniel how the Kateri road epitomised all that she most feared about God, and she felt deeply saddened that she had strayed so far from her ardent faith in what the pastor always called her "Loving Saviour". The God she now believed in was punitive, a God to whom she dared not pray at all, a God who had turned away in disgust.

Daniel had not hurt the whole of her, she reflected, but only the part that remained a child, the child who had adored, without question, the adults in her life. She had always tried too hard to please – small wonder, then, if she was left feeling bruised!

She got up stiffly, dragged the top blanket off the bed, wrapped it around her shoulders and went to the window. She twitched the curtain aside and peered out. The rain had ceased and the front garden was deserted. It gleamed wetly below her, the trees dripping and swaying slightly, their scant dry leaves rustling like whispers.

Her conversation with Stephen had left her with extremes of feeling. On the one hand, he had offered her the riddle of her 'self', though he had made it plain that she alone could decipher it. On the other hand she was now no longer convinced that she must end her relationship with Daniel, and that gave her some frail hope that he might yet be waiting for her. Yet she still felt deeply offended by him. To go back to him now – wouldn't that be risking further hurt? How long would his present contrition last? He wasn't needy in the way that she was needy, not at his core...

What grieved her most was that the fervent sense of purpose that she had carried with her from Nigeria had not sustained her. None of her dreams had their roots in reality. What she had longed for – marriage with a man who was respected, a decent home, being esteemed by her peers as someone of worth – was sheer fantasy. But her dream of working among the maimed and wounded victims of the road, albeit not in Kateri but in the pristine clean environment of hospital wards and operating theatres – that had also been fantasy. What had she done, other than to aspire to a badge of uniform that would merely set her apart and give her status, while simultaneously making her – what did Stephen call it? Inviolate? A quality she now knew had been stolen from her.

But, she reflected, her aspirations had not, entirely, been a pose, for during her few days back at Kateri she had begun to feel a genuine, if belated, concern for the people there, and that feeling must have originated somewhere. Even now, she could visualise herself living at the clinic and walking among them with her saving, healing arts. She would have real status, and she didn't have to try very hard to be able to see herself surrounded by little children, wiping away their tears, bandaging their wounds, giving them inoculations, and seeing the grateful and smiling faces of their mothers. Not just the mothers, but all those whose lives she would be there to transform.

Yet was this not simply replacing one fantasy with another?

The reality was more brutal and had even a doom-filled nightmarish quality about it. She might have status, but she would be ill resourced, her energies stretched to the limit, the responsibilities endless, the work unrelenting. In addition, she could not avoid being the prodigal daughter, even with a badge of status, if she returned unmarried and with a child. Yet, what was the alternative? Her funding came from Nigeria – they'd consider it a betrayal of the worst kind if she refused to go back. Not that she wanted to stay in England…

As she had parted from Stephen, he had intimated that all this was part of the riddle that only she could solve. She had not known what he had meant, and had turned her mind from his words, shrugging them off, exhausted.

"If you are only concerned with serving your own self-image, Hadissa, whether you go back to Kateri, or anywhere else for that matter, nothing will change. And your spirit is crying out for change. It's your real identity you must discover, not who you were in the past, but who you are now."

What he'd said rang true. If all she could accomplish by going back to Kateri was the bolstering up of her own self-esteem, then her life would continue to be ruled by daydreams, and real happiness would continue to elude her. Her spirit was as rebellious and self-centred and self-opinionated as Daniel's – worse, for she had cloaked it under a veneer of altruism and false piety! She had failed to see, or refused to see, beyond the road and the blood. Her eyes had been blind to the suffering of her village, which was even more desperate because it was hidden and long-term. She'd used the road as an excuse, a means of escaping a life that was hateful to her. She had not recognised it as a way *in*, where she might discover richness and spiritual fulfilment.

When he had gone into Stephen's study she had expected, even hoped, that he would have blamed Daniel as much as she did, but secreted within everything he had said had been compassion for him. At that moment, she recognised that she and Daniel, in their separate compulsion to determine and manipulate their own identity and future, were by nature more similar than she had realised. It was almost a familial resemblance. This recognition that they were, in truth, one flesh, bound together not only by their unborn child, but also temperamentally, was startling. What right had she, therefore, to criticise Daniel?

It was very dark, but from the window she could just discern the cold grey trunks of the winter trees that separated the garden from the road, swaying slightly, the lattice of their boughs a stark net against the luminous night sky. Beyond was a single street lamp, brightly lit, and across the face of it, a twisted branch, like a scar. It was a dark, dread thought, but with a cold, strange prescience, she realised that maybe she could only truly relate to someone as equally scarred and vulnerable as she was. Then she thought, but if I look beyond the scar, all I see is light. Abruptly, the lamp went out, and the garden was shrouded in darkness.

One generation is about to be born, she thought, her hand gentle over her warm stomach, and somewhere another is dying. But we, Daniel and I – and John-Sunday, my beloved brother who weeps for me and misses me, and my mother who has turned her face to the wall – we are still passing through. Only out of what we do, and who we are, can something come that is new. Have I the courage to accept the gift? The gift of life, and new life? And will I ever measure up to what will be required of me in Kateri, in spite of never, perhaps, understanding who I really am? Of never knowing, perhaps, why I'm there?

She and Daniel had sown the seed, and their child would reap the harvest for their people. Could she find a way to trust in her new, painfully acquired self-knowledge to see her through, to forgive where she had not forgiven? It would take a special kind of love, she thought, turning back into the room and beginning, wearily, to undress. Unconditional love, absolute love, mind-bendingly sacrificial love. But I have hope now; a hope that's earthed in the memory, not of darkness and confusion, but of light. The clue to the riddle was in the light, the light in the trees. It wasn't veiled or hidden. I only had to look up to discover it, and I had to look up at the right time, or I would have missed it. And if I can look again to God, there will be no counterfeit or flickering light, no false revelation, for he is no snake in the grass to deceive and frighten me. Nothing is promised, neither success nor happiness, only the gift. That must be enough for us all.

She lay down on the bed and pulled the blankets up to her neck. A great sense of warmth and serenity began to suffuse her whole body. She felt that she was not lying in a cold, dark room in a foreign country in winter, but in a great pool of radiance and luminosity, like an African landscape drenched with sunlight. At that moment, the child within her moved for the first time, a calm, but unmistakable pulse, deep in her body, as if in recognition of its roots.

# CHAPTER 15

In the days immediately after Christmas Dan lost count of the number of times he sat in the car outside Joanna's house, hoping to catch a glimpse of either her or Hadissa. He could not believe that he had entirely lost Hadissa; he thrust that image away from him and, on each occasion wrote a note, begging one of them to get in touch with him, and posted it through the narrow letterbox.

It was to no avail. He knew that on Joanna's part, at least, this was not indifference; she would hardly be so callous, and although he was less sure of Hadissa, she could hardly ignore him forever. She had said she needed some space. Well, presumably she'd had it in Ely. The fact that she had told him not to come round to the house again, that she had nothing further to say, he was less prepared to accept. He was resolved to lay siege to her until he had told her what was on his mind.

Often he waited for an hour or more, sitting in the car or leaning against the lamppost or the wall of the house, and by the time he had gone through this ritual for a week or so, frustratingly monotonous as it was, every feature of the place was irrevocably imprinted on his mind. He knew every crack and crevice of the pavement, every detail of the pitted wood of the window frames and the way that the damp drained downwards from the windowsills, making a glistening green stain on the crumbling red brick. Walking up and down the street to keep warm, he felt there was no other street in the country that he knew so well, and that he would remember it all his life.

He saw very few of the occupants of the other houses, but once, when the man opposite put his head out of the door and frowned at him pointedly he began to feel uncomfortable, as if he was a stalker, which in fact, he thought wryly, he was. That day he cut short his visit and walked rapidly back to his car with his face averted.

Only a few days remained of the school holidays. By

310

next week, he would be back in the classroom with only the evenings available to visit the house. He began to panic and to think wild unreasonable thoughts, which inevitably alternated with surges of resentment, anger, self-pity and absolute dread. He wondered if all this time Hadissa and Joanna had been staying in the Nurses' Home, and if so, he was waiting in the wrong place. During this time, his temper was more volatile than ever, and the interior of his flat was as untidy and dishevelled as his mind. Overtly, he tried to hide the turmoil he felt. He dressed meticulously and shaved twice a day just in case he ran into Hadissa on the street. At night, he lay awake for hours, replaying their conversations over and over again, each time with a different, more positive, outcome. His dreams were riven with wild imaginings – that they were never coming back, that Stephen or Verity had forbidden it, that Joanna had transferred to another hospital and taken Hadissa with her, or that she had been sent back to Nigeria.

One night he had a nightmare from which he woke sweating and crying out. In the dream, Hadissa, clothed in native dress, was retreating down a yellow sandy track into the bush, her bare feet raising little clouds of dust as she walked. Although she had her child in her arms, she looked deeply unhappy, and she was calling to him, perhaps speaking words of farewell, except that the dream was soundless, and though he strained his ears to hear what she was saying, he could hear nothing. Her hand lifted as though to explain or justify why they must separate – or perhaps to ward him off – again he could not tell. Her presence was almost tangible. He felt that if he could for a moment remain absolutely still he would be able to sense the slight rise and fall of her breath, but he could not be still; it was imperative that he should reach her, talk to her, caress her. Even the contours of her face and the colours of her wrap-around skirt against the red earth were so intense and vivid that for a few minutes, caught between sleep and waking, he even questioned whether it was dream or reality. He was aware, in the dream, of shouting her name, but his voice was mute as if his vocal chords were paralysed.

Behind her, was the shadowy figure of a man, a black man, his face turned from him, out of focus – John-Sunday? – and he became possessed by terrible grief and anxiety. He hastened towards her in the dream, yearning, pleading, but

311

although his feet moved with immense strides, each step was painful as though his feet were blistered, and he came no closer. His shoulders ached as though he was carrying a huge burden that was becoming heavier with each step, impeding him so much that he thought he would surely fall under the weight of it. He must shrug it off, this burden, whatever it was, and lay it down; yet, in some elusive way, it seemed vital that he hold onto it, that it was fundamental to their happiness. Nonetheless, he must rid himself of it, for otherwise, he could not reach his beloved, and to come face to face with her was crucial.

His arms flailed upward, painfully making contact with the wall behind his head, bruising his outstretched fingers, and he woke. The crystal clear image of Hadissa trailed away into the far recesses of his mind and she became gradually more amorphous, like a wraith, until she faded altogether into the shape of the uneven gap between his bedroom curtains, through which gleamed a faint cold light.

Dan swung his legs out of bed and fetched a drink of water, dismally aware of the drabness of the room and the residual odours of his abandoned supper. He took the glass to the window and looked down into the wet street. Across the road, the sluggish river glittered between the shiny black trunks of the trees. The grief he had felt in the dream had not left him and he was suddenly convinced that he would never see Hadissa again, and that her last words to him had been final. When she had walked out of his flat, she had gone forever. The door was closed against him. He knew now that what he had lost was beyond measure.

* * *

Almost completely hidden under a large umbrella, Joanna walked briskly down the street towards where Dan was standing. After a week of persistent rain, the street looked sodden and dreary and it had matched his mood. Now, at last, and if she deigned to speak to him, his patience might be rewarded, but he was slow to react. He had waited for so long and on so many occasions, fruitlessly, that Joanna now seemed like an apparition. He remained as motionless as a statue, rigid with cold and misery.

"Oh, it's you!" she exclaimed. She had been about to

312

cross the road but now she stopped abruptly and faced him. "Been waiting long? I've been at work. I got your notes, but only last night, when I came back. A great pile of them on the doormat." She looked at him more closely, observing his white face and his gaunt cheeks and the new lines of strain about his mouth. There was something in his eyes, too, that spoke of... could it be desperation? Was this arrogant, selfish, self-opinionated bastard *suffering*?

"Hadissa's not back, you know," she said lightly. "It's pointless waiting here."

He roused himself. "Not back? Is she coming back? I mean, she hasn't gone home?"

"To Nigeria? How can she? She's starting her new module next week. She's due back tomorrow, actually. Look, we can't stand here," she added decisively, quelling her dislike of him. "Come in the house. Come on," she insisted as he wavered. "Don't stand there dithering. You'll get wet through." She took his arm. "You *are* wet through," she exclaimed. "God, you must have been standing here for ages!"

"The coat doesn't dry off from one day to the next," he murmured, following her across the road.

"You've got a car, haven't you?"

"You can't always park very near. I was afraid to miss her."

Joanna dropped his arm and felt in her bag for her key.

"You've been before?"

"Every day since Christmas."

Joanna opened the door and they went into the house. Once inside she flipped the light switch on and off rapidly.

"What are you doing?"

"It's the switch. It's knackered. It sometimes works if you... God, it's cold in here!"

"It's fused, I expect."

"Hell, that means a ladder!"

Dan found himself smiling. "Joanna, you'd hardly think your father was a..." She glared at him furiously, and he backed off. "Okay, just show me where the trip switch is."

"If you think you can manage," she said stiffly. "I'm going up to change. If you can make the kettle work," she added grudgingly, "I'll get us some coffee in a minute."

*Later, the house warm, she began to calm down. She*

313

*was wearing a heavy sweater and tracksuit trousers, her feet enclosed in thick socks rolled down over her ankles. They stayed in the kitchen, where she sat opposite him on an upright chair, clutching her mug, her legs crossed in a position that he could only admire but not attempt to emulate.*

*It was only the second time they had had a conversation but neither of them wanted to recall the first. Dan spoke for a long time and he felt that this time she was really listening to him and taking in what he was saying.*

"You've changed somehow," she said at last, shaking her head. "You're not the man I met in this kitchen that first time."

"I'm the same," he said quietly. "People don't change that quickly, Jo. You're just seeing a different side of me."

"One you don't recognise either, I bet."

He was silent.

"Okay, I'm convinced," she said, dropping her legs from the chair and leaning forward on the table. "You really do love her. But she's had a hard time, Daniel. What are you going to do about that?"

"When's the baby due?" he asked evasively.

"About May, I think. She needs to get checked."

"I've got to see her, Jo."

"Yes, well… But will she see you?"

She got up and put the kettle on to make herself another cup of coffee. She looked at Dan questioningly, but he shook his head.

"How was she in Ely?" he asked.

"Troubled, since you ask. At least at first. Very quiet and withdrawn. Then she had a long talk with my Dad."

"And after that?"

"She seemed better. Happier, perhaps. No, she *was* happier," she added, turning towards him. "You could see it in her eyes."

"What did he say to her, do you know?"

"If I did, I wouldn't tell you. It's up to them."

"Your dad. You don't say 'father'. I never called my father 'Dad'. Actually, I wanted to ask you something about him."

"Go on."

"Well, I'm… No, it's just curiosity, really."

314

"Oh, do get on!"

"Well, I've known Stephen for quite some years now, and I just wondered what it was like for you, as a child, with him for a father." Seeing her balk, he said, "I ask, because I never really knew my parents, understood them, I mean. They were quite old when I was born. I just wanted to get away. Oh, I still visit them, but they've no real idea what I do, or anything else about me..."

"You don't tell them?"

"Not anymore, no. It's pointless. I cut the umbilical cord, ages ago. They're both in their sixties now. They were born in a different era. I see them about twice a year. Frankly, so long as they know that I'm earning, that's enough for them, and they lose interest if I try to say any more. I come away as soon as I can. But it can't be like that with your parents. Are you close to your mother?"

"Very," she answered crisply. "As a child Ma was always there for me. Dad had a succession of parishes then and he was always out. When you work for God, you know," she added cynically, "there's no clocking in and out. The work is never-ending; it's relentless, and he was the sort of person who always felt guilty if he wasn't at it all the time. It was his calling, he said. Didn't seem to understand, or didn't want to, that marriage and parenthood were, too. He came late to that, if that's any excuse. Mum had a hell of a time with him. Things got better when he joined the college. Much better. He was a different person, even in that esoteric atmosphere. Ironically, much less cerebral, more human."

"What happened to change him, do you know?"

"I know a bit. He was a personal tutor, and apparently one of his students was really obnoxious. Wouldn't leave him alone, and they spent the whole time talking about this guy's faith, or the lack of it..."

Dan interrupted. "Did he say that?" he asked uneasily, his face flaming. "That this guy was obnoxious and wouldn't leave him alone?"

"No, but that's how it seemed to me. Dad would never use that word. Actually, what he said was that he ended up loving him. That's how Dad speaks, a bit OTT, as you know. But I got the picture. You know how it is: he talks, you listen, he talks some more, and in-between the bits of holy language and

315

the cliches, you put two and two together and make…"

"Five," he interrupted. "Joanna, unless he had a whole load of disaffected students, which isn't impossible, I suppose, that guy was probably me."

"God, *no!*" She clapped a hand to her mouth, beginning to laugh.

He smiled at her. "God, yes."

"Dan, I am sorry!" she said, still laughing but patently embarrassed. "I remember now, he said his name was Daniel. God, I'm so *sorry!*" She slapped the table. "You've got to admit though, it's funny. So it's you I've got to thank for his change of heart! I never thought I'd be thanking *you* for anything. *God!*"

"I wish you'd stop calling me God."

"Don't be facetious," she said, "It's just the way I speak."

"I've noticed. That, and a whole lot more…"

"Prig." She grinned carelessly, getting up to take their mugs to the sink. She ran some hot water and rinsed them out, then went back to her chair. She was finding him strangely attractive, and it confused her, that she had softened towards him. "It started as a sort of adolescent rebellion. Swearing, I mean. With him, there was always too much 'ought' and 'should' and 'must'. Too many rules. Too much time spent pleasing God and too little with Ma and me. You got sick of the sound of it, God-this, God-that – and here I am, doing it all the time! But you see, I hated it, and it showed. It hurt him – I refused to go to church anymore. I used to lie in bed on Sunday mornings instead, and it really gutted him. So I thought it was all my fault, how their marriage was, because it felt like I was in the wrong all the time, a misfit, or as if I had some sort of congenital defect."

"You weren't responsible for how their marriage was working out."

"Try telling that to the sort of child I was! Anyway, since then I've been less of a rebel. I've sort of returned to their values. And they've worked through it, given each other more space. Things are very different now."

"You love your father?"

She looked surprised. "Of course I do. I've always loved him; that was half the problem. I idolised him, but he was just never there for me, as if he didn't see me. Perhaps it's just that he's never been very good with children."

"As simple as that?"

"Perhaps. Anyway, it doesn't matter anymore. I do think, though," she added, "that you don't really grow up until you learn to forgive your parents." She grinned. "And I'm *very* grown up, as you know, so I must have forgiven them, though there was never much to forgive with Ma."

She walked to the window and looked out to where the overgrown garden reached back to a low wall that bordered the next-door property, the mirror image of her own, but separated from it by a narrow alleyway. Over the wall, she could see her neighbour hanging out clothes, the line bouncing and sagging as it became increasingly loaded with washing. She turned back, pushing her hands into her pockets.

"Dan, I wanted to ask you something as well."

"Go ahead."

"You won't like it," she warned.

Dan sighed, slightly exasperated. "Oh Jo, if this is about Hadissa, I thought we'd got past that! No more recriminations, please! Surely you're convinced now that I love her? I'd do anything to get her back!" He looked down at his lap, not knowing what to expect. "Well, all right then, go ahead."

"It's not about Haddy. It's about Ellen."

Dan's head shot up. "*Ellen*? How on earth do you know about Ellen?"

"I've met her."

"Where, for heaven's sake?"

"In church, actually. She told me about you and her."

"I bet she did!"

"I told you, you wouldn't like it..."

"Jo," he pleaded. "We're friends now, aren't we? Don't let's spoil it. That was... another life. Ellen and I... We split up over a year ago. It was never going to work. Neither of us was in love. It was... something or nothing."

"You've had girlfriends before?"

"So?"

"Live-in girlfriends?"

"What *is* this?" he asked irritably.

"And now you love Hadissa."

Dan leant over the table towards her, his fists clenched. "*Yes*! Haven't I made that obvious? D'you think I'd hang about

317

like I've been doing if I wasn't...? What d'you take me for?"

Joanna grinned, raising a placatory hand. "Okay, calm down. I only wanted to know. This Ellen of yours, actually I didn't particularly take to her, myself, to tell the truth..."

"Oh God, Joanna," he said, clutching his hair. "What about Hadissa? What the *hell* am I going to do?"

"Well, she's coming back tomorrow, as I said. Why don't you come round in the evening?"

\* \* \*

When Luke arrived back from a parish visit to find Dan's car standing in front of his house he was not surprised, for Stephen had forewarned him. He took him through to his study, and they sat in two battered leather armchairs in front of an equally battered desk. The walls were filled with antiquated leather-bound books, which Dan doubted Luke had ever opened.

"You were right all along, weren't you?" Dan said ruefully. "You knew it needed to end like this, if it wasn't going to end in tears."

"There've been tears enough, from what I hear," replied Luke dryly. "So, you're going to make an honest woman of her?"

Dan flared up immediately. "Oh, don't be so crass! I *was* going to ask you if you'd be my best man!"

Luke was amazed and slightly affronted. When Stephen had brought him up to date he had assumed that Dan was marrying Hadissa merely because she was pregnant, and he was indignant. He'd always felt that in making decisions Dan usually chose what was most convenient to him, but he reckoned that this time he'd been well and truly chastened Now, looking at him more closely, he thought that, although events might have run away with him, he seemed content. Perhaps I've misjudged him, he thought, and he reached out, took Dan's hand and shook it.

"I'd be glad to," he said simply, "but I'd like to know why you're going down this road. I mean, are you really in love with her?"

"Luke, I'd go through fire for her."

Luke smiled. "That shouldn't be necessary."

"No. Fact was," Dan confessed, "I missed her like crazy when she went to Ely. Then, afterwards, when I thought she'd

318

gone back to Nigeria, I thought I'd blown it. I had this terrible dream... I was carrying this terrible burden; it was stopping me reaching her and I wanted to put it down, but it seemed really important that I carry it." He laughed, slightly embarrassed. "Boring, isn't it, other people's dreams? There's no actual need to know, is there?"

"Was it the child that you wanted rid of?"

"No!" Dan exclaimed. "No, not at all! It's natural you should think that, after... but no. By then I'd accepted that the baby was... part of her, part of *us*. No, it was probably guilt. I suppose I needed to hold on to it until I could give it to her, even, perhaps, for her to take it from me, if that doesn't sound too trite."

"It's called forgiveness."

Dan looked at him almost with dislike. "You and Stephen are a right pair, aren't you?"

Luke ignored this. "Dan, dreams help us face up to things. Guilt and forgiveness – they're two sides of the same coin. Anyway, what happened next? I'm all agog."

"Don't be too agog, will you? It's still none of your business!"

"No, it's not," said Luke quietly. "Not any longer, if..."

"Okay, I'll tell you," Dan said, surprised at this sudden abdication of responsibility. "Then you can close the chapter. I went round to the house, saw her through the window. I stood outside for a long time – didn't dare go in, or try to go in. She's very pregnant, now, you know." He leant forward. "Luke, I felt such a... I don't know. You've no idea how scared I was! What if she still refused to see me? Anyway, we went to her room – Jo stayed upstairs – and we just talked."

"Jo's a great girl."

"Yes, she is. She's not in any doubt about this, you know. She thinks it's right for both of us."

"Well, Dan, I hope it is," said Luke gently. "I sincerely hope it is."

"It *is*," Dan insisted. "I tell you, I'd go through fire for her. I'd never seen her as she was that night. You know that particular dignity she has? My God, she was formidable! I felt I'd never seen her properly, before, as herself, I mean, rather than just in relation to me. I tell you, by then I'd reached the point when I thought, if I could just see her again, hold her in my

319

arms, I'd…"

"What?"

"…I'd spend the rest of my life at her feet!"

Luke made no reply. He looked away, apparently embarrassed. Yes, thought Dan, thrilling with comprehension, it must be a dull life that knew nothing of love. Never again, if I have any choice in the matter, will Hadissa and I be separated as this has separated us.

"But, Luke," he went on, "I did try to convince myself that what happened to us before Christmas wasn't the main thing… I mean that she'd get over it and come back to me, that we could continue as we were. But I was deluding myself. Things could never have been the same, could they? No, we had to move on. And perhaps we had to hurt each other first, to discover what was… true."

"What are you going to do now?" asked Luke. "Is she going to stay on in England?"

Dan met his eyes. "Yes, well, that's the rub, isn't it? She said that if she broke her promise to the bishop, to work in the clinic, I mean, she'd never forgive herself. It was a sort of defining moment. Scary. But, you know, Luke, I'm not particularly rooted in this country. I like Cambridge and I enjoy my teaching, but I've never had the sort of driven-ness and vision that she has, except, maybe once, and even that was in Kaduna, not here. I still wonder whether I can actually cope with Africa, long-term."

Luke was startled, and he leant forward on the edge of his chair. "You're going *back* with her?" he asked incredulously.

Dan laughed slightly. "Well, I'm hedging my bets a bit. Any child of mine gets educated here," he said pompously. "So I offered to box and cox. Go back to Africa together after the baby is born, spend some time with her family, get the clinic functioning, and then, after a year or two, come back to England for a while. Box and cox, as I say."

"You'd do that?"

Dan pulled a face. "Luke, it's a question of needs must. And she had another suggestion, something about the headmaster of the makaranta being ill – she thought I could take his place for a bit. They'd build us a concrete house, put me on the village Council…" He began to laugh again.

"Sounds electrifying…"

"And she said something else, and you'll appreciate this. You said something like it, yourself. When I asked her to marry me, she said, 'You remember the bird with the broken wing?' She said she'd set it free."

"Ah yes," said Luke quietly, "like a phoenix from the ashes."

# PART 3
*Kateri*

# CHAPTER 1

After Hadissa left for England time passed very slowly for John-Sunday, especially since her promised letters failed to materialise. Daily he presented himself at the pastor's door to enquire for mail, and daily he was disappointed. After a while the pastor began to wait for him at the bottom of the hill, and as soon as he caught sight of him, would wave eloquently and shake his head, whereupon John-Sunday would turn back. The pastor shared John-Sunday's concerns, for Hadissa was a child of Kateri, and was not a voyage into foreign lands a most alarming venture?

By the end of two weeks, when there was still no news, John-Sunday became extremely exasperated with his sister. He had asked her to write – why, then, had she not written, and why was she not more considerate of his feelings? One evening, unable to bear anymore delay, he sat down at his rough wooden table and, by the light of his hurricane lamp, composed a brusque note, full of reproaches. He sat looking at it for a long time, wishing there was another way to say what was in his heart, but in the end he sighed heavily, sealed it, and put it into the pastor's mailbox for Kaduna. He told himself that it was not only for his own peace of mind that he wanted to hear from Hadissa, but for his mother's sake, too.

A few days later Hadissa's parcel arrived, containing a fine cotton shirt and the silk blouse that she had purchased from the charity shop in Ely, and a postcard of King's College, on which she had simply written, The course is going well, a module on preventative medicine. I will write more soon. John-Sunday handled the shirt with mixed feelings; pride in the apparently costly fabric and the figure he would cut, wearing it, and remorse that he had sent her such an angry letter. If only he had waited a day or two longer! He resolved to be more patient in the future. The two of them sat over the postcard for a long time, frowning silently over the paucity of the words.

325

"She does not speak of how she is," said his mother shrewdly. "Only what she's doing. Do you think, John, that she can be happy in a place that is not her own? What about church? Do you think she has found a good pastor?"

John-Sunday could not answer, for his heart was heavy. England seemed to him like one vast city, Kaduna writ large, but how large he had no idea. He knew Daniel Marsden was there, and this filled him with unease. He felt a tightness in his gut that he could not explain, but he wrote a brotherly letter of thanks and some village news and waited for the next letter, which he hoped would be more enlightening.

More weeks passed without further intelligence. His mother ceased to enquire, and a deep sadness descended on their hearts, which neither expressed in words although they saw it in each other's eyes. John-Sunday felt bereft and isolated, and he tormented himself with doubt. In sending Hadissa to England he had interfered in affairs far beyond his domain; he lacked maturity and wisdom and once more he felt the burden of his father's absence; had he been there, he would never have allowed her to go. When he worked in the fields, he would find himself scanning the sky for planes; he knew it was senseless; this part of Middle Belt Nigeria was not even under a flight path, but he could not prevent himself. Or he would raise his eyes to the distant hills where a white shimmering nimbus of light hung over the horizon, suggesting an infinitely remote country that could only be traversed in dreams. In the evening the shape of these hills flattened to dark, two-dimensional images, giving the illusion of a high wall or the very edge of the world. The illusion persisted until in his imagination he could see himself gripping the sharp edges of the hills, and peering over endless miles of distant seas to find some hint of her. He remembered, then, that she had said she would be at the edge of a sea – might she not, at the same time, be looking for him? Or calling, even before it had occurred to him?

If John-Sunday had been given any sign that what he had initiated was wrong for her, he would have willingly have fetched her home. He longed to take matters into his own hands and go in search of her, yet his obligations to his mother frustrated the desire at its very inception. As the days passed, the walls of his house and the boundaries of his field became like a prison from which he could not break out, either physically or emotionally, and his mind turned inward upon itself, so that he mourned for Hadissa as though she was dead. Just as, earlier, he had ceased to look out for a letter, now he ceased to watch the hills. Instead he threw himself into the routines of his work, toiling endlessly in the fields until early evening, and occupying himself late into the night with sundry small tasks at his mother's hut.

One afternoon, early in November, the long-awaited letter arrived, and the pastor took it to the field where John-Sunday was working. He stood where the long yellow grass made a natural margin with the tilled soil, shouting and waving the letter until he had attracted John-Sunday's attention. John-Sunday came fast, ripped open the small blue envelope, and together they looked at the single sheet of notepaper and the slightly crumpled photograph of Hadissa and Dan, standing under the sunlit archway of the cathedral ruins.

"Of course, she'll be making friends," murmured the pastor, but John-Sunday was silent. He rapidly scanned the thin paper, but Hadissa's writing was more cramped and spidery than before, and he found it difficult to decipher.

"What does she say?" asked the pastor, leaning over the letter with him. "Read it…"

"I'm trying to! It says something about 'college' and 'study' and… and 'house'… She talks of a priest called Stephen who she stayed with in Ely – I can read that bit… And there's another name…" He knew full well the name was Daniel, and his heart sank.

"Well, that's good if she's found a priest!" exclaimed the pastor. "What else?"

"I can't tell…" he lied.

"Read it out! Put the letters together – here, let me…"

John-Sunday snatched the letter away.

"I'm not completely illiterate!" he said angrily. "And it's my letter! Wait," he added, trying to distract him, "here's the word 'happy', I think."

"She's happy?"

"It says, 'happy'. It says it here." John-Sunday jabbed his finger at the page.

"Not 'unhappy'? Just 'happy'?"

"Yes." Their eyes met, and they were still.

"So, my son," the pastor said quietly, taking his arm,

"you can rest your mind at last."

Miserably John-Sunday looked into his mind, but all he could see was his own inadequacy because he could not read his sister's letter, and bewilderment because he was once again thwarted by the lack of any real information. The sight of Daniel Marsden standing so close to her in the photograph filled him with resentment, and his mouth twisted in a grimace of real pain. He could not share his fears; it was not for him to divulge her secrets. But he suddenly felt more alone than ever.

"It says 'happy'," he said at last, his expression inscrutable. He folded the letter carefully. "And I give thanks to God for that. But I don't know what she is talking about, the studies or her own spirit. I can't read what it says," he admitted quietly. "I still don't know how she is. I shall just have to wait a little longer."

*   *   *

He showed the letter to his mother, but the photograph he kept for himself. He cut a piece of duct tape and stuck it on the wall of his bedroom, then he stood back and fixed his eyes on the tiny image of Hadissa's face, no bigger than the nail on his thumb. He tried to send his spirit into her mind, but something prevented him, and he did not think it was merely distance; his anger stood in the way. It was Marsden, he reflected balefully, this alien intruder, this meddling impostor, who was standing between him and his sister. Always, *always*, he had known how to look into her mind! If he couldn't, now, it was because this man's spirit was standing in the way. He did not ask himself whether the enigmatic smile on his sister's face meant that Hadissa was colluding with this; that she might be deliberately choosing to distance herself from him.

Calmly, and quite coldly, he peeled the photograph off the wall. He held it gently in the palm of his hand, then he closed his eyes and prayed. He thanked God for Hadissa's life and he prayed for the preservation of her innocence and he prayed for the safety and well-being of her soul. He tried to pray for Daniel, but could not form the words.

"Devil! *Devil!*" he said aloud, through clenched teeth. "Keep away from my sister! Just… just keep away!" Controlling his shaking fingers with an effort, he carefully tore off the side that contained the image of the smiling devil, and crumpled it in his hand. He laid the laughing face of his sister on the pillow, strode into his workshop and tossed the screwed-up piece of paper into the hot brazier, where it curled slowly, as if alive, before finally bursting into flames. The last that John-Sunday saw of it was the scorched face of Daniel, smiling into the flames. For a moment he felt a frisson of fear, as though he had committed a diabolical act, then he shook himself, and turned away. Ah, he thought malevolently, if he so much as harmed a hair of his sister's head, he could burn in hell!

\* \* \*

John-Sunday became increasingly busy in his field for it was harvest time and there was much to do. There would be no rain until March, if then, and the stemmed crops, especially the maize, would shrivel if not cut at the right time. For this he used a *noma*, a broad, long-handled blade sharpened to a razor edge. He worked methodically, rhythmically scything the heels of the cobs until they fell in a dusty yellow heap at his feet, to be collected at the end of the day. Then he dug up the yams, slicing through the thick yellow stalks, and left them piled on the ground. He worked fast, with all the pent-up energy of his youth, and he became less fretful.

Others were similarly engaged with sorghum and potatoes, and as the harvest progressed, the high pyramids of vegetables transformed the entire face of the village landscape. As they laboured, the men bare-chested and glossy with sweat, the women carrying their infants on their backs, they chanted a strangely modulated assortment of spiritual choruses and repetitive native songs. Their deep bass voices were lilting and melodious, and the fields rang with their pulsing harmonies. There was an unusual urgency about their movements, for the weather was changing daily, threatening a cold winter. At midday, the older women came out to the fields with water bottles and corn cakes. The labourers took this refreshment standing, leaning on their nomas, the men making crude, surreptitious jokes about the size of the corn – a phallic symbol – and speculating about whose harvest was poor and who would be needy that winter.

The day came at last when there was no more to do and

the burning of the fields could begin. The men took huge cooking pots filled with burning twigs and ran to the edge of the field and scattered them over the stubble. Then they stood back and leant on their shovels, wordlessly observing the course of the flames, the smoke rising upwards through the blue sky to form dark dusty clouds of ash that settled on their clothing and on their sweat. The fire seemed curiously inert, soundless; it was only when they approached that they could hear the crackling of the stalks and saw how far and fast the flames had moved. During those days the women and children were closely confined to the village, for the sharp stalks, which were all that remained from the dying embers, would have cut their feet to ribbons. When it was over nothing could be seen for miles except blackened and charred fields that, during the day, glowed with a dark metallic light, but by evening were transformed to a melancholic, silvery grey beneath an intensely roseate sky.

Meanwhile, friends and relatives from out back of Kateri, Taha, and other bush villages, started to arrive. They huddled in groups, squatting to examine the vegetables, weighing the huge yams in their hands, scraping the skin on the potatoes to reveal the white flesh, pricking the corncobs to test their moistness. While family news and gossip was shared and old feuds settled in the Council, their barefooted children played on the edge of the scorched field, testing each other's endurance, for the white ash kept its heat for days.

The celebrations, repeated each year and familiar to all, took place on the Sunday following the last day of fieldwork. Clad in native dress – vividly patterned, full-length skirts, anklets of dyed feathers and feathered headdresses – they marched in a slow, measured procession to the church, chanting and stamping, while the drums beat and innumerable pipes pierced their ears with melody. Offerings were brought for the poor: baskets of maize or homespun bundles filled with vegetables, crates of live chickens, even a tethered goat or piglet. Once in the church, the pipes and drums reached fever pitch as slowly, their eyes dazzled by the bright sun, they progressed up the central aisle to where their pastor was waiting among the clusters of lit candles.

The service of thanksgiving lasted all day, and everyone prepared food for each other. Small children, driven wild by the smells of cooking, poked up the flames with sticks, and were indignantly slapped away. The drums persisted late into the night, accompanied by sporadic bursts of wild barking from scavenging dogs as they fought over discarded chicken bones. When the sun rose, there was no one to be seen other than an occasional insomniac, and the dogs lay stretched out, replete, among the abandoned cooking stones and upturned plastic bowls. The only sound from the circles of huts was a loose shutter or piece of broken palisade, banging in the wind.

For the wind was coming, the fearsome red harmattan to which Hadissa had likened Dan, and the days were becoming hotter. Each night the sky was a vivid red as though jealously guarding its heat, and during the day people would gaze mutely towards the russet haze of the horizon. It was a time of feverish activity and the village was full of sound again; the sound of the axe and the hammer, the frenzied lowing of corralled animals and the squawks of chickens rounded up for slaughter. The larger branches of outlying trees were cut down and split into flat, wide staves for new palisades to safeguard the animal stock; running repairs made to wooden structures; new thatch cut from long maize stems and pampas reeds, and the roofs of the huts patched and tied with nets. The working clothes were washed out and hung on long lines of twine stretched between the huts, and the women dried vegetables and smoked chicken and bush meat, each evening cooking up the trimmings for the exhausted men.

As John-Sunday worked alongside the people he knew so well, in complete accord with them and land that had nurtured them, he rediscovered, at last, his own inner peace and harmony. By the time the wind finally came, late one night, roaring across the fields with a deafening rush to thunder against the side of his house, he was no longer questioning, but merely waiting, his heart acquiescent, and when he prayed it was with a word borrowed from the Muslims, *in sh'alla.*

# CHAPTER 2

It was then that Zac came. John-Sunday was in his workshop overhauling his farm implements, which he had carefully laid on the ground with the deadly blades pointing away from him towards the light. Wearing just a loincloth and squatting on his heels, he oiled the curved wooden shafts with a clean rag, then he rubbed dust into the blades with newspaper. Completely absorbed, he worked in this way for some time, with a repetitive sliding movement of his whole arm, which soon became shiny with sweat and oil.

His workshop was a rectangular structure of mud brick built against the wall of his concrete house, open on one side and supported at each corner by strong vertical beams covered by a sloping, corrugated-iron roof. He kept the earthen floor scrupulously swept and on the wall he had fastened hooks on which to hang his long-handled tools.

The noise of the road hardly disturbed him, but it also obliterated other sounds, so that when a shadow suddenly darkened the doorway he looked up, startled. Silhouetted against the bright sun was the diminutive figure of a man clad in a travel-stained tunic and battered sandals. His face was almost completely obscured by a white *keffiyeh*, but his eyes were deep-set and the bones of his forehead prominent. Casual visitors to Kateri were rare, and John-Sunday looked up at him warily.

The stranger opened his mouth to speak, but something caught in his throat and he coughed, turning his head away and swallowing convulsively.

"I am Zac," he said hoarsely.

John-Sunday stared at him blankly and his visitor glanced back the way he had come as though disappointed that John-Sunday had not recognised his name.

"I am Zac," he repeated, his voice slightly muffled by his *keffiyeh*. "Zacarias Ibrahim Umkole. I am sent by the bishop. I asked in the village and they told me I'd find you here. You're

John-Sunday. You know me as... as the bomber from Kaduna. I've a letter for you... from the bishop."

It was a long speech and it finished on a dying fall, which spoke equally of exhaustion or reserve.

John-Sunday got to his feet and wiped his oily hands on a rag. Face to face, the contrast between them was clearly evident. John-Sunday stood a head taller, his thickly muscled neck more robust than his visitor's, whose body seemed fragile and emaciated. He seemed nervous, and as John-Sunday advanced and held out his hand, he retreated a step.

"Forgive me," John-Sunday said. "I've had no word. You're welcome. Give me the letter, then."

To his relief, it was typewritten, but it was more than a simple letter of introduction, for it contained news that delighted and amazed him. Not only would the Bishop fund his new workshop, but he was sending Zac to work alongside him, as he had promised. If Zac was a criminal, thought John-Sunday, he was also an experienced mechanic, and if the bishop had chosen to overlook his crimes, why should he complain?

"You've read this?" He frowned to disguise his excitement.

"No." The voice behind the *keffiyeh* was stronger now. "It's private to you, but the bishop told me we might work together, if... if only you can forgive, and make me welcome."

"Forgive?" answered John-Sunday placidly. "It's not for me to forgive. Take down your *keffiyeh*, Zac. I would see your face."

Briefly the stranger's eyes narrowed, almost with hostility, then he shrugged and complied, revealing the terrible scar across his face. "*Am* I welcome?"

John-Sunday laid his hand on his wasted shoulder. "You are welcome," he repeated.

The man gasped with relief and fell to his knees, laid the palms of his hands flat on the ground and, to John-Sunday's consternation, kissed his ankles. As he rose he wiped his face with the *keffiyeh*, and John-Sunday saw that he was near tears. He looked gravely into his eyes.

"You mustn't kneel to me," he said, "if you're to be my *malama*." The term he used meant teacher, and the man's eyes glistened.

"I didn't know if you'd welcome me," he muttered

harshly, shaking his head. "I've been three days on the road. All the time I thought, after what I've done, why should you welcome me? You know what I did! I... I am a murderer."

John-Sunday gripped his thin arms and shook them gently.

"All that is past. Make your home with us!" The man would not meet his eyes. "Zac, *look* at me. I've been praying you would come. I've been waiting for you these long weeks. Listen. We'll look after you and you'll forget all that's troubled you, and your soul will heal."

"My soul cannot heal," Zac said mournfully. "I shall never forget..."

"You *shall* forget!" John said passionately. "And I thank God for you. You will teach me what you know about mechanics and we'll work together. Shall it be so?"

"Why should you do this?" Zac asked tremulously, looking up at him. His tone was anguished, and his whole figure was quivering under John-Sunday's hands. "Why should you take in a stranger, a man who has stolen life?"

"I lost a brother," said John-Sunday simply, embracing him closely, "and I'm not without guilt in the matter. Come, let me show you where I live."

They walked over to the house. John-Sunday's own room was simple; a plank bed and foam mattress, and a rail for his clothes, but he had kept the second room empty, except for his father's possessions, and he took Zac there. After the dazzling intensity of the sunlight the room seemed dark, but in one corner it was possible to distinguish the wooden tea chest that contained his father's personal effects, and his plank bed, which stood upright against one wall. Leaning against it was a thin rolled up mattress, on which could still be discerned the sweat stains marking the imprint of his father's body.

After Stanley's death his father had sat for a long time in the unforgiving darkness of the hut, refusing to eat, and when he eventually emerged, he was like a beaten cur. His mouth was set and grim, his eyes bloodshot with incessant weeping, and his skin was the colour of ash. His figure, once so upright, was now stooped as though he had stayed too long in the hut, or as though his sorrow had accelerated the passage of time. John-Sunday was frightened. His father had become an old man who could never again threaten or intimidate him, but although John-Sunday saw all this instantly, he saw it with horror and dread. It was at that moment, when he realised how fragile was his father's mental state that he began to fear for them all.

Shortly after, he had gone to his parents' hut and found his mother alone and wailing. It was almost with relief that he realised that his father had gone, for with a new, acutely perceptive but premature maturity, he recognised sadly that nothing could have consoled his father for the loss of his favourite son. Then, one day, in a sudden desperate fit of uncontrollable rage, his mother began to rampage around the hut, her dishevelled hair falling about her forehead and her heavy body shaking with a tirade of invective so wild and vehement that John-Sunday had backed away in fright. As he waited, hunched and trembling, some small distance from the doorway, the treacherous tears staining his cheeks, she had cast out of the hut everything that had belonged to her husband. After the dust had settled John-Sunday had crept forward. Amongst the tumbled heap was the marital blanket from their bed, his father's work clothes, his embroidered festive robes, his city jacket, his Bible, a little drum that he used in church services, and a few bent and battered tools. He took the blanket, made a huge bundle and, in full view of the inquisitive eyes of the village, he had humped the whole lot down the three-mile path to his house. There he had once more folded the clothes as he had seen his mother do, carefully wrapped the Bible in cloth, bound it with twine, and laid everything in the tea chest. Then he had shut the door on his memories.

Since then he had hardly entered this room except to check on the state of the wire mesh against the window or to lay down ant powder on the floor. Now, standing in the entrance with Zac, he observed that despite his precautions, insects had indeed penetrated, for there were faint trails in the dust that had accumulated on the floor, and the telltale glassy smear of a snake on the smooth surface of the concrete walls. The room was stiflingly hot and close, and John-Sunday was deeply conscious of the lingering smell of his father. He took a deep breath.

"We can make this room fit for you," he said to Zac, "and there are some clothes here that you can use. They were my... my father's, but I think my mother will agree. They'll be too big for you, but they can be made to fit."

"If they were your father's – may he rest in peace – will

335

your mother not mind?" Zac spoke hesitantly, assuming John-Sunday's father had died.

"I don't think she'll mind. Let me take you to meet her, then after a few days, when she has got to know you a little, we can ask her."

"What will you say about me?" Zac's voice was fearful, his eyes bleak. "If you tell her... She may not want to meet me."

"I needn't say anything," answered John-Sunday mildly, "beyond the fact that you've come from the city to work here and you need something clean to wear. I could say that the bishop sent you... You're my guest, but it's for you to tell her... what you wish."

"Don't think of me as a guest," Zac said vehemently. "I pray you, give me work!"

For the remainder of that evening John-Sunday was distant and preoccupied. Zac rightly supposed that taking him into the room had resurrected memories of his father that were too painful to discuss, so he set himself to match his mood, saying little more than a few inarticulate words of gratitude. When offered food he told John-Sunday that he had already eaten on the road, and John-Sunday did not insist, for his own meal was frugal. He gave him candles and matches and they said goodnight awkwardly. For the next few hours Zac busied himself in his new room, sweeping the floor of dust and insect droppings, and assembling the plank bed. When he had finished he went outside again, but there was no sign of John-Sunday. The fire had burnt down and the hurricane lamp was cold. Zac went round to the back of the house, closed the shutters, wrapped himself in a blanket, and went to bed, falling immediately into a dreamless sleep.

The following morning he was woken by the sound of traffic thundering by on the road. It was still dark, and for a moment he had no recollection of where he was. Then he remembered, got up, draping his blanket around his thin shoulders to keep out the early morning cold, and went out. He found an empty pail and followed the path until he came to the borehole. The water was shallow, muddy and yellow where it had been churned up by people's feet, and there was no clear water beyond. He saw that the bore was broken, and as he washed himself and filled his bucket, he set himself to think how it might be mended.

He found John-Sunday preparing the fire, gently blowing on the tiny flames, coaxing it into life.

"I've been to the borehole. We could mend it if we had some new pipe."

"We only use it for cooking," said John-Sunday, glancing up. "And there's no money for pipe." He spoke dismissively, and Zac felt rebuffed. "I wondered where you were. You couldn't sleep?"

"I woke early. The road..."

John-Sunday grimaced. "Yes, it's very noisy here. It's like that where you come from, though, isn't it?"

"In Kaduna, yes. But in Nasarawa there's much less traffic. The nights are quiet except for the dogs..."

"There are always dogs," said John-Sunday. "Well," he added, "this will be hot enough soon. Pass me the bucket and I'll heat some water in the pan."

"Don't you have a woman to do this?" asked Zac, before he could stop himself.

"I am alone," replied John-Sunday calmly, "except for my mother and she is out back of the village. I have a sister, Hadissa, but she is not here. She is studying overseas, in *England*," he added significantly, pride overcoming him.

"England!" Zac was overawed. "And studying! And is she alone there?"

This was too near the mark for John-Sunday, who was already regretting that he had named his sister to one who was alien to his family.

"We will not speak of her yet," he said sharply, his brows furrowed. "Eat now," he said with difficulty, attempting a milder tone. "There's bread and sugarcane. Afterwards I'll go up and see my mother. Come with me if you wish."

"I do wish," replied Zac politely, "but I also want you to give me work. It's a long time since I've worked. Give me *work*," he pleaded, spreading his hands, "for how else can I be part of your family? Let me work for a while, and if you're satisfied, *then* take me to visit with your mother!"

John-Sunday saw the sense of this and after they had eaten he set him to clearing the piece of land in preparation for the building of the new workshop. With the agreement of the village Council, he had already chosen a site. It must be near the clinic, he'd said, if there was to be a clinic, so they could run a generator from it, if they could get a generator, but distant enough for the noise from the machinery they hoped to acquire not to disturb the sick who might eventually inhabit it. He had laughed at this convoluted way of putting it, and the village elders, who trusted him, had laughed with him, not knowing why he laughed.

They began work the very next morning. At first, John-Sunday, conscious of his comparative wealth and status, stood over Zac like an overseer, but he soon abandoned this attitude and, over the next few days, worked side by side with him, digging and clearing the land. They marked out the corners of the site with staves, stringing lengths of twine between them to ensure the walls would be straight. When this was done Zac said that the site was too small, and, to John-Sunday's amazement, he strode out across the uneven ground, pulled out some of the staves they had just planted, and, brushing aside the prickly scrub, he replaced them almost into the bush.

John-Sunday was pleased that they seemed to be working happily together, so he was taken aback when Zac soon made it clear that he preferred to work alone. He started to keep his distance, as if embarrassed by his initial emotion, and eventually John-Sunday took offence. During the few days of their companionship he had assumed that their frequent consultations implied mutual respect, but now he felt baffled and confused by the man's change of mood. He became wary of him, and wondered how wise it was to trust him. He sensed that there were darker forces at play in Zac's mind, which he felt incompetent to deal with, so he took refuge in his workshop, ostensibly cleaning the rest of his tools, a task that had been interrupted by Zac's arrival. He felt disappointed and unsure of himself. He did not want to take sole responsibility for the new building. The sheer scale of it daunted him and gave him restless nights. Although he was eager to realise his dream of becoming a fully-fledged mechanic under Zac's tutelage, he knew it was a risky endeavour, involving a great deal of expenditure. Deep down he felt that although they were of a similar age, Zac's greater experience of the world only emphasised his own youthfulness. He knew that he would have felt more comfortable if they could have simply collaborated, but now, unaccountably, Zac seemed reluctant.

John-Sunday was also quite simply curious about what

338

had turned Zac into a criminal. He hoped Zac would have confided in him, but of this he had yet he showed no sign. The unease between them continued for some days, Zac working at one end of the site, and John-Sunday at the other.

Lying in bed one night, his hands behind his head, he tried to see things from the other man's point of view. In the end he realised that if Zac was going to open his heart to him, he would do so in his own time. After all, he'd spent the last two years on the streets, and before that he'd seen his family massacred before his eyes. Small wonder, then, if he was unforthcoming. John-Sunday found himself wondering how long it would take before he could completely trust him, or whether he would prove to be just too unstable.

The following morning when John-Sunday went to the site, Zac was already there, digging trenches for the foundations. When he started to dig sideways, at an angle to the main trench, John-Sunday went up to him.

"Zac, what's this for? It's not in the plans."

Zac hardly paused in his work. "A gully from the borehole," he panted. "When we've mended it. We'll build pipes out of wood if we can't get clay."

"There's clay on the riverbank," said John-Sunday, ashamed he had not thought of it before.

"Then we'll use that."

"And oil won't seep? Pollute the water?"

"Water goes downhill."

John-Sunday saw the sense of this but when he saw him marking out an inner rectangle near the door, something in him snapped.

"If you make changes, Zac, tell me! I'm part of this, too!"

"Inspection pit."

"No way!" retorted John-Sunday. "It's pure rock under here!"

"I know. I'll use iron wedges. Break it up."

"Iron wedges? Where from?"

"Old tools, car bits, anything."

"Huh!" said John-Sunday scornfully. "I'll believe it when I see it!" Yet he was secretly attracted by the idea, and after a respectable time had passed he capitulated. That night he slept more easily and early the next morning, as they trekked harmoniously into the bush together to cut enough planking to shore up the pit and to build pipes for the borehole, he suddenly realised that the tension between them had dissipated. That evening, in a subdued voice, Zac told him why he had planted the bomb, and the names of his wife and his two children. It was an intensely precious gift, to be given their names, and John-Sunday was moved. The following evening he took Zac with him to his mother's hut, and subsequently to the gatherings around the night fires. He proved to be a good listener, compassionate and discreet, and on the day that he stood up to read the lesson in church, John-Sunday knew that the villagers had accepted him.

Zac developed a strong affection for John-Sunday's mother, which was reciprocated. Every evening after they had finished work, Zac would touch John-Sunday on the shoulder and say, "Right, I'm going up the hill," and John-Sunday would know that when he reached his mother's hut later that night, he would find Zac already ensconced by her cooking fire, or she would be preparing the *fura*, the small balls of compacted flour softened with sour milk, which the two men would consume next day for lunch. Her mood became lighter and the strain and acrimony between them lessened. She even suggested, laughingly, that if they were playing with concrete they might as well build her a house and she would come down out of the bush to care for them. When they agreed she went suddenly silent; until then, such a move had been inconceivable.

Another thing that John-Sunday noticed, and that intrigued him greatly, was the discovery that while Zac rarely smiled, his mother's laugh, which for years had been little more than a scornful cackle, had become, with this stranger, almost flirtatious. She was tender towards Zac in the way that she might have been tender with his father, had John-Sunday not been too young to realise that there had never been tenderness between them. With a total absence of resentment, he understood that if his mother was treating Zac like another son, it was not as a replacement for her lost Stanley, for that was impossible, but as a gift from God to brighten her days.

# CHAPTER 3

The work gathered pace over the next few weeks, for Christmas was approaching, when all labour would cease for the duration of the holy days. Both men worked on the site late into each evening by the light of their hurricane lamps, even, one night, fetching a concrete mixer, hired from the Muslims on the other side of the road. They brought it over like thieves, while the road was quiet, giggling like schoolboys, trundling the heavy iron machine across the ditch of the central reservation. Then they stood and gazed at it wordlessly before bidding each other goodnight. That night John-Sunday could not sleep for excitement, for it was a significant act, this acquisition of a concrete mixer, the beginning of the realisation of his dream.

The road was not always quiet at night, as John-Sunday knew to his cost. Zac had more than once commented on the perpetual noise of the traffic, the sheer proximity of the road and the potential danger it created to the safety of the village, but both men knew that it was also a prospective source of business. One day, however, this was brought home to both of them in a way that underlined with gruesome reality the urgent necessity both of the clinic and the workshop.

The noise of the crash woke them from their sleep, a hideous rending sound that reverberated through the night and brought the nearest villagers running. They struggled into their clothes and joined the rush towards the road. The sight that met their eyes was appalling. An oil tanker had collided with a family car, shunting it off the road into a concrete dwelling, one side of which had completely collapsed. Though the tanker was erect, it was spilling fuel along the roadside, and the driver was weeping with shock, plucking at his clothes, and protesting his innocence. The women led him away and he fell against the wall of the house, shaking.

"I didn't even see it!" he mumbled repeatedly, "I didn't even see it... Why were they travelling at *night?*"

In the half-demolished house a woman and two of her children had serious head injuries. They carried them out and laid them on the ground and wrapped them in blankets. The sky was intensely dark, and the pastor moved from one to another with a hurricane lamp, comforting them until they could be attended to. The car, half obscured by rubble, was a twisted wreck.

John-Sunday knew about wrecks. He knew he must go and look, for there must be people in the car, but he feared what he would see. He dared not take a flaming brand, so he ran to the workshop for a hurricane lamp, and hurriedly wound tape around the glass, afraid that if it shattered it could cause a conflagration. Then he approached the car cautiously. The driver was already dead, his wife in the passenger seat critically injured by the force of the impact, but their four children in the back were hysterical, and he could not tell how badly they were injured. When they saw him, they held out their arms to him, and he felt a surge of anger against the road. Yet by then word had got round, that the car had had no lights.

He turned on his heel and yelled at the top of his voice.

"Zac! Over here! Here! I need *help*!"

It took the rest of the night to free them. One child, trapped between the seats, had a broken arm through which the bone protruded whitely. No one except John-Sunday and Zac would approach the car for fear of an explosion. They said it was their job, and they must do it, so he and Zac crept underneath to wrestle with the twisted chassis until at least one door could be wrenched open and the child released. It took hours, and he was ready to tear out his hair with frustration, especially when the elders came to urge more speed, for the victims were still lying on the bare earth. By then the sun had risen, casting long purple shadows across the ground, drying their wounds to agony and traffic was mounting on the road, their brakes squealing as they encountered the spilt oil.

"Look," he exclaimed finally, scrambling out from under the car, his face smeared with oil and grime and sweat, "we can't do more than we are doing! I don't have cutting equipment! And if I did I don't have a generator! We'll have to use what tools we have. We can't even see properly, but for God's sake," he added urgently, "don't light any lamps. And get the women to rake the sand over that fuel on the road – I know it's dangerous, but *do* it.

342

And bring water...! And, for God's sake, take the injured to the clinic."

"But the clinic isn't ready... It can't take casualties..."

"It has first aid!" he replied grimly, wiping his forehead with an oily cloth. "At least it's clean and out of the sun. Get women in there, and some water, and start cutting bandages."

"We don't have the key to the gate..."

"Get the pastor's wife!" he roared. "She has a key! Or break down the gates, but get them *in* there!"

Again he struggled under the car to rejoin Zac, who was quietly wrestling with a car door, his hands slimy with oil, his shoulder bloody and bruised under his torn clothes.

"I can't shift it," he gasped, blinking away sweat. "I can't see what I'm doing... We can't do it without cutting equipment!"

"Well, we don't *have* cutting equipment!"

"I have cutting equipment."

It was a deep quiet voice and seemed to penetrate the noise and confusion so that for a moment John-Sunday marvelled. He twisted round to see who had spoken, but all he could see was a pair of feet in clean sandals, and the bottom of a white tunic, also clean. He rolled out from under the car, rearing his head to see who had uttered such redeeming words. The figure squatted down in front of him, bearded and bareheaded.

"I am Hassan. I am the mechanic from the other side of the road. I think perhaps you need me. I have cutting equipment, and I have a radiotelephone. Let me work with you, why not?"

* * *

Christmas passed with no message from Hadissa, and once again John-Sunday fretted, but he was diverted from his anxiety by sheer hard work. The accident had impressed on the whole village the absolute urgency of a decent workshop, so with Hassan's help he employed men from both sides of the road, Christians and Muslims. Friction was inevitable, because of the call to prayer and all that it implied. John-Sunday quickly became impatient with both sides, thus relinquishing what little authority he had achieved. Bitterly, he put Zac in charge. Zac called a meeting and talked to the Christians quietly, squatting with the workers amidst the rubble and dirt. He pleaded with

343

them to emulate the punctuality of the Muslims and to respect their prayer time.

"They're different from us," he said, "but that's no reason to mock their faith. I've learnt this for myself," he added, lying through his teeth, "that we have much in common. Can you not be reconciled? They work as hard as you do, and there's enough work for all." He spread his hands to encompass the half-constructed site. "Even when this place is built there'll be work for everyone who wants it, for although they'll cope with accidents on their side of the road, we have the clinic, and when it's built we must maintain it, and whatever vehicles go to the city hospital. What we have to do now is deal with the wind."

For the harmattan was blowing with a vengeance. Red dust began to accumulate in Zac's inspection pit and in his drainage tunnel. Everything became filthy; the dust clung to all the oily surfaces, and they were compelled to work all day with rags around their faces. Many men stopped coming. It was not the time of year to build, they said; either the dust or the heat would kill them if they worked all day in it, and they walked off the site. There was a few days' hiatus while Zac and John-Sunday scratched their heads, but then the wind dropped a little, and the men returned. They worked hard to make up for lost time, and the mood was better; their wives had sent them, they said sheepishly, angry at the loss of earnings – promised, when money arrived from the bishop.

By this time John-Sunday had his radio link and his telephone cubicle in the clinic of which he was very proud, for he had his own key to the gates and could come and go as he wished. The radio made him think about Hadissa. It bewildered him that, while he now had the sophisticated technology of a radio link, his spiritual ties with his sister seemed to have completely vanished. He put in a call to Cletus, begging him to ask Stephen to find his sister and tell her to write, and with that very indirect and uncertain request he had to be satisfied.

Conditions in the workshop improved slightly when they got the roof on and the doors in place, but the dust was still a problem, and one day it became intolerable. They were working on a tractor that had been brought in for an overhaul, and the dust was penetrating all the delicate mechanism of the carburettor. Raging, John-Sunday left it, and wiping his hands roughly on a clean rag and tearing off his overalls, he went angrily over to the clinic to telephone the Peugeot factory for advice. The result of that was an invitation to view the factory and to find out for themselves how the difficulty could be managed. After a quick call to the bishop's house to beg accommodation for one night, he returned to the workshop to tell them what he had done.

Hassan suggested that he and John-Sunday go on their own, leaving Zac to manage the men, and to this Zac reluctantly agreed. He did not, as yet, want to show his face in Kaduna. He was afraid of being arrested, but he was jealous of Hassan. He also felt that he and John-Sunday were getting above themselves. After all, he thought, they were only building a very small garage. Yet he was also deeply anxious about the expedition itself.

"Have you not considered," he said, "that you'll be a Christian and a Muslim travelling together, and how risky that is? Also," he added vehemently, "you're my younger brother, so you should take direction from me!"

John-Sunday looked at him in surprise. Was that how he thought of him? He didn't reply, and soon after they left in the truck.

That evening after work, Zac did not go up to the mother's hut, but instead prowled around the house in a desultory manner, finally going to the door of John-Sunday's bedroom, as though by doing so he could conjure up his presence. He was anxious and afraid. Outside the wind gusted furiously, and he could hear something banging against the side of the house, but inside all was still and calm. He lifted his lamp and peered around. John-Sunday's bed was neatly made and in the alcove he could see his familiar clothes on the metal rail. His attention was caught by a small photograph above the bed, and he raised the lamp to examine it. One side of it was torn off, but what remained shattered his peace of mind.

It was a picture of a young girl – she could only be Hadissa, John-Sunday's twin. She was standing in front of a sunlit arch, a foreign place unlike anything he had ever seen, and she was beautiful. A tremulous, slightly knowing, smile hovered about her mouth, as if she was on the very edge of womanhood. Carefully Zac peeled away the tape and carried the photograph outside, where, in the light of the evening sky, it was instantly suffused by a reddish glow.

He gazed at it closely. It seemed to burn in his hands. She had a look of John-Sunday, and a separate look of the mother, but the resemblance was partial; the rest was herself, youthful and intensely female, and Zac drew in his breath. Surely they were meant for each other, and he would have his joy of her!

He sat on the bench for a long time, holding the photograph in his hands. He stayed there until it was too dark to see it any longer, then he carried it into his room. He had one night in which to take pleasure in it, even if it made him miserable, for John-Sunday would be back the next day and he must not find it missing. One night and one morning in which to enfold and clasp and cherish the image of this girl – who was so far away, so absolutely out of reach, and so utterly unattainable. For was she not virginal, and he, a murderer?

\* \* \*

The two men returned elated. Zac went out to meet them and he and the workers crowded round the truck jubilantly, for it was laden with heavy rolls of thick rubber sheeting.

"This is for a curtain in the workshop," explained John-Sunday triumphantly. "We'll mount it on a frame, and it'll keep out the dust. That's what they do in the factory. You cut strips and the sections overlap... and we have enough for all the doors in the clinic, inside and out, which will stop the dust getting into the wards... I don't need to tell you what this means for us all!"

However, he did not wait to unload the sheeting but disappeared into his house and closed the door.

"He's had a letter," explained Hassan, smiling at Zac. "He wouldn't read it on the journey. The bishop gave it to him as we left. I think it's from his sister in England."

\* \* \*

John-Sunday sat on the edge of his bed, the tears coursing down his face, his body convulsed with grief. She was coming home, but married, and she had married *him*. What had happened to his prayers? Was God indifferent? Or just not listening? If that was not bad enough, she was pregnant. But to bring Daniel with her – that was even worse.

346

*Do not be angry with me, John-Sunday, that I have not written as much as I should have done…*

To his amazement he found he could read her handwriting quite clearly. It was as though scales had fallen from his eyes, or that, previously, she had been writing in distress and now was free of it. Its tone, though apprehensive and tentative, read as though something deep within her had been resolved.

*…It has been more difficult than I expected to settle in this cold and rainy country. I did not want to write sad letters when you have done so much for me.*
*The course will finish in May and, God willing, I will qualify. I have already qualified in preventative medicine and pre-natal care. Diagnostics are more difficult as some of the diseases we study are not common to Nigeria. For anaesthetics I can always seek advice from Mr Boseh, who will be visiting the clinic on a regular basis.*
*John, I am coming home! I cannot wait to see your beloved face again. Times have been hard.*

This was scribbled out blackly but nevertheless he could discern the letters as if some miracle had made him more acute.

*….John-Sunday, you must* promise *not to be ashamed of me. I have earned your anger but I do not want you to be ashamed as well. But I must tell you that Daniel – who you will remember from Kaduna last summer – has been very kind to me and a good friend. By the time you receive this we shall be married. I am expecting his child and we do not want to wait…*

This also was obscured, the force of her pen indenting the page.

*I know that this is not what you or our mother would have wanted for me. Marriage to one of the boys at Kateri was always the plan, wasn't it? But it could never be, I have known that for years. I had to get away from Kateri, for many reasons. Daniel wants to work with us in Kateri and Kaduna, perhaps as a teacher. You remember the headmaster of the makaranta can no longer work? Well, Daniel could take his place! Imagine our village kids learning maths again, and English, and learning really well!*

*I will write again with the details of our flight. Will you meet us from the plane? Come in a car if you can. The baby will be very small and a car journey will be smoother.*

A *car*? But he had never even driven the truck on those roads, let alone a car! So short a time, and already she had forgotten their ways...

*Do not grieve that my life has turned out like this. I have prayed to God that he will give me a new start. I am sure that when you meet Daniel again you will come to respect and admire him as much as I do.*

There was a space as if she was deep in thought, chewing her pen as she was wont to do. In his mind's eye, he could see her as a child sitting on the bare earth with her paper tablet and a stub of pencil. The soft pigtails of her childhood...

*John-Sunday,*

*Is there a concrete house where we can live? I do not think Daniel will be happy in a hut. Perhaps near the clinic?*

*I send you my love. Do not stop loving me, I beg, but greet me with the warmth that I know is in your heart to give.*

*Greet our mother, tell her of the child.*

*Your loving sister,*
*Hadissa*

John-Sunday slowly bent his head into his hands, the letter clutched in his clenched fist. She did not speak of loving Daniel, he thought dourly, but only of respect and admiration – words more appropriate to an arranged marriage. They sent a frisson of dread through him, and his anger mounted. In spite of his passionate prayers Daniel Marsden had, after all, meddled in her life.

He was also angry with his sister. Almost he would have cast her off, yet he could not sustain his rage. She was still

Hadissa, and had he not seen her face, sitting on the bare earth with her paper tablet, tapping her teeth with her pencil? Well, he would do as she asked. He would build her the house she wanted, though every brick would tear his fingers. His mother's house would have to wait a little longer... He regretted this deeply, for it had taken a great deal for his mother to agree to come down out of the bush. Yet he was bound to Hadissa as to no one else. He would prepare lodging for her and her baby. And Daniel. It would sicken him, but he would do it. He and Zac would do it together.

# PART 4
*The Road*

# CHAPTER 1

The moment they stepped on to the plane at Stansted she said she was already in Kateri. Struggling along the aisle with the swaddled figure of Habiba clasped in her arms, she had tilted her face towards him. "It's just a bridge of air."

Dan felt differently. All he could think of was what he had left behind: his racial roots, his occupation, the familiar streets of Cambridge, the motorway steaming with rain, the pale sky above the terminal building and a swift, silent fly-past of starlings in the bright, light air, which he had glimpsed as they walked along endless carpeted miles of glass-fronted corridors, pushing the heavily laden trolley. He took out the in-flight magazines from the pocket in front of him – a futile attempt, he thought, to ground them in the illusion that they were not in some half-world unconnected to anywhere else. He caught Hadissa's eye, gesturing with the magazines.

"You want these?"

She shook her head. Habiba whimpered and she opened the front of her blouse and adjusted the baby so that she could feed. Dan watched for a while, gazing at the little red-brown curly head that brushed his arm, and at the soft, olive swell of Hadissa's breast.

The engines roared and swelled, and as the plane rumbled forward and began to speed down the runway, Dan could feel each bump and pothole and he glanced at Hadissa to see if she was anxious. She smiled at him, her eyes dreamy, oblivious to everything but her draining breast and the suckling child. Then they were in the air. The plane rose, settled back, then climbed again in a sweeping turn. The land receded, its houses, factories, buildings, roads, hedges, fields, traffic, *people*, paling into insignificance – like Stephen, he thought suddenly, in the departure lounge, his arm upraised, an expression on his face almost of consternation, as though he had suddenly remembered the one, final, most crucial point, the point that would make or

353

mar everything. Whatever it was, it was already immaterial, the green land diminishing as though being sucked into unreality, for the reality was here, now, on this cramped plane, and there was no way back.

Food came, and Dan balanced their plastic trays on the small shelf in front of him. Instant breakfast, re-heated in grey filing cabinets at the back of the plane. A child-support system of geometrically arranged containers and plastic cutlery, and elongated paper tubes of sugar and salt – economically apportioned items of coagulated additives, he thought, masquerading as a menu. Amused at himself, he glanced at Hadissa to share the joke, but she was gazing at it in wonder and delight.

Stephen had handled the wedding very well, he thought, as he settled back in his seat after their brief, unappetising meal. Hadissa had gone to sleep, one arm protectively around the baby, fastened once more into her seatbelt. The short ceremony had been conducted at Stephen's church in Ely, before a full congregation titillated by this extraordinary alliance of a white man and a very pregnant, very black bush village girl. They had come in their Sunday best, and everything was hats.

Of course, Stephen had done his work impeccably, and if he'd disapproved he hid it well. Dan grinned to himself. Poor Stephen, it can't have happened to him very often, that he should be faced with a mixed marriage where the bride was heavily pregnant, yet completely unfazed by the figure she cut in her wrap-around skirt, hastily made from a length of patterned cloth bought on Ely market, and no family to bear witness! There was one particular hymn, though, the words of which still rang in his head.

*Breathe through the heat of our desire*
*Thy coolness and thy balm;*
*Let sense be dumb, let flesh retire,*
*Speak through the earthquake, wind and fire…*
*The still, small voice of calm.*

A strange choice of hymn for a wedding, Dan reflected, with its sexual innuendo, which the sacrament of marriage, however overdue, now cloaked in respectability. Stephen had spoken well, though, he thought, as he shifted his legs once again. Of course, he'd been bound to speak about God, but something else, too, something about "being and doing"... connecting it, in that devious way most clergy seemed to have, to the hymn.

"You see before you, standing here," he'd said, his voice even more parsonical than usual, "a young couple on the edge of a great adventure. Both of them are *do-ers*, and both are well equipped to meet the challenges that life will throw at them. Now, life in Africa will be a huge challenge, but make no mistake," he'd said emphatically, "compared to the supremely demanding challenge of love, it will be trivial. For without love, how can we face the trials that may be in store for us? We can't see around corners! We set out blithely enough on the road of life, trusting in our own abilities, and a certain amount of sheer good luck, to get us through..." He'd paused for effect, then said more quietly, "Yet we are, each of us, ignorant of all but a fraction of the truth about what *love* may demand of us... We see but dimly, and perhaps it's just as well. But if we can't see round corners, you say, at least we can *trust*, at least we can *hope*, at least we can have *vision*! Yet I tell you that they, on their own, are insufficient. Hopes may fade, vision might be thwarted, and often is, to become as leaves blowing in the wind. I tell you that what is left, if we have not love, is no more than a watery, self-seeking..." His voice rose suddenly, "*compromise!*"

At the time, standing awkwardly in front of Stephen, a mere arm's length away from his projecting voice, Dan had almost reared back.

"Yes, compromise," Stephen said quietly, looking directly into Dan's eyes. "The time may come when we do lose hope and we do begin to fear; when, in spite of all our efforts and all the purity of our first vision, life itself, in all its complexity and all its reversals, seems to be beating us. So what do we do then?"

He paused, and looked around, his expression grave – too grave for the occasion, thought Dan, wilting under Stephen's inflexible gaze. "I will tell you what we do," Stephen continued quietly. "We do nothing. Yes, we *do* nothing. That is the moment when we must *cease* doing, and learn to be *still*, so that we can hear the still small voice of God. In listening to that voice, if we let ourselves hear it, we will be given strength; strength to go on, strength to learn again of trust and hope and vision, and strength to go on loving. There can be no exceptions to this," he said softly, "if only we can allow ourselves to be embraced by the fire of love, and if we desire that love to be blessed by God. For he, alone, in his great wisdom, knows what is the best that we can become." He paused significantly, and then raised his eyes to the congregation and finished on a rush. "And now to God the Father, God the Son and God the Spirit, be all praise and honour…"

Serious stuff, thought Dan, dreaming on the plane as it tore across Hadissa's bridge of air. He was surprised he'd remembered so much of it, but that almost-shouted word "compromise" stuck in his mind.

Yet, why shouldn't he compromise, he thought rebelliously? He couldn't take the sort of risks he was taking without, at the same time, making contingency plans, having an exit strategy, some back door out of which he could escape. And he had it. His work permit was for one year; he'd renew it once, he'd said, coolly unrelenting, and after that they would return to England, for a while at least.

Hadissa hadn't liked the idea, but he thought she'd get over it once she put her head down to work. He had always felt, instinctively, that he needed to leave room for manoeuvre, and if that was manipulation, it was from the best of motives. Though perhaps Stephen had been right about doing, he reflected sombrely. To always want to organise, and to always impose structures – as though by sheer force of will he could choreograph the people around him – might be his particular curse. If so, and if he and Hadissa were to be happy, he must not take that curse to Kateri.

\* \* \*

Hadissa was not asleep but deep in thought. She had not realised how much she had been clinging to her images of Kateri, how much she had unconsciously stored them in her mind, vivid and colourful – light-hearted, too – not plagued by demons of poverty and injustice or the unwanted sexual attentions of her father. She was still bruised, still wounded, but she was married, now, safe from the prying plans of the elders, and now all she wanted to see John-Sunday. And her mother. She wanted to lay the baby, with its red brown hair, in her mother's soft, welcoming arms, and see her tawny skin, striated like parchment, tighten, as she clasped the child to her chest. She wanted to see her mother's wide smile, hear her bark of triumph – for here would be the unforeseen, yet longed-for, seed of her own renewal. She wanted her mother to forget the past, as she, herself, was endeavouring to do, or put it safely behind her.

The thoughts rushed in on her. She wondered whether she'd start work immediately, or whether there'd be that long-drawn out African interval before anything could be accomplished. She no longer deluded herself that her presence, of itself, would revitalise the village life of Kateri. She had set aside those romantic fantasies. All she could do was live on the land and bring what help she could, both to Kateri and to its outlying villages. She knew her presence would make little difference to the way in which women, in general, were treated, but she could diagnose and treat basic illnesses, and maybe save a life or two on the road, or in childbirth. She might even, with Boseh's help, get some people to hospital. But she couldn't do anything about the tribal or religious conflict, or the hopelessness of the poverty-stricken lives that most people lived. She might be able to do something about their diet. She might even do basic operative procedures. But she couldn't do anything about the fear and the hate, or the lack of education and opportunity, which drove young men into religious fanaticism, or worse, banditry, to roam and terrorise the road.

Her mind drifted into sleep. *Here are the villages and the people who dwell there, and you have a story to tell, for once you were a child of the bush but now you are a woman of authority, with a career all your own. Once Kateri was mineral rich* – and it still is mineral rich, she thought, starting awake. Much of the soil is barren and unfarmed. I will talk to John-Sunday, if he'll listen to me. He'll know what to do. The wellsprings and boreholes will breathe again – the children, too, for Daniel will teach them. Yes, she thought, clean water and education are the key to renewal. Your sons and daughters will prophesy, your young men will see visions, your old men will dream dreams... Young men do not run away to the cities, she thought, when they can find life and hope within their own village.

Could she be a blessing to the land, she, John-Sunday and Daniel?

# CHAPTER 2

The plane was due in at three in the afternoon, and by the time it landed John-Sunday and Zac were already in the arrivals lounge. They had brought a Peugeot Estate, a demonstration car acquired at a cut-down price, courtesy of the factory in Kaduna. It had a powerful engine, and with the seats laid flat it could double up as an ambulance for the clinic.

They were not unduly worried by the time, for they only had fifty miles to go and it would be light until five, but there was a long delay while they waited for Hadissa and Daniel to come through customs. They were both nervous but for different reasons; John-Sunday, because he was apprehensive about meeting Daniel again, and Zac, because although the girl he secretly loved was irrevocably out of reach, he could not help but cling to the idea that their futures were somehow bound together. How should he greet her? How would she respond to him when she saw his scar? It was imperative that this first meeting should go smoothly. Later, when she learnt how indispensable he was to John-Sunday and her mother, when she had heard his side of the story of the bombing and had come to terms with what he had done, surely she would give up this unnatural liaison with the white man, and then, then... He could not decently finish the thought; it was pure fantasy.

There she was, more than an hour after the flight had arrived. A lonely, isolated figure, but unmistakeably Hadissa, her belly still slightly swollen from her pregnancy, her breasts full and round, carrying her baby in her arms – as beautiful, Zac thought, as in her photograph. Not looking particularly happy though, he realised suddenly, but worried, upset. She came up to them swiftly, embraced John-Sunday, cast a momentary, panic-stricken look at Zac, and then burst into tears.

"Hadissa!" John-Sunday clasped his arms around her, and glanced at Zac in bewilderment. "What's the matter? Where's Daniel? Didn't he come with you?" He looked back the way she had come, his mind reeling, his eyes alive with hope.

She frowned and shook her head. "Of course he came with me! But they stopped us, made us empty our suitcases..."

"Well, that's not unusual..."

"But they took him away! I thought he'd catch up with me, so I waited. Then I had to change the baby's nappy, and I thought I'd missed him, so I went back to where we were... and he's still in there! I didn't know what to do," she said despairingly. "I thought you might think we hadn't come, so I came on through."

"Well, let's wait a bit, see what happens," said Zac encouragingly, determined she should notice him. "I'm sure it'll be fine."

She hardly glanced at him. "No, it won't! It won't! He was carrying..."

John-Sunday frowned. "What? Something illegal?"

She gave an almost imperceptible nod. "Second-hand medication," she whispered, glancing fearfully around. "And currency. Lots and lots of English currency."

*　*　*

"As I say, sah, I cannot let you go until I know why you carry one thousand English pounds in your toilet bag, and another thousand hidden about your person. Here's this wallet, thick with paper money, more in that pouch in your jacket pocket, yet more in your shaving bag – and your socks – do English usually carry money in their *socks*?" he scoffed. "Do you think we're stupid? Why didn't you declare it? Or bring in a banker's order, or make the exchange in your own country, and bring in naira?"

Because you're corrupt, Dan thought wearily, oblivious that corruption was what the official, himself, was alleging. Because the rate of exchange makes nonsense of it when I'll lose so much through *baksheesh*. Because I don't want anyone to know that I've got it. Because I may want to buy a decent car, or clothes, or a decent meal occasionally. Even, for God's sake, a proper toilet. Because, you stupid twit, I may need it to get home again.

"I've given you my explanation," he said, running a finger round his collar. "I'm a teacher. I shall be living in the bush and I want to buy equipment. A lot of equipment. And we're newly married. There're things I want to buy for my wife..."

"Ah yes, your wife." It was a sneer and Dan bridled.

"Who I'm married to is none of your damn business!"

"We make everything our business, sah."

"I bet you do!"

The man inspected him silently. "And the medicines, sah?"

Dan sighed. "For the clinic at Kateri, as I've already told you. My wife's a nurse. And I'm a British citizen. I've told you that, too, more than once."

Perhaps, he thought uneasily, he should get himself a lawyer. This gave him inspiration.

"I wish to see the British High Commissioner," he said, with mock pomposity. "His residence is here in Abuja. I think you'll find him easy enough to track down."

His bluff worked. The man blinked nervously and spoke with more courtesy.

"That won't be necessary. Wait here, Sah."

He went out and closed the door behind him. Dan saw him looking at him through the reinforced glass and he turned away. The tiny, windowless room was brightly lit with the harsh white glare of strip lighting, and there was no fan. As the minutes passed, he began to sweat profusely. He wondered where Hadissa was. Had she already met up with John-Sunday, and at this very moment was enjoying a cold drink in the cafeteria?

Time moved slowly, and he began to worry about the road. They had two or three hours' travelling ahead of them and it was already after four. Suddenly he was aware of being scrutinised, and he looked up sharply. Someone was watching him through the small glass panel in the door. Even as their eyes met, the door opened and the customs official came in.

"All's well, Sah," he said cheerfully. "We've checked your papers and everything's in order..."

"I think I knew that, didn't I?" Dan replied scathingly, getting to his feet.

"...So you may go now."

"Well, thank *you*!"

"But first there's the little matter of the currency..."

Dan knew what was coming.

"There's a small fine to pay..."

"Small, you say."

"Yes, Sah, very small..."

"Okay," Dan sighed. "How small is small?"

"Only small, Sah. And Sah..."

"What now?"

"We are not concerned about the medication – we hope you will use that for our people!"

They took him to back to the room where they had previously examined his luggage. The room was empty, and his huge case and the flight bag lay open on the rickety tables, the clothes strewn about haphazardly. He began to repack his trunk carefully, then, glancing at his watch, he hastily bundled everything else on top, but it refused to close. He managed to lock one side of it, and secured it with the strap. He stuffed the thick wads of notes from his the toilet bag into his flight bag, thinking, at least they hadn't taken all his money; he still had his escape route. But his wallet was empty and there was no trace of the cellophane packet with its four hundred pounds for emergencies.

* * *

The airport was empty, and it was now dark outside. The night was humid, thick with particles of red dust. They went quickly to the car and loaded up.

"God, it's heavy," John-Sunday grumbled, hefting the trunk into the boot. "And it isn't even fastened properly!"

"We're staying a while..." Dan felt irritable and uncommunicative, and he was slow to recover his humour. The atmosphere in the car was tense. Zac drove with Dan beside him, John-Sunday in the back with Hadissa and the baby.

"We're now *very* late," growled John-Sunday, sounding morose and tetchy.

"John-Sunday, leave it." Hadissa gripped his arm. "Daniel knows how late we are. It can't be helped. We'll get there all right, with God's help."

They didn't pray, Dan thought. God's blood covering the vehicle. Coming safe through the Red Sea. All that business, they've left it out this time. We're on our own. It was now intensely dark, with no lights showing on the land as far as the eye could see.

After a while John-Sunday thawed and began to talk more easily, but he turned his head so that he spoke exclusively to Hadissa, and so quietly that Dan could hardly hear what he was saying. He caught snatches of news, and the clinic was mentioned several times. Occasionally Hadissa urged him to speak louder.

"Daniel would be interested in that."

"Say that to my husband…"

Huddled over the wheel, Zac grinned maliciously to himself.

"John-Sunday, Daniel can't hear you. Tell him what you've just told me."

"John-Sunday, that's terrible! Daniel really needs to hear that!"

"*Okay*," John-Sunday said, raising his voice at last and swinging his body forward. "Okay, you do need to hear this, Daniel. There've been more riots."

Dan turned and stared at him. "Riots?"

"Extremists from both sides," said John-Sunday shortly. "Up the road from here, at one of the checkpoints. It's only happened recently but it's serious. Some people don't like it, that we employ Muslim workers in the new workshop. Word gets around, so they're making a point. Anyway, a Christian was shot dead in his own office. He was an official at the checkpoint – another Christian shot him. A case of mistaken identity, but revenge was taken against the Muslims. Now both sides blame each other."

"The old story." Dan turned back to the road.

"It's not all bad," said John-Sunday defensively. "I only told you because we're late! There's good things happening all the time. For instance, there's a Muslim businessman in Kaduna who is supplying shrubs for the children's garden there. You remember, at the mosque?"

"How could I forget?"

"And we have a Muslim mechanic working with us at Kateri, and the mosque is donating money to help our workshop project. So you see, it *is* possible for us to work together, in spite of many setbacks."

"Win some, lose some," said Dan indifferently.

"But *your* country's not helping!" John-Sunday leant forward again, his mood swinging abruptly. "We've had news... You've been selling Christian land to the Muslims!"

"What on earth...?"

"Your *country*!" John-Sunday almost spat the words, and Dan turned his face away, repelled.

"I don't know what you mean," he muttered. "*Christian* land..."

"It was on the radio, and Cletus – you remember Cletus? He showed me a cutting..."

"I don't know what you're talking about."

"You have these old churches," John-Sunday explained derisively. "Where you can't get Christians to worship anymore! So the Muslims say they'll buy the land. Well, of course they'd say that! So you sell it to them...! Well, we're not so polite! We'd rather any use was made of it, than the Muslims have it! But *you, hah!*"

Hadissa groaned with exasperation. "Must you quarrel? He's my husband!"

John-Sunday ignored her.

"*We* don't stand in the corner out of the way, like you do, and say, 'oh, by all means buy our land!'" His voice was heavy with sarcasm. "'What a good thing it is that the land will be used for religious purposes!' No! When you sell off church land to the Muslims, for them it is a victory! And they tell it around the world! A *victory!*"

"Not me, mate," replied Dan quietly. "Not my land. Nothing to do with me."

It was no good. He couldn't make the effort. Too much had already happened to overwhelm him, even before they had reached Kateri. What the hell did he think he was doing, coming to this God-forsaken place? What on earth had possessed him? He looked out of the window at the African darkness. In England he had left behind a rainy autumnal day, the trees heavy with leaves, dripping and sodden, the roads and the fields laden with pools of water, but here, beneath the impenetrable dark sky, there was just a vast, empty savannah, the soil cracked and pitted into deep crevices, hung with blackness.

"Fires ahead," said Zac, calm, fatalistic, his eyes on the road.

# CHAPTER 3

Blazing torches lit the area, chasing long, horizontal shadows across the road. Hadissa moaned in fear, and Dan reached behind and clutched her hand. As Zac slowed down John-Sunday was at last silent. They joined a short queue of cars and trucks on the inside lane, the wheels bumping along the uneven surface of the hard shoulder. A handful of men in camouflage gear ringed the place, some waving flaming brands. The short, staccato sound of rifle fire stabbed the darkness, spreading alarm and confusion among the drivers. Then it was their turn.

*If it all goes bad on us, we'll run... if we can.*

Cletus, on Dan's first journey on this road. But Cletus had prayed...

They pulled up and Zac wound down the window. In the light of the torches Dan could see beads of moisture on his forehead and his upper lip. Hastily he wiped his own face on his sleeve. He could smell the sweat in his armpits, and then he jumped as the boot was thrown open and the suitcases were wrenched out. A dark figure, his face tense and glossy with sweat, banged on Zac's door with his fist. Jerking the muzzle of his rifle, he motioned to Zac to get out.

At that moment John-Sunday remembered Zac's dread of the Muslim fanatics in Nasarawa, and his machete wound, and he touched him on the arm.

"Stay where you are, Zac," he said brusquely. "And keep the engine running."

He opened his own door and got out.

"*No*, John!" Hadissa reached for him, clutching at air.

John-Sunday ignored her and slowly went forward to stand by the front of the car. He leant back against it, but feeling its heat on his thighs, stood upright. Someone gestured for his papers, examined them in the light of a hurricane lamp, then glanced at him suspiciously.

"Are you a Christian?"

Momentarily John-Sunday closed his eyes. *Stanley*, he thought bleakly, *Stanley...*

*They had run into bandits who had made him get out on the side of the road and asked the usual question: are you a Christian? And when he had said yes, they shot him.*

He crossed his arms over his chest, averting his eyes, trying not to show how afraid he was. He wanted to say, defiantly – bearing witness – yes. Yes, I am a Christian. Yes, I believe in the one true God – but he lowered his head and nodded instead, and then couldn't stop nodding.

Inside the car Dan saw his movement. It was the action of someone at bay. For God's sake, he thought angrily, he's only a boy! Then he remembered Stanley. He'd been even younger when he was killed on the road. Sighing inwardly, he moved. He snatched up his flight bag and flung open the door of the car. Hadissa grabbed the back of his seat.

"Daniel! What are you doing? Don't..."

There was the sound of a shot, a deep explosion in the night, and John-Sunday disappeared below the bonnet of the car.

"*No*," Hadissa screamed, and as if in response, the baby began to cry, a startled, breathless half-choking wail that tore at Dan's gut. He could no longer see John-Sunday.

"Dammit, dammit, dammit," he muttered, and leant across to Zac and spoke in his ear. "If you get a chance, gun the engine, and go!"

Zac's jaw dropped. "But what about John?"

Not, what about you, but what about John? Well, it was predictable.

"I'll get him back in, somehow. Then *go*. Just drive, and swerve like crazy."

He clasped his flight bag to his chest and got out. John-Sunday was crouched on the ground clutching his stomach, his head drooping. Dan could not tell if he was hurt. He held up the flight bag.

"Money," he shouted. "Lots of lovely money! English pounds, not your bloody *naira!* Come on, you bastards! You can have it if you let him go!"

Playground games. He circled round them until he was away from the car, and they followed him, as if mesmerised. They looked at each other incredulously. He took the wad of notes out of the bag and waved them around in the air.

"Get in the car, John-Sunday," he called urgently. *"Get back in the car!"*

He was aware of John-Sunday stumbling away, clutching his stomach, and he shouted louder to distract from his shambling figure. Then he rushed at them, yelling like a banshee, the notes in his hand. He tossed them up in the air, trying to get into a position where he could get back to the car. He was a wild sight, his jacket flapping open, the money falling about him like leaves, his red unruly hair, his pale face lit red by the torches, shiny with sweat, and his mouth wide open in a hoarse shriek of rage and contempt. But John-Sunday was back in the car and Hadissa was screaming and Zac was revving the engine hard.

At that moment Dan saw, quite clearly, almost dispassionately, that he had no chance of reaching the car. He tossed the last of the money in their faces, then rammed the empty flight bag at the nearest one's chest. He was close enough to see his broken teeth and his wide, astounded eyes.

"That's it, mate," he grunted, then turned and ran.

He ran for the darkness beyond the fires, towards a steep bank that bordered the road. He climbed it on all fours, his fingers scrabbling for a hold in the compacted soil. Beyond was high scrub and dense shadow, but the further away from the road he could get, the less likely they would turn back and shoot at the car. Once in the thick scrub, he thought frantically, he could hide for a while, and then hike up the road to Kateri. It couldn't be too far. At the top of the bank he turned for a last sight of the car, but it was his undoing; his white face shone like a beacon, and there was a shout of rage behind him. In that split second he saw Hadissa's face at the window, her mouth wide open in a silent shriek. He saw Zac hunched over the wheel. It was too dark to see John-Sunday, but his door was swinging shut. Then, with a screech of tyres, they were away, swerving, accelerating up the road, the lid of the boot bouncing. Mixed with the sulphurous fumes of the torches was the acrid smell of burning rubber.

He ran like one demented, the prickly shrub tearing at his clothes. The land was uneven and pitted with stones which bruised his heels and scraped at his shins. His ankle turned and he nearly fell. There was a gap in the scrub, and he saw, ahead of him, that the land was rising again. His chest was constricted, tight with exertion, and his heart thumped, but he surged up the incline like an athlete, his breath catching in his throat like bile. He was not alone, for behind him he could hear a strange animal throb on the ground, the relentless, pounding footsteps of his pursuers. He felt a fierce exultant joy that, with each step, he was taking them further away from Hadissa.

\* \* \*

There was chaos in car as they left. Hadissa was punching John-Sunday, weeping, screaming out her terror and relief. Zac drove hunched and grim-faced over the wheel, deafened by the shrill, piercing wails of the baby. As for John-Sunday, he sat clutching his head, silent and ashamed. For he was not hurt. The shot, which he had expected and feared, and which seemed, at point blank range, incapable of missing him, had been a bluff. He had vomited with fear and now he smelt it, pungent and sour, mixed with the other human smells in the car. They wanted to frighten him, he thought, and they succeeded. Now Daniel had taken his place. He felt mortified, dishonoured, disgraced beyond measure.

\* \* \*

Dan had been running for nearly twenty minutes. At one point, the thunderous sound of the road came to him, and he realised that he had been moving in a wide arc, and he turned away into the bush until the noise receded. Night had fallen and it was utterly quiet, as though all life was watching and listening. Once he heard the clumsy startled movements of some large animal nearby, and he stopped for a moment, holding his breath, but whatever it was moved silently away into denser foliage.

He bent and rested his hands on his knees, panting heavily, inhaling the cool air. The sounds behind him had diminished and he wondered if they'd given up. He couldn't hope to outrun them, for they were native to the bush and must know the territory. Then, with dread, he heard the rhythmic thud of boots on the hard earth. They were still coming, slowly but inexorably, not tearing through the bush as he was, but conserving their strength, steadily, methodically, tracking him. He knew they were close – no more, he judged, than a couple of hundred metres. He began to run again. The moon was out, illuminating the landscape with its pale green glow and creating harsh elongated shadows on the stony ground. It helped him to see his way, and he ran on, faster, but staggering slightly now, his ears straining for the sounds of thudding feet. They did not call out or shoot, for the range was too uncertain and the light treacherous and inconsistent. They came after him silently, like ghosts. They were tenacious, and with reason; he had fooled them on the road. In his mouth he could taste the sickness of despair.

*Hadissa, be safe! God, make her safe!*

He realised that he was no longer wearing his jacket. The second jacket lost to Africa, torn off in his headlong flight, but he hardly cared. Now there was some kind of level path, and taller trees. It made running easier and he sprinted on, the shadows and patches of moonlight patterning the ground. But if it was easier for him, then it would be easier for them too. Almost he could feel their breath on the back of his neck, feral and predatory, and his shoulders hunched defensively. What would it be, a shot? Or would they use their machetes? Then, through the encompassing bush, he was aware of signs of habitation, lights, the swirling smoke of night fires, and the round indistinctive shapes of encircling huts, and his spirits lifted. Nearby he could hear the soft murmur of people talking, but behind him, even closer, the accelerating throb of pounding feet.

Bent figures of women by the cooking fires; the smell of cooking fat and something else, he knew not what, and did not take the time to think, for they were upon him. His breath rasped in his chest, but he was within the circle of light. The women were calling out fearfully, backing away; a black cooking pot toppled, spilling its contents into the embers. The fire blazed up and Dan stopped short.

At that moment he felt a deep shock to his back, high up on his spine near his neck. I'm shot, he thought drearily, and lurched forward, his arms flailing.

The fire came up to meet him. His face flamed, and his hands scrabbled in the fierce white ash. The pain was horrendous. Every nerve in his body shrieked in protest. His mouth opened and he roared with anguish and disbelief, a high-pitched sound, ugly and obscene, like a trapped animal. The white-hot ash burst in a cloud about his head, and with his next tortured breath, seared his lungs. Images of cold stone danced before his eyes, a chill cavernous interior, a charred cross....

*To the glory of God this Cathedral burnt.*

He did not lose consciousness but tore himself out of the fire, scrambling away from it, crawling blindly on the beaten ground, his head shrouded in burning ash. The women looked at him in horror, their hands to their mouths. The men stood motionless, stunned and silent, their guns still raised, as Dan's body, contorted with agony, thumped against the walls of a hut and recoiled, before finally coming to rest against the cool palisade of a nearby chicken coop.

# CHAPTER 4

In the car a grim silence descended. The lid of the boot was still flapping but Zac did not dare to pull over to shut it.

"You think he got away?" he murmured, but no one replied. Hadissa seemed sunk in a stupor, bereft of hope, the child suckling at her breast for comfort. John-Sunday lay collapsed against the window, his eyes half-closed, his hands flaccid on his lap. He seemed to be sleeping, but it was not far to Kateri, and when he saw the familiar concrete houses he roused himself.

"Zac, take my sister to the house, and light some lamps."

Zac looked at him apprehensively. He seemed grim, determined.

"What are you going to do?"

John-Sunday knew what he had to do, but first he had to see Hadissa and the baby settled, and fetch his mother. He disappeared up the track at a run. Zac carried in Hadissa's bags and watched as she laid the sleeping child in the middle of the bed, then he left to fetch the lamp. Shivering, Hadissa sat down on the edge of the mattress, and began to nurse the baby again, staring into the darkness. She felt intensely cold, inside and out, her mind paralysed. Eventually, hearing Zac again at the door, she got up wearily, laid the now quiescent child on the mattress, and gathered a blanket around her shoulders.

"You can have my room tonight," he said uncomfortably, handing her the hurricane lamp. "I'll sleep in the workshop." She took it from him awkwardly and he watched her, embarrassed by the proximity of this sweet vulnerable girl whom he loved. "We've built you a house," he added diffidently. "But you won't want to be there alone tonight."

"Where's my brother?" she asked him, calmly enough.

"I think he's gone to bring your mother. She can have this room if that's well with you."

"Where will he sleep, then?"

370

Zac hesitated, avoiding her eyes. "I shouldn't tell you... He's going back, I think."

"Back?"

"To the road. He says he's going to look for your... husband."

Hadissa said nothing. She knew Dan was dead. She sat and waited for her brother. It would be futile to dissuade him, and she would not attempt it. He would need to reclaim his honour, for otherwise he would not live. She waited, immobile, for a long time, while her baby slept. Then she heard them coming down the path, John-Sunday's steadying voice and her mother's breathless, anxious wails. Then she was at the door. She burst in and flung herself at Hadissa, her arms stretched wide, her tears flying out on her fat cheeks. She gripped Hadissa by the shoulders and squeezed her painfully.

"A year! A whole year and you're come at last! He fetch me from my sleep, and I think, she's come! *Ai-ee*, he bring me down the path in the dark!"

"He told you what happened?"

"He told me." She shrugged and turned to the bed. "No matter. He'll sort it out, with God's help." She peered inquisitively at the baby. "So, this is your child."

"But, Momi, my husband..."

"Oh, John'll take care of that," she said indifferently, bending over the bed. "Red hair," she muttered, stroking the dusky dark hair of the sleeping child.

"Daniel is red," replied Hadissa faintly.

Her mother looked up, startled. "Your man is red? How, red? He's a white man."

"He has red hair."

"So," breathed her mother. She gave Hadissa a significant look. "It starts again, yes?"

Hadissa frowned, bewildered. "What starts?"

"Your father had red hair. You and John; you're dark. I thought the redness all gone, and now you've started it all over again."

"Started *what*?" Hadissa asked impatiently.

"Your ancestor, Hadissa. He was a white man and he had this same red hair. Didn't you know?" Her eyes glinted. "It came out in your father, but my family were very dark and you are, too." She giggled inanely. "Oh, Hadissa, you must have loved your Dadda very much…"

"*Loved* him?" She flushed. "How can you *say* that? I *hated* him! You knew how he was with me, and…" She thought she had forgiven her mother, but it was not so; she was filled with resentment. "You did nothing about it, Momi! You just let him…"

Her mother reached out and slapped her cheek. "Don't *talk* to me like that! I'm your mother!"

Hadissa rubbed her face. "I was a *child*, Momi!" she said dully, tears forming in her eyes. "You should have hated him too, for what he was doing to me." She turned away and went to the window. "But you didn't care, did you?"

"Well, see what *you've* done!" said her mother sharply. "Perhaps you didn't hate him so very much after all! *Something* made you choose the red man! How long will it take this time, you silly girl, before the redness disappears?"

She clutched at Hadissa, her nails digging in to the tender flesh of her arms.

"To think you should come back in this way!" she exclaimed. "Lord a'mercy! *Lord* a' mercy! And your husband lost!"

Yet her eyes gleamed with triumph and satisfaction, that Hadissa should arrive without the white man.

\* \* \*

John-Sunday loaded the truck, throwing in blankets, a couple of bottles of water, and an old mattress, in the event of finding Daniel alive. He checked the air pressure and the fuel gauge and fetched a battery torch from his workbench. Zac watched him uneasily, but John-Sunday refused to meet his eyes. He got in and started the engine. Then, at last, he looked at Zac.

"Take care of Hadissa."

"I can't come with you? You've never driven south before."

"I know how to drive and I must do this alone. Take care of Hadissa," John-Sunday repeated. He drove the truck slowly along the path from the workshop towards the road. At the grass verge he paused, waiting for a break in the traffic, then he turned the truck towards Abuja, swerving diagonally across the wide central reservation, scattering the goats tethered there, and waking the herdsman.

"Who's that? John-Sunday? What is it, John-Sunday, that you steal my rest? The end of the world?"

Above him the night was profoundly dark, an infinite expanse of firmament shot through with bright stars, but towards the horizon the sky was changing to a luminous encircling mass of radiant blue above shifting clouds. How many hours had passed since they'd been stopped on the road? Three? Four? If only he'd not had to fetch his mother! The three-mile run up the hill and her ponderous walk down in the darkness, impatiently urging her on, had been unbearably time-consuming. But he could not have left Hadissa, a married woman, alone with Zac at night. Part of him hoped, treacherously, that she was not, still, a married woman, but he thrust that thought from him. If Daniel died tonight, it would be his fault. His fear, his utter cowardice, had lost Daniel for her at the very start of their marriage. It was the most shameful moment of his life, and as he drove, he wept.

After some miles he slowed the truck and began to scrutinise the opposite lane, searching for anything unusual. A hard knot of anger was forming in his stomach and he found himself hoping that the bandits would still be there. If necessary he would confront them and demand to know where Daniel had been taken. Then they'd shoot him, and it would all be over. If they shot him it would be no big deal, he thought despondently, for he could not go on living with this shame, with Hadissa's accusing eyes fixed on him, or the ignominy of Zac's sympathy and his collusion, or his mother's prying mockery. At last, seeing debris in the other lane, he pulled over on to the hard shoulder, skidding slightly on the loose gravel, and stalling the engine. He left his lights on to illuminate the place, and reached for his torch.

The wind was up and a wall of traffic was coming towards him, and again he had to wait before he could cross. He dashed across to the central reservation, and then across the two lanes on the other side. As his figure was caught in their headlights the drivers blasted their horns and taunted him, their shouts fading into the night as they passed him, stolen by the buffeting wind. He shone the torch around, but he could see no sign of activity here, no telltale spent cartridges, no abandoned flight bag, no burnt-out torches. Only the usual litter; a twisted strip of tyre, and battered and rusty drinks cans that might have

373

been thrown out of any passing vehicle. He shone his torch into the ditch and up the bank, and for a moment he was elated, for in the ditch he could see huge bundles of firewood, and up the bank a piece of fabric had been caught on an overhanging branch. He scrambled up and shone his torch on it, but it was only an old shirt, torn, filthy and full of lice. He threw it down in disgust, and wiped the palms of his hands on his trousers.

He went back to the truck and drove slowly up the road, about a quarter of a mile. Traffic streamed past him, honking and hooting, braking hard as they saw the red lights of his tailgate swerving in and out. Again he searched, but it felt wrong; he knew it was not the right place. He ran his hand through his hair, baffled. Perhaps he had started his hunt too close to Kateri. Zac had been driving very fast as they made their escape, and it had taken them another three-quarters of an hour to reach home. Perhaps he had not gone far enough down the road.

He climbed back into the cab, slammed the door, and set off again, driving more slowly now, scanning the hard shoulder. He drove for another half hour, then pulled in again. At this point there was a slight bend in the road, and he knew that it was a favourite ploy of the bandits to mount their ambush beyond a bend where drivers would come on them unawares.He had no need of his torch, for a faint gleam of dawn was lighting the sky, and he could see that although there was the usual debris, there was no bank of earth rising out of the ditch for Daniel to climb, no overhanging scrub in which he might have hidden. The ditch fell away into wide white fields of sorghum, and he was aware that the land beyond was treeless, merely low hills and valleys. A little way back from the road he could see a circle of mud huts, and a long rectangular building covered by a tin roof.

He drove on again, deep in thought. He stopped twice more, each time scrutinising the place, each time disappointed. There was a lull in the traffic, the brief quiet time when hardly anything travelled on the road. He was very cold, and he had not eaten since his breakfast the previous day. His mind felt dulled and there was an unpleasant taste in his mouth. He rubbed his eyes, and opened one of the bottles and took a long drink of water, tilting his head back, steering with one hand, his eyes fixed firmly on the road ahead. He felt angry, bitter, thwarted. Now that he had found the courage to confront his enemies they were not to be found. They had simply disappeared into the night.

The rising sun cast a fiery red glow over the horizon, transforming the cloud mass over Abuja to an intense violet blue, and the land seemed to open up in front of him, the colour flowing across it and revealing myriads of tiny insects dancing in the air. He drove on hopelessly. The surface of the road was steaming and his tyres sounded wet. He thought he would drive nearly to Abuja; perhaps he would see more clearly when he came back on the other side.

As he came into the outskirts of the city he saw a fire burning, far back from the road, among the low shantytowns; dense black smoke rose in a narrow column into the sky, and he could smell the acrid stench of burning rubber. Ash was drifting across in the slight breeze, and bits of paper, still smouldering at the edges.

It reminded John-Sunday of something, but the memory was elusive. Then, horrified, the tiny hairs rising on the back of his neck, it came to him, the torn photograph of Daniel that he had burnt in his brazier. He stopped the truck, and lowered his face into his hands. He remembered the anguish of that time, the deep animosity he had felt towards Daniel, his unthinking, blind anger, and how it had evoked in him an intensely urgent longing to use what power he had, however malign, to intervene in their relationship. He had not, at the time, questioned his motives, and had little regret for the dormant superstition that had led him to burn the image of Daniel in his own fire. Now he comprehended the malevolence of that act, and he saw too, how it might have been a curse. He had cursed Daniel and Daniel had died.

It was now mid morning. Wearily he drove back towards Kateri, but though he scanned the road, he no longer believed that Daniel was alive. The road was now crowded with vehicles of all descriptions, completely filling the two lanes of the dual carriageway. Frequently he saw burnt out cars beside the road, and trucks with their wheels missing, collapsed on the hard shoulder, and then he saw a battered tanker on its side, and a woman, bent over, filling a water pot from a ditch. Behind were ramshackle huts and shanties, and John-Sunday drew in his breath. He had never seen such squalor.

He pulled up beside the tanker and stopped. Chickens scattered, squawking, and a grimy child peeped out from the window of the derelict cab. A man walked round the back of it, wearing a soiled *keffiyeh* and the distinctive collarless tunic characteristic of Muslim workingmen. John-Sunday got down from the truck and went up to him.

"*Assalama alaikum*," he greeted him, bowing deferentially. He had a crucial question to ask and he needed this man's goodwill and cooperation.

"*Alaikum salama.*"

"You speak English?" asked John-Sunday.

"You want something?"

He was a slight, thin, olive-skinned man with a rasping voice, and his eyes showed the persistent inflammation characteristic of those who lived by the road. His eyelids were half-closed and bloodshot, his mouth and his thin straggly moustache stained with betel juice. When he spoke he revealed broken, infected teeth, the betel stain like blood on his gums.

"I am seeking someone," said John-Sunday nervously, unsure how much to divulge. "Someone lost on the road."

The Muslim looked at him closely. "Yes," he muttered, "he said he was lost on the road."

John-Sunday could not believe his ears. Daniel Marsden, here, with a *Muslim*?

"A white man?" he said eagerly. "Red hair? Injured, perhaps?"

"A *white* man?" His tone was scathing. "There's no white man here."

"Who, then?"

"Come and see." The Muslim turned, and led the way to the tanker. "You have waited long," he said over his shoulder. "It is time, and beyond time, since he came."

Even as he peered into the cab John-Sunday, with a strange prescience, knew what he would find. The child had disappeared and another figure lay there, huddled in blankets, apparently asleep, but John-Sunday saw the gleam of his eyes and the colour of his hair. There was no mistaking that hair and John-Sunday drew back in horror, his worst fears realised. It was his father, thin, unkempt, his mouth wet and drooling, covered in flies. Beside him was an empty wine bottle. John-Sunday pulled at the blanket, the better to see his face. One side was twisted, as if he had been punched, as if the punch had imprinted itself on his features.

"Is this whom you seek?"

376

"No," said John-Sunday with loathing. "No, another."

"You are sure? You have the mark of him."

"No," John-Sunday repeated dully. He turned away. "It is another I seek."

"I did not expect you would take him," said the Muslim with disgust. "*In sh'allah* – he will stay with us. It is best. He is among friends."

"He takes strong drink?" John-Sunday spoke with difficulty, his mind reeling, but the Muslim laughed scornfully.

"Once he did, but this is something I make for him, since Allah struck him for his sins. He came from nowhere and worked with me, since two years. But it is not your business, if he does not belong to you. You seek another, you say?"

John-Sunday pulled himself together. He could deal with this later, he thought, if he could face up to it; not now, while he must look for Daniel Marsden. Later, he thought; he'd come back later, but he knew in his heart he would not come back. He could no longer envisage taking his father home. He looked again, and groaned inwardly. His father had hidden himself here, working for this man? He, who would not work with Muslims? It was a mystery.

"I must go," he said. "I have stayed too long."

"This other, you hoped to find him here?"

"Word travels quickly... A white man," he repeated, "hurt on the road."

"Alone?"

"Not alone," said John-Sunday uncomfortably. "There were others. They escaped."

The man looked at him closely and he saw comprehension dawn.

"Bandits?"

"Yes. Last night. We lost him, so I look for him all night. He only came to Abuja yesterday. Now he has disappeared."

"Many disappear..." the man said, spitting long stream of liquorice-coloured liquid on to the ground near John-Sunday's feet. He recoiled, and man laughed sardonically. "I would disappear, myself, if I had the chance!"

John-Sunday turned away. Stopping here had been fruitless, after all.

"If you see him..." he said, turning back. "If you get

word of him… will you send to Kateri?"

"Kateri? Which side of the road, Kateri?"

"This side."

"You are Christian?"

John-Sunday could say it now, when it didn't matter. "Yes."

The man looked at him impassively, his expression enigmatic. He felt in his tunic and brought out a battered packet of cigarettes. He tipped one into his hand and put it to his mouth and lit it, eyeing John-Sunday intently. He seemed to be measuring him up. He inhaled deeply, then blew a cloud of smoke into John-Sunday's face.

"There are many here." He indicated the camp. "None of them are white. We do what we can for them, which is not much. They also come from nowhere."

"You take in the homeless?" John-Sunday was incredulous. To find kindness here, amidst such poverty, was one thing; to learn that there were many utterly confounded him. Truly, only the poor served the poor! It turned his prejudice on its head; it shamed him, and he felt it shamed his church. Had this, then, been his father's penance?

"Allah is merciful; they do not live long, generally." The Muslim indicated the cab. "This one, he will die, perhaps soon. You deny him, but you still expect me to help you?" The compassion in his eyes was almost unbearable, and John-Sunday hung his head.

The Muslim nodded. "This white man," he said. "I will send to Kateri, if I hear of him."

*  *  *

John-Sunday returned to Kateri, parked the truck by the house and went in to wash. The baby, Habiba, was lying on his bed, asleep, but there was no sign of Hadissa. Cautiously, he lay down on the bed next to the child, marvelling at her tiny hands and feet, and her delicate rosebud mouth and observing the red-brown fuzz of her hair. Eventually he roused himself and went across to the workshop. On the bench was a covered plate of food, and he ate hungrily, standing at the door. He knew they would not leave the baby alone for long.

At last Zac appeared. John-Sunday saw him enter the

378

house and emerge with Habiba. He glanced up when he saw John-Sunday.

"I saw the truck. I was coming to find you. Any news?"

"None. No trace of him. He's dead, Zac."

Zac stopped in his tracks. "You don't know that!"

"I'm not even sure I was looking in the right place."

"Walk with me," said Zac. "I'm going to the clinic. Hadissa wants the baby with her."

John-Sunday paused, incredulous. "She's working in the clinic? Already? With her husband dead?"

Zac looked at him. "He's *missing*, John, and she wants work. She's checking the stocks. It's right for her to do this. Believe me, I know the feeling. But what will you do," he asked, "now that you haven't found him?"

"I shall go back," said John-Sunday simply. "Try to talk with the bandits, if they appear. But it's no use."

"You want me to come with you, this time?"

John-Sunday hesitated. He was still very afraid, but it was his offence that had landed them all in this mess. It was up to him to make what atonement he could.

"No," he said heavily. "Someone must stay here, manage the work, look after Hadissa. It had better be you."

"You'll see her before you leave?"

"No, I'm going almost immediately." He was not yet ready to face her reproachful eyes, not until he was sure. He would go now, before she saw him. "Fill up the tank, would you?"

He turned and went back to his house for a jacket, and climbing once more into the truck, he drove away. Zac stood with the empty can in his hand, watching him go and wondering, not for the first time, what was in store for them all.

I will marry her, he said to himself, hugging himself with anticipation. If this white man does not return, I will marry her. I'll ask John-Sunday to give me her hand.

*   *   *

Once more John-Sunday drove down towards Abuja, but this time he stopped short of the city, parked the truck in the shade of a tamarisk, and threw himself on the ground to sleep. He was convinced that Daniel was dead. How could he have

379

survived? To carry on searching was futile.

He woke, dripping with sweat, for the sun had gone round and it was nearly evening. He got up stiffly and climbed back into the truck. His bottle of water was tepid, but he drank thirstily, and poured some of it over his head, rubbing it into his mat of hair.

He set off again slowly, hugging the hard shoulder as though his engine was faulty, and whenever he saw people walking on the hard shoulder, he stopped and talked to them. Some of them carried huge bundles of kindling scavenged from the bush, others large amorphous bundles covered with tarps, still others crates of honeycomb, fruit and vegetables balanced on their heads. It was getting dark and all of them were frightened when he stopped; they slunk back, avoiding his eyes. He could understand their fear, but he left the same message with all of them, that if they heard news of a white man, they should send to Kateri. They stared at him, unblinking, incredulous.

He sat for a long time in the cab, wondering what had happened to Daniel. In his mind's eye, coldly, dispassionately, he saw his body lying somewhere in the scrub, prey to any passing animal. And it was his fault. There was nothing left to do, and his own life was forfeit; the future held nothing for him now. He was dishonoured.

His lights lit up every detail of the road ahead, but for some unfathomable reason there were no bandits. At a snail's pace he drove all the way to Abuja, only turning round when he reached the outskirts of the city. Here he left a message with a Muslim mechanic in a shanty by the roadside and finally, at dawn, he returned to Kateri. Wearily, he threw himself on his bed and tried to sleep, but for a long time his eyes stayed open, staring into the dark. He had failed.

# CHAPTER 5

Dan woke to nightmare. He was in complete darkness and his body felt numb. Instinctively, he jerked his head to shake off his stupor and an intense pain shot through his neck, but ominously, there was no pain in his limbs. Terrified, he panicked, and as his muscles tensed the pain shot down his spine and he almost passed out. At least, he thought, relief surging through him, he wasn't paralysed. He tried to look down at his body, but he could see nothing. Was he blind, as well? Then he saw a gleam of light and realised his eyelids were partially fused together by what seemed like a viscous glue. His arms and legs felt heavy, as if some weight was pressing down on them, and his hands were stinging. He could sense air on his body and he realised that he was totally naked except for his wrists and ankles, which seemed locked to the bed. He could feel harsh fabric chafing his burnt skin. Was he a prisoner, then?

His mouth felt gritty with ash and his throat was sore, but his chief anxiety was his bullet wound. A neck wound could prove fatal, and if he was a prisoner, how on earth could he survive? The pain was shooting through his body – an unfortunate image, he thought wryly, his pedagogic humour re-asserting itself, but he thought it dispassionately, as though he'd been drugged, or as though it had all happened to someone else. He remembered the fire, and that had been real enough.

At last he managed to force his eyes open, still terrified at the thought that they had been burnt, and felt particles of gritty dust fall on to his cheeks, like flaking leaves. The same stuff was on his body as well; he could feel it dry against his skin. His first sight was the cloud of mosquito net under which he was lying, suspended from the roof of whatever dwelling he was in. He breathed a sigh of relief, but his chest hurt with the effort and he remembered that he had inhaled hot ash.

This was not the first time, he recalled, that he had woken in this place. The taste of the hotly spiced food that they had brought him still lay on his tongue, and had left a residue of grease around his teeth. He had woken to the sound of people moving about, and the clatter of cooking pots, and two women had come. They had tried to spoon-feed him, but the food had stung his lips, and he had roared hoarsely in pain and fear into the darkness. They had fled, screaming, and since then they had only given him water. He found himself wondering if it was clean. He himself was not; he could smell his own faeces and the mattress was damp.

Under the mosquito net it seemed a half-world of partial hearing and even more partial sight. The net was thin but it was opaque, and he could not see beyond it. His depression mounting and the tears forming in his eyes, he asked himself, then, what he had done, that life should treat him so unjustly? It was unbelievable that, just yesterday he was observing a fly-past of starlings, already feeling nostalgic about rain even as he boarded the plane; that, a week ago, he had been standing in front of Stephen, being married, and that not so very long ago his mood in Luke's study had been jubilant and optimistic. Where had he gone wrong? And look what he had come to! He was isolated, cut off from all that he knew, hundreds of miles from his home, and separated from Hadissa both by distance and misfortune. Even so, he could not find it in himself to regret meeting Hadissa; far from it. At the thought that she was ignorant of what had happened to him, even, perhaps, believing him dead, he groaned aloud.

Immediately he heard voices at the door; a woman's voice, deep and tranquil, and the voice of a man, rich, deep-toned, that spoke with authority. They pulled aside the shutters and the sun rushed in, and it was only then that he realised that his mattress was lying directly on the floor, and he raised his eyes and squinted up. What he saw was not reassuring. The man was dwarfish and very fat, his face matt-black and pockmarked. He was in native dress, his belly hanging over his belt, and his cheeks were pendulous. Over a homespun tunic he wore a skirt made of a tattered assortment of animal skins, and his thickly muscled legs were covered with numerous feathered anklets. Dan suddenly realised he was a pygmy, but what he was doing in the Nigerian bush, he couldn't imagine. He was probably some sort of *obeah* man, or bush doctor. He was surprised how little alarm he felt, and put it down to shock, or the drugs they'd given him. The man looked intently into Dan's face, his eyes glowing.

"I am out of Chad," he said, confidentially, and waited.

Dan grunted an acknowledgement of this, at which the man seemed gratified, his chest swelling pompously.

"I speak English, see," he said, with a broad smile, his chins wobbling. "I come help you. I bring good medicine. You have pain?"

Dan tried to nod, and winced.

"Ah, no move! What your name?" He squatted down, revealing that he was wearing nothing under his clothes, and Dan averted his eyes. "Give me name," he said, wagging his head and smiling broadly, "and you come no more harm. Ah, no move!"

Dan had shifted uneasily, and again he winced with pain. Despite his overt good humour, the man somehow seemed sinister, and Dan stayed silent. He felt wary of him, but when he was asked again, he capitulated, and told him his Christian name. Nothing worse could happen to him, after all.

"Ah, now *I* give name, and you not fear!" He laughed gently, his chins shaking, and pointed to himself. "Akuleki. I am doctor. Ak-u-le-ki, see? You know what village you come? No? I tell you. You come *Muslim* village! You Christian, yes? All white men Christian. Here, *Muslim*. They make you well. Put leaves on you with gum for burns. It is very good; look, see?" With stubby fingers he gathered up some of the green flakes that had fallen on to the mattress, and let them fall again. Dan felt reassured, but he wanted to ask, What about a proper doctor? Why had they tied him to the bed? What about getting him out of this place, wherever it was? And why hadn't they sent him to hospital? This last question he managed to ask.

"No, that bring police!" Akuleki gave him a wide, white-toothed grin. "Not good – white man burnt."

White man shot? In the end he put the words together.

Akuleki laughed dismissively. "No, not shot, but six days you lie here, hurt bad with stick of rifle." He pointed to his neck, and nodded significantly. "And burns – hands, knees, face, hair, feet, all *burns*," he said with macabre satisfaction. "Not chest, not back, not toes…"

He seemed proud of his English vocabulary, and Dan would have grinned if he could. He imagined the English lessons, the words chalked up on the board, a pointing stick – *learn these*! Then he heard the echo of the words.

"My face?"

"Ah, one side bad, very bad. Two side, fine." For a moment he seemed professional and intrigued. "Like vitiligo disease – we have that here. Make dark skin pale pieces, with you, black pieces!" He smiled encouragingly. "See, you are one of us. Now, we rope you so you don't pick, but now, not rope. And do not worry, leaves grow here for healing. And we have Vaseline and pepper."

*Vaseline and pepper?*

Akuleki untied him, fastened a loincloth over him and he drifted off to sleep. The next time he woke the pygmy had gone, but apparently he had left instructions; beside the mattress, was a lid-less bottle of water. He could read the label: Fanta. Before long the two women returned, carrying a length of thick homespun fabric that they laid on the ground beside him, then they pulled aside the mosquito net and made to lift him up. He shrank back, groaning, making himself heavy, and lifting his arms weakly to fend them off. Again, they fled and the bush doctor came quickly into the hut. This time he did not squat but addressed Dan from his full height.

"You bad man," he exclaimed sternly, raising an admonitory finger. "You make women fear! They come help you, see? You need piss water. They take you! They take you *now*!"

He summoned the women and together they lifted him, smiling uncertainly at him and chattering in their own language. The pain returned, but he made no further protest. They were doing what they could, and he should be grateful. He *was* grateful, for without them he would have died, but he longed for his own home and his own bed and the feel of his own sheets. As they laid him on to the makeshift stretcher, he could see figures crowding the doorway, hazy in the sun. Akuleki sent them packing, angrily waving his arms at them as they retreated, giggling, as the women struggled with Dan through the narrow door.

Outside the heat struck him like a knife and as the light caught his eyes his nerves juddered. He closed them, and when he next opened them, he was in a narrow cylindrical hut with a thatched roof. The stench warned him. The women were panting now with the effort of carrying him, and when they removed his loincloth and sat him on a hard wooden plank, he knew he had not been mistaken.

"Oh, God, no," he protested weakly. "Well, okay, but leave me alone, will you? Bugger off."

He waved his hand towards the door, and they left, hooting with laughter, covering their mouths with their hands.

He urinated, and then looked down at his body. On his feet and hands, through the thin poultice of leaves, he could see angry marks and ominous raised white blisters, but he turned his mind from it all, did what he had to do, and then called out. The women appeared immediately and they hauled him off the plank and washed him like a child. It was good to be clean again but it was humiliating and he kept his eyes closed until he was back on his bed. Later they brought food: plantain, mashed sorghum, chopped tomatoes and sweet peppers, and small pieces of bread soaked in sour goat's milk. The combination of tastes was not unpalatable, and he made himself swallow. The juice of the sour bread, as it trickled down his throat, was immensely comforting, and he began to feel a spark of hope – no, he thought, not a spark, never a spark! – but an inkling, like a distant voice. This reminded him of Stephen and what he had said about being still and taking things in. He thought ironically, well, I'm keeping very still and I am taking things in. I might yet survive this. It helped to think about Stephen. Somewhere, he thought, he's praying for me. The thought gave him strength. Later still, they lit a hurricane lamp and placed it behind his pallet, where it sputtered feebly and soon went out.

He was woken by a nightmare in which he was being tossed about in liquid flame. The shrill pulse of the cicadas in his ears and he was drenched in sweat, his face flaming. He quieted himself, conscious of his throbbing heart, and that day he was feverish again. Akuleki came and changed his dressings, his swift dexterous fingers mixing the herbs and the Vaseline together in a wooden bowl, and then spreading the fresh poultice over his body.

"Open wounds," he grumbled, as though Dan was to blame. "I give you something for the pain."

Dan had been half-conscious throughout his ministrations, but when the pain-killing draught touched his throat, he almost screamed. It was as hot as chilli and it burnt and wrenched at his throat.

"No, no, is good," murmured Akuleki softly, as Dan

385

choked and writhed on the bed, gasping for air. "We treat fire with fire, like on your face. Now sleep! In the morning, better!"

The next day he pricked the blisters on Dan's hands and feet with a hot needle and squeezed out the pus. Dan gritted his teeth but could not help a groan escaping him. The dressings that went on then were different, cooler, and his hands and feet felt better.

"Not my face," he'd gasped, during all this. "Leave my face alone!"

Akuleki agreed. "No, the pepper is enough. *Now* you will be well!"

He was not well, but he was marginally better. The fever had gone and he was lucid again. Also, he was calm, acquiescent, and he lay quietly, savouring the stillness. Akuleki had succeeded in keeping the villagers away from the hut, and the only other people he saw were the two women. He asked them their names, and they told him, giggling. One was called Hamseen, and because she was gentler than the other, and less friendly, he favoured her. When they carried him to the latrine he no longer dismissed them, but leant against Hamseen's shoulder while she cooed over him. It came to him that, since they were Muslims, ministering to him in this way probably rendered them unclean, and he was sorry about that. He pictured them eating alone, reconciled to their sacrificial giving. This, according to Stephen, was love.

Yet, why hadn't they got him to hospital? No vehicle, he supposed, and no telephone. Too far, and too little money. And, of course, their fear of police. He comprehended, then, how people could die in the bush from injuries such as his. But why not a Muslim medic, then? The whole village knew he was a Christian and it hadn't stopped them caring for him. He didn't think Akuleki was a Muslim. Perhaps he was an animist. God, that explained all those feathers – he was a witch doctor! Then he realised that the last time he'd seen Akuleki, he'd simply worn a patterned tunic over a pair of conventional trousers. Why the feathers, then? To impress him? Okay, he thought, I'm impressed. And in the morning, he told himself, I'll ask him about a Muslim medic, see what he has to say.

His mind wandered and he thought of Hadissa, and Habiba, his child. He thought of John-Sunday kneeling, injured, in the dust on the dark road. He thought of Zac, emaciated and angry, planting the bomb. He thought of the children trapped in the bus. Again, he thought of his wedding day, and Stephen's words about compromise. Compromise? That was a joke! When he'd stepped out of the car, he'd had no choice. He had to do what he did, and he'd tell Stephen so, if he got out of this alive. He remembered something else, too. Stephen had quoted something about God not just being in the earthquake, the wind, or the fire – the *fire*? – but afterwards, in the still, small voice. The only voice he'd heard like that was Hamseen's. Was God in *her*? Or Akuleki, heathen though he was, was God in him? Had the fire literally been a baptism, an indication of ownership? If so, he'd not sought it, and he still, rebelliously, thought of himself as free. Nevertheless, he was conscious that he was no longer angry. He had accepted the simple attentions of the women. He'd drunk their water, clean or not, and eaten their food, and although all that was unforeseen and unsolicited, and he himself was desperately ill, he felt at peace with himself. He thought that it was unlikely he'd ever feel so reconciled to himself again, as he did then, lying in that thatched mud hut deep in some anonymous valley somewhere in Africa. Things were out of his hands. He could no longer manipulate events. He could no longer even control when he ate or slept or went to the latrine. They, the two women and Akuleki, they decided for him.

In his ears, the persistent sound of the cicadas was like the ticking of a clock. It will not last, this calm, he thought, even if he recovered. It would evaporate, and be replaced by struggle; the struggle to make a life with Hadissa, the struggle to relate to John-Sunday, the struggle with Kateri and Kaduna, with life in Africa – the whole nameless, amorphous struggle with life itself.

Yet for the moment, half sedated by shock and painkillers, greasy and uncomfortable with the layers of bitter smelling herbs that tickled his bare skin, stiff, bruised, and most definitely isolated from all whom he loved, he was at peace. He asked himself why. Because, he thought, striving for clarity, because I didn't try to manoeuvre out of this. I could have left John-Sunday to his fate, but I didn't. I could have left everything to chance, but I chose to do differently. And I'm glad I did what I did. Hadissa, he thought, half asleep, I did it for you; you know that? John-Sunday's your twin and you love him. I did it for you. Okay, he thought languidly, to the glory of God this body burnt.

# CHAPTER 6

Five days had passed, and John-Sunday had never been so fraught. Each day he rose early and went to the fields while Zac and Hassan worked in the new workshop. Early in the afternoon he returned home, washed and ate, and then had an hour or two on his bed. He was no longer sleeping in the workshop, but in the new house that he and Zac had built for Hadissa. Daily, at the end of his siesta, he would dump the old mattress, the blankets and the water bottles into the truck, and set off down the road. He stopped at every village and encampment and tested them for rumours, although he knew his heart wasn't in it. He was doing all this driving and using all this fuel, not for Daniel's sake, but for Hadissa.

At the end of the night, when the dawn was approaching, he would drive slowly back up the road to Kateri and fall into bed. Formerly, he had slept on his back, his arms wide, a way he had of staying cool. Now he slept on his stomach, his head buried in his arms, as though he was trying to suppress the deeper darkness of his soul. He slept soundly and woke drenched in sweat, stiff and cramped. During the day, he was morose and introverted. He hardly smiled, and was tense and abrupt with all comers. The other villagers knew of his trouble, for Zac had told the story, but they were afraid of his temper and after a day or two of voyeuristic interest, they kept away.

Except for the pastor, who came daily, sometimes twice a day, asking for news. It reminded John Sunday of how they had waited for Hadissa's letters, and it irritated him. He hated his pontificating, fussy manner and he wanted to shout at him. He would watch him from the workshop window, shambling away on his bare feet in his dusty dark suit. He meant well, but John-Sunday found him intolerable, and on the Sunday, when the pastor urged John-Sunday to come to church so that the whole community could lay hands on him for healing, he almost snapped.

"You do the praying, Pastor. I've work to do."

The pastor looked at him. "My son, you should be listening to God," he said sternly, "and you should at least keep a Sabbath rest!"

John-Sunday shrugged. He had no answer.

\* \* \*

Hadissa missed England, or if not England exactly, its advantages. Running water, electricity at the flick of a switch, law and order, a balanced diet – all things she had rapidly taken for granted. She missed the polished furniture of her room and its fitted carpets. She missed her English clothes, most of which, to their bewilderment, she had donated back to the charity shop in Ely, feeling they were not appropriate for Kateri. She missed the cathedral in Coventry and as she compared the richness of its art with the paucity of imagery in her own church building, she felt impoverished. She recalled how the eyes on the tapestry of the risen Christ had called to her, and how, for a time, she had answered the call. Now it was merely a distant echo to which she couldn't connect.

Each day she worked long hours in the clinic, putting Habiba to the breast when she was hungry. The child was growing quickly and her lusty cries brought women running, but Hadissa fended them off, and after a while they let her be, though they gossiped among themselves that she neglected the baby and let her cry too long. But Hadissa was busy. Supplies had arrived from the hospital in Kaduna, accompanied by a note from Boseh announcing his imminent arrival, and she was trying to organise the stock before he came. The clinic was open each day, and when she unlocked the green iron gates there was a silent queue of people waiting to see her, their eyes keenly watching her for any display of grief. She dealt with them as best she could, briskly efficient, ignoring Habiba's pitiful, kittenish cries from the next room. On the Sunday, she sat at the back of the congregation with her mother and Habiba, but slipped out before the end of the service, unable to tolerate their avid stares and whispered comments. Neither could she face the ritual laying-on of hands. It seemed hypocritical, to ask for healing from a God who she no longer trusted and who had abandoned her to widowhood so young. Again, she questioned her future –

who would marry her, now? Her vigil in the cathedral, her tortured struggle to perceive God's will, the vision of light on Christmas night, she now regarded as risible.

One afternoon Zac drove her to Taha, a remote bush village, where a woman was having difficulty giving birth, and on the journey, she sat in the back of the truck and breastfed Habiba, while Zac tried unsuccessfully to avert his eyes. She had grown accustomed to his scar and she smiled at him shyly, acknowledging his interest. As they approached the dilapidated mud hut village they could hear the woman's screams and Hadissa hurriedly handed the baby to one of the women to look after while she examined the mother in the hut. It was a breech birth and Hadissa was apprehensive, so it was a good moment when she brought the new infant out into the sun, still blue and bloody from the birth. Habiba had not been as tiny as this one, she thought complacently. Her milk flowed with the contact, and she knew that her own child was developing well.

She spent so much time with Zac that on one occasion she told him he was like another brother. Zac's face twisted ironically and, gladly, intuitively, she realised that he did not see himself as a brother, but was attracted to her as a woman. Sometimes she found herself thinking that if Zac had been at Kateri when she was growing up she would never have left. At night, alone in her bed, she pictured his scarred face bending over her and imagined his touch. She did not mind his scar; on the contrary, it filled her with compassion; like her, he had sinned and was vulnerable. There was equality between them that she hadn't known with her dead husband. That Daniel was dead, she did not doubt. Far from grieving, it set her free. At least she had arrived married – a guilty thought, flickering through her mind and then gone, dismissed by her own shame and her uneasy conscience

Her mother cooked the food at night, and she, John-Sunday and Zac ate with her, although sometimes Hadissa gave her mother a rest and cooked the meal herself, Habiba lying on the ground playing with her toes. They were like a real family, she thought, and it would have been a good time were it not for the guilt. She could hardly believe that it had only been five days since Daniel was lost, so comfortable was she in her new routine.

\* \* \*

"Do you think he's dead?"

"Yes, I think he's dead."

"But does your sister think he's dead?"

"Who knows what my sister thinks?" asked John-Sunday bitterly. "She's a mystery. *You're* closer to her than I."

"In that case," said Zac quickly. "Will you, one day, give me her hand in marriage?"

John-Sunday was not surprised, but still he hesitated. "Wait two moons. If it's what she wishes, ask me again. Until then, don't speak of it, either to me or to her. Have I your promise?"

"You have my promise."

\* \* \*

One afternoon, a week later, John-Sunday was out in the fields when he caught sight of Hassan at the edge of the field. Earlier in the month, heavy rains had washed away the soil from the new yam plants, but since then it had become cracked and dry, and the roots were withering. John-Sunday had spent the morning re-heeling the plants and trenching up the soil. With only a hand-hoe it was backbreaking work, and the ground seemed to vibrate with the heat. He stretched and wiped the sweat from his forehead, and it was then that he saw Hassan. For a moment, he was alarmed, for Hassan never usually came up to the fields. A few days earlier, a new motorised drill had been installed, donated by the Peugeot factory in Kaduna; it had a half-inch bit that could take off a man's fingers. They had never set eyes on such a thing before.

God in heaven, he thought. Let there not be an accident to add to our troubles!

He threw down his tools and made his way across the field, but when he came up to Hassan, he saw he was grinning.

"You look like you're expecting disaster."

John-Sunday grimaced. "Would that be so surprising? What's the problem? You need some real work to do?"

"You have a visitor. You'd better come down."

John-Sunday hesitated, looking back over his half-trenched fields. "Will it take time, do you think?" he asked. "Because I've no way finished here."

391

Hassan looked at him gravely. "I think you should come, John, and come now. It's news, I think, if it's to be trusted. You may need to act."

"I'll fetch my tools."

*   *   *

Their visitor was squat, almost dwarfish. He was barefooted, and his tunic was travel-stained. He seemed on edge, as if reluctant to be there, but Zac stood squarely in front of the door, ostensibly examining a manual. He looked up as they walked in.

"John, this man has a strange message. You should hear it."

John-Sunday went up to the stranger and greeted him politely in Hausa. "You've had something to drink?"

The man shook his head. "Spik English," he said firmly. "I am *Bayaka*."

Bayaka? Surely not, John-Sunday thought. The man was short, but still too tall for that diminutive tribe. He was immediately suspicious. "Yet you speak English?"

"A missionary came to our village in my grandfather's day. He built a school."

"I know about missionaries," said John-Sunday bitterly. That explained his stature, too, he thought. "But you, yourself, are not Christian?"

"Some things we forget. It is better so."

"Why?" John-Sunday indicated Hassan. "He's a Muslim yet we work together."

The stranger looked at Hassan with contempt and then spat on the ground. Angrily Hassan took a step forward, but John-Sunday put a conciliatory hand on his arm.

"Fetch us some water, Hassan," he suggested. "A message is more difficult to give when the throat is dry."

Glowering, Hassan slipped out and the three men appraised each other silently. When he returned they each drank from the bottle in turn, and the stranger seemed to relax. He drank noisily, wiping his mouth on his hand, then he cleared his throat and once more spat on the ground. Zac looked at the globules of spittle staining his scrupulously clean floor and raised his eyebrows, but made no comment.

"Now," said John-Sunday, "you have a message for me?"

The man stood up. "Akuleki works at a Muslim village in the bush…" He spoke in a singsong voice as though he had learnt his message by rote.

"Akuleki? Who's Akuleki?"

The man looked incredulous. "A very important man. Bush doctor, very clever, out of Chad…"

Light dawned. Was this, at last, news of Daniel?

"Is that all your message?" asked John-Sunday, frowning.

"No… there is a burnt man…" Zac leapt forward and took the man by the scruff of the neck and shook him.

"You speak the truth?" he demanded threateningly. The stranger twisted and squirmed in his grasp.

"I spik truth! I spik truth! I am to say there is a burnt man in a village off the road…. And Akuleki was there! That is all!"

They looked at each other.

"Where?" Hassan asked. "What village?"

"Not very far! Machacho. Up the road to Kaduna, then west!"

"Impossible!" said John-Sunday. "*Up* the road?"

"Wait a minute," said Hassan excitedly, gripping his arm. "Maybe you were looking in the wrong place…!"

John-Sunday threw him off. "Of course I was looking in the wrong place," he snarled, "otherwise I'd have found him…!"

"But you looked *down* the road! This man says *up* the road! *Think,* John-Sunday! Maybe Daniel went round in a wide arc!"

"You mean, ended up north of here?"

"Why not?" said Hassan. "He's an Englishman," he added scornfully. "He can't travel by stars as we can! So he's ended up in the bush…"

Zac had been silent, but now he interrupted. "No, it's not that," he said. "After we were stopped *we* went north. Daniel went up the bank. There'd be no track there. Perhaps the only way to this village is by track, and it starts further up towards Kaduna. But you say he's burnt?" he asked turning to the man.

"*They* say…"

"How was he burnt? Have you seen him?"

"I have given message," he said mulishly. "That is all. I go now..." He turned to for the door.

Hassan grasped his arm. "First, tell us where! How do we know it's not a lie?"

"I can show you," said the man with dignity, looking into his eyes. "Even though you are Muslim and they..." he thumbed at John-Sunday and Zac. "...they are Christians. The village is several hours off the road. I am a hired man..."

"I'll pay you," said John-Sunday, "if you promise to lead us to this place! If not, if you cheat us..." He made a quick movement across his throat.

"I do not cheat. I will show you... for two hundred *naira*."

"Hah!" said Zac, accustomed to haggle, but John-Sunday interrupted.

"You can have the money," he said. "All of it, if you take us to Machacho."

"And then you will kill me!"

"No, you'll be free to go. Until then you stay here with us. You can eat and rest. We'll go this evening, and by cockcrow, we'll know if you are speaking the truth. *Then* we will pay you. You have my word."

\* \* \*

John-Sunday was reluctant to tell Hadissa what had happened, not wanting to raise her hopes, but Zac was wiser. If Daniel was burnt, Hadissa needed to prepare medicines and a clean room. While they were away she could move all her belongings from John-Sunday's house to the new place, so that if they brought Daniel back he could go straight into the new dwelling. He went over to the clinic to break the news to Hadissa. He found her in her little office, sitting at her desk.

For the first time since her arrival in Kateri, her control cracked. She looked at Zac, her eyes wide, then she began to tremble uncontrollably, her hands flapping among the papers on the table. She stood up, put a shaking hand to her forehead, and then walked to the door and back again, unable to be still.

"Is it good news?" he asked softly.

"How do we *know*!" She almost shouted the words at him and Zac stepped forward to take her in his arms. She didn't

394

resist but sobbed inarticulately against his chest, her fists clenched.

"I thought he was *dead*! Now I don't know how..." She raised her face to his, her eyes unseeing. "Where is he? What's happened to him? Burnt, you say? How could he be burnt? I can't..."

"Be still," he murmured into her hair. "Be still, little one. And be brave. You need to be strong, now, for both of us. For all of us, I mean. For all of us."

"I can't... I..."

"And for Habiba. His child."

She sobered, and stepped back from him, smoothing her uniform.

"I'll get some medication..." she said more calmly, turning away, "and a bed ready... And I'll radio Boseh for antibiotics... Boseh will come, I think. He's due here any day as it is."

For the first time she met his eyes. "Now is the time," she said enigmatically.

"The time?"

"When it all begins."

He did not know what she meant. For him it was an ending.

"When what begins?"

"Oh!" she said heavily. "All of it."

She opened the door and went out, leaving him baffled.

\* \* \*

Hassan drove. He told John-Sunday that since they were going to a Muslim village it might be useful to have a Muslim with him. John-Sunday did not demur, and the two of them set out towards Kaduna in the truck, their little guide perched on the front passenger seat. They drove fast up to the next intersection, then more slowly, looking for the track west into the bush.

"This can't be right," John-Sunday frowned. "He'd never have made it this far!"

"It *is* right!" said their guide insistently. "I have run it. Look out for the track. There!" He pointed with his finger. "There! Now! Turn now!"

They swung off the road on to a narrow, uneven track

half hidden by trees, which led uphill at right angles into the hinterland. Hassan drove carefully, apprehensive about the suspension, changing gear often, and their guide, at ease now, watched his every move, smiling and clapping his hands softly.

"I cannot drive…" he commented at last.

"You've no vehicle?"

He gave a twisted smile and shook his head.

John-Sunday was curious. "Where do you live?"

The guide pointed west. "Over there, in the bush, some thirty miles."

"And you ran all the way?"

The man shrugged. John-Sunday was aware that in the deep valleys there were many settlements, unconnected to the main thoroughfare, where people lived who never visited the city, who were neither Christian nor Muslim, and who had their own tribal religion. It must have taken a great deal of courage, he reflected, to come down out of the bush to the road and enter a Christian village.

"How far is this place, Machacho?"

"Two hours by the sun, running."

They knew how these messengers travelled. They ran easily, even in the heat, with a steady loping gait that allowed them to go for miles without a break. Two hours of that, by the sun. John-Sunday looked at his watch. He guessed that the speed of the truck was slower than that of a running man and, while he could have cut across country, they would need to keep to the track.

"Add another hour, then," he estimated. "We should be there by nightfall."

The little man turned.

"You cannot go all the way in the truck," he announced. "The river bed is dry and you cannot get it across the rocks. You will have to walk. I will show you which way we go, but we shall not be there by nightfall."

John-Sunday sighed. How on earth, if it was dark, were they to get an injured man back to the truck? He decided to wait and see what arrangements could be made at the village.

They drove many miles over the beaten track, bumping and swerving over the rough ground, and by the time they came to the riverbed it was late afternoon and they were tired, for both of them had been up since dawn and done a day's work in the heat. They parked the truck, and taking only a water bottle, made their way across the rock-strewn river bed. Ahead was a slight incline, and beyond, stretching for miles, was vast uncultivated grassland copiously dotted with stunted trees and prickly shrubs. Hassan and John-Sunday were filled with awe, for they had lived the whole of their lives by the road, and neither of them had ever seen such fertile countryside. As they descended the hill they began to speculate on the quality of the soil and how a road might be made through the bush, and a bridge constructed. For a while, distracted by these thoughts, they forgot their weariness but after another hour, they were nearly exhausted, for neither was accustomed to walking long distances. Once on the downward track their guide kept so brisk a pace that John-Sunday and Hassan were left behind, and he was frequently forced to stop and wait for them. Despite his small stature, he seemed more resilient, and he grinned condescendingly at their discomfort, watching them as they squatted on the grass and drank from the water bottle. He refused to share it with them, and stood long-sufferingly on one foot, resting in his own way, but obviously impatient to get on.

"Come-come! Come-come!" he said eventually, and far too soon. "We go now!"

Already the sun was setting, transforming the grassland to a lush vivid green, interspersed with dark blue shadows that hugged the contours of the land. To the south-west, the ground rose to form gently rolling hills punctuated by rocky escarpments, gleaming red in the dying sun. To the north-east was a harsh, inhospitable landscape of ravines, devoid of vegetation. In front of them, the track inclined steadily downwards until it gradually disappeared into a wide gorge lined with tall trees and massive boulders. Once they saw a circling kite, and to John-Sunday, its high-pitched haunting cry sounded intensely poignant, like a farewell; eerie, utterly wild and unearthly. For a moment he paused, transfixed by its gliding passage, the tilt and twist of its forked tail. By now, the familiar horizon of their purple hills was obscured by dense, overhanging branches, and the gorge had narrowed to become a deep cleft in the surface of the earth, mysterious and impenetrable. When the track completely petered out to no more than a steep, narrow slope between the trees he stopped in alarm.

"We go down there?"

397

"Yes. Machacho."

John-Sunday stood irresolute.

"Can this be right?" he asked Hassan uncertainly. "Daniel couldn't possibly have done this in the dark…"

"You forget, John, he'd have come from the other direction, from the road. We've probably made a wide sweep round. Come on, it's not so dreadful."

Yet dread was what John-Sunday felt. It was a wild, secretive place, a place, he felt, where man had never laid his imprint, but when the guide began to scramble down the precipice he followed without further argument. There was silence for some minutes, then John-Sunday stopped again, and with an exclamation reached out at the cliff and scratched out a handful of dirt, moulding it in his fingers. There was still some light in the sky and he could see that what he was holding was not soil, but crumbly, slightly damp, clay.

"There's water here?" The guide watched impassively as he touched the clay to his lips.

"We are below the river bed," he said. "There is water all the time, all year. All you do is dig for it."

John-Sunday was incredulous. "*Below* the river bed? How can we be *below* the riverbed?"

"The gorge takes you deeper," said their guide succinctly.

"How far, now?" asked Hassan, impatient to get on.

"Not far," he answered, looking at the sky. "Some small way."

Night came quickly, a velvet curtain falling almost visibly before their eyes, the stars obscured by the thick foliage. As the gorge levelled out, they saw the path had deviated to accommodate fallen tree trunks and rampant, prickly scrub, higher than a man. The noise of the cicadas was loud in the long grass; they throbbed incessantly, an electric hum of sound. The vegetation was thick and lush and, to John-Sunday, distinctly oppressive. Huge clumps of tall green creepers hung over them, the dry stalks rattling like angry snakes.

"Give me the open field any day," John-Sunday moaned, gazing around uneasily, his black eyes rolling. "I do not like the spirits of the trees!"

Hassan chuckled and clapped John-Sunday on the back.

"The spirits of the trees?" he repeated scathingly. "And I

thought you were a good Christian, John!"

At last, they arrived in a clearing where an attempt had been made to control the encroaching scrub, for the ground was covered in wood shavings and, in the shadows of the trees, they could see logs piled high in tidy stacks. It was very dark now and they clung close to their guide, who seemed totally unconcerned by the darkness and maintained the same speed as before. In fact, they had now joined the same path that Daniel had taken, so it was not long before they saw lights and smelled the wood-smoke of the village.

John-Sunday put his mouth to Hassan's ear. "What do we do when we arrive?" he whispered. "How do we play it?"

"I think we ask to see the elders. Beyond that..."

"One of us must lead. You're older, and it's a Muslim village..."

Hassan demurred. "But Daniel's your family, John. You're related to him."

John-Sunday grimaced. He had thought of Daniel purely as Hadissa's white husband. It had not crossed his mind that he was now his brother-in-law, and Habiba his niece. For the first time, he felt a lessening of his hostility and the first stirrings of compassion.

"If Daniel's here we *must* find him," he whispered passionately. "We can't leave without him. And if they lie to us it'll be difficult to come back again."

The guide stopped suddenly, and putting his hands around his mouth, uttered a prolonged high pitched call. He waited, listening, then turned to them.

"Machacho," he announced, beckoning gently with his cupped hand. "You come now."

# CHAPTER 7

Wood-smoke hung in a haze over the thatched huts, but through it, John-Sunday and Hassan could make out a circle of figures sitting around a small fire. Apart from the crackle of the flames and the spitting of wood, all was quiet, and when they looked round for their guide, he had vanished. Then, as they waited, uncertain and tentative, on the edge of the circle, a figure stepped out of the gloom. Although he was wrapped in a simple earth-stained blanket, and his hands were hidden, he stood erect, a person of authority; probably, thought John-Sunday, the elder of the village. He was not tall, but he had presence. His face was narrow and lean, his high cheekbones heavily scarred with slanting tribal marks, his nose aquiline, his lips thinner than the Igbo or the Yoruba, and he held himself with dignity.

John-Sunday and Hassan found themselves silently examined by a pair of inscrutable deep-set eyes and they moved closer to each other. Neither of them spoke.

The man bowed, the merest hint of an acknowledgement.

"*Assalama alaikum.*"

His voice was unexpectedly high pitched and rasping and they realised he was very old.

"*Alaikum salama,*" Hassan replied, imitating his slight bow. They waited.

The old man suddenly gave a piercing cry, like a whistle. "*Why* do you come to our village?" he shrilled. "*Why?*"

This was unusual, for it was more customary to perform a leisurely, highly intricate ritual of welcome, and for intent and purpose to be revealed only gradually, as the visitor took his ease. It was considered rude and inhospitable to ask such a question outright and it boded ill. John-Sunday hid his disquiet.

"We had a message," he answered politely. "A message that's vital to the happiness of our family. Your own guide brought us here."

The elder waved his hand disdainfully, half turning to glance across the fire to where others listened avidly. "*What* message?" he demanded, barking out the words. "*What* guide? *What* family?" He gave a small, childish giggle, peeped round at his companions, and cupped a hand over his mouth in glee.

John-Sunday took a deep breath. "The family of the man who was burnt…"

"*What* man?" Another inane giggle.

"A white man. Hurt on the road some days past."

"A *white* man?"

"Yes," said John-Sunday firmly. "A white man. Is he here?"

"If a white man was here…" said the elder merrily, shaking his head. "We would know it." Everyone nodded solemnly – colluding, John-Sunday thought, in the lie. For it was a lie, of that there was little doubt, otherwise, why the messenger? There was some hidden reason for this deviousness, some unknown factor that necessitated this absolute denial. It could only be that, after all, Daniel was dead, and his heart lurched.

"Is he dead?"

"*Who*, dead?" the man snapped back, laughing derisively. The sound of his laughter acted like a trigger, and a wave of hilarity rippled around the camp. He bent almost double with laughter, then abruptly he stopped, like a tap turned off. John-Sunday thought, Now what? He could hardly accuse the man of outright deception. He decided to take a risk, a risk that was the more perilous because he and Hassan were alone and far from home.

"Ah, I see it! You're ashamed," he stated provocatively. "You've failed in hospitality and now the white man is dead."

Their response was instantaneous and predictable. There was an immediate uproar as the whole group got to their feet and surged forward, shouting belligerently, imprisoning them in their midst, but John-Sunday realised that, although they were shaking their fists at them, none made contact. The smoke swirled, harsh and acrid.

"This means trouble," Hassan said in his ear.

"No," panted John-Sunday. "It's a sham… Watch this!"

To him, their anger seemed artificial, their reaction part of an elaborate and convoluted game. He took a deep breath and filled his lungs with air.

"*You* are not the elder here," he roared, pointing contemptuously at the man. "No, you are an *impostor*! Take us to your headman! Take us to your *real* wise man!"

He had not anticipated the effect of his words. The whole group subsided and their hostility seemed to evaporate. Once more, there was a wave of unbelieving laughter, and the circle opened to reveal a small, wizened figure seated by the fire, muffled in a cloak of grey sackcloth.

"Shaba is old," he said in a cracked voice. "But I am older. I am the leader here. My name is Okonwo. You have come for Dan?"

\*   \*   \*

They gave John-Sunday a hurricane lamp and took him to Dan's hut. Inside all was dark and quiet, as if the sick man had slept through the commotion, but when John-Sunday bent over him, he could see that his eyes were open. One side of his face, deep into his hairline, was covered with a poultice of fresh green leaves, and his lips were swollen and charred almost black, except where they had cracked and bled. John-Sunday realised to his horror that the guide had been right. Daniel had indeed been burnt. The hair had completely gone from his forehead as if seared away in one stroke, and his right ear was blistered, angrily inflamed.

"Not... the lamp!" It was a mere whisper of protest, and John-Sunday gasped. He obeyed immediately, moving the lamp away from Dan's face and putting it on the ground, where the flame flickered for a moment, then burnt up brightly.

Dan licked his lips and winced. "Who's this?"

"John-Sunday."

"John-?"

"Hadissa's brother."

"Ah yes." He began to cough, his chest heaving. "So, you've recovered?"

"Recovered?" repeated John-Sunday, bemused.

"The road. Weren't you shot?"

"No, I... No, they didn't shoot me. They..." he stopped, humiliated by the recollection of his cowardice.

"You've taken a long time, then. Never mind, you've

come for me at last…"

"We didn't know… I looked for you, but…"

"You thought I was dead, best forgotten." He spoke matter-of-factly, without resentment, and tears of shame mounted to John-Sunday's eyes.

"*No*! No, I… I gave up. I didn't know where to look anymore."

"No. Well. Funny place, isn't it? But they cared for me."

"But they said you weren't here!" said John-Sunday. "They tried to deny it!"

Dan grinned weakly. "They would. They're ashamed…"

"But why?" asked John-Sunday. "They've looked after you, haven't they? And why didn't they fetch us straight away? Or get you to a hospital?"

"*Us?*" Dan tried to raise himself. "Who's with you? Not *Hadissa*?"

"No, no," John-Sunday soothed him. "Lie back… It's all right. She's safe at Kateri. I came with Hassan."

"Hassan?"

"The mechanic from the other side of the road. The Muslim. Remember? I told you about him in the car."

"Ah, that fellow! You made contact with him at last."

"Yes. Zac and I work with him now."

"Zac?"

"The bomber from Kaduna. He drove us up from the airport…"

"Ah, yes, of course! That's good! *Good*," he repeated softly. "I'm glad about that. And Zac lives with you?"

"We all work together."

"*Good.*" His voice faded, and John-Sunday realised he was drifting into sleep.

"Daniel, listen to me!" he said, bending closer. "I must find a way to carry you. I need to know, are you very… burnt?"

"A little…"

John-Sunday looked down the length of Dan's body. The poultice did not entirely conceal the scarred and blistered skin, and he found himself thinking: this could not have happened at the road. It couldn't, for example, have been the result of burning brands thrust in his face. No, this was something else. Daniel must have had some sort of accident while he was running away.

"How... How did it happen?"

"I told Hadissa, one day, when we were... talking." His voice was faint. "I said... I said I'd go through fire for her. It seems... I have."

"My God! But *how?*"

Dan sighed, rousing himself once more. "Oh... it was there. So I fell in it."

For a long time after Dan had fallen asleep John-Sunday stayed by his side, squatting on his heels and gazing at him, and it came to him how easily and spontaneously he and Daniel had talked together. Daniel no longer seemed as abrasive as he had been at the airport, and his own hostility seemed to have vanished without trace, to be replaced with a kind of calm acceptance. He marvelled, too, how tranquil and sweet-tempered Daniel appeared, in spite of his horrific injuries. It seemed uncharacteristic of him. Perhaps, he thought, it was just exhaustion, but he appeared gentler, somehow, and calmer than when he had first encountered him.

After a while, he rose and left the hut. He found Hassan sitting by the fire alone, waiting for him, drinking tea.

"We'll have to stay the night," said John-Sunday as he joined him. "We can't move him back up that cliff in the dark."

"We'll need help, in any case."

"Perhaps there's a shorter route," mused John-Sunday. "If we take the truck further down the road, maybe we can arrange to meet them somewhere."

Hassan got to his feet. "I'll ask."

John-Sunday was suddenly furious. "Yes, and ask them, too, why they tried to hide him from us. We might have left without him!"

"No chance. You were right, it was only bluff. They were going to show him to us anyway."

"Then why bluff, in the first place?"

"I've already asked them that."

"And?"

Hassan squatted down beside him and said calmly, "It's because they're Muslims, John. And Daniel was attacked by Muslims. You might have threatened them with the police."

"I would have done! I *knew* he was here! If they'd delayed any longer that's exactly what I would have done!"

"They're ashamed," said Hassan quietly. "Those bandits,

404

they're... exiles. The village no longer recognises them as their own. The people here, they believe in God. Allah the Compassionate, remember? They *live* their faith. They're hospitable, gentle people. They hate violence and law-breaking. And, remember, John, Daniel's a white man and therefore trouble. They were terrified." He stood up. "They've done their best for him, you know. They even brought in a bush doctor, a *pagan*, John, to look after him. They could not have done more for Daniel if he'd been one of their own. Tell me, John," he demanded sternly, "would you have done the same?"

\* \* \*

In the morning, John-Sunday stayed with Dan while Hassan trekked back to the truck and then returned to Kateri to collect Hadissa and Zac. Hadissa took her medical bag and they made a bed in the back of the Peugeot so that Dan would be comfortable on the return journey. They set off again in convoy, this time towards Abuja. They had agreed with the villagers at Machacho that they would carry Daniel to the road, then wait beside it until John-Sunday recognised his own truck.

Dan was feverish after being manhandled through the bush for a couple of hours, and Hadissa had no time to prepare herself for their reunion. When she saw him lying on the stretcher, his ugly, blackened blisters still covered with leaves and an unnatural pallor beneath his skin, she became very emotional and almost threw herself over his body. The Machachoans averted their eyes, scorning her, a black woman embracing a white man. As they had finished loading Dan into the car, John-Sunday turned to give them his last thanks but they had silently and unobtrusively melted away into the bush.

Hadissa was silent on the brief journey, and when they arrived back at Kateri, she left to feed her crying baby. Her mother had been looking after Habiba, and was angry because she had to move out of the house. Zac and John-Sunday accompanied her back to her old hut, the woman complaining the whole way.

Afterwards Zac made himself scarce, and for the rest of the day he worked, disgruntled and miserable, under the tractor in the workshop. At the end of the afternoon, he did something he had never done in his life, and went for a long walk across the fields. John-Sunday decided to distance himself from all this emotion and he returned to his mother's hut. Some of the thatch had fallen in, and few a few days he busied himself there, repairing the roof and finishing his hoeing in the field. He had much to think about.

\* \* \*

Every morning Dan woke to the sound of the dogs. John-Sunday had warned him about them and about the noise from the road. If he woke during a certain hour of the night, he could listen and not hear the road. The nights were short, the cooking fires not lit until dusk, and for hours he was aware of women passing in front of the house, the muted sounds of their deep contralto voices. He reckoned it was nine or ten o'clock before they were settled, and they woke with the dawn, once more treading the path by the house. So at night there would be only a couple of hours of complete silence, the penetrating silence of the bush, broken at last by the five o'clock call to prayer from the mosque and the sound of the dogs, eerie and disembodied in the cool green light of early morning. And in the background was always the road, its deadening row, its permanent howl, its thunderous rush of sound. It gave him nightmares.

He missed Machacho. There it was quiet and he could sleep in peace. He remembered the closeness of the trees and the gentle whispering of the leaves at night, and the fresh air beneath them. Here the sun beat down remorselessly; there was no shade and the air was always stale and fetid. The cooler hours of the night never seemed to freshen it, and there was always a hint of traffic fumes to add to the heat. In Machacho, the thatch of his hut had kept out the heat, but here the tin roof of the new house seemed to vibrate with it, reflecting it downwards, so that it burnt and tormented his skin. There was no curtain to the small window, and since Hadissa kept the shutters closed the air was stifling. He was frequently beset by thirst, for although she placed a bottle of water by him when she left in the mornings, it seemed muddy and glutinous compared to the clear spring water they had given him in the village, and he was afraid of infection. He was loath to make a fuss in front of Hadissa; he desperately needed her approval. He wanted, above all, to keep silent about his ordeal, but the water worried him and on the second day, he asked her about it.

"The water here seems different," he said diffidently, his voice still harsh. "In Machacho it seemed clearer, somehow, colder. I think they dug for it. Or perhaps," he said, gasping slightly. "They kept it in a container buried in the ground. Do you think they did that?" He felt he needed to know so that he did not become more ill. "They said their water was fresh, but I think they boiled it for me, anyhow. Do you boil it?"

She seemed strange to him, foreign, elusive, as though she had withdrawn from him, and she had come without the baby, as though he was infectious. She sat listlessly by his bed, unsmiling.

"I can boil it," she said, apparently unconcerned. "I have a large pot in which I boil the nappies. I can use that."

He was taken aback. "No, Hadissa, not that one," he said with difficulty, not wanting to overrule her but dismayed by her apparent negligence. "Haven't you got another one? One you can just keep for water?"

She looked at him. "I can buy another if you wish."

In Machacho, the food had been plain but succulent. He remembered savoury broth, juicy tomatoes, sour goat's milk, curd cheese filled with herbs, and some sort of greens, which had the texture of spinach. His mouth filled with saliva at the thought of it. Even the meat, which he suspected was bush meat, had been leathery but nutritious, and it had given him the satisfaction of chewing. In Kateri, the food that Hadissa or her mother prepared was always bland: mashed plantain or boiled yam, cooked to death, except for the hard bullets of half-baked corn. There, apart from the women who had attended him, he was always conscious of movement around him and chatter, but here, he was left alone for hours until the silence rose within him like fear.

*He asked for candles, and she brought some, but they did not last long and he could not bring himself to face the matches – he was still afraid of fire; he hated the reflected light from the flames of the cooking fires, dancing up his wall. Later he asked Hadissa for a mirror. His request broke through her apathy, and she began to cry. He insisted. He said he wanted to see what the damage was. She fetched one and wiped it on her skirt, protecting her hands against its sharp edges with a piece of rag.*

*"You shouldn't look," she said. "It's bad for you. I never let my burns patients look at themselves. I warn you, you'll be shocked, but it looks worse than it really is."*

*She handed it to him tearfully, and for the first time since leaving England, he sought his reflection in the glass. He looked a mess. His eyelashes had gone, one eye was bloodshot and his lips were black. Yet, although half his face was still covered in the layers of dark green leaves that had been applied in Machacho, and that he knew, now, to be infinitely effective, his skin was gradually healing, the scabs breaking off to reveal clean pink skin underneath. Some kind of local herbal remedy, perhaps, its origins lost in the mists of time, but in this culture universally recognised – like in the film, what was it,* The English Patient? *Well, that was appropriate enough, except that he had not found it easy to be patient, except, perhaps, outwardly.*

*His reflection looked back at him, patchy, faintly inquisitorial, mild, baffled. I'm not a monster after all, he thought, remembering his mirror in Cambridge. I'm damaged, but I'm not a monster. He let the fragment of glass drop on the bed, and only then realised that Hadissa had left the room.*

*During his silent hours he found himself trying to identify sounds, some more distant, some nearer, some within the room. Over time, some of the leaves on his body had withered, and when he moved his legs to adjust his position, he could hear them crackle where they had fallen off his body onto the bed. Or perhaps it was his skin. Whatever, it was a not unpleasant sound. It reminded him of autumn leaves in English woodlands, rustling under the touch of some passing bird.*

# CHAPTER 8

At first Hadissa slept in the same room with him, curled up on the floor with the baby. Several times during the night he would hear small muffled noises as Habiba woke, and then Hadissa's crooning voice as she comforted her, or tiny gulps and burps, the unmistakeable sounds and smells of the breastfeeding infant. It should have bound him to her, he thought mournfully, but instead he felt like an interloper, his presence within her room an intrusion, an unwarrantable infringement of her privacy. The truth was he missed his village woman, Hamseen, against whose shoulder he had lain at the most intimate of moments. When he suggested that it should be John-Sunday who should take him to the latrine, he thought, wryly, that Hadissa agreed with just a touch too much alacrity, as if she did not like to come too close, or was afraid of him. At the same time, when Zac offered to change his dressings, she refused, preferring to do it herself. Yet she removed the dried and grease-saturated leaves so briskly that it hurt, poking at them with her fingernails to lift them from the skin.

"Slowly, go slowly," he gasped, wanting to keep silent, but writhing under her fingers.

"I've seen worse," she said. "And you don't want these old leaves. I'll give you a sterile dressing. I've just the thing for burns."

No mention was made of how he became burnt, or that he had taken John-Sunday's place on the road, or that he was her husband, or that Habiba was his child as well as hers. She did not mention it, and neither did he, though he did ask her, once, why she no longer fed the baby in front of him. She was embarrassed and avoided his eyes.

"I... I don't like to disturb you," she said. "You need your rest."

"I *like* to watch you," he said softly, his eyes gleaming. "You're my wife. I *like* to watch you."

409

He saw distaste in her eyes; it made him feel lonely, defective, repulsive, old. She cleaned the soiled nappies with a sharp knife, scraping off the liquid excrement into a plastic bucket, and dumping the filthy towelling in an old cooking pot, which she boiled over the cooking fire in the evening. The smell wafted in to him through the open door. Then it was his turn to show distaste.

"I've run out of disposables," she said, referring to the packet of nappies they had brought with them on the plane. "There's no washing machine here," she added defensively, catching the expression on his face.

He softened. "We can change that. I've money, and Zac has a generator..."

"You don't have money," she said cruelly. "You lost it on the road."

It was the first time she had referred to the road and what had taken place there, and only then to speak of what they had materially lost! He was incredulous.

"There's some in my trunk," he said mildly.

"What trunk?" she said contemptuously. "The trunk is gone."

"Gone? How? It wasn't even opened, on the road!"

"Well, it's gone," she said uneasily. "Don't ask me how. Perhaps it was never in the car at all."

But it was. He remembered, vividly, that he hadn't been able to close it properly, that he had closed it with the strap, and that John-Sunday had complained as he loaded it into the car. What could have happened to it? He felt it was better not to ask, but it sowed a small seed of doubt in him. Their cultures were so different!

"Well, there's still my bank account – I can get more," he said lightly. "I'll need new clothes soon, and other things." She shook her head dismissively, as if to say, you want to make your life at Kateri, but you want the luxuries of Western life as well. She did not say so, but bending forward, picked up Habiba, deftly swinging her on to her back, and knotted her shawl across her chest. Then she collected the armful of wet nappies, picked up the bucket and the heavy cooking pot, and bending slightly under her load, went to the door.

"I must go to the clinic. John will come soon, to take you to the lat."

For a moment she stood motionless, balancing her burden, her eyes distant and unhappy.

She looks, he thought sadly, like a trapped bird...

*   *   *

Boseh arrived, bustling into the house as if on a hospital ward, with a bulging medical bag. He hummed and hawed and with his tweezers took particles of dry skin from Dan's burns, scraping the flakes into a specimen bottle, and then took another and demanded that Dan urinate into it. As his sleeve brushed against him, Dan wondered if he had washed his hands, but dared not ask.

"No fever, but we'll see what all this tells us. I'll let you know, but it seems to me..." he bent and peered into Dan's eyes, lifting the lids with his thumb so that Dan winced, "... that you really ought to consider going back to England."

"Why? Why on earth?"

"Because, my dear chap, you have a fair skin and you have serious burns, and fair skin and Africa do not live well together when you have burns as bad as yours. You need specialist care, which, with all the goodwill in the world, we cannot give you. You'd stand a better chance of recovery in England. We don't want soft tissue sarcomas, do we?" he added cheerfully.

"Well, I'm staying." Dan felt mulish and resentful again.

"Hmm, you think so, do you? And what does your wife think, may I ask?"

"I just need time!" Dan said desperately, avoiding the question.

"Daniel, time will only help so far," Boseh said seriously. "It won't cure. As long as you have unhealed scar tissue, you stand a real chance of infection. And even when scars are properly formed, you'll have to take immense care. You can't, for instance, go out in the sun. Have you thought what that means? And you need a proper diet, vitamins and minerals and so on, and enough to drink. It's not fair on Hadissa..."

"She's said so?"

"No. She's too loyal."

"You've asked her? You've asked her what she thinks?"

"Daniel, she's terrified. Why, I don't know. But you

need to ask yourself whether looking after a sick man, and a white man at that – not that I am making a racial comment, you understand, heaven forbid! – but a pale-skinned man with serious burns – is quite the life she ought to be leading, what with her duties at the clinic and her baby. The clinic means a very great deal to us, you understand, and after all, it's why she went to England in the first place. If you won't think of yourself, then think of Hadissa. I'm sorry, Daniel, but you must try to understand what I'm saying to you."

Dan was silent, then he lifted his eyes. The expression in them was bleak, but defiant. He would not, on this occasion, he thought, compromise.

"I understand you very well," he said quietly. "But you seem to forget that I'm married, with a wife and a child here in Kateri. Hadissa may be your resident nurse, but first and foremost she's my wife."

He thought he would have the last word, but he reckoned without Boseh.

"In that case," he said, squatting on the ground and packing the specimen bottles into his bag, "we'll wait and see what Luke thinks."

"Luke?"

"He's coming. The bishop sent for him. And he's talked to Stephen, the priest who sent you here. They're of one mind – they think you should go home."

"Luke, coming here?"

"Any day. The bishop thinks it best. And now I have to go to the clinic. It is, after all, why I came."

\* \* \*

The day came when he felt stronger and they took him outside. It was late afternoon and though the sky still gleamed red from the sunset, the colour of the land and its stern light was gradually being absorbed into the less brutal darkness of evening. It was not too demanding on his eyesight, and he found that he could even walk the short distance to the mattress that they had laid on the ground for him.

It was a motley crowd, he thought, looking at the group of waiting men standing in the shade of the single tree outside the new house. All failed and damaged people, all disfigured and somehow wounded. Including me, he thought wryly. Including me.

Zac, the bomber from Kaduna, was there, his scar a pale crescent against his black skin, and Hassan, the rejected Muslim mechanic from the other side of the road. John-Sunday was there, whose family paid such a price for their denial of Hassan, and the pastor, guileless but infinitely malleable. And, last but not least, Cletus had come, guilty and ashamed, yet of all of them the most innocent. Quite a crowd, he thought, quite a reception. They helped him on to the mattress and then settled awkwardly on benches above him; a circle of politely evasive eyes, not wanting to be seen observing his deeply inflamed skin, on which small patches of dried leaves still adhered. Dan wore a loose shirt over his chest and his own trousers, which had been washed and patched but now hung on him so limply that he had asked for a length of twine to tie round the waist. Hovering at one side were Hadissa and the baby, and her mother. The child wailed suddenly, a desolate keening sound in the silence, and turned to Hadissa's breast so avidly that finally she went back into the house to feed her.

The pastor spoke first, courteously.

"Are you well, Daniel?"

"I thank you, Pastor," Dan replied evasively, aware that formalities were being observed. His lips were dry and cracked and he spoke with difficulty. "Are you well?"

"I am quite well," the pastor assured him, raising a hand. "You know all here? Cletus you remember from Kaduna, but Hassan you may not know. He is one of us."

"I know Hassan."

"Of course."

Despite his reddened burns, the green residue of herbs on his hands and the patchy healing of his facial skin, Dan suddenly felt very white. It isolated him, and he felt a mounting anger that he tried to subdue. He made an effort to sit up, but fell back on the mattress weakly. Why could they not have given him a pillow? He tried to support himself on his elbows, for at all costs he must not show how very vulnerable he still was. Who could tell what they might do with him? Yet the time to keep silent was at an end. He would not set himself above them, or against them, but he saw with peculiar clarity how it would be.

In the prison of his illness he had seen much that would

have been invisible to him had he been free to go outside, but he had deluded himself that it was only part of the whole, and not necessarily a true part. Now he could see in their faces what in their hearts they, perhaps, had hoped was well hidden. He saw that they secretly feared him. He had not, he realised, kept his racial distance, as a white man should. He knew too much about how they lived here, both what privations they suffered and what violence ensued from it. For that reason, and because he had been a victim of their country's violence, they were bound to want him gone. It was all suddenly very obvious, and it was to do with hospitality. He was an impossible burden, not just economically, but on their imaginations. He was quite simply too much for them, and they just couldn't cope. The black man's burden, he thought wryly, role-reversal with a vengeance.

*Vengeance*, he thought, *yes*. If he'd been one of them, the fact that he was injured wouldn't have been significant, and that was suddenly very difficult to accept. The subtle distinction in how they regarded him, compared to how they might have regarded one of their own, lay not in the fact that he was injured, but in the simple fact that he was white, with all the terrible history it implied. Their collective memories and attitudes were just too entrenched. Given the history of his country's involvement with their nation, Dan didn't blame them.

As if reading his mind, John-Sunday leant forward and addressed him formally.

"With respect, Daniel, will you now go back to England?"

For a minute, Dan took refuge in the old silence, then he said, his voice brittle with tension, "So that's what this is all about! And here was I thinking it was a celebration! Anyone would think you wanted rid of me!"

The men looked away, embarrassed, but tranquil, confident, and Dan knew his reasoning had been correct.

"You must listen, young man," said the mother, her tone grave and serious. It was the first time he had ever met her, ever heard her speak, this mother of Hadissa and John-Sunday, for she had kept her distance from the house. She was a heavy-bellied woman, very black, her hair scooped carelessly about her glossy face, and even from where he was lying, he could smell her body, the sour odour of stale cooking fat and old fires. "My son is only thinking of you…"

"Is he indeed?" he rejoined sarcastically, raising himself again. "Then I must thank you all. But no, I'm not going back to England, unless..." He hesitated, then chanced his arm. "Unless I take my *wife* with me, and the baby."

"But Hadissa is needed here!" said Cletus, his voice raised, resisting him. "And, whether you like it or not, Daniel, you still need hospital care; care that we cannot give you here or even in Kaduna. Skin grafts..."

"Ah, you've been listening to Boseh! And why on earth *can't* I have skin grafts in Kaduna, if I need them? They must have seen burns before, the life you lead!"

His voice was faint and he could feel the sweat breaking out painfully on his skin, and running down his back.

"Forgive me," Cletus hung his head. "Mr Boseh said, the colour of your skin, and the texture... it's different..."

Furious, Dan interrupted. "He could take it from my bloody thigh, you know!"

No one swore in the village, and there was a ripple of disapproval. Still Cletus was polite. "No, you should go where you can find the best help. Luke is coming..."

"You plan to send me away with him? To lose my child, my..."

He couldn't continue, but lay back, exhausted and dispirited, refusing to listen anymore. They can go to hell, he thought bitterly. Time passed dully. He was aware of them talking among themselves, then suddenly Hadissa was standing over him, the child on her back, asleep now. He could feel her cool breath on his face as she bent over him briefly, and he could sense her anger. Not with him, though. She turned away and he heard her voice lifted in quiet contained fury. This is a new Hadissa, he thought, or the old one come back, the one who was straight and true, the one who could not stand a lie, the one who bore my child, the one I love. Suddenly, the loneliness, which had threatened to engulf him, and which had been his constant companion since his arrival in Nigeria, dissipated. He heard a ringing in his head, as though all around there was a high melodious tune. It spelled hope and joy. The still, small voice again; accessible, dependable, and singing.

He realised the men had left. Only Zac remained. His last sight of Hadissa, before he finally succumbed to the immense vertigo that assailed him, was when Zac took the baby

415

from her and kissed it tenderly, his scar distorting as he formed the kiss.

The singing voice in his ears stopped, cut off sharply as if a door had been shut. By what right, he thought, with a surge of anger. Habiba was *his* child! *His* black-white child, *his* daughter, seed of *his* seed! What right had Zac to touch his child? He was too far gone to observe Hadissa's reaction, but at that moment, a spark of hatred and jealous rage glimmered within him, and the loneliness returned in waves. *That man, Zac,* he thought furiously, *I shall have to watch him*!

# CHAPTER 9

When John-Sunday looked back over Daniel's brief but humiliating interrogation, he was filled with shame that he had not risen to his defence and, for days afterwards, he hid himself in the fields and refused to come down to the workshop. Despite all the pressure that he and the others had heaped on him, Daniel had remained adamant and John-Sunday could not but admire his courage, both his courage with his burns and his determination to remain in Kateri. He had also seen his sister's anger. He felt he should have asked her first, before submitting Daniel to the indignity of that cross-examination. Even now, it was not too late. If she pleaded with him to make it easier for Daniel to remain, he would do what she wanted, as usual.

Yet she did not plead and he did nothing. He knew that both of them were waiting for Luke, as if, somehow, he could provide the answer to the simple and infinitely complicated question of what they must do about the sick man.

John-Sunday had much to preoccupy him, apart from his work in the fields. He was conscious of a vague, persistent doubt that had nagged at him ever since the episode on the road, but which he could not identify. For a while, during the expedition to Machacho and after Daniel had been brought safely back, the doubt had receded, but the less he consciously thought about it, the more it grew in significance, until it became a constant companion to his thoughts. It rushed in upon him in the morning when he woke. It brooded over him during the day, and at night, it harassed him in his dreams. There seemed no respite from it, yet he could not put it into words.

At last, one day, when he was hoeing in the fields, the doubt formulated in his mind, and he confronted it. The facts were clear: he, himself, was at fault. Daniel had risked his life for him, and he had turned his back and rejected him. That was what it amounted to. Again, he had not borne witness. He had not said, this man, he saved my life and the life of my beloved

417

sister and her baby, and for that reason alone he is one of us, and will be kin to me until the end of his days. Daniel had shown the greater courage, the greater strength, the greater love, and the utmost self-sacrifice, while he, a coward, had fallen to his knees on the road and later, neglected to take his part. He had let Daniel, the man he hated, bear the whole intolerable burden of their lives. He could more easily have come to terms with it if Daniel had died on the road. But Daniel, living? That was another matter.

*Greater love hath no man than this: that he lays down his life for his friend...*

It was hardly surprising that those words came to him then. Yet he had never perceived Daniel as friend.

And there was a greater love even than that for a friend, he reflected bitterly; the sacrificial giving of one's life for someone who was so utterly different from himself that he was almost an enemy. It was one thing for Daniel to have offered his life for Hadissa and the baby. That was natural. But it was not they whom Daniel intended to benefit; it was he, kneeling, petrified, in the road; he, John-Sunday, who had cursed him in his prayers and burnt his image in his fire!

If only Daniel had not been an Englishman...

If he had, indeed, been one of them, a Kateri man, for instance, or someone like Zac, a brother by adoption, related by mutual suffering, would he have treated Daniel the same way? What had Hassan said, about the villagers in Machacho? *They* looked after Daniel, he'd said; they showed him love. "Would you, John-Sunday," he'd said, "would you have done the same?"

It dawned on him, then, that Hassan must be perfectly aware what he was thinking and feeling, what he was struggling with, and that, subconsciously, it was to avoid him, too, that he hid himself in the fields.

No, he would have treated one of his own kind as a brother; not only because it would have been natural, but also because he sensed that Hadissa would, and he was accustomed to take his lead from her.

If only Daniel had not been *white*!

If only, being white, he had not been prepared to forfeit his life!

If only, being white, with red hair like his ancestor, he had not therefore resembled his father! And if Hadissa had not, all those years ago, been a victim of their father's malign attentions!

If only she had not fallen prey to Daniel, in England...

If only he had not perceived Daniel as a predator...

For all that, it had been other than revenge, it would simply have been a failure in courage, but it was more than a failure in courage, it was the complete absence of love. This was childhood teachings come home to roost, with a vengeance!

He would go to the pastor and ask for forgiveness. *No*, he thought wretchedly, lifting his eyes, unseeing, to the sky. That would not be enough; not when his victim hung in burning limbo in his own house. He must go to Daniel. He must make his peace with Daniel, and then, let come what may. He had been in Hadissa's thrall for far too long. It was time to make an end, to grow up, to become his own person, no longer bound by her whims and inconsistencies.

* * *

"What I don't understand," said Dan painfully, "is why you should be so conscious of my *colour*. Honestly, I was never conscious of yours. And as for Hadissa, well, her colour was never something that got in the way. Far from it, it was something beautiful to me... It gave her an added richness. Have you never heard the saying, 'black is beautiful'?"

He sighed, conscious as never before of the gulf that separated them.

"Well, perhaps it never reached you here. I can understand why the colour of my skin should be a problem because of the *climate*, but that's my problem, not yours. What I don't understand is that for you it's become an issue of *race*."

"It's not really an issue of race," said John-Sunday uncomfortably. "It's more... difference. You see, we have a history..."

Dan was mute.

"You mean slavery, don't you?" he said after a minute. "Colonialism. But that's ancient history now, surely?"

"I don't mean that, not exactly."

John-Sunday was kneeling by Dan's mattress like a penitent, the rays of the sun slanting downwards over the floor, creating a strong purple shadow over the sick man's face. It was midday and the room was very hot, much hotter, he thought, mortified, than his mother's hut. He had not treated Daniel well. He had built this new house hurriedly, without thought, and it was no more than a concrete shell, completely lacking in design. He should have built it in the shade, further into the bush, where the vegetation was tall. He should have thatched it for coolness, not given it a tin roof. He should have put the window on the other side, away from the direct heat of the sun. He should have used his powers of problem solving of which he had been so proud, and *imagined* what it would be like for a white man to live at Kateri. But he hadn't thought. He hadn't reckoned with Dan's determination and his obviously deep desire to succeed in his new life with Hadissa. He had not taken on board his *separateness*, but only seen his *otherness*, his strangeness, his foreignness. He had not perceived him as family.

"I don't mean just slavery or colonialism," he said. "There's something more. I mean our personal history, what's shaped us. We're... different, Hadissa and I."

"Different? In what way? I don't understand."

John-Sunday looked away. "She doesn't know this, but we had an ancestor who was... who was white."

"Ah! And that makes a difference?"

John-Sunday shook his head incredulously. "Think about it, Daniel!" he said with sudden heat. "Just think! He was a missionary, a *Christian*, who should have lived a Christian life! He came here to spread the Gospel – *Good News*, Daniel! But it wasn't good news for *our* family! My father, even my *father* was pale," he added insistently, "even after so many generations. And he had reddish hair!"

"Reddish hair?"

"And Habiba has reddish hair!"

"But that's natural! I've got red hair and she's my child!" He coughed, a prolonged harsh sound in his throat. "And you and Hadissa," he said weakly, when he had recovered, "are very dark. There's no sign..."

"It's not just colour, Daniel," said John-Sunday wearily. "You still don't understand, do you? It's what it does to you, knowing you were sired by a white man, outside marriage. That your great-great-grandmother, or whoever, was probably raped, or at least *owned*, by a person of faith, a *Christian*." He laughed derisively. "You don't throw *that* off! You think you do; you

420

spend your life not even thinking about it; you're brought up black; you pray as black; you worship as black; but then... when it comes back to haunt you..."

"You start to mind."

"...Yes."

Dan sighed.

"I see. Well, it seems to me..." He shifted slightly in the bed. "John," he said abruptly, interrupting himself, "don't you think I could get up? I feel much better. I get so fed up lying here. I'll be as weak as a jelly if... I want to catch up with things, see what's going on."

"The sun... Boseh said..."

"Well, in the mornings or in the evenings, then. I can't just lie here! Hadissa..."

"She's in the clinic every day?"

"Yes. I hardly see her. And I think she'd feel better, too, if I were up and about. She's not used to seeing me helpless. Maybe she'd be less anxious..."

"You think she's still anxious for you?"

"I don't *know*!" said Dan impatiently. "Anxious for me or for herself, what's it matter? If I could get around a bit, see what's going on, share things with her a bit more, well, maybe we'd... stand a better chance."

Words failed him. He averted his face, his mouth twisting, and John-Sunday saw with some compassion that he was struggling to hide his tears.

"I understand," he said quietly. "I'll see what I can do. I'll tell Zac..."

"*No*, not Zac! Come yourself, old chap, if you can. Get me *up*! Get me out of this!" His hands made a spasmodic movement on the mattress, then his bandaged fingers quivered and lay still.

"I will. We'll begin tomorrow."

They were silent for some moments then Dan said, "I started to say, but I got side-tracked... It seems to me that I ought to ask *your* forgiveness. For the sins of my ancestors, whoever they were." He gave a short laugh. "Not that any of my ancestors were missionaries, but nevertheless..."

John-Sunday bent his head. "You don't need to ask my forgiveness, Daniel. It's rather the other way round. You risked your life for me on the road. You had no idea what might happen. You might have died. We thought you had." He put his hand gently on Dan's arm. "In God's name, I am glad it didn't come to that. I rejoice! You're my brother, Daniel, and I thank God for you! I never understood... I never wanted to. I only saw the colour of your skin. Can you ever forgive me, Daniel?"

"Just get me out of here, and I'll forgive you anything!"

\*    \*    \*

That night Dan dreamed he was tied again to his bed, petrified with fear. On the floor something had moved, a brief, slightly menacing movement. A lizard, perhaps, or a snake. He would have called Hadissa to chase it out, but he remembered her fear of snakes. John-Sunday, then? No, he was up at their mother's hut.

In the dream his arm reached under his bed. He saw his arm go under the bed and bring out a heavy boot, the thick leather scuffed and dirty, the soles worn to holes, a boot such as the bandits wore who had chased him from the road. He lifted it high in the air and waited for the thing to show itself again. Then he saw it. It was black, bulbous, and obscenely shiny, like a single eye, surrounded by thin wiry legs. A spider, but unlike any spider he had ever seen. It was enormous. He brought the boot down on it. He felt, in the dream, the resistance of its leathery skin, and he hit it again. The boot seemed to go down in slow motion, not nearly hard enough to do any damage. He struck at it frantically, and at last he pounded it into the ground. He leant down and looked at it. It was still alive, but the wound had cleft its head. It reminded him of something. He concentrated hard and as he woke, the answer came to him. It was Zac.

\*    \*    \*

They worked each day in the clinic, she and Zac. She became accustomed to seeing his face in the mornings through the partition door of her office, and they would go into the treatment room together, where he would help her to prepare the medication for the day. Or he would stay on in the afternoon after the patients had gone, and scrub off the floors with clean sand so that it would be ready for her in the morning. When the patients came he helped her by fetching things and holding

422

things as she directed. Then he made himself scarce, watching and waiting for the last one to leave, waiting until she came out to lock the gates, shutting them both inside. They talked and she fed Habiba, and he watched, and she no longer minded that he could see her with such intimacy, and afterwards they talked some more.

Hassan was annoyed with him, he said; accused him of shirking his duties at the workshop, but he had finished his work on the tractor so it was all right. He laughed about it. He said Hassan should spend more time with his wife, and Hadissa was surprised. She said she didn't know he had a wife, and Zac said in that case he should stop meddling and go find one.

"Maybe you shouldn't come here so much," she said awkwardly, "if you have other work you ought to be doing."

"There are other men who can do my work; it's good training for them."

She wanted to believe him, but she looked her doubt.

"No, it's all right. Really. Anyway, I'm a free man and I want to come."

Hadissa wondered if he remembered at whose behest he was free, but made no reply. It was like a conspiracy between them and she started to avoid Hassan in case he said something. She already saw less of her brother, for he was up in the fields and her mother was busy in the house or at the market. Only in the evenings were they all together, to eat.

During the day she and Zac were often on their own, and they were alone, now, except for Habiba, who lay on a blanket on the floor, chuntering softly. He told her about his family in Kaduna, how the Muslims had come one night and burnt their house. There had been riots, he said, but distant, far off, and he'd gone out. He did not think it would reach his house. When he returned it was to find his house burning, no screams or cries coming from inside, but only the crackling of the flames, and people crowding round helplessly. Nothing to rescue, no bodies to bury. His past, he said, had been scribbled out, the way you wipe a slate in school. They told him later, how he took his machete in his hand, and about the expression on his face as he took it. He went in search of Muslims, any Muslims, to hack and burn as his family had been hacked and burnt. And they turned his machete on him, so that his face was cut.

Hadissa watched him tremble under the weight of his

memories. She had been waiting for him to tell her of his life. It was what she had been wanting. She wanted to reach up and cup his face in her hand. She wanted to touch and stroke his scar.

"Daniel found me. In Kaduna, the day I planted the bomb. It's because of Daniel they sent me here." Zac was struggling to be honest, even if she found it brutal. He had to be fair to the sick man lying helpless and immobile on his bed, while he...

"That's why I'm here, because of Daniel and John-Sunday, what they said to the bishop. The bishop, he told me. Daniel suggested it."

She did not want to hear Daniel's name repeated like this from his mouth. She only wanted to take away his heaviness, give him joy, heal his memories, let him talk and let his memories be healed in the telling. She did not want to hear how Daniel had met him, or what Daniel or John-Sunday had said to the bishop.

"You lost a brother to the Muslims, to the road, and I am come instead. I shall be brother to you now." He had said it before, but when he said it now, and how he looked at her when he said it, it was not "brother" he meant.

No, he was not a brother, but she did not tell him so. She did not feel toward him as she would a brother. No, never a brother, but a friend, perhaps, someone to whom she did not have to excuse herself, or pretend. Yet their talks had sealed something other than friendship. What this was, she dared not think. Was deception, she wondered. Riven in her soul? For it was Zac she thought of at night when she lay tossing and turning on her bed, not Daniel. It was Zac who made her smile and feel glad. It was not Daniel who she wanted to touch her as husband, but Zac.

# CHAPTER 10

"Luke's coming in a few days and he's bringing a visitor to see you. We've had word."

"You said he was coming."

"You want to know what visitor?"

"Cletus, I expect," Dan said dourly.

"Not Cletus."

"Who then? You talk in riddles, John."

"You know the priest Stephen? His daughter, for some reason."

Dan looked at him, amazed. "*Joanna's* coming? Why?"

"She's a nurse, apparently. They'll take you home if you wish."

"I don't wish. You know that."

"Think about it. It may yet be best for you."

Dan and John-Sunday were making their way over to the clinic. Dan was wearing dark glasses, which John-Sunday had bought on the market. He walked slowly, holding John-Sunday's arm with one hand, the other supporting himself with a stick. His burns had mostly healed but his legs and his face were still painfully inflamed and his heels were sore from lying in bed. His lips cracked open when he talked. When he walked any distance he coughed harshly. John-Sunday was patient with him and did not hurry him.

Their walk had become a morning and evening routine, for John-Sunday had been true to his word. Immediately after their conversation, he came down out of the bush and settled again in his old house to be at hand in the mornings, and take Dan out while it was yet cool. They walked a little further each day; up the path into the bush and back again, down to the road and back to the house, to the new workshop where Dan rested, and then back again, where he would collapse thankfully on to his bed. It exhausted him, but he was stronger each day.

In the evenings the pattern was repeated until Dan felt

strong enough to walk by himself. He would go up the path into the bush and sit on the roots of a tree to catch his breath. The sun slanted down and the only sound was of the cicadas; it was peaceful and he could sit and think. Frequently children passed on their way from the makaranta, and they would hide from him in the long grass and shout, "*Bature*! *Bature*! White man!" He would call out to them but they always scattered, timid as the mangy bush rats he had seen creeping under the huts after dark. They reminded him of the children at the school in Kaduna, in those two untroubled days before the bomb.

He considered the injustice of it all, but without rancour. Perhaps, he thought, his sickness and slow recovery had dinned into him a tranquillity of spirit, and an absence of bitterness, which hitherto had been foreign to his nature. John-Sunday's apology had helped. It had gone a long way to reconciling him to his condition.

Hadissa was another matter. Things between them were still strained, and he had ceased trying to talk to her as a husband. She did not touch him except when she changed his dressings, and then she was perfunctory, efficient, as though he was no more to her than just another patient – less, for she was less tender. Understandable, in a way, considering what a poor failed thing he had become. He was no use to anyone, a drain on the village's meagre resources, and yet the injustice of it rankled. For Zac, the bomber, was here, safe and thriving, while he, who had poured out his soul to save the children, victims of Zac's aggression and violence, was ailing, diminished and scorned by the very community to which he had been willing to sacrifice everything. Zac the *spider*, was he not standing between him and his wife, catching her each day a little closer in his web? He had not dared to confront Hadissa with it. Perhaps he should. Perhaps things were not yet so far advanced that they could not turn back the clock, and retrieve something of what they had known in England. Yet he was not, any longer, the same person as he had been in England. Things had happened, sudden, terrible things. He was weak, scarred, marred, *charred* – the rhymes rang in his head – no longer the energetic man he knew himself to be, for all the faults in his character. But was not Zac scarred, too – and perhaps John-Sunday and Hadissa as well, perhaps irremediably? Who could know? He and Zac had that in common, as well as their mutual adoration of Hadissa. Both of them had lost their

426

home, their material goods and their health, and to what purpose? In heaven's name, he asked, raising his eyes behind their dark glasses to the hot incandescent sky, to what purpose?

*To the glory of God this cathedral burnt?*

\* \* \*

"They're bound to try to take me home. Tell me, John, tell me again. Why should I go? I've no life there anymore. My life's with Hadissa and the baby. Habiba's *mine*, for God's sake!"

"But not to own," replied John-Sunday mildly.

"Oh, John, I don't mean own, like... like a slave-child or something! I mean bone of my bone, flesh of my flesh – oh, you know what I mean! Why can't we make a life together, here in Kateri, or in Kaduna, perhaps? I could teach... Hadissa could nurse. I've money. I could pay back what I owe Kateri..."

"You owe us *nothing*!"

"Well, we could buy things for the village, things that you need. Seeds, tools, a water-purifying tank, things like that. Mains drainage – though I don't know what it would cost. Books, electricity..."

"Western things."

"Don't be ridiculous, John! Anyway, you want them too."

"Yes."

"Well, that's what we intended all along. That was our plan before all this happened, before the accident... Money goes a long way in Africa."

"*English* money."

John-Sunday did not know how to reply. As far as he was concerned, there was now no impediment to this arrangement taking place in its entirety, other than the fact that what Dan had euphemistically called the accident had made it utterly impossible. His antipathy towards Dan was spent, dissipated by proximity and his greater understanding, both of Daniel and of himself. He no longer perceived him exclusively in relation to his father, or what his father had done, or what his father had become. On the contrary he now regarded him with something like love, certainly with deep and growing affection

427

and respect. As far as he was concerned Daniel was his brother. He felt closer to him than he ever had to Stanley. He did not feel guilty about this; a little surprised, perhaps, but he could not accuse himself of disloyalty to Stanley, when Stanley had been in his grave these three years or more. And there was compassion between them, and a genuine, very gentle desire to give each other *space*, which had never existed with the brother of his blood. Yet Daniel was still not well, and John-Sunday doubted he would ever be fully well. Since he had taken to walking about, his cough was worse and his skin more inflamed than when he was confined to the house, and the skin on his ankles had flared up into tiny ulcers, blistered once more by the heat, which oozed and wept alarmingly. Hadissa had scolded them both, but John-Sunday could almost be glad of her reproaches if, in any way, they indicated that she cared about Daniel, but he could not be sure. He no longer knew what was in her mind.

There was nothing to say that he had not said before, nothing to repeat about the sun, the climate, and the damaged skin, which were the only reasons he dared suggest that might encourage Daniel to go home.

"We could walk up and see Hadissa," he suggested. "If it's not too far for you."

"If you like." Daniel did not expect to find her anything but occupied.

The green metal gates were wide open, and a small group of people waited patiently, huddled on the ground in the scant shade against the compound wall. They watched silently as the two incongruous figures approached, the white man hobbling painfully on his stick, his legs and feet and hands covered in dusty white dressings, his flushed face smothered in grease. The truck was parked beside the clinic and John-Sunday realised that Zac was probably inside. For a moment he hesitated, wanting to protect Daniel from further hurt, but there was no reason he could think of not to go in, now they had arrived.

The waiting room was full of patients and there were no empty chairs. They stood at one side of the room, against the wall, and Dan took off his dark glasses and leant his head back gratefully. The door to the treatment room was open, and from where he was standing John-Sunday could see Hadissa bending over a patient, someone else supporting the patient's leg while she worked on it. It was Zac, in a white overall. John-Sunday glanced at Dan furtively. His eyes were glittering with utter fury. Even as they watched, Zac lowered the leg gently to the floor, and Hadissa poured a few tablets into a jar, handing it to him with a smile of such sweetness that John-Sunday almost gasped. Zac turned and passed the little jar to the patient, and it was then that he caught sight of the two men, staring at him from the side of the waiting room.

If he had in any way acknowledged them, it might still have been all right, but instead he stared back, unsmiling, then turned to Hadissa and spoke the single word, Daniel. She looked up, startled, and twisted her head to peer down the room. She frowned, and whispered something to Zac, then she made her way through the rows of people until she was standing in front of Dan. She spoke to him crossly.

"Why are you here? Is something the matter again?"

She ignored her brother, but he answered nonetheless.

"Nothing's the matter, Hadissa," he said quietly. "We came out for a walk, and we thought to come and see you."

People had turned to listen and she indicated them. "I'm busy. As you see."

"Then we'll go away again."

"Where's the baby?" asked Dan, straightening himself and folding his arms. "Who's looking after her?"

"My mother, of course, on the market. I'll fetch her soon."

"When?"

She shrugged. "When I've finished here."

"When?" he repeated.

"*I* don't know! About half an hour."

John-Sunday interrupted, "Hadissa, there are more people outside. You won't be finished in half an hour."

"Zac'll see to them. I'm training him here. I must go now," she said, her eyes sliding sideways. "Otherwise I'll be late for the baby."

"You're *not* training him here!" He thumped his chest. "He's training *me*, in the workshop!"

It was their first quarrel. She saw the hurt in his eyes and would have said something but Dan spoke first.

"We'll go, and not take your time," he said politely. "Or we could wait and walk over with you."

At last she looked straight at him. "It's not necessary," she said firmly. "And it's too far. You must take more care in the sun, Daniel. I don't want you to get worse."

"No," he said coldly. "I can see it would be most inconvenient for you."

He and John-Sunday stood in the corridor. He wouldn't go back to the house immediately, he said. He wanted to wait a bit, and, in spite of what Hadissa had said, perhaps walk over to the market with her. John-Sunday shook his head helplessly, but Dan was adamant; he would wait for Hadissa to come out.

Outside was the sultry heat of the evening. John-Sunday took him thirty yards away into the meagre shade of a nearby bush, and waited with him. They sat on the ground and waited. Dan made knot after knot of the long dry grass, his eyes darting occasionally to the door of the clinic. The road roared past, raising the dust and litter. Two children were playing, barefooted, amongst the rusty debris beside the road, their shadows dancing. Behind them, higher up the bank a man walked by, driving two goats in front of him, occasionally tapping their flanks with his stick to encourage them. Across the road someone came out of the Muslim teashop and threw back the awning and a lorry pulled up and stopped with a judder of brakes. The driver got out and slammed the door, then disappeared into the teashop. The traffic whined past in both directions.

The sun was brutally hot. Daniel had stopped fidgeting with the grass. He sat with his back against the smooth trunk of the tree, his hands limp on his spread knees. The children had disappeared. The sky darkened, casting long shadows across the ground.

They waited for more than an hour and still Hadissa did not emerge. The queue of waiting patients slowly dwindled, and still they waited. Suddenly they saw her at the gate, walking with Zac and a few patients towards the truck. They helped the people into the back of the truck, then Zac got into the driver's seat.

John-Sunday thought, she'll surely come now, and for a moment it seemed as though she would, for she turned back, but it was only to shut and lock the gate. They heard the metal bolt slide across, but she seemed unaware of them. She went back to the truck and climbed into the passenger seat. The engine started up, and Zac reversed, and they drove off along the track beside the road.

Dan gave a long drawn-out sigh, and coughed.

"When they come back," he said, wiping his mouth on his sleeve, "they'll be alone together. Is that the custom," he asked John-Sunday deliberately, "to be alone with a man who's not your husband?" He coughed again. "Is that the custom, here in Kateri?"

John-Sunday was uncomfortable. "It's not the custom," he said dully. "She shouldn't do it." He felt ashamed of his sister. What did she think she was doing? Didn't she care who saw her? It was just as well, he thought, that they did not have to live with Shariah law. The way she was behaving, she could be stoned to death.

"I thought not. How long do you think they'll be gone?"

"It depends how far they go."

"Yes. I wonder how far they *will* go." A euphemism that, he thought, John-Sunday could not possibly understand, but he was mistaken. Under his black skin John-Sunday flushed.

"Their way lies past the market," he said, awkwardly, hoping it was true. "Maybe Zac will drop her off."

"And maybe he won't. Maybe their way lies on a different track. Do you think so, John?"

"Do I think, what?"

"That maybe her way… is on a different track?"

John-Sunday made no reply. He was deeply disturbed by what he had seen, and frightened for them all. His heart felt leaden, full of dread.

"Let's go back," he said. "I'll make you something to eat."

"Women's work."

Zac, when he first came to the village, had said something similar, and John-Sunday groaned. He'd given Zac her name, but he'd taken more than her name. He had stolen her soul.

\* \* \*

Hadissa had never in her life been out back of the village in the dark. The lights from the truck gave the uneven track an uncertain glow, and made the thorny branches of scrub seem shafts of light against the mysterious darkness beyond. Fallen

431

trees and the occasional, abandoned hut loomed at them out of that darkness, like an accusation. Even Zac became fearful. He drove anxiously, uncertain of the direction, leaning forward to peer out of the dusty windscreen, his jaw tense, the muscles of his strong bare arms wrestling with the wheel over the rutted track, his right knee braced against the side of the cab.

They did not speak. Their secret time, the time of conversation and intimacy, was past. Now she huddled into herself, the baby in her arms, her expression inscrutable as she tried vainly to mask her own disquiet.

"We're very late," she said once, uneasily, into the darkness.

"I know. I didn't expect us to take so long. I'm doing my best."

That was all.

"There it is," he said, eventually, a sigh of relief in his throat.

"What?"

"The road."

"Were we *lost*?"

"A little. Not now."

Neither of them spoke again until they reached Kateri. Zac parked the truck outside the workshop.

"Will you be all right?"

Either of them could have asked the question, but it was Hadissa who spoke.

"Of course," he answered. "And you?"

"I must go and do Daniel's dressings…"

"One thing." She stopped and he took her by the arms. "Hadissa…"

"Yes?"

"We've done nothing wrong."

She raised her eyes. His face was lit by the beams of light from passing traffic, pulsing on his skin like a heartbeat, and she saw that his eyes looked guilty.

"No? Well, then…"

He watched her disappear into the darkness, then drew in his breath heavily, and went to the house that he still shared with John-Sunday. He closed the door as quietly as he could, but John-Sunday heard him.

"Zac? That you?"

432

Zac went to his door. John-Sunday was sitting fully dressed on the side of his bed. A candle burned.

"Where have you been? We were worried."

Zac sighed. "Taha and beyond."

"A long way."

"Yes."

"Have you eaten?"

"No."

John-Sunday looked at him. When he spoke his voice was tight, repressed, as though he was holding himself in check. "What you did tonight, Zac... It wasn't right."

"No... I know. It won't happen again."

"She's *married*, Zac. My sister's *married*."

"I know," he repeated. He paused, then he added gravely, "I know, but they..."

"There are no 'buts', Zac. Be careful, that's all, that you do not dishonour her."

"There's *no* dishonour," Zac shouted, suddenly furious.

"No?" Again that repressed, slightly scathing voice in the candle-lit room, where shadows danced on the wall with their every breath. Zac suddenly realised that John-Sunday was very angry. Under the force of it his own fury evaporated, leaving him drained.

"Be careful," repeated John-Sunday, "...that you do her no ill. If you hurt her, Zac, if you *dare* bring shame on our name, be sure..."

He hesitated, wary of threatening this man whom he had regarded as a friend and a brother.

"Be sure I will send you from here," he said tightly, turning his face away. "If I do not kill you first."

433

# CHAPTER 11

Dan could not explain to himself why his sleep was plagued with such vivid dreams. Night after night garish images assailed him, and he often woke sweating and miserable. During the day he rationalised it as best he could, reflecting that, since his days were troubled, his nights were bound to be disturbed. Pain of the body or of the spirit, both could cause nightmares, and he had both. In England, Hadissa had told him nightmares were a sign that God was speaking to him. He wondered what it was that God was trying to say, and why he sent such awful, incomprehensible images. She had seemed to sure that it was God who sent them, but he doubted that she would be so confident, now.

One night he dreamt that he was watching his own feet deliberately walking into white-hot ash, which rose and fell around him like butterflies, dancing about his head and brushing against his face with their delicate, burning wings. Each touch of them on his skin was like a new branding, and he found himself rubbing his arms against his face to sweep them away. He woke to pain and fever and the smell of his own fear, to the sound of his own hoarse cries ringing in his ears and the feel of fresh blood running down his cheek. It was the time of the night when there was no sound outside, even from the road. He felt horror rising inside him, and a dreadful fear that everyone had abandoned him, that he would be condemned to lie there in this foreign place in his own sweat and filth until finally his body became utterly corrupt. Unaccountably, he found himself repeating his marriage vows in tune with the pulse of his blood – *for better for worse / for richer for poorer / in sickness and health / forsaking all other / keep you only unto him...* but it was Stephen's voice, not his – and when the response came – *I do* – it was the merest echo of Hadissa's softly-spoken African inflection: *Ah-do.*

Vows, promises, good intentions, visions, hopes and

434

dreams – they were as transitory as falling leaves and, like fallen leaves, blown away on the first intemperate wind.

* * *

That night, as Daniel wrestled with his nightmare, Stephen, in Ely, woke from an equally troubled sleep. He got out of bed, and throwing his dressing gown round his shoulders, he went downstairs to his study and knelt down at his prayer desk. In front of him his prayer book was open at the night service, Compline, which he had read before going to bed. The psalm allocated for that evening, had he known it, was the same psalm that Luke had read to the bandits on their way up the road from Abuja.

Stephen read through it again, murmuring the words out loud. He had reached the fifth verse – *thou shalt not be afraid of any terror by night: nor for the arrow that flieth in the daytime –* when, inexplicably, he stopped short and raised his head. Had he heard something? Could someone be at the front door, so very late? He listened, but heard nothing further. He returned to his prayers and finished the psalm. A few minutes later he heard the noise again. He got up, his prayer book still in his hand, and went to the front door. He flicked the switch for the porch light, unbolted the door, and flung it wide. The porch was empty and the wind was up, for the tall trees in front of the house were rustling, their branches grinding together slightly in the breeze, and a few dried up leaves fluttered in at his feet. The garden and the drive were deserted. He glanced down at the book in his hand, and in the light from the porch, his eye was caught by the middle stanza of the hymn that followed the psalm. *From all ill dreams defend our eyes, from nightly fears and fantasies...*

Stephen was deeply disturbed. Returning to the study, he knelt down and earnestly prayed for all those he knew who were sick or in distress, and all those he could think of who might be awake that night, unable to sleep, or overwhelmed by anxiety. Among them was Daniel.

* * *

The door opened and Hadissa came in, carrying a candle. "Daniel," she whispered. "Are you awake? What is it?

435

Were you dreaming?" She bent over him, then seeing his face, she stopped short, aghast, her hand to her mouth.

"Oh, my God, your *face*, Daniel," she exclaimed. "What have you done to your *face*?" She raised the candle to see him better. He had rubbed his blisters raw, leaving open, bleeding wounds above his eyes, on his cheekbones and on his lips.

He coughed harshly and groaned, striking out to ward her off and nearly upsetting the candle. "Oh, *God*," he cried, in anguish. "Why do you torment me so?"

Assuming he was addressing her, Hadissa reared back, her hand still clasped round her mouth.

"I am so *sorry*," she whispered. "Oh, I'm so very, very sorry!"

She backed away, and left the room. She stopped only to pick up her shawl then she ran for John-Sunday. Barefoot, she ran across the path by the side of the road, ignoring the speeding traffic, and up the track that led to John-Sunday's house. She burst into his room without knocking, but he had heard her step and was already sitting up in his bed.

"Come! Oh, *come*," she shrieked at him, snatching him by the shoulders. "And bring water!"

"What...?"

She shook him and punched him. "Oh, get up and *come*! Bring water! It's Daniel! He's ill! He's terribly, terribly ill!"

John-Sunday felt clumsily for his candle.

"Oh, why do you *wait*?" she cried petulantly. "Come to *Daniel*! I must... I must go to the clinic. I must fetch medicines and bandages. Oh, why do you *delay*?"

"Go from the room, then," he said harshly. "I cannot dress while you're here!"

She looked at him, eyes blazing, then stumbled from the room.

John-Sunday hurriedly threw on his clothes, then ran to the latrine, where he picked up a bucket of river water, slopping it. He paused, considering, then put it down again and dashed over to the workshop where they kept bottled drinking water. He picked up a full crate, hefting it in his arms, and he was reaching for a new packet of candles when he suddenly became aware of Zac, standing by the door.

"Is there something the matter?"

"It's Daniel," he answered shortly, pushing the candles

into his pocket. "Go back to bed, Zac. You can do nothing. You've played your part!"

Zac gazed at John-Sunday, his eyes pleading, haunted, and he retreated. Then he turned back, suddenly furious.

"Always you leave me out of things!" he shouted, stamping his foot. "Always you leave me behind!"

John-Sunday stopped short. "What...?"

"You went to the *bishop's* with Hassan! You went to the *factory* with Hassan! Not *me*," he cried childishly. "No, not *me*! When Daniel was missing, you didn't take me with you then! And when you went for him, you took the *Muslim*! You took *Hassan*!"

John-Sunday pushed past him and hurried over to the new house. Hadissa was already there. She must have gone like the wind, he thought.

"Take this," she said crisply, handing him a large plastic bowl. "Oh, good, you've brought clean water. And candles – I was going to suggest... Light them, will you, but keep them off his face. Here, open a bottle. Pour it into here..." She handed him some cotton wool. "Here, soak this in the water. Wait, I'll put in some iodine..."

"That'll *sting*!"

"It can't be helped," she snapped turning on him. "Do as I *say*! He'll die, else. Give me another bottle. I need to clean away this blood. And fetch a hurricane lamp. And get some more candles and melt them. I need the wax..."

"You'll put hot wax on his *skin*?"

"No, no, on the dressings. It'll seal everything. It'll seal in the wounds. And get those bandages. No, wait, get me a cup. I need to dissolve some aspirin, if I can get it down his throat..."

For all her frantic activity she dealt with the sick man efficiently. John-Sunday did as he was told, and found time to admire her calm dexterity as she gently cleaned the burns and dressed them with clean lint. Daniel had ceased to rave and thrash around on the bed. His eyes were wide open, gazing at her as she hovered over him, and straining to see her each time she turned away. When she turned her attention to his feet, where fresh blisters had formed, he lay back quietly, and did not flinch as she gently peeled back the old dressings and laid fresh grease on his inflamed shins and ankles. He seemed pacified, soothed by the touch of her fingers, and after a while he fell into a deep sleep. She finished and sat back, looking at him closely.

"How did this happen?" she whispered to John-Sunday. She sounded bewildered. "Did you walk too long in the sun?"

"We *sat* too long in the sun, perhaps."

"But why, John? You must know the danger... How *could* you?"

"Well, how could *you*?"

Her face fell guiltily.

"We stayed," he said gently. "We were waiting for you."

She turned to him, and he saw that her eyes were blind with exhaustion. "I don't understand."

"After the clinic," he said simply, reluctant to accuse her of anything. "He wouldn't come back to bed. He wanted to wait for *you*. Be with *you*."

"I see."

"*Do* you? *Do* you see?" he asked intently. He loved her very much but he wanted her to realise what she had done, to be aware. He wanted, if at all possible, to fend off the menacing threat of Zac, to safeguard, if it was not too late, her virtue. "*Do* you?"

"I have said so," she sighed. "Now, John, thank you for your help, but leave me with him now."

"You can manage?"

"Well, you can boil the bowl for me if you would, and bring it back. I don't want to leave him alone again. Oh, and Habiba will wake soon. Bring her, would you? I must feed her."

\*   \*   \*

Dan lay for the rest of the night without waking. Occasionally his head twitched feverishly and he seemed restless, but when Hadissa laid her hand on his head, or squeezed more water into his mouth, he quickly subsided. It was a long night. In the morning John-Sunday appeared at the door with Hassan.

"Hassan has brought you something."

Hassan came tentatively into the room. He was carrying a wide flat fan made of banana leaves and a large meat hook, which he fastened to the ceiling over Daniel's bed, with a length of twine attached to it to work the fan.

"I'm sorry," he said shyly. "I should have thought

438

before."

John-Sunday was grim. "We should all have thought before."

Hassan looked down at the bed. Dan was still asleep. Some of his hair had grown back and his forehead was the same colour, an angry red, and his nose was raw where he had rubbed away the newly healed skin. It will scar this time, Hassan thought. The rest he could not see for it was covered by dressings.

"Is he very ill?" he asked timidly, glancing at Hadissa.

"He's better," she replied tentatively. Her voice was subdued and he knew that she spoke from hope rather than certainty. "But he had first-degree burns, Hassan, and now he has a high fever. He should be in the hospital... but we cannot move him now. It's too late."

"*Too late*? Will he die, *in sh'allah*?"

Hadissa sighed. "I think he will not die. But he's very ill, and with such a high temperature... the brain..."

"You want me to radio Mr Boseh?"

She hesitated, then shook her head. "I don't see he could do more for him then we're doing. He should have gone home to England. It's my fault," she said bleakly, smearing the sweat off her face with her hand. "Others tried, but if *I'd* urged him he might have gone. But I didn't... I wanted him to do what he thought best. Oh, I don't know what I wanted! But I'd hoped he would have been better by now. This has set him back."

"He didn't want to go, in any case," said Hassan. "Well," he added after a pause. "I will pray for him, and for you, too, with your permission. Allah is merciful."

"Someone should pray," she sighed, "...for I cannot."

John-Sunday said nothing, and soon after, they both left.

She sat by Dan all day, working the fan and feeding him endless bottles of water. Once her brother came to the door and said, "Hadissa, there's been a queue of people outside the clinic all morning. What do you want me to say to them?"

"Oh, I don't know," she said wearily. "I can't go over now, John. You'll have to send them away. And put a notice on the gates, will you, saying we're closed for a couple of days. Word will get round to those who can't read. We can't do anything else. I can't leave Daniel while he's like this."

"I'll bring you some food."

439

"I'm not hungry."

"You must keep up your strength, Hadissa…"

After a while Hadissa dosed fitfully, starting up at each small movement from the bed, but Dan did not wake. His body seemed flattened somehow, as though he was sinking into the mattress. When darkness came once more John-Sunday renewed the hurricane lamps and brought her a plate of food. She ate some of it, kneeling on the floor by the bed, and the whole time she did not take her eyes off Dan, but he did not wake. In spite of the small metallic sound of the spoon against the enamel of the plate, the creak of the fan and, outside, the thundering road, he did not wake.

\* \* \*

"Oh, my husband, what have I done to you? Forgive me, I've hurt you so much! I didn't mean to hurt you, Daniel, truly I didn't. There, is that better now? Cooler? Oh, Daniel, what's happened to us?"

Daniel shifted slightly on the bed. Around them the night was quiet and there was no sound from the road.

"Oh, Daniel, try not to mind the pain. You *will* get better again, and then… Oh, what have I *done*? Why has this happened to us? We hoped for so much, didn't we? Such promise. Such hope. I didn't realise, Daniel, I didn't know… Forgive me. You couldn't possibly know what I was feeling. I was so confused. Daniel, I thought you were *dead*! And you were there all the time, waiting for someone to come, and I didn't know… Oh, Harmattan…"

"You have not… called me that… for a very long time."

His voice was almost inaudible and his hands in the bandages fluttered on the bedclothes.

"Oh, you're awake! Oh, thank *God*," she gasped, and the tears spurted from her eyes. "Oh, Daniel, I'm so sorry. This is all my fault…"

She was weeping now, openly, the tears coursing down her cheeks.

"No," he said faintly. "Not… not your… fault."

Weakly, he lifted his hand to her face and now, at last, she did not avoid his touch, but leant into his hand so that her cheek was cupped in his bandaged fingers.

"You're crying," he said wonderingly. "Don't cry, dear one. I'll go soon. It's best."

"Oh *no*, Daniel!"

"Can you... some water?"

His lips were swollen and dry, but she raised his head so that he could drink, and he lay back again, panting. "How long," he asked feebly, "...have I been ill, this time?"

"A couple of days."

"What about the clinic? Don't people need...?"

"Oh, Daniel, you think of others all the time!"

"No," he muttered. "I think of myself."

He was quiet and she thought that he had gone away from her again, but at length he roused himself once more. His voice was a little stronger, and she saw that he was less feverish.

"I... I found myself... praying, you know," he said gently. "If that's what it was."

"That's good..."

"Is it? Yes, well..." He paused, trying to collect his thoughts. "At first, in the hut... in the village... I found myself thinking... I was talking to some sort of god, I think. I thought, if he would just look away for a while – God, I mean – *then* I would be ready to go..."

"You meant...?"

"I thought I was going to die," he said quietly. "But something was preventing me. Don't worry," he added gently, "I forgot about it later."

He couldn't see her eyes, but she was biting her lip. Her body was very still but it was the stillness of utter defeat. He looked at her hands, motionless on her lap, and thought how capable they were; they dealt out medicines; they washed and cooked; they threw his child over her back; they did a thousand things during the day; they could repulse or beckon him – did she not know her power? Yet her posture was so much that of a servant that he could hardly bear it.

"Yes," he said, observing her. "I have to go, I think. The heat, the sun... I must let you go. I don't belong here. I thought I did, but I was wrong."

She met his eyes. "Because of me? Me and... and Zac? We didn't... We haven't..."

Even the 'we' hurt; the sheer fact that, even at this moment, she could align herself with the man – how it hurt!

"How *could* you?" he asked, suddenly harsh. "The man's a criminal! And he's... He's ugly; disfigured!"

"As I am," she replied simply. "And..."

He finished her thought. "As I am, now. Okay, but do you love him?"

It was the same question she had asked her Igbo lover, and she recalled his answer, that love was not a word he recognised. She knew, now, what he meant.

"I needed..." She stopped helplessly.

"You needed someone who needed you," he said quietly. "One of your own kind. Well, don't blame yourself for that. It's what we all need."

He said, following his train of thought, "It was natural in a way. I should have expected it. Two very vulnerable people... But I was vulnerable too. You didn't know that, did you? But I was. But never mind..."

She was unable to speak. She couldn't find the words to answer him.

"No, I must go," he continued after a moment. He felt hot, drained. "Not because of... you... Because of the fire... and because I am no longer fit... I must go home." He shifted uncomfortably on the bed. The talking had exhausted him, and as his temperature rose the blood suffused his face. "I *must* go home, I think, I *must* go home. Hadissa, I'm sorry," he said feverishly, "But... Oh, think of it as God's will, Hadissa – it was never meant to be. I *must* go home, I think. I *must* go home, I *must*..."

She saw that he would leave. She saw, too, that the thought tormented him, but still she couldn't speak. He would go, and she would be alone again, this time with a child... *I've lost everything*, she thought dismally. The bandits, when they took him, they took everything. Yet she knew that was false. She would not have lost him, had she loved him.

She laid her head gently on his chest. He jerked slightly, then he said, "Oh, my darling... I can feel you... I can feel your little head."

"It doesn't hurt, to...?"

"No, it doesn't hurt. Everything's all right, Hadissa... I love you, you see.... I've always loved you. You're my beauty..." His voice trailed away. "You're my black, black, black, black... beauty."

# CHAPTER 12

Dan's fever did not return and he became patient once more, sweet-tempered and acquiescent, except that he could not abide Zac's presence in the room. When Hadissa needed help to move him and suggested fetching Zac, he refused point-blank, and afterwards there was a tacit understanding between them that she would only ask John-Sunday or Hassan. Dan had lost weight during his illness and he was not heavy to lift, but any contact with his skin was an ordeal. He bore it silently, without complaint, thanking them so warmly that even Hassan was discountenanced and had to go outside to hide his emotion. John-Sunday followed him.

"You think he's going to die," he said. "That's it, isn't it? That's what's upsetting you?"

"It's not just that. He shames me. He shames us all. But he does look ill. He's very weak."

"Hadissa doesn't think he will die. She says the fever's gone."

"But he's worse than when we brought him home!"

"He *looks* worse," said John-Sunday. "But I think he's over it. I think he's picking up again."

"But how can he stay here, John?" asked Hassan. "He can't possibly, even if we could get him to the hospital..."

"I don't think he *will* stay."

Hassan looked at him. "Does Zac know? Does he understand what's happening?"

"I've no idea." John-Sunday shook his head indifferently. "And I don't care. I haven't seen him, and even if I had, I wouldn't discuss it with him. I... I couldn't, and anyway it's not my place. Hadissa must..."

"What does the future hold for them, do you think?"

John-Sunday laughed bitterly. "You, a Muslim, ask me that? And who d'you mean? Hadissa and Dan, or Hadissa and Zac?" He shook his head. "Who knows? I've stopped thinking

443

about it."

"Do you pray, John?"

John-Sunday scowled dismissively. "Who to?" he asked bleakly. "And what for? The pastor asked me the same thing. He said he would come and lay hands on him, for healing."

"What did you say?"

"I said he could come if he liked, but he wouldn't be able to touch him. He was angry. He thinks I've lost my faith. I haven't. I give thanks all the time. For Daniel's life, for my life, for the family's life, for the life of the workshop, for *you*, but..." He looked away, to where the traffic was roaring past. "Ask me what I *want*, what to pray for, and I wouldn't know how to answer you. I don't know what I want. I don't know what to pray for. What's best, perhaps, whatever that is. I can't see into the future. I can't see anything clearly anymore."

He hesitated, feeling a lingering trace of his first ambitious dreams, like marks in the sand obliterated by passing feet. The memories dwelt with him – how he had hoped to redeem his brother's death; how he had hoped to wipe away the stain of his father's betrayal; how he had longed for family harmony – and what had it come to? To a burnt man in a primitive concrete house? To his sister's *shame*?

"What *should* we pray for, Hassan? What do *you* pray for? It seems to me my prayers have been for all the wrong things. Or that God doesn't listen. So why bother?"

"No, you're wrong," Hassan said quietly. "Allah is compassionate – you'll see."

\* \* \*

He followed her with his eyes wherever she went, as she moved about the room. She brought Habiba to see him, and the child lay on the bed at his side, her hair longer now, a glowing auburn, tightly curled. Once more she breastfed the baby in front of him, and as he looked at them, the black girl and their half-blood child, he avidly stored up in his mind the images they presented, as though gorging against a later time of famine. After a few days, she resumed her work in the clinic, leaving him in the care of Hassan or John-Sunday, but he hardly noticed them, and took refuge in sleep. When she left him to fetch food from her mother's cooking fires, or to do the washing, or even to attend to the baby, he chafed impatiently until she returned. At night she slept at his side, but he often stayed awake until morning, just to see the early light blossoming on her sleeping face. He could not bear her out of his sight.

During the long nights, weary with his vigil, he had much to occupy his thoughts. He knew that it had partly been jealousy, but also the very naturalness of Hadissa's relationship with Zac, that had triggered his relapse. He wrestled with the thought but finally, reluctantly, he was able to admit it. Whatever the deceit, and the deceit still angered him, he conceded that Zac was probably a good man with a genuine love for Hadissa, which in spite of his anger Dan felt compelled in some way to acknowledge. Both of them were complicated and damaged people, as he was, now – and maybe had been before – and the attraction between them may have had something to do with that. Perhaps, Dan reasoned, desperate to find logic in it all, Hadissa saw herself as some kind of personal redeemer to Zac, or he to her. Certainly, the man drew out of her a deep compassion, but Dan knew he wouldn't have wanted a relationship based on that. He must set her free to go her own way and make her own life, whatever it would be. There was a bird, once, a trapped and frightened bird... but in another life.

\* \* \*

One afternoon Hadissa was in her dispensary when a shadow filled the doorway. Patients were not allowed to disturb her there, and she turned, prepared to be severe. Joanna stood in front of her, smiling. For a moment Hadissa did not recognise her, then she dropped what she was doing and rushed forward.

"Jo! I'd forgotten you were coming! When did you arrive?"

"Just now. We flew in yesterday. Stayed the night with the High Commissioner in Abuja, so what do you think of *that*? Came on this afternoon..."

Hadissa threw her arms around her and laughed excitedly. "I'm so glad to see you!"

"You too, Haddy, you too. Things have been happening here..."

Hadissa's face changed and she looked down. "Too many things..."

445

"Well, I'll hear later." Joanna turned around. "This your dispensary? It's great! Where d'you do the treatment? I saw a whole gaggle of women outside."

"Its Women's Day – they come for gynae things…"

"You didn't *do* gynaecology…!"

"No, well… I have to learn, don't I?"

Joanna was dismayed. "But there're so *many* out there!"

"Yes, it's never-ending, and it's worse at the moment because I had to shut the clinic for a time. Daniel was ill…" She turned away, and began to sort things on the table, putting bottles away and shoving things into boxes.

Joanna looked at her closely. "How's the baby? How do you manage?"

"I manage. My mother looks after her during the day. I go to the market and feed her in her stall."

"Your mother works on the market? You never told me."

"It's something new. She has a Singer sewing machine, and she sells what she makes. She never used to do it but… she does it now."

"A Singer? God, I remember those at school."

Joanna propped herself on a stool, folded her arms and prepared to listen.

"So, you want to tell me what's been going on?"

"Daniel… He's been very ill."

"Well, I know *that*! That's why I came. But *you* didn't tell me, did you? You haven't written to me at all," she said, punching her lightly on the shoulder. "Not a single, single letter!"

Hadissa looked down. "I couldn't, Jo. So much happened. It wasn't as simple as just not writing. It was because…" She met her eyes. "I didn't know *how* to tell you."

"Oh? And I thought we were friends."

"We are! Nothing can change that!"

"Yeah, well, never mind, I'm here now and I'll see for myself. Dad sent me. Phoned me up suddenly, told me to come quick-sharpish."

Hadissa looked puzzled. "Quick…?"

"As soon as I could. What's been happening, Haddy?"

"Are you with Luke?" asked Hadissa obliquely. "I mean, did he come with you today?"

"Yes, he's nattering to the pastor at the moment. I said

446

I'd come and hoick you out. Your dishy brother showed me the way."

"My *dishy* brother?" Hadissa began to giggle. "You don't change, do you?"

"Why should I?"

"No reason. Oh, it's good to see you! Things have been... It's been... Oh, we never thought, when we set out, that..." She stopped, and looked down helplessly.

"Come on, Haddy, spit it out. I know most of it anyway. I've come to take him home, take him off your tiny little hands."

Hadissa shook her head. "You know, a week ago, even a week ago, he wouldn't have gone, but now..."

"What's changed?"

"Oh, he can't stay here, Jo, and I think he knows it. You'll see, when you speak to him. I think he actually wants to go now. And he really can't stay. His skin is really bad, and his cough... He needs specialist care, and a cool climate."

"Well, he'll certainly get that in England. It's bloody cold at the moment. But you'll stay on here?"

Hadissa looked at her sadly. "I must. The clinic..."

"Well, let's go and see him, anyway," said Joanna decisively, getting off her stool. "You can tell me what's happened on the way. What changed his mind, I mean. Don't fret," she added, putting her arm through Hadissa's and walking with her to the door. "Let me deal with him if he's difficult. He won't get past me."

"You won't find him difficult," replied Hadissa as they left the clinic. She shut the gate and locked it under the disappointed eyes of the women gathered there. "He's changed, Jo. He's not the same man you knew. Now wait a moment while I have a word with these people. I'll tell them I'm coming back, shall I, and you can give me a hand, if you like."

"Be glad to. That's what I've come for, to give you a hand."

\* \* \*

"God, Luke, what a rabbit warren! All these dilapidated huts and horrible shanty houses. Some of those women looked absolutely destitute. And that dreadful road! God, the noise! To have to live with that, all the time! It would drive me barmy!"

It was evening and nearly dark. They were walking up the path to John-Sunday's house where he had prepared a meal for them. Joanna had been working with Hadissa all afternoon and had only left when Hadissa had gone to feed Habiba.

"Jo, you can't compare it with England," said Luke. "And at least it's clean…"

"*Clean?*"

"Well, you should see some of the townships near Kaduna. The litter there, it's indescribable. It's surprising anyone lives to adulthood." He indicated the village with a wave of his arm. "Here, they really try. They live hard-working, honest, decent lives. As for the road, well, I expect they get used to it."

Joanna snorted in disgust. "I'm sorry, that sounds like the worst kind of patronising. As for getting used to it, I wonder if they do. You make it sound as though it's somehow… noble, or something – to live like this. I don't think it is. I think its squalor and poverty and deprivation, and I don't think that's in any way noble."

"I didn't use the word," said Luke, mildly. "Of course it's not noble, not in itself. But, how they cope with it, there *is* something noble about that. And I'm not being patronising. They're a clean-living, honest people, struggling against all odds to survive in very harsh surroundings…"

"You can say that again," Joanna snorted scornfully. "I bet if you had to live here you wouldn't think like that. *God*, no! Think what it does to them! That's a Western idea, anyway, natives living unsullied lives close to nature. It's an out-of-date myth to salve your conscience with!"

"Which is why we're helping to build the clinic," said Luke quietly. "And why we got Zac out of Kaduna, and why we're working with the faith groups, and why we're financing the workshop. And we won't stop there. We'll carry on helping, but they'll be doing the work, Jo, the hard graft. There's nothing patronising about it. And if you want to compare it with England…"

"I never said I did. Wouldn't dream of it. That was your idea, not mine. I'm just looking at what's under my nose, and there sure is something under my nose all right!"

"Well, there's poverty in England, too. People who slip through the net. The mentally ill, the homeless. But compare their faith, for instance. The church in Nigeria is the fastest growing church in Christendom. You just compare the quality of their faith with what you see in England, even in your father's church. Ask Hadissa. She's experienced both. It's much more alive and much more vital, more *immediate*, than in England..."

"It has to be, doesn't it?" she asked curtly. "A perpetual state of life and death, all the bloody time. They *need* religion to prop them up!"

"Jo, you're impossible! They just pray it how it is. Everything: the seasons, the crops, the road, childbearing; everything's a source of prayer. And, by the way, rejoicing, too."

"Bet they don't do much rejoicing!"

"They do, you know. They know the things of the spirit more than we do. Ask John-Sunday... Or Dan, if you don't believe me."

"*Dan*? I wouldn't have thought..."

"You'll see. I think you'll find he's changed his ideas about that."

"He'd have had to," she said grimly. "He should never have got involved with Hadissa. You missed that, didn't you, Luke? I'd have frozen him in his tracks. I did warn him, you know. I said..."

Luke raised his eyebrows sceptically. "And when does warning people ever do any good? They have to find out for themselves. And I didn't miss it. I warned him too. I admit it was later, when I thought he meant to keep Hadissa in England. When I discovered he intended coming out to Africa, I changed my mind. In my opinion he's done his utmost to fit in with her needs. He was prepared to sacrifice everything..."

"She never really loved him, you know, not in the way we understand it. She just wanted security, that's all. She didn't love him enough to stick with him. And now he's lost everything, even her. You think it was worth the risk?"

"Whose risk, Jo? Not yours or mine or Stephen's. Or even Hadissa's. No, *he* took the risk. Even Hadissa was on firmer ground. She was, after all, coming home. No, it's Dan who's taken all the risks..."

"Could it have worked, do you think, but for..."

"You'll have to ask him," said Luke. "I'd say, in theory, yes, but in Nigeria, no. Too many imponderables. The tension here, for one thing. The difference in culture, for another. You can try to ignore cultural differences with all the will in the world, but they don't go away. Apart from the food, the climate, things like that, people's expectations are different. Dan's a natural organiser, but you can't organise people if they don't want to be organised, and you can't impose your own ideas. You have to wait and hope that maybe, one day, and just perhaps, they'll see things as you do. And if you think you know what's best for them because you're British, and you think the British way is best, well, it hasn't always been, let's face it. Would he have been that tolerant, d'you think? That patient? Even assuming his ideas *were* what was best for them? They might not have seen it like that, and what then? And the fact that she's black and he's white might one day have become a difficulty. It might still be, for her. Not here, perhaps, but in the city. That child, Jo, at school, and afterwards, trying to marry her off, and she half-caste – think of that! But how can we know? We can never know for sure. It might have worked, if what happened on the road hadn't happened." He took her arm. "Come on, let's go. They'll be waiting for us."

They began to walk up the path. All around them was the smell of cooking fires, and the intensely pungent smell of spiced food. The air was full of smoke. It hung over the roofs of the houses and drifted down over the road, where the lights of the traffic illuminated the darkness with a dull red glow.

"You know," Luke continued. "He had vision, did Dan... He was quite prophetic in Kaduna, and some of his ideas have already taken root. You won't get him to talk about them, though. He's too modest, or he dismisses his part in it. Or he genuinely doesn't realise it. But in Kaduna some of the projects we're now working on are a direct result of his perceptions and his ideas. It's a tragedy he didn't have more time. It's an utter tragedy."

"I know," she said surprisingly. "I suppose I'm being a bit fierce because... I thought he was a complete bastard, Luke, a manipulative, selfish bastard, but that was only at first. For quite some time..." She paused, unsure how much to divulge of her own feelings. "Let's just say I was completely wrong about him. I was happy to admit it to him once, and I shall tell him again when I can get him on his own."

Luke laughed. "What, *you*? Eat humble pie?"

"I shall do more than that, Luke. I shall look after him if he'll let me. Not here. I don't mean here. But when we get back.

I intend to take very good care of our friend Dan."

"He's badly disfigured, you know," Luke warned.

"I saw. That won't last, though. Don't worry about it," she said confidently. "We'll sort him out in England."

* * *

Later, that evening she asked him, "Luke, do you believe in telepathy?" and he frowned and said, "I believe in *God...*" and she called him a pompous ass. She didn't say anymore. She had been going to tell him about the night her father sensed a presence at the door, how disturbed he'd been, and about his prayers, but she changed her mind. Stephen hadn't used the word 'telepathic', however. The Spirit, he'd said, was not bound by time or space, so was it so surprising that just when Dan needed his prayers most, he was moved to pray for him? Joanna thought it was ridiculous to make that sort of link, as if there'd been some sort of supernatural propinquity. She thought it was bizarre, almost creepy. It made her shiver.

* * *

Dan's trunk had turned up, but empty. The pastor brought it over rather sheepishly, explaining that it had been in his house some days. A trucker, he said, had dropped it off on his way up to Kaduna, and there it had stayed. Dan remembered how he'd suspected the trunk had been stolen, and overtly they vied with each other as to who should feel the most shame. Possessions were few and this had been a suitcase full of them. He also wondered how it could have lain forgotten for so long in the pastor's house. *Et tu, Brute*, he thought, you also were tempted; then dismissed it from his mind.

He was up and about again by then. Every day he could be seen, walking on the paths with his stick, as if to imprint every detail of the village on his mind. In his Western clothes, his feet bandaged and a white *keffiyeh* wrapped round his head, which Hassan had lent him to keep off the sun, he cut a strange figure, one they would never forget.

The day he left they crossed the road as a tight-knit group to see him off, and as they stood on the central reservation, waiting for a gap in the traffic, he told John-Sunday, "You can have what's in the trunk. It's only some clothes and a few textbooks; they might come in useful, mostly maths, but you said you were interested in maths, so anyway, take them if you want. You're too big for this place," he added seriously, "...but I know you'll help it grow around you."

The car was waiting on the hard shoulder, Luke and Joanna already inside, and he turned to Hassan and said, "Hassan, look after John-Sunday. He's like a brother to me now. And let me know how the workshop goes. I'll send you some money, not much, I don't know how things will be for me at home, but it might buy something." He put the borrowed *keffiyeh* in his hand, loosely folded, but Hassan pressed it back, saying, "No, keep it to remember me by," and he tucked it away again in his pocket, then turned to where Hadissa was waiting.

"Hadissa," he said. "Don't cry." Lovingly touching her with his bandaged hands, wishing he could feel her skin, wishing he could lay his cheek against hers, but unable to because of the dressings. "Let me know how Habiba is. Maybe you'll come to England? No, forget I said that. Don't plan for that. Be happy here. I'll write, but not yet. Not for a while. Don't cry, Hadissa, don't cry." He kissed his half-blood child quickly, and turned away.

"Zac," he said, at last – and then he didn't know what to say, so he said nothing.

His last sight of them as they drove away was Hadissa, clutching the baby in her arms and behind her, Zac, the shadowy figure of his Cambridge dream, identified at last. Hassan stood apart, a sentinel in overalls. John-Sunday ran beside the car with his hand on the bonnet, then, as they gathered speed, he thumped it hard, a gesture of finality, and then fell back.

Dan looked back over his shoulder. John-Sunday was standing on the hard shoulder, frantically mouthing something – a last, inaudible message, then one arm shot up high above his head, his pale palm a gesture of farewell. Reminded of Stephen at Stansted airport, Dan thought, maybe humankind is the same everywhere, no matter who they are or where they live. We're not so very different. The last message is always half-heard, and always the same: Go with God.

\* \* \* \* \*

452